BUILDING
THE
BRITISH EMPIRE

TO THE END OF THE
FIRST EMPIRE

CONTENTS

CONTENTS

INTRODUCTION

As our story is to deal with the development of the British Empire and of the British themselves, we may pause for a few moments at the beginning to consider what these people are who have so puzzled the world. For they always have and still do puzzle the rest of mankind. Critics and analysts of almost every other nation—German, Italian, French, Spanish, American and others—have written great numbers of books about the character of the English, or more generically the British, only to express their bewilderment. Even the British disagree about themselves.

They are, indeed, a singular race, one which has prided itself on being "a little mad," but critics have never been able to decide whether they are in truth mad or cunning, honest or hypocritical, stupid or deeply clever, unthinking or very far-seeing. About no other race has the clash of opinion been more violent. It would be better to say nation than race for, as a matter of fact, there is today no such thing as a "pure" race. The British are, as we shall see in our narrative, made up of the crossing of many races, and if there are in truth such things as racial characteristics, that may in part account for the innumerable contradictions in the national character and in the opinions held of it by those of other nations.

There is, at any rate, such a thing as national character though no historical problem is more difficult than to analyze it and to trace its origins. Probably some of the origins lie in those obscure questions of race of which we know far less now than we thought we did a generation ago. We shall have to guess at some of these.

There are also the circumstances of location, geography, soils, climate and such, although these have to be considered in connection with other more subtle conditions. It is easy, for example, to talk glibly, so long as we do not think too much, about those favoring the rise of Greek civilization, but the physical conditions have remained much the same for several tens of centuries whereas a few generations cover the whole of "the glory that was Greece." Combined with other factors in the right proportion and at the right moment, physical factors, however, have their importance and we shall have to glance at them from time to time. Religion and language have also their influence and will have their place in our narrative. There is, in addition, that immensely important factor of what Renan called "a rich heritage of memories," of efforts directed in common for a common purpose through centuries. These build up traditions, and traditions, common to a whole nation, are most powerful compelling and cementing forces. But the core of the problem still does and must elude us. Why should the Greeks, as we have noted, rise for a few dazzling decades to the intellectual and æsthetic leadership of the world, only to descend again into mediocrity? Why should the population of the British Isles, small until a century or so ago, have produced according to the American student of genius, Professor Cattell, one-quarter of the most eminent men of all the world? Incidentally we may note that of the foreign-born in the United States who have achieved sufficient eminence to be in *Who's Who*, about fifty per cent of the whole came from the British Empire. Whatever these figures may be worth it is certain that the British from their small island have overrun the world until they own one-quarter of its surface and govern one-quarter of its population. Of the two billion or so of human beings on this earth, five hundred million are under British rule. Here is a problem that cannot be solved by any one single or simple formula, such as race. We can only tell the story, pointing here and there, as we come to them, to factors that appear to have helped in the process. In that way we may learn something even if we cannot explain all.

National character and aspirations do not always remain the

same. The British of today are in many respects different from their ancestors of the Tudor reigns. Nor does history move in one straight line of progression from start to finish. It is a zig-zag, depending on altering conditions; on changing moods of the people; on international relations, which like the force of gravity may swing a nation out of its orbit for a while; on the appearance at the right moment of great men, or their non-appearance. But on the whole the history of the British Empire possesses a unity, and the Britain and British of today are what the past has made them.

What of the British of today? What have they and Britain developed into? Here at once we run into difficulties which will confront us throughout the narrative. When the present King, George VI, was crowned in Westminster Abbey in May, 1937, he had solemnly to promise and swear that he would "govern the peoples of Great Britain, Ireland, Canada, Australia, New Zealand and the Union of South Africa, of your Possessions and the other Territories to any of them belonging or appertaining, and of your Empire of India, according to their respective laws and customs." This oath, and indeed the entire ceremony, gradually altered throughout more than a thousand years, may be taken as shedding the first light on our problem. Let us consider only a few points with their contradictions. Here is the greatest congeries of democracies in the modern world held together by a King who "reigns but does not govern." Nevertheless, the moment that the monarchy was overthrown, the Empire would dissolve. It would break into many component parts, each weak as contrasted with their united strength as units in the Empire. They are held together by neither logic, law nor force but in the main by sympathy, affection, tradition and loyalty to the Crown. By the Crown I mean neither its peculiar legal position as the keystone in the constitutional arch of government nor the person of the monarch who happens to be ruling at a given moment. "The Crown" to the British signifies the entire past, present and future of the British peoples. It sums up in itself as one symbol the entire strivings, hopes, aspirations, and loyalties to God, King, the Commonwealth and to each other as individuals, of all the peoples of the Empire. It is conceivable that the island of Great Britain might some day become a Republic, although unlikely. But it is impossible that the Empire should ever as a whole become one. Both the political and the spiritual difficulties would be insuperable. It would be impossible to elect a temporary President for one-quarter of the earth, and, even if elected, an official constantly changing in the heat of controversy could not serve as that symbol which we have just described. The British people are intensely interested in the monarchy and royal family as persons but as the Crown has become increasingly important as the symbol which holds the Empire together it has become increasingly important that the man who wears it should himself typify the highest and often conflicting ideals of his subjects. That was what caused the personally tragic matrimonial problem of Edward VIII to become an imperial constitutional crisis.

We may note one or two other points as to the coronation. Much of the ceremony goes back for a thousand years. No other Western people has as strong a sense of continuity and tradition as has the British. They love pageantry for itself but when on great historic occasions the old customs and even the old costumes reappear it is more than pageantry. It is a linking together of a single event with all the past of the nation. It is a largely unconscious realization, unspoken like much else British but none the less deeply felt, of the unity of history and the steady flow of life from generation to generation which give a higher value to the mite that each individual can contribute to the whole in his or her own day and sphere. It is an almost mystical identifying of one's self, however important or unimportant, with the larger society of the race over space and time. It is the enhancing of individual dignity and the securing of a certain sense of immortality. The British are not mystics in the sense that a Latin mediæval saint was a mystic but however inarticulate they may be about it they have a sense that enables and forces them to plumb to the depths of life.

Closely connected with all this is another notable trait, one which in my years in England struck me almost more than any

other. This is their extraordinary social cohesiveness and sense of
social responsibility. This is the more remarkable because in ordinary social life, in the usual sense, the Britisher does not greatly
put himself out for the sake of others. He is aloof. He loves privacy. He is ill at ease in a garden which is not hedged or walled.
His house is his castle and he well knows how to keep it closed
against unwelcome intrusion. The most successful of all races, perhaps, in government, he wants as little of it as possible. He wants
freedom of every sort to be himself and live his own life as he
pleases. And yet I do not know any other people who so simply
and spontaneously undertake duties, social, humanitarian or political, for the sake of the whole. "England expects every man to
do his duty," and duty, though rarely if ever talked about, seems
to bulk large at the base of the nation. You may call on an old
man and find that he is out, visiting two or three prisoners who
are his special charge, not as a member of an organization but just
naturally as an individual. At tea at a country house, you will hear
the local cases discussed—perhaps illness, poverty, or a young
Communist whom some one has been talking to, trying to teach
him something of the English system. No organization. Just individuals doing this and that by instinct and sense of duty to the
whole. A few years ago, when the Government faced bankruptcy,
it asked the people to pay as much of their taxes due in July as
they could in January. Queues lined up at six in the morning at tax
offices to pay. This is a very different sort of living for the State
than is preached by Mussolini or Hitler. It is not control from
above but, as I say, a spontaneous attitude toward society from
below—effort given freely.

This extends to personal relationships. There are plenty of
crooks and bounders in England, as I found to my cost, but a nation has a right to be judged by its ordinary sound people and not
by its worst. The United States cannot be judged by its kidnap-
pers and gangsters. One of the traits of the sound Britisher, known
all over the world I find, is that, as the phrase goes, "he will not
let you down." He is a "good man," as they also say, "to go tiger
hunting with," and the same man whom you may have thought

surly or offish in a drawing room would stick by you to the end if you suddenly found yourselves together in a tight hole.

This "will not let you down" goes through all ranks, and it gives one that sense of being able to depend on the others that made the queues line up to pay their taxes. You knew that if you did your duty, others would also and that you would not be "made the goat." All these traits are of enormous social value. They enable the Empire to function in what other races, more logical perhaps, but less socially cohesive, consider an extraordinarily haphazard fashion. The traits have been molded, I think, by four forces in large part—religion, sport, the ideal of the gentleman, and "snobbishness."

In spite of modernism in all forms, religion, whether "Church," "Chapel" or other, is still a great power in British life, and it would be fatal to overlook it. Sport, which for centuries has played so large a part in British life, has had enormous influence in fields apparently wholly remote from it. It is not a matter merely of health of body, strength of muscle or quickness of eye. It has meant much more than that. Every outdoor sport is a contest between opposing teams, and from this fact have come certain notable traits, such as the characteristic English one of compromise. Unless games are all to end in fights and bloody noses, there must grow up a willingness to give and take, to accept decisions in good spirit whether winners or losers. There must be team work within each team, but in addition, and from this comes one of the greatest of British political discoveries, the two teams must be considered as each playing its part in the larger whole, that of the game itself. Applied to politics, the British eventually found that an orderly opposition in Parliament was as necessary to Parliamentary self-government as was the Government temporarily in power. Complete recognition of this fact was given in 1937 by the granting of a salary to the "Leader of His Majesty's Opposition." One has only to realize that a century or so ago, opposition might be construed as treason, and that today in many of the great countries such as Germany, Italy, Russia and others, no voice in opposition is tolerated at all, to understand the importance for human liberty of this British mode of "playing the game," for there can be no safety for the liberties of a people if there can be no criticism of those temporarily in power.

The ideal of the "gentleman" has also been peculiarly British, and exerted great influence. It has altered through the centuries but is quite different from anything in the rest of Europe. For the most part on the Continent, society historically was sharply divided into a permanent noble class, whose children were nobles, and the ordinary people. British society has been much more fluid. It has been easier to rise to the nobility, and, as younger sons descend to the rank of commoner, there is a constant movement up and down. From this freedom of movement, to a considerable extent, has arisen the modern gentleman. He may have a high title or none, but he is supposed to have certain qualities and qualifications, such as education, good manners, and especially some of the deeper qualities such as the "not letting you down" already mentioned.

Two things have helped to spread these ideals among the people at large. One is the British trust in leadership, which comes largely from the belief that the leader has the last quality just mentioned. The other is, if you like, snobbery, which usually comes in for unmitigated scorn but which has had much to do with the molding of the manners and ideals of the people. British society is hierarchical, descending from the Royal family, the nobility, through the county families, lower middle class and so on. Each class, below the Royal, would like to find itself in those above it and as far as they can, they model their behavior on those in them. Until lately, perhaps, the model has to a great extent been the gentleman, who has been found in all the higher grades of society. We may smile at the valet who calls himself "a gentleman's gentleman," and throw all the scorn we will at snobbery as a whole but it has been better to try to copy the speech, manners and to some extent the ideals of conduct of a gentleman than those of the merely powerful or rich.

Connected with many of the points we have mentioned is that feeling for law and order which strikes almost every visitor to

England. It is a trait with a long history behind it but seems to have become deeply imbedded in the race, for it is found in the Dominions under frontier conditions as well as in the heart of Empire where in London the patience, good humor, and orderliness of the crowds are noticeable on every occasion of the massing of the people.

It is impossible in one short chapter to run over all the traits which make the Britisher so enigmatic to others. In his study of *Englishmen, Frenchmen, Spaniards,* Madariaga has alluded to the Lion and Unicorn of Great Britain's armorial bearings as indicating the contrast between some of the aspects of the British, the one majestic, powerful, the "King of Beasts," and the other a freakish fanciful creature. The list of contrasts is endless. We have Puritanism and a nation above all others devoted to sport; inarticulateness and one of the greatest of national literatures; apparent casualness in all they do and the ownership of a quarter of the earth; a "nation of shop-keepers" who have given us some of the world's greatest poetry; unsocial in many ways yet with an extraordinarily close-knit social fabric; lovers of home above all other peoples yet the greatest wanderers in the world; shy and yet completely assured of their own superiority; devoted to baths and content with the fewest and worst bathrooms in Western Europe; a people who assure us they have no imagination or sentiment but who set up statues of Peter Pan and carve fairies on oak stumps in Kensington Gardens. And so we could go on. Santayana quotes a saying: "One Englishman, a fool; two Englishmen, a football match; three Englishmen, the British Empire." He justly notes that the first phrase of the epigram is absurd, and objects to the last that it is untrue because one Englishman is enough to win an empire. Anyway a remarkable people, whose course of history we are now to follow.

BUILDING
THE
BRITISH EMPIRE

TO THE END OF THE
FIRST EMPIRE

CHAPTER I

BEFORE AND DURING THE ROMAN PERIOD

THE MOST OUTSTANDING fact which has influenced British history is that Great Britain is an island. It is true, however, that Ireland and Iceland are also islands northwest of Europe and have had a quite different history. It is obvious, therefore, that other factors will also have to be taken into consideration, and these we shall note presently. Great Britain itself was not always cut off from the main continent. There was a time when the present straits of Dover were dry land, and the east coast of England stretched far out into what is now the North Sea. Then came a period of subsidence of the land facing south and east, and possibly between 2500 and 2000 B.C. the waters of the North Sea and the Atlantic Ocean cut through the lower lands between what are now France and England, and created that vast moat which has until the present day of aerial warfare been England's best protection.

Earliest man probably either walked into England over where are now the Channel waters, so detested by travellers, or paddled his way in primitive boats across a narrow and very shallow stretch of sea between the east coast and the mainland. There were various races in Continental Europe even in those prehistoric days. Our knowledge of them is scanty, but evidence shows that they pressed or were pressed steadily westward, pausing at mountain or other natural barriers, until pressed again, and finally brought to bay with their backs to the wild waste of the

Atlantic waves. They were driven into the Spanish peninsula, into the Breton peninsula of France, and into Great Britain over the land bridge and narrow waters, and there farther into the mountains of Wales, Scotland, or farther again into Ireland, as other tribes, peoples or races continued the inexorable pressure.

These mountains of Wales, northwestern England, and the highlands of Scotland have been of great importance in our story. There the first invaders turned against their pursuers of later waves of migration and successfully maintained themselves.

There is much confusion about these early tribes and migrations, and scholars are far less willing to make positive assertions or even ambitious guesses than they were a generation ago, but with the help of geology and archeology a few facts for our purpose emerge from the darkness of these prehistoric days.

These are, chiefly, that Great Britain became an island, with all which that has since implied. Also, probably about the same period, the climate greatly changed from warm and extremely moist, to what it is today. The modern climate has been an important factor in developing temperament, character, and ways of living. For one thing, unlike the climate which most Latins enjoyed, the British one, although not severe, drove—by its mists, fogs, and rains—people indoors so that the home, and not the sunshine of the *piazza*, became the place where they met and carried on their life. If there are no open squares in British cities as on the Continent, no open-air cafés, and life goes on inside the front door instead of outside it, it is largely because of climate, which created the habits of privacy and seclusion which this indoor home life bred.

It also appears that whoever the early migrants may have been, and whatever their distinct racial traits, they came in wave after wave, settling here and there in varying numbers and in different sections, so that the inhabitants were a highly mixed race long before the later migrations after the Roman period. The later comers, too, found different conditions. Not only had the land bridge long been submerged but the earlier races or tribes had become widely spread over the islands. Later invaders, as we shall see, were able to conquer the earlier up to the mountain barriers we have mentioned, but as the mixed population became more numerous and more squeezed into the mountains it became more difficult to conquer and pass them. For the most part, therefore, later ones, such as the Angles, Saxons, Danes, and others, did not cross into Ireland. Thus, the later mixture of blood, which has meant so much to England, did not affect Ireland, except for some raiding by sea, around the coast, and left fewer traces on the mountain peoples than on those in the south and east of England.

Although Great Britain became an island, the waters did not for long offer either that protection or road to wealth and power which they did later. The scattered British tribes were neither better sailors nor had better boats than their neighbors on the opposing coast of the mainland. The shoreline of the south, and particularly that of the east, of England, with their numerous rivers, inlets, and havens, and the coastal plain stretching back, offered easy access to those who sailed over on surprise attacks.

Several things were to be necessary before the island position of Britain could be made to yield its full advantage. Among others there had to be a strong and unified government to resist attack. This was to be developed under the Normans. There had also to be a growth of over-seas commerce with distant lands, and along such trade routes as would place England in a position to participate. If we look at her place on the map we can realize why these things came to pass under Elizabeth, and why southern England could benefit whereas the northern part of the island, Scotland, and the other islands of Ireland and Iceland did not. England alone was geographically so set as to be able to make the most both of the routes over the Atlantic to distant lands and of the growing trade of northern Europe, many of whose most flourishing cities at the end of long trade routes were just across the narrow seas within easy reach of such of England's own ports as London and Bristol.

It is true that there was some trade even as early as the Stone Age, when there are indications of exchanges with both Spain and Egypt. Later, in the metal ages, there was trade along the great

3

amber routes, such as in gold with Ireland and tin from Cornwall. About 50 B.C. the last was largely destroyed, as far as Continental exports were concerned, by the destruction by Cæsar of the port of Corbilo, but the Belgæ who had invaded England and established two kingdoms had also set up a somewhat high standard of civilization on the Continent, and there was in consequence a considerable trade with southeastern England. But in all these earlier trades, Great Britain's position as an island was a hindrance rather than a help. It was to require centuries of international change and of internal development in England to make London the crossroads of the world.

It would be interesting and perhaps important if we could describe the sort of people these early inhabitants of England were, their habits and customs and mental outlook, but we really know practically nothing about them. Apparently as early as the Stone Age, during which Britain ceased to be an island, there are evidences of settled agricultural life, of considerable wealth, in the barbaric sense, and of political and religious organization. From this age date the great stone circles at Stonehenge and Avebury, the significance of which is not fully known. During the succeeding Bronze and Iron Ages there were many shifts in location and population, in which soils, upland and lowland, and other geographical features played their parts, but where so little is definitely known we may well pass directly to the coming of Cæsar and the shedding of historical light on the scene.

In the preceding centuries British culture had been successively influenced by the cultures of different Continental districts, and as a result the lives of the people in various sections differed widely. In some we find undefended villages and in others hill forts, massive and intricate in design. Some of the tribes preferred the lighter soils and higher open land; others, especially with the coming of the Belgæ from Gaul who had inherited from German ancestors the technique of woodsmen, to some extent penetrated and cleared the forests.

Cæsar tells us several things about these Belgæ with whom he was familiar in Gaul (France). These people who had crossed

4

the Straits to plunder, and then to settle, in England still bore the names of their Gaulish tribes, and he says that the Gaulish King, Diviciacus, governed not only a large part of northeastern Gaul but Britain as well, meaning by that the southeastern part of England. There was apparently close connection between the peoples on the two sides of the Straits. Contingents from Britain helped their kinsmen in Gaul to fight the Roman legions, and refugees from Gaul found safety in England. It is probable that the reason for the Roman invasions of Britain is to be found in Cæsar's belief that it was necessary to pacify the rich province of Gaul as a Roman province, and that, owing to its relations with the Gauls in southern England, it was equally needful to exert authority across the Channel.

His first expedition, which may be considered as in the nature of a reconnaissance, was made in the late summer of 55 B.C. He sent in advance a subordinate, Gaius Volusenus, to explore the coast for a good landing place, and, unfortunately for Cæsar, Volusenus did not sail farther than the Downs, off Deal with its sloping beaches, missing the fine harbor which he would have found some distance beyond. Cæsar finally embarked with ten thousand men, though his cavalry were late in getting on their transports, and the wind, which has so often come to the aid of the British, swept them down channel instead of in the direction of Deal, where Cæsar landed his infantry. That night there was a flood tide and both the vessels which he had beached and those which he had anchored were heavily damaged.

Cæsar had no supplies for a winter campaign, and had conflicts with the British while foraging among the rich fields back of the shore. The ships were repaired as rapidly as possible. The British played fast and loose, sometimes despairing of beating off this new band of invaders, sometimes fighting pluckily against them. One day they attacked the Roman camp but could not stand before the solid formation of the legions. Cæsar, however, realized that his situation was precarious in the extreme, and that night re-embarked his troops and sailed back to Gaul.

As an attempt to conquer Britain, the expedition was obviously a failure, but Cæsar had learned a good deal. Among other things he now knew that the southeast of England was a rich grain country; that the British, unlike the Gauls of the Continent, used war chariots which, although the wheels were not provided with scythes as has often been said, were an important arm of offense and could only be well met by cavalry; that the British could not stand up against legions in formation, and that their morale crumbled under defeat. Of the naval aspects of the problem of conquest, and of the geography and resources of the island farther back from the Kentish coast, he learned little. Back in Gaul, however, he prepared for a more elaborate expedition in the following year. He had discovered, at least, the interesting fact that the hitherto unknown land, from which reinforcements came to his enemies in Gaul, was rich in food supplies, as far as he had explored it, and might have a value in itself apart from the control of the island Belgæ who intervened at inconvenient moments in his control of their Continental kinsmen.

At the beginning of his next expedition his fleet of 28 warships, 540 transports and some 200 merchant vessels was detained for three weeks by contrary winds. During that time an event happened of prime importance. Cæsar knew that the allegiance of the Gaulish tribes was uncertain and therefore he meant to hold them by taking some of the chiefs with him. Among these was Dumnorix, who had personal grievances against Cæsar, and who, after trying to persuade Cæsar to allow him to remain, escaped from camp with his cavalry. Pursued, he was cut down, asserting his freedom of Rome.

That night Cæsar sailed and disembarked his forces next morning, apparently somewhere near his former landing place, not yet having discovered the harbor of Richborough. Beaching his vessels, he at once marched inland and defeated a force of British near Canterbury. A gale having totally destroyed forty of his vessels and heavily damaged the rest, he had to return to the coast and waste ten days in repairs. He had again proved careless as to the naval aspect of his problem, and the Britons took their advantage. The strongest chief was Cassivellaunus, King of the

6

Belgæ, with his capital in Hertfordshire. He had unsuccessfully been trying to assert his power over the other Belgic tribes, and those of Kent now offered their submission if he would come to their help against the Romans.

When Cæsar renewed operations he found himself pitted against probably the ablest man in Britain. In the course of the campaign, however, although the British proved themselves better foes when well led, Cæsar was able to defeat them and to destroy the headquarters of Cassivellaunus about two miles from St. Albans. The mixture of tribes and the small extent of the real power of any of them are ·indicated by the facts that the Trinobantes of Kent deserted Cassivellaunus, and five tribes gave their submission to Cæsar. On the other hand, other Kentish tribes attacked his fleet and the camp about it, so that Cæsar had again to hurry back to the coast after making peace with the Catuvellauni.

Meanwhile trouble had broken out in Gaul which required Cæsar's immediate presence. As his fleet had been reduced in size and he had many prisoners, he had to make two crossings but reached Gaul in safety. From that night in 54 B.C. for nearly a century until 43 A.D., no Romans again molested the island, and the fear of invasion passed like a bad dream.

It is not definitely known why, under the Emperor Claudius, the subjugation of Britain was again decided upon, and in the course of some years carried out up to the Scottish border. Britain became a Roman province and so remained until the early part of the fifth century, though the exact date of the passing of the Roman civilization and power cannot be accurately determined. The Britons, however, did not consent tamely to subjugation, and the exploits of the chief, Caractacus, who fought bravely and organized opposition to the Roman advance only to end his days as a captive in Rome, deserve to be recalled. Doggedly refusing to accept defeat, three times he organized armies which fought the Romans in open battle, and his name stands above all others of the British in this first period of conquest.

Another to be remembered is that of the Queen Boadicea (or

7

Boudicca, as some scholars now prefer to spell it). By the year 61 much of England had been organized, and there were Roman cities or settlements at London, Verulamium, Chester and elsewhere. With conquest and organization had come the tax gatherer, the usurer, oppression and mismanagement. The people were groaning under their losses and burdens. Boadicea's husband, as head of the tribe of Iceni, had submitted without a blow to Claudius and become a "client king." As on his death he left only his widow Boadicea and two daughters, the Romans declared the royal line extinct and confiscated its property as well as that of all the Icenian nobles. Boadicea was publicly flogged and her two daughters raped.

Smarting under her injuries, the Queen called upon the entire British people of the east and south to rise and slay their oppressors. Suetonius, the governor, was in Anglesey, where he was massacring Druid priests, when the storm broke. So strongly had the Romans felt themselves entrenched in power that London and other towns were unwalled. Within a few days over 70,000 Romans, it is estimated, had been killed in three towns alone, which gives some idea of the size of the Roman population only eighteen years after the beginning of the conquest.

The Ninth Legion had been wiped out. The leader of the Second Legion showed cowardice and refused to come to the assistance of Suetonius who had marched south in haste. With only about 10,000 troops he met the mob of British, for, with their families with them, they were more that than an army, and in a surprise attack the Romans annihilated them. It is claimed that 80,000 men, women and children were slain. Suetonius was a capable soldier but not a statesman, and thought only of more vengeance. A new Procurator, however, was appointed who was both more humane and statesmanlike and, having secured from Nero the recall of Suetonius, a policy of conciliation and good government was inaugurated. The three names of this dark period to be recalled are those of the British heroes Caractacus and Boadicea, and of the Roman Procurator Classicianus, who stood up against the successful general and brought a measure of peace to the tortured people.

8

The last died in England, and his tomb, identified in 1935, is now in the British Museum.

Agricola, who governed well from 78 to 84, completed the conquest of all the island, including Wales, except in the far north, where the wild tribes then known as the Caledonians could not be beaten in their equally wild mountains, and who yet could raid the lowlands. A series of forts was built across this northern frontier and after the Emperor Hadrian had visited Britain in 119 the famous Hadrian's Wall was erected. At that time, the Wall and other frontier defenses apparently called for the use of approximately 19,000 troops including cavalry.

It is now time to turn from war and bloodshed to enquire what was the nature of the Roman civilization as established in Britain, and what, if any, were its lasting effects. Unfortunately, in spite of the numerous Roman remains and the fact that we are now well within the period of recorded history, much less is known than we would desire.

We do know, however, that under the new arrangements made for the government of the Empire by Augustus, Britain was regarded as one of the most important provinces, usually governed by an ex-consul. There are no statistics available for population but from various evidence it has been recently estimated that the people may have numbered between 500,000 and 1,000,000, of whom perhaps half were fully Romanized, including an uncertain number of Romans themselves in addition to the four legions stationed on the island. This population was distributed more like that of prehistoric days than of modern England.

The earlier peoples had mostly settled where tillage was easiest and the soils lighter and more cleared. The great change, which brought woodland and marsh into cultivation on a large scale and so greatly expanded the tillable area, potential food supply, and population, did not come until later, although it was well under way by the time of the Domesday Book. Probably about 100,000 immigrants had come into England, including the 40,000 legionnaires together with their families, camp followers, merchants, and so on. These, however, were of all races, such as

9

Burgundians, Vandals, Goths, Saxons and others, including comparatively few pure Romans. Although the racial melting pot thus continued to boil, these newcomers were mostly assimilated into the long-headed type of British, and it is impossible to say how far or in what direction racial character may have been altered.

In considering the life of the people in Roman times we may begin with the distinction between town and country, and in England the country naturally comes first.

For the most part there were two types of country settlement, the villa and the village. These represented two distinct economic and agricultural systems, and it may be possible that these two systems extended into the distant past before the Roman conquest, although the evidence is yet scanty. There may have been the individual separate family farm and the communal group, the one developing into the villa and the other into the village.

At any rate, the villa of Roman days was the residence of one family, with their dependents, standing isolated on its own farm lands and not grouped with any community. There are some exceptions, for there are cases found of several villas grouped together within a common enclosure but this does not invalidate the general rule. There were also some villas in which the owner was engaged in mining or pursuits other than agriculture but these exceptions, again, do not alter the general rule of farm life.

The villa itself may have been large or small, depending on the wealth of the owner, and with or without outbuildings. It was usually Romanized in style, as were its furnishings. The walls of the rectangular rooms were generally decorated with painted plaster, something like those we see at Pompeii, and the inhabitants, unlike the dwellers in so many modern English houses, enjoyed the luxury of central heating and suites of baths. The surrounding farm was divided into large open fields.

The whole establishment was an independent, compact economic unit, and the servants and laborers were usually provided with quarters within the main building of the villa itself. Villa life was in general the privilege of the well-to-do but had nothing to do with the later life of the manor house, which belonged to an entirely different system of society. The villas were scattered over the countryside, their numbers varying greatly with the locality, and there was a more or less steady increase in both numbers and size from about the first to the third century.

The other form of country life in Roman times was the village. This was the abode of a communal group, living in small and almost invariably one-room circular huts, the whole group surrounded by a ditch or fence. These people, judging by the remains found, were only slightly if at all Romanized, except in the south. They were evidently poor, though the village owned the surrounding lands, which were farmed in common, small plots seemingly being allotted permanently or annually to individual villagers. It is interesting to note that much of what we know about the shape and arrangement of these old fields of fifteen centuries ago and more has been due to the recent development of aerial photography from airplanes. They were usually only one or two acres in extent, and, as always, the small farmer had less efficient methods of cultivation than the large landowner, as witness the small light plow of the villagers as contrasted with the large heavy one of the villa owner.

It is impossible to say definitely what was the status of this British peasant, or whether the villagers owned their lands in fee or were the tenants on a private or imperial estate. If they were free, the tendency was probably, as in Gaul and Germany, gradually to transform them into dependents of large landowners. The workers on the villa estates were likely to be slaves. In any case, the Romanizing of Britain seems to have brought an increasing degree of peace, as the formerly constant and often unrecorded wars between innumerable small tribes appear to have ceased. It is notable that the villagers' huts yield few weapons of any description.

Another feature of the Romanizing of Britain was the growth of towns. As we noted in the Introduction, one of the great differences between the northern and the Mediterranean peoples is that the latter have been profoundly urban, whereas the former find their deepest satisfactions in the life of the country. The republics of Greece were "city states," and the Roman Empire took its name from and centered in, not a country or nation or race, but a city. When the Romans organized Britain there were no cities and scarcely a town of any considerable size. To the Roman, however, civilization spelled cities, and in Gaul he provided the tribes with capitals, and soon began to carry out the same policy in England. Verulamium, London, Chichester, Canterbury, Dorchester, Exeter, Silchester and others were built. Agricola and other governors encouraged town life, and money was spent lavishly, indeed much too lavishly. It has been said that even today no English town is so supplied with public buildings as were these small tribal capitals. For example, at Silchester, which had at very most a population of 2000, housed in eighty buildings, a basilica was built which would accommodate 4000, and hundreds could bathe simultaneously in the public baths. As another example of waste, huge baths were started at Wroxeter, although there were few to use them, and they were never completed.

Government spending was on an enormous scale and towns were built with streets on the familiar rectangular pattern, with the usual forum, market square, and so on to which the Roman officials were used. Not only apparently did they wish to indulge the Roman love of building but it was also hoped to Romanize the population by having large and fashionable centers where they would speak Latin and live in accordance with the Roman style. To some extent they succeeded, as for example in London, which in the Antonine age may have had 15,000–25,000 inhabitants, in Verulamium, which may have had 5000, and some other places.

But there are two points to note. One is that the Romanizing influence of the towns extended very little beyond the few acres on which they stood. The richer villa dwellers took on a Roman veneer, but the great mass of the people who lived neither in towns nor in the villas of the wealthy seem to have remained largely untouched. The grandiose building plans would indicate that those who laid out and built the towns expected that their populations would grow rapidly, but the alteration in habits and tastes was too sudden. In fact, even down to the present day, the British have remained essential lovers of the country rather than of cities. The Britisher grows best with his feet on the soil and not on city pavements. In time, he has found both cities and country useful for a complete life, but he has never shaken off his love of nature. The most inveterate Londoner still speaks of the "town" and not the "city" (unless he means the financial district), and of "roads" and not of "streets," and no other city in the world at all comparable in size is so rural in its aspect and ways.

Gradually the Roman cities or towns declined. At Silchester the forum was burned down in 160 and rebuilt, but when it burned again in 300 it was not rebuilt. There is other ample evidence in many places to indicate the slow decay of town life, a phenomenon which to some extent in this period seems to have been true of the whole empire. By the fourth century a number of the towns, such as Verulamium, were practically deserted, and squatters were living in the abandoned houses. The causes of decay are obscure, other than those already mentioned. One may have been the cessation of spending for building. Another, the heavy taxes, and yet another the great inflation in the currency which raised the cost of living exorbitantly. Between the first part of the third century and the reign of Diocletian the price of grain rose 6000 per cent in Egypt and probably the same effects were felt in varying degrees in other parts of the empire.

Both the villa and the village, as we have seen, were for the most part self-contained economic units. The people, rich or poor, who could not exist at the cost of living in towns could live off the land. The position of the villa owner, as contrasted with the former rich man of the town who had depended on an income earned there, was indeed a happy one. There may have been few luxuries but life went on in at least modest comfort, and hunger and nakedness did not stalk at the door.

Commerce and industry, other than agriculture, consisted chiefly in the export of raw materials, such as copper, lead, iron, hides—to which should be added slaves and hunting dogs—and the import of manufactured articles, thus reversing the later history of Great Britain. There was a marked tendency toward concentration of capital and mass production, as well as the draining of

money into the hands of traders, and the accumulation of un-
payable debts by the richer patricians. The situation was not a
healthy one, and in some respects resembled that of today. Intellectually and æsthetically the Roman period was barren. British
art had been brilliant but to a very large extent under Roman influence became debased and vulgarized, becoming rather a branch
of manufacture than of art. Nor had the Romans done anything
for the religious life of the British. Roman religion with its Pan-
theon of gods was itself on the wane and did not replace to advantage the innumerable tribal gods of the natives. Before the end
of the Roman régime, however, Christianity had obtained a foothold, not only in Roman Britain but beyond where the power of
Roman arms extended, although its origin is too obscure to be
traced.

Gradually the unconquered tribes on the borders became more
restless and aggressive—the Scots, who were Irish, and the Picts,
who were in Scotland. The whole Roman Empire was weakening
from internal causes, and Britain felt the retreating tide. Many
reasons have been assigned for the slow deterioration and final
collapse. As far as Britain is concerned—and here again we glance
ahead to the present day—the government had become more and
more centralized from a distant center, and bureaucratic. Local
and individual ambition and initiative had been gradually extinguished. The Romans devoted themselves to breeding ordinary
men. The extraordinary were outside barbarians. As has been well
said: "The Romano-Britons, trained for generations to obedience,
were a ready prey for any upstart of coarser fiber and more brutal
energy who should learn the easy trick of turning their docility to
the service of his ends."[1]

Somewhere between 417 and 429 apparently, the Roman Empire simply faded out of Britain, and the last of the legions were
withdrawn. The island was left to its fate. No such impress had
been permanently left on Britain as on Gaul, the future France.
On the other hand, slight as the traces might appear in the tumul-

[1]R. G. Collingwood and J. N. L. Myers, *Roman Britain and the English Settlements*,
Oxford, 1936, p. 307.

tuous centuries to follow, it would be unwise to say that the occupation had meant nothing. In part the Roman twilight, deepening into night, may have been due to the fact that about the beginning of the fifth century there had been a renewed Celtic immigration from Ireland. As the Romans may have had to withdraw westward from the south and east of England before the invaders from over the water from the continent, they would thus find themselves in a Celtic zone where both the Celtic race and culture triumphed. It is interesting that the British historian Gildas, who wrote in that century and knew Latin, appears to have known nothing of Britain as a Roman province. So rapidly did the memory of Rome fade from the minds of even the more cultivated Britons.

The Romans had founded London and had built a system of roads which were long to last and not to be equalled until the eighteenth century. These gave to England a system of transportation and a certain unity which she would not otherwise have possessed in the following centuries, even though the bridges fell and the roads were allowed slowly to decay.

There had also been a further mixture of races, a training in the ways of comparative peace and of efficient if rather dull and stupid government, a contact of some centuries with an alien people with different ideas and a higher standard of material life, the clash of Mediterranean city culture with that of British country life ideals, and the hazy recollections of a centralized State, with power and glory instead of the everlasting bickerings of small tribes. It was to be many centuries, however, before the Norman William was to centralize the State again, and the effects of the Roman occupation, if any, were to lie deep in the subconsciousness of the British (soon to be mingled with hordes of new invaders), rather than in any continuous memory or tradition. The Roman period is rather the painting on the drop curtain of the stage on which the British drama was to be played than the first act of that drama itself.

CHAPTER II

FROM THE FALL OF ROME TO THE
NORMAN CONQUEST

THE DECLINE of Roman power and of the social structure of Roman Britain had been gradual. We have already alluded to the fact that the full value of Britain's island position was not realized until late in her history, and when that position coincided with other factors. For the past three centuries and more she has played a dual role. From about the sixteenth century she has been caught in, though not a part of, the affairs of the European continent with its wars and politics and has also been the head of a world empire which has little or nothing to do with Europe. But until the age of exploration opened the non-European world to her, she was, apart from her own island life, concerned with the Continent, and for centuries was subject to raids from thence, both of the civilized Romans and of the uncivilized barbarians.

For a few centuries, beginning with Elizabeth, world power and control of the seas were to render her practically immune from continental attack but with the shift of sea power to air forces that immunity may again pass, and we can understand the earlier conditions better when we think of the gas masks provided for the entire British population today. A glance at the map shows how open to attack were England's southern and eastern shores, and we may think of the boats launched against her in the early days in terms of the airplanes which now may overleap her navy and attack her cities in this new world into which we have lived and which, in large part, is again becoming a struggle between civilization and barbarism.

The Romans had crossed the channel to conquer yet they also brought order, centralization and a higher standard of life. But the same waters which they had crossed, and the North Sea, were also the routes by which the barbarians of those days could fling themselves upon the island for marauding raids. The Saxons, from the German coast, of whom we shall speak presently more in detail, began their onslaughts in the third quarter of the fourth century. Within a generation or so we find in the North a "Duke of the Britons" stationed at York with a legion and auxiliary troops, and a "Count of the Saxon Shore" (note the title) with his center of defense at Richborough. Perhaps somewhat later there was also a mobile field force, ready to strike at any point, under a "Count of Britain." The details are unimportant, the main fact being that the protection of the island was still considered to be on the land and not as later on the sea.

In the year 360 both Picts from Scotland and Scots from Ireland broke through the defenses of the frontiers. In another four years the Saxons and others were joining heartily in the game of loot. As the most recent authority, Hodgkin, has said, "the years from 360 to 367 were a crescendo of ravage."[1] The world as known to Roman Britain was being destroyed, and if, in the days of inflation, the villa owners had fared better than the town dwellers, in the years of barbarian invasions, they fared worse in their isolated homes. A civilization was in its death throes, and we know less of the years from 410 to 450 than of any other historical period in British history. We do know, however, that British were carried off as slaves to Ireland and that the Picts ravaged from the north and the Saxons from across the North Sea.

The future was to lie with the Saxons, but opinions as to them have changed greatly from the days of Freeman, Stubbs and Green. The more one attempts to delve into the origins of the various Germanic tribes—Angles, Saxons, Frisians, Jutes and others

[1] R. H. Hodgkin, *History of the Anglo-Saxons*, Oxford, 1935, Vol. I, p. 49.

—that crossed the water to harry the English lands, the more complicated the problems appear. The matter may profitably be left to the specialists. Where so little can be definitely known as to the origins, movements and characteristics of the various small tribes, it may suffice to class them as merely Germanic. Whether Hengist and Horsa, who used to loom so large in the history of this period, and whose figures Thomas Jefferson wished to place on the seal of the United States, were in truth real or legendary persons is now a matter of doubt. That being so, it is not worth while for our present purpose to argue whether they may have been Jutes or of some other tribe.

Before the Saxon, or Germanic conquest of Britain, various obscure German tribes had been gradually pressed from the interior of what we may call Germany to the coast, and then as pressure increased on them from behind, they were driven over the sea to England. The reasons are obscure but we may note the arrival of the Huns and other wild tribes from far to the east of continental Europe, and also perhaps the subsidence of the coast line which was reducing the habitable area for those caught between the pressure from the east and the waters encroaching on them from the west.

Whatever the causes and whatever their tribal affiliations, there was a mass of humanity being pressed across the North Sea to seek land, plunder and safety in England. The result was the Anglo-Saxon conquest, though to be accurate we may have to add other tribes to these. There are two problems: who the tribes were and where they lived on the continent, and where they settled in England. Place names, burial customs and other evidences have all been brought into play, but interesting as the surmises and inferences may be to the local antiquarian in England, we may disregard them in the larger story of empire. Whether the folk-lore story that the "proud" British King Vortigern invited Hengist and Horsa to come over to help protect him from attacks from the north has any truth or not is of less importance than the actual fact of the Germanic conquest, and its effects.

The problem of the invasion is a dark one, but whether a real

Vortigern did or did not invite over a real Hengist and Horsa to help him against the Picts and Scots, it seems fairly certain by the analogy of contemporary events elsewhere in that period that in the confusion of the times some ruler did invite some leaders of one set of barbarians to help him against other sets, and that the "saviors" got out of hand and became themselves conquerors and plunderers. It was a common story in those days. The first comers found the plunder and the land good. Word went back. Others came, and so it went on.

Probably the bands were not swarms of any one tribe but were made up of members of many—Jutes, Angles, Saxons, Frisians, even Franks—each succeeding band united for an expedition under one popular leader. There was no "invasion" in the modern sense of a great army operating on a unified plan, but scattered bands landed and conquered here and there—in Kent, up the Thames, along the Humber, in Sussex, and elsewhere—each on its own, picking out lands where they chose, and slaying or uniting with the native Britons in a bewildering variety of ways.

There was, of course, opposition on the part of the natives. Out of the mists and shadows of the time, comes, for example, the figure of a certain Ambrosius, "the last of the Romans," who is said to have united forces against the invaders. A generation or so later we encounter an unknown Welsh character who as the legendary King Arthur gave rise to one of the most prolific and poetic cycles of myths in British history. He is said to have gathered to him the "kings of Britain" and their followers, and to have fought the Saxons in twelve great battles in the last of which, that of "Mount Badon," he slew 960 enemies with his own hand. This may mean that he had been deserted by the other chiefs and that he fought at the end with only his own followers, but we do not know who he was, whence he came or where the battles, if any, were fought. It is certain that the legends connecting him with Cornwall were false as it was too far out of the fighting zone, as were also the legends of his Round Table and his "Knights" who, as myth paints them, belong to a social period centuries in the future. On the other hand, there probably was some such leader and the incrustations of legend are gathered around some solid core of historical truth.

Of more importance than historical origins is the influence that this hero of the Welsh continued to exert for at least a thousand years, from the ninth century to our own, on British literature and thought. English, Welsh and Scotch have all used and contributed to the Arthurian legends which have passed through many phases. The enormous and continuing popularity and vitality of the Celtic stories of Arthur and his knights is sufficient indication of the strength of the Celtic strain in Britain and the instinctive response to the Celtic soul which must be taken into account in trying to understand the race of today. Many qualities were to be contributed by the Germanic tribes, so opposed in many respects to the Celtic, but although the Briton of today may understand the German better than the Latin, he himself is different from either, and we may not be wrong in ascribing some of the more subtle elements of difference to the early Celt, of whom, however, we know but little.

For the understanding of the later Celtic spirit, however, there is a rich and fascinating literature, the high point in which is the collection of tales and legends known as the *Mabinogian* in which we find the choicest expression of the "Celtic magic" which merges the natural and supernatural in an enchanted world in which not only British poets but ordinary every-day common British folk still love to wander. It sets them as much apart, for instance, from the common folk of America, as the appreciation of the whimsicalities of a Lewis Carroll sets them apart from any race of the European Continent. Not only have the British inherited much of the Celtic "melancholy," but it is to the Celtic wonderland that we can trace most of the fairy lore of Shakespeare and all English tradition, and from whence we yet hear

"The horns of Elfland faintly blowing."

In any case, the conquest, infiltration, or whatever we choose to call the process by which a vast body of Germanic people settled themselves throughout England, became fairly complete, and in the following centuries we have to note the rise and warfare among themselves of Saxon kingdoms, notably at first that of the West Saxons. The first question to be considered is how far was this new blood mixed with the older British and how far did it replace it?

No definite answer can be given, for we are now dealing with the mistiest centuries in our story and have to find our way through a fog. Even the latest authorities admit that only a blurred impression can be got of the process at work. We may say, however, that it was markedly sectional. The heaviest Germanic settlements were in the south and east of England and survivals of earlier races in other parts would therefore be correspondingly greater. Moreover, different types of life suffered to different extents. The towns appear to have been generally destroyed, and although the evidence is not positive, it seems probable that the existence of even London was broken for a time. The old villa life appears also to have been rather widely wiped out. The villages and peasants may have fared somewhat better, although the not certain evidence of place names would indicate, as far as it goes, a more or less complete obliteration of the old population except in Cornwall, Wales, and on the borders. Using all sorts of evidence the problem of what proportion of the old British blood the new English race was to possess remains insoluble as to any definite figures. They would probably vary for every region and indeed for each small locality. In language and other ways the people in England became overwhelmingly Teutonic as a result of the happenings from 500 to 700, but this is far from indicating that the original Britons were wholly destroyed, though they became culturally submerged. Some of them moreover took not only the inevitable westward way to Wales and Cornwall but also crossed to the northwestern corner of France, where the Celtic language as spoken today is British Celtic.

It is hard to say why they failed so completely, but they seem to have been an unstable people. As we have seen, the centuries of Roman rule had left no such lasting impression on them as on the Gauls. When the hand of Rome was withdrawn they slipped back to old characteristics. They preferred constant civil war among

themselves to combining against the common enemy. They ran
the whole gamut from the utmost religious asceticism to the most
unrestrained indulgence of their lusts and passions. There is little
to be found of that balance, co-operation, compromise, and practical common sense that we find in the later British of our story,
though their blood and some of their traits were to be mixed with
other races to form the complex British character and temperament
of today.

It may be that the Unicorn mentioned in the Introduction owes
much to the first British whereas the Lion owes more to the Saxon.
The latter was a barbarian and he showed it in his demolishing of
the last remains of Roman culture. He was also a heathen, though
before the process of assimilation was over both conquered and
conquerors were to be Christian. But the Saxon had certain high
and needed qualities, such as co-operativeness, loyalty, steadiness
in defeat, and a courage that did not fail. He came, moreover, in
two roles. He was not simply the plunderer but also the pioneer
settler who wished to gain and cultivate land and to build up an
agricultural civilization.

Up to the middle of the sixth century the fate of Britain was
by no means certain, except as hidden in the nature of the two
peoples. All the west and north of the island, the larger part, was
yet in British hands, and there were still many British in the
midst of the Saxon settlements. The British, however, were divided into a lot of petty kingdoms, whose incapable kings could
not unite.

The Saxons were even more divided but they had within them
the germs of a genius for government which the British lacked.
Ethelbert of Kent, for example, managed to combine, without
civil war, most of the small kingdoms south of the Humber with
his own, although there was disintegration after his death. There
were kingdoms of Sussex, Essex and East Anglia, and, on the
Welsh and Scottish borders small kingdoms coalesced to form the
larger ones of Wessex, Mercia, and, most important, of Northumberland. The historians of the Victorian Age seemed certain
as to much of the history of this period which is now matter of

violent controversy, and we may pass from these shifting combi-
nations to consider the political ideas of the Saxons from which
their development came.

Here, again, we have to forget, or certainly to question, much
which was formerly taught by Stubbs and others. Trying to steer
a middle course between the old certainty and the new agnosticism,
we may accept as most likely that the Germans in coming to England brought with them preconceived ideas, of which we may note
three in particular. These were that war leaders, great or small, had
their bands of devoted followers. These might be scarcely a handful, for a raid, or after the coalescence of smaller bands under one
great leader, like the King of Mercia, might number 15,000. The
main point is that men naturally grouped themselves about a
leader whom they served loyally and from whom they in turn
received benefits. We shall find this thread running through most
of our subsequent story.

The leader, however, and this is the second idea in the Saxon
contribution, was no tyrant. He could maintain himself and his
position only by consent. The band or the people were free. Too
much stress used to be laid on "folk moots" and "Witenagemots"
as the origin of free institutions and even of Parliament. The
English, from the Saxons down, have not cared much for political theory. The point was that both leader and people knew that
the choice of a leader was a free one. Consent can be won in various ways, as the later Tudors, who made themselves almost dictators, well knew, but when a leader, monarch or other, forgets the
principle of consent, there has almost invariably been trouble in
British history from this early period down.

A third strong idea in Anglo-Saxon society was that of kinship,
but although Stubbs transferred the Germany of Tacitus to England, this wholesale transfer fails to take account of the influence
of the migration itself. The idea of kinship which was basic in
Teutonic society did apparently remain but had been much weakened by the fact that the innumerable separate bands which crossed
to England did so as mixed adventurers and not as kindred
groups. In Germany the kin group, in case of crime, for example,

could be held as a whole for compensation, and the group of the injured person shared in the receipt of the payment. In England, even in Kent, which probably remained more German in this respect than other parts, the chief responsibility was put on the offending individual. The breaking down of long-established kin groups by the method of invasion was probably responsible for this change. The old system had bred a strong sense of joint social responsibility, and the new one that of the independence of the individual, and it may not be wholly fanciful to find the germs of much in later British character in the conditions of this disturbed period.

A brief glance at the lives of the people in the heathen centuries of the conquest will let us realize the complete break with Roman Britain. The towns, as we have noted, practically disappeared. Moreover, in place of the large stone buildings in classic style, England became a land of wooden structures, the largest of which were the halls of the leaders of different bands. These were of all degrees from those of a small local magnate to those of a king such as described in the old poem of *Beowulf*. Though varying in barbaric magnificence, they adhered to a type, something like those of the later great barns, a few of which yet remain. The large room was covered by a lofty ceiling supported by huge open beams, and it is worthy of note that in a recent series of sketches in *Punch* illustrating traits in "the British character," love of such beams appeared as one. In spite of all changes since, the English find a deep satisfaction in this wooden architecture, so utterly different from the Roman, which had been swept away, after dominating for some centuries, and it indicates one of the elemental cleavages between the northern and the Mediterranean peoples.

The dimly lit hall had running down the middle the long hearth on which logs blazed, the smoke finding its way out through mere holes in the roof. Weapons and trophies hung on the walls, and benches ran round them for the retainers. High seats of honor were reserved for the lord and lady, or whatever the leader and his wife might be. In their dress there might be much of barbaric splendor, such as tunics gold-embroidered and with gold ornaments, and the Kentish jewelry in particular was among the finest in the world at that time. The drinking horns and other vessels were mounted in gold or silver gilt, often of beautiful design. In the evenings at the feasts, which played a large part in Saxon life, there would be heavy drinking, and the exploits of the leader and other warriors would be extolled. The characteristic feature of the Saxon settlements was the *ton*, now the final syllable of so many English place names, which meant merely an enclosed group of buildings, which was also, on a large scale, called a *burh*, another lasting place name ending. Surrounded by a stockade of logs set upright in the ground the appearance must have been much that of one of the early settlements on the American western frontier. Within this might be the large building of a lord, with outbuildings and cottages or merely a group of hovels of the poor.

These latter buildings were small and mean, usually built partly below the level of the soil, and of wattle and mud with thatched roofs. They were dark and, as appears from remains, frequently filthy. We have indeed got a long way from the towns and villas of the Roman period with their fine buildings, central heating and private and public baths. Socially, we have, on the one hand, the war bands who spent their lives fighting foes or wild beasts and, on the other, the ceorls and serfs who cut the forests and tilled the soil like other peaceful, hardworking pioneers.

In such poetry as has come down to us, notably *Beowulf*, we find, mingled with the glorification of heroic deeds and fights, the more somber notes of the loneliness and weariness of the laborious days of the poor, the dread of the wild wastes which still surrounded them, "the terror of the grey wolf" and other real or imaginary animals and monsters who preyed on human beings, such as the mysterious and terrifying Grendel. The Saxon poetry is as different from the classical literature of Rome as later Gothic architecture was to be from Roman, but there are deeps of feeling, sensing the sadness and mystery of life, which were to remain permanent in the English mind and readily fused with Celtic traits.

It may also be noted that Saxon poetry was deeply concerned with nature in all her moods, and especially with the sea in its every aspect. The love of the Saxons for their vessels, their fear-lessness and delight in battling with the storms with their mighty winds and waves, every change to be noted in sea or sky, are all set forth in Saxon poems with a fineness of perception and a wealth of imagery and words that mark a race which not merely used the sea but loved it. There was to be later a long period in which the English became a land-keeping rather than a sea-going people, but when England did turn again to the sea, to become its undis-puted mistress, the passion with which her mariners took the wild waves again to their hearts, delighting in their dangers, may well have been the revival of the old Saxon love of the sea. At any rate, no other races have loved, known and understood the seas as did the early Saxons, the Vikings, of whom we shall soon speak, and their descendants, the later English.

Much of the religion of the old Continental Saxons seems not to have survived the emigration, and such religion as they possessed in England bears but faint resemblance to the Scandinavian my-thology. Thor and Odin become shadows of themselves, and the great gods were apparently less important to most of the Saxon population than were a vast number of minor supernatural be-ings, such as elves, giants, sea monsters and a miscellaneous crew for which the English have never lost their love. These were all to remain in one form or another, but the Saxon, whether warrior or back-bent serf, was ready, in his increasing religious vacuum, for a new belief which should fit his moods and needs.

Christianity had been extinguished in the area which was now peopled and governed by the heathen Saxons, but not among some of the remaining British, notably in Wales and Ireland. A Celtic Church yet remained, though it had no unity, and showed no in-clination to extend the benefits of Christian faith to the heathen. It may, indeed, have taken a certain satisfaction in feeling that the hated heathen if left alone in this world would be certain to go to Hell in the next.

Celtic Christianity had received a great impetus in Ireland from St. Patrick, and in Wales from St. Illtud, both of whom had been in France and brought back the most strict form of monasticism.

26

One of Illtud's supposed pupils, David, became the patron saint of Wales, and in his monastery at St. David's the monks practised the most austere severity of life, yoking themselves to the plow in place of oxen, eating but one meal a day, and spending entire days fasting and in prayer. Irish monasticism was less rigorous, but in that island many hermits lived alone, devoted to their visions and religious life. Although the two churches were distinct, there was much intercourse between them, and Welsh and Irish monks went back and forth across the Irish Sea to teach and learn from each other.

Until the tenth century the Irish was also the Scottish Church, for we must recall that it was the Picts who lived in Scotland and the Irish were called Scots. The latter had planted a few colonies in Scotland and also started monasteries there, of which the best known was that on the island of Iona founded by St. Columba. He was of royal blood in Ireland, but decided to help the spread of Christianity in Britain and his influence from his lonely isle became widespread, for monasteries were centers of learning and missionary endeavor as well as refuges for those who wished to escape from the world.

The Irish, however, were divided into a great number of petty and warring kingdoms, and there was as little unity in Church as in State. Each king had his own monastery, and the Church as a whole was without centralization or order. Nor, although St. Patrick, who was not a learned man himself, had brought Latin to Ireland and some ideas of the Roman Church, did the Irish Church have any connection with Rome. Irish Christianity, coming down into Britain from the north, was soon to encounter Roman Christianity coming up from the south. Scotland itself was divided between Celt and Saxon, the latter having conquered the southeastern lowlands up to Edwin's Burgh (Edinburgh) built by King Edwin.

All the rest of that country, and by far the greater part, was in the hands of the original inhabitants, and, as the distinguished English historian Trevelyan has said, "the history of Scotland is largely the history of Anglicizing the Celt" without much change of race.

The work of the monks of Iona, in which they were to a considerable degree successful, was to Christianize both the races of Scotland in their day.

In 590 Gregory the Great became Bishop of Rome, with momentous consequences for all the world. The Roman Empire was in ruins, and anarchy reigned in its former provinces. Upon the seemingly weak foundation of the Roman bishopric, Gregory in a few years built up a new spiritual empire in Europe and laid the basis for a new unity and central authority. To England he sent Augustine, who landed in 597 in Kent, which he soon converted to Christianity, although he made little progress elsewhere and the Welsh Church denied his claimed authority. Thirty years later Paulinus, another emissary from Rome, converted King Edwin of Northumbria but King Penda of Mercia remained stubbornly pagan though not persecuting. The new religion had not yet taken deep hold on the people and changed with the deaths of kings or fortunes of war. After the death of Edwin, who had been conquered by Penda, Northumbria relapsed into heathenism but became Christian again when the next king, Oswald, invited the monks of Iona to send down missionaries. Thus both the Roman and the Irish Churches played parts in the conversion of the most important Saxon state of the time.

Trouble arose, however, when spheres of influence began to conflict. Rome, which had first attempted to convert the Saxon kingdoms, wanted that sphere for herself. The ostensible differences, when King Oswy of Northumbria called a Synod at Whitby in 670 to decide on the claims of the rival churches, seem today of slight importance in themselves. The Celtic Churches, both Welsh and Irish, for example, celebrated Easter on a different date from the Roman, and their monks shaved their heads in a different manner.

We must consider, however, as we shall have to do in following the religious thread all through the rest of our story, that questions which seem minor or even absurd are often but the focal points of a whole complex of racial or political emotions, traditions and outlooks, and become symbols of things that lie far deeper. In many cases the minor points may be seized upon and disputed in preference to avowing the real differences at issue. In this case the issue was the fateful one of whether the future English Church should be of the Roman or the Celtic type, and whether for many centuries ahead it should be an organized part of western Christendom or remain isolated and aloof. King Oswy's decision in favor of Rome settled the matter, and the Celtic monks and missionaries withdrew to the Celtic parts of the island.

The English, as we have seen, had already been moving away from the tribal and small-kingdom organization of society, which the Celts were yet unable to get away from, and toward consolidation and centralization. In fact, they were groping their way toward an *England,* instead of a group of warring tribes or petty states. This is largely what gives importance to the Synod of Whitby and has nothing to do with whether the skull should be shaved in front or back. Although many troubles in later days came from this first decision in favor of Rome, we have to consider each period of history to some extent by itself, and it is unquestionable that the establishment at this time of the Roman rather than the Celtic Church among the Saxons did much to create the unity and character of later England.

Accepting the unified Church of Rome assisted the unification of the state. Order and authority in the ecclesiastical realm tended to be reflected in the political, just as the disunity in the Celtic churches tended to perpetuate the disunity of the Celtic people. The statesmen, here and there, in England who were striving toward power and unity gained valuable help from the bishops and clergy who were striving toward the same goals in their own sphere. The churchmen were the learn   men of their time, and served the kings, who joined with them, by their minds as the warriors did by their arms. Moreover, the nature of kingship in public estimation was strengthened by gaining, besides mere lay power, that mystical quality which has appealed to men throughout the ages and which yet so strongly characterizes the coronation service of the present day.

The process of conversion and acceptance was gradual, as we

have seen. The fact that London was slow to accept the new order led Theodore of Tarsus, a Greek, who was Archbishop from 669 to 690, and one of the ablest in the long line of English churchmen, to establish the headquarters of the Church at Canterbury, and for nearly twelve and a half centuries his successors, the Archbishops of Canterbury, have remained the Primates of all England. The new church brought with it learning and the love of it which had long been absent, together with books, its indispensable tools. Alcuin, in his library at York, and "the venerable Bede," father of English history at Jarrow, were among the notable scholars of this period.

Slowly, also, the parish system developed, so that each parish came to possess its local church and its endowed priest, often married at that time. This system grew up together with the townships under both Saxons and Danes, of which latter we shall speak presently. If a clergy were to serve the people, to help civilize them, to pursue learning and found schools, both taxes and endowments were necessary. The churchmen were the "clerks," the men who knew law and how to write, and by deeds and wills both kings and thegns transferred property to the Church for the above purposes. While the power of the Church was thus consolidating, so likewise was the lay power. In the early part of the seventh century the so-called Heptarchy, or seven kingdoms, although their number and bounds had varied, had become practically a Triarchy with the powers and overlordships divided only between Northumbria, Mercia and Wessex.

The Saxons had thus advanced considerably since they had driven out the British from parts of the island and completed the overthrow of the Roman civilization which had been fast decaying, but it needed more than the old Britons, the Romans and the Saxons to weave the thread of British story and character before the Norman Conquest, many of which threads stretch down to the present century. The Saxons were largely men of the woods and clearings, pioneer farmers. They left the sea behind them and forgot their sea-craft. They were never men of towns or cities. Nevertheless, it is in such groupings of population where men can constantly exchange ideas, that civilization develops and that the "urbanity" grows which takes its very name from *urbs*, the Latin word for city, as opposed to the countryside.

In spite also of the advance toward unity there were still needed other forces to further that process. Among tribes or kingdoms, constantly warring among themselves, civilization is necessarily retarded. It is true that before his death in 839 Egbert, King of Wessex, had made himself to some extent over-lord of all England but he was far from being the ruler of all the English which his descendants became after the struggles with a new series of invasions by the Danes or Vikings. With these our story takes another sudden turn. As the Saxons had added their contribution of blood and traits, so now other invaders were to add theirs, and fresh and important strains were to be mingled with the already complex racial combination of the English.

Who and what were these men who were first to harry England and then contribute much to her character and later history? Without going into all the surmises and conflicting evidence of modern scholars it is sufficient to say that they were the Scandinavian peoples who lived from Denmark north. There were many local differences among the Danes themselves as well as larger differences between them and the Northmen, or Norwegians, but we can arrive at a general approximation. At home they were tillers of the soil and hardy fishermen, but everywhere had unusual access to the sea. Their history shows beyond question that they were perhaps the most remarkable of the successive invaders of Britain, for they were not merely harriers of the near-lying British Isles, but voyaged to Greenland, went conquering overland to Constantinople, won and settled Normandy in France and established a kingdom in Sicily, then the key to the Mediterranean. They were evidently an extraordinary folk and no mere barbarians.

They were, it has been said, "the wild progeny of wild lands," and that is true, as is also the fact that they could be guilty of almost inhuman crimes and blood lust, especially when the "berserk" fury was upon them. But to paint them all as fiends of cruelty is evidently quite wrong. Starting out on their overseas career as pirates and raiders they were able later to live on ordinary terms with the peoples among whom they settled, and to establish firm governments. They did, indeed, hold life cheap but with this trait went other qualities not wholly disconnected with it. They were courageous in danger, fearless, and not to be discouraged by adversity or defeat. They loved fame and admired their heroes. They were reserved, taciturn and resolute. They worshipped will power and suppressed all evidences of feeling. As seamen, they were magnificent, and were the first of European peoples to explore the wider oceans and to carve out an empire over sea routes. In their characteristics we come on a rich mine of qualities foreshadowing those of the later British race, and we cannot but believe that the strain which they were to contribute was an important one for our story.

What suddenly propelled these people on their extraordinary career of conquest it is impossible to say. It may have been unknown pressure from the east of the old sort, or the known pressure of Charlemagne on their neighbors to the south, a famine, or what-not. At any rate, a stream of peaceful emigration of farmers set in from Scandinavia to the Shetlands and the Orkneys, which became important in the eighth century. This was followed by the sudden unleashing of the warrior class. In 793 a party of Danes or Vikings raided the monastery at Lindisfarne. About the same time and in quick succession after, other parties raided the coast of Dorset, and monasteries in Scotland, Wales and Ireland, burning, plundering, murdering or carrying off the monks to slavery. Along the shores the shrieks of the peaceful inhabitants so unexpectedly given over to massacre by these terrifying strangers rose against the lurid background of flame from their burning homes and churches.

Then, for some decades, the English were left alone, though elsewhere the Viking activity was incessant. They had learned, moreover, their own power at sea and that both the British Isles and the empire of Charlemagne on the Continent had no adequate defence against them. Sea power, combined with their own character, was the road to their success, and in yet another point they resembled the British of later periods, particularly the Elizabethan. They were not merely conquerors at sea but traders bent on building up business. Professor Trevelyan notes a Viking tomb in the Hebrides where the dead warrior's pair of scales was buried with his sword and battle axe, a presage of India and much else in the British Empire of the future.

The boats of the Vikings formed the decisive military invention of their period. Long, low in the waist, open, with but one sail and perhaps sixteen oars to a side, they were enlarged and improved so as to carry a hundred warriors. So shallow that they could penetrate far inland by small rivers, moving faster than men could follow them on the banks, they were also remarkably seaworthy, and a replica of one crossed the Atlantic in 1893 in four weeks. Of the quality both of their boats and their seamanship it is enough to say that the Vikings discovered America nearly five centuries before Columbus. They also perfected their armor and weapons for land warfare so as to make them practically irresistible. Increasing in numbers, skill and knowledge (they even learned, primarily seamen as they were, to use British horses to form cavalry troops), they finally secured possession of the North, the Midlands and the East of England, and raided King Alfred in Wessex. If the blood of these folk could be peaceably blended with that of the Saxons and the underlying strains of earlier British races, the fusion might indeed produce something unique.

Alfred was easily one of the most remarkable men in English history. He was the youngest brother of Ethelstan, King of Wessex, and was chosen to succeed to the throne on his death as the ablest member of the royal house although the late King had had sons. At that time, however, the line of succession followed that of ability rather than of direct descent and minors were excluded. He had been to Rome in his early youth and throughout his career showed a far wider understanding of life and the world than any other English king of the period. We shall note presently his labors on behalf of the education of his people, but both during the reign of his brother, who steadily defended his kingdom against the Danes, and the earlier years after he himself

33

came to the throne, Alfred had to devote himself to war rather than to learning.

Experience soon taught him that the unmounted, badly equipped "fyrd," or mass rising of the people, mostly farmers, was no match for the new methods of the Danes, who had also reintroduced into England the building of fortified towns. However, when the new enemy raided his own kingdom many of his subjects fled, he himself holding out on the "Isle of Athelney" in Somersetshire, now merely a small eminence rising in a meadow, but then an actual island in undrained marshes. It was one of the critical moments in English history, for Alfred was not only threatened by the Danish hordes under their leader Guthrum, but also in the rear by the Welsh of Cornwall. His reputation, however, was so great that the thegns answered once more to his call, and, as the result of the decisive victory in the battle of Ethandune, Guthrum was forced to sign a treaty according to which he and his followers became baptized Christians and agreed to withdraw and remain within the limits of a section which became known as the "Danelaw" on the east coast.

A few years later, Alfred was strong enough to make another treaty, limiting the boundaries of the Danelaw so as to give London to the English King, who promptly fortified it. The Danes were indeed rulers of northeastern England but were becoming Christianized and also more and more settling down to the peaceful life of farm and small town, so that they themselves were ready to resist further attacks from overseas of their own kinsmen who might raid them as they themselves had raided the Saxons. Moreover, even within the Danelaw, there were many Saxons left now mingling with the Danes. To the north there was still a small unconquered Saxon section, which, however, was to become more closely allied to Scotland than to England, all of which south of the Danes was now united under Alfred. There were still minor wars but Alfred had built a navy, as well as fortified London, and the danger from across the water was much lessened.

The great Saxon King was now able to devote himself largely

to the task of repairing the ravages to learning which had been made by the destruction of the monasteries. He brought scholars from the continent, established schools, reintroduced the knowledge of Latin, and himself founded English literature by translating the work of Bede into Saxon and writing various volumes himself in that tongue. Learning and the ideals of peaceful civilization had been all but extinguished during the long dark night of brutal warfare lasting for generations, but at last the torch had been at least kindled again, and the rise of towns presaged a revival of intellectual life. Alfred also reorganized the machinery of government. Besides the creation of a fleet, improvement in the army, and the erection of forts, he developed the best civil administration the kingdom had had, until it became stronger than the less well-organized Danelaw. The political qualities of the Saxon began to outweigh the fighting qualities of the Dane.

On the other hand, the Dane was to contribute much, particularly in the field of law. The very word, law, is Danish and the "Danelaw" signified that part of England where Danish law was current. Alfred's work had not only been solid but, fortunately, his descendants proved able men, and in the next two generations were able to conquer the Danes and unite all the island, except Wales and Scotland, under themselves, whom we may regard as the first "Kings of England."

Even so, however, the Danish law remained. In fact there was a wide variety of laws and customs, and although later both the "common law" and statute laws for the whole realm were to develop slowly and naturally, it is perhaps not fantastic to consider the long history of English tolerance of local varieties as building up that vast variety which is the law in the British Empire today, and which appears in the Coronation Oath, quoted in the Introduction, in which the King has to swear to govern all the Dominions and other possessions "according to their respective laws and customs"—not British laws and customs but those of manifold communities all over the globe.

We may note that in a sense British history has always been "imperial" in that British rule and life have always had to take account of managing and understanding different peoples and races. If the British, better than any others, have learned the art of ruling by conciliation and allowing freedom to the various component races and sections of empire, their training has been a long one. The fact, however, remains, that even given so long a period in which to learn, they had, somehow, the innate qualities to profit by it.

After the reconquest of the Danelaw by the Saxons, or English, as we may begin to call them, the two peoples gradually merged, and it is interesting to see how each contributed something to that pattern which became "England." In his reorganization of government, Alfred had built up the shire, so familiar today, as a unit of administration. On the other hand, the Danes had organized a system of towns or burhs, our boroughs, each centering about a military commercial town, such as Lincoln, Derby, Leicester, Stamford, and so on, and ruled by an earl.

Both systems continued and developed. As the English extended their control of the Danelaw, they imposed their administration through shires but also they developed among themselves the system of boroughs which were to become more and more important both in trade and administration as time went on. There were innumerable local differences, as there always have been and still are, among the almost uncountable units and sections of the Empire but the form of modern England was beginning to take shape. It was not difficult, after all, for the two peoples to merge because they were of the same general racial stock, German and Scandinavian. They had many qualities in common, and others which happily supplemented each other. England, however, was not through with foreign invasion and there was yet to be heavy hammering before the welding of the modern race was complete.

Before we have to turn to the inrush of new invaders and the din of new battles we may glance for a moment at one or two aspects of the late Saxon period. This civilization, although of infinitely greater influence on the future than the earlier Roman occupation, has left fewer tangible traces. Of the great halls and homes of the nobles or thegns nothing can be seen by us, for they were made of wood. What remains we find are not of buildings but of jewels, utensils and, above all, of institutions. In spite of all the improvements in the organization of government, we must not think of the State in modern terms. That as yet did not exist. Tribal wars, along with tribal organization, were indeed disappearing, but there was as yet no "King's Peace," no police power of the central government. If England were to advance in civilization, however, men must somehow be protected in their peaceful work in villages or lonely clearings, and the organization which provided this protection, with all its faults, was the feudal system of which we now find the beginnings.

Two classes emerged, the military which maintained order and afforded protection, and the peaceful class of farmers, traders and others. The king looked to the thegns to follow him and raise troops in war, and the thegns in turn protected those locally about them. "Every man had his lord," to whom he looked for protection and justice in exchange for service. This was the general system and theory, and as we have already found the village, borough and shire of later England, so in the armed thegn, although primarily a warrior, we glimpse the future peaceful squire and Justice of the Peace. The earlier courts of justice, such as they had been, tended more and more to be replaced by feudal lords or magnates, secular or religious, as the king alienated his right to administer the law himself.

In fact, although England had been united under one Crown, it was too large and scattered, with the means of transportation and communication, to be administered from one center, and the feudal system took another step forward in the creation of a half-dozen—more or less at times—large earldoms, the earls owing duty to the king but responsible for their own sections.

We have spoken of the religious magnates, and may here note that during the tenth century there was a marked revival of the monastic life, and of religion in its various aspects. Monasteries and abbeys sprang up in all parts and became heavily endowed with riches and lands. This movement, fostered by Dunstan who

rose to be Archbishop of Canterbury from his abbacy at Glaston-
bury, resulted in a considerable part of the feudal power passing
into the hands of churchmen instead of into those of the military
leaders.

Especially noteworthy is the Saxon "wyrd" or sense of fate
which permeated all Saxon thought, and like the belief of the
Mohammedan made the warrior resolute and fearless. "Wyrd
goes ever as it must," Beowulf said when he faced destruction by
the great dragon Grendel, and the sense of a fate fixed for each
individual against which he cannot struggle contributed not only
to the reckless courage of the Northern races but to a certain gen-
tleness and especially to their grave melancholy, all notes to be
found in later English character and literature. Allied to this
theme we may find many a passage even in the earliest Saxon
poetry which might belong to any period of English character,
such as the line in *The Lament of Deor:*

> That passed over, so also may this,

or those in the *Far-Traveller:*

> Who before the host   his fame would raise,
> Manfully act until   all depart,
> Both light and life: who lives for honor
> Hath steadfast glory   under the stars.

As the world slowly emerged from the barbarism following the downfall of Rome, the Church was to be the main factor in preserving and nourishing learning and civilization, and
the work of Dunstan, afterwards made a saint, had an important
lay as well as clerical significance. A Celt, he combined the temperament of that race with the cooler statesmanship of the English, and for long he was the most influential adviser of the
Crown. Not a great deal is definitely known of him and the body
of popular myths which grew up around his name may be disregarded save in so far as they point to a figure who in striving
for learning and order was ahead of his time.

In this period it looked as though a united England was
developing naturally toward a strong feudal state of the later

type of the Middle Ages. The situation, however, was not nearly as sound as it appeared. The real condition had been somewhat obscured by the fact that four generations of the House of Alfred had been men of marked ability, but in spite of mixture and nominal peace, Saxon and Dane had not really coalesced and the Danelaw separated the strong southern part of Saxon England from the weak northern portion, so that the new structure might crack either if an incompetent king came to the English throne or if invasions should again occur on a grand scale. Both of these possibilities eventuated simultaneously.

We may stop for a moment to glance across the channel. There, in Normandy, the Northmen had built up a powerful and compact duchy. From the duke down through a series of gradations, the feudal system of lands and other benefits conferred in exchange for military service was a fact and strictly enforced, whereas in England, although the system was similar in theory, there was much more looseness and less efficiency in its practical working. The earls with their large territories, and the religious and lay lords of lower ranks, formed no such unified military machine as was at the command of the Norman duke.

In 975 Edgar, last of the able descendants of Alfred, died, leaving two sons, both children. As we have noted, there was no formal rule of succession and the monarchy was largely elective within the royal family. A quarrel broke over the two boys, Edward and Ethelred, the former being favored by the lay lords and the latter by the ecclesiastical. Edward was elected king, only to be assassinated four years later, when the crown fell to Ethelred, then a boy of ten. He was entirely unfit for the office, and his nickname of "Redeless" meant that he was without advice, especially after the death of Dunstan.

Probably he could not have controlled the forces making for the internal weakness of England in any case, but in 984 the Vikings, or Danes and Norse, began a new series of descents upon England which were designed for plunder and not for settlement. Alfred had had, on occasion, to buy the Vikings off by tribute but now the Danegeld began in earnest. Ethelred first

39

gave them £10,000, a sum vastly larger in purchasing power then than now, and in later years sum after sum was thus extorted. This Danegeld, or tribute to the Danes, had far-reaching effects. It was the beginning of direct taxation. It ruined the peasantry, hastened serfdom, and later as a matter of convenience made the lord the tax gatherer, with the eventual implication that he owned the lands for which he was made responsible for the taxes.

To add to the confusion, the King of Norway and the King of Denmark, both of whom had been driven from their thrones at home, joined forces, and with their followers attacked London. That city put up a stout fight and repulsed the attackers, but as a result of their plunderings and burnings in the country they were bought off with £16,000 by Ethelred, though only for a respite. Sweyn of Denmark recovered his own kingdom and became more formidable than ever. In the hope, perhaps, of help, Ethelred married the sister of the Duke of Normandy, and began that Norman connection which was to last until William I himself conquered England and became king.

Meanwhile, Sweyn returned again and again to the attack, and so conquered the ill-knit kingdom that he was accepted as King of England. Ethelred fled to Normandy. Monasteries were sacked and ruined. The Archbishop of Canterbury was murdered, and the country overrun. When at last Sweyn died after an attack on the monastery at Bury St. Edmunds, his followers chose his son, Canute, as his successor and in spite of the opposition of the English he forced the Witenagemot, or assembly of the Saxons, to choose him king, so that he became the ruler of all England.

The choice was a fortunate one, although for the first time the Witenagemot had gone outside of the royal family to choose a monarch. This body, we may here note, was not made up of popular representatives nor was it the origin of Parliament as many of the nineteenth-century historians of the German school liked to believe. It was composed only of magnates, both lay and ecclesiastical, and royal officials on a more or less chance basis. Although it served a useful purpose as a sort of great council of the realm, bringing together many of its leading men, it was never the direct precursor of any later body known to the British Constitution, and its importance used to be too highly rated.

Canute, though he preferred his English kingdom, came by his brother's death to rule over an empire which included both England and Denmark and later by conquest Norway. He governed England well, however, and after his firm establishment on the throne instead of paying off his followers in confiscated English lands, he paid them in a Danegeld and sent them back to Denmark. A heathen in his youth, he had become a thoroughly conforming Christian, and not only enriched the Church but advanced Englishmen to its high offices, and chose his friends and advisers from among these ecclesiastics and leading English laymen. Among the latter the most notable was the Saxon Earl Godwin of Wessex, whose career now began. The Court language was both Saxon and Danish, and under Canute's rule there was little or none of that dislocation of institutions and ways of living which was to follow the later conquest of the French-speaking Normans under William.

Canute himself died in 1035, leaving two sons, Hardecanute and Harold, born of different wives. Godwin, with his great influence, and the West Saxons generally, declared for Hardecanute, whereas the North and Midlands chose Harold. It is sufficient to give the bare outline of events up to the Norman Conquest of a generation later.

Canute's empire broke up on his death, and after fighting for the English throne between his two sons and Alfred, an exiled son of Ethelred, who was murdered, the English chose Edward, another son of Ethelred.

Brought up in Normandy, which was more cultivated than England, Edward not only preferred the French language but the French-Norman ways and men, and filled his court with Normans, although Godwin managed to retain power over the weak King who was capable of making trouble but not of ruling. The earl by the marriage of Edward to his daughter even became the King's father-in-law, but his own dislike of the Normans, and the evil doings of his son Swegen, a young brute apparently, led finally to Godwin's downfall and banishment. During his absence the young Duke of Normandy, William, came over to pay a visit to Edward, who agreed that the Norman should succeed him on the English throne.

The English were growing weary of having the high offices filled by foreigners and were becoming so restive that Godwin felt it safe to return from exile, and was reconciled to the King, who restored him to his earldom. Within a year or so, however, Godwin suddenly died while dining at the King's table. He had had six sons, of whom the eldest, the good-for-nothing Swegen, was now happily dead. The eldest surviving son, Harold, succeeded to the estates and power of his father and practically governed England in the name of Edward. He was a man of great ability, though the King preferred the next younger among his brothers-in-law. In any case, Edward lavished titles and lands on Godwin's sons until the brothers came to rule the richest and most populous part of England—the south and east. Another family, the descendants of the great Earl Leofric of Mercia, ruled the Midlands and most of Northumberland, the two families thus dividing all England between them and being rivals for supreme power.

Meanwhile the question of the succession to the throne in case of the death of the childless King Edward had arisen. Another Edward, a son of Edmund Ironside, who had lived in exile as far away as Hungary, was recalled and accepted as heir but died almost immediately on arrival, leaving only an infant. It was obvious that, with the danger impending from William the Norman's claims in case of the King's death, it would be utter folly to place a child on the throne. The expected death and crisis occurred in 1066. Harold, the son of Earl Godwin, although not of royal blood, had shown himself a man of unusual capacity, and had recently conquered Wales. On the death of Edward, January 5, Harold was at once chosen king and crowned in the earlier Westminster Abbey which Edward had built on the site of the present one.

Meanwhile, Duke William in Normandy had increased his power by the conquest of the French province of Maine. We have already seen how the English kings were chosen in this period, and William obviously had no valid claim whatever to the kingship of the English. Of the several reasons he put forward to assert his right, the best-sounding was the promise of the late Edward to him of the succession, a promise, however, which had no validity whatever in English law or custom. Nevertheless, the prize was great and, although not without some difficulty, William persuaded a large number of his feudal followers to adventure with him into England, promising them lands and plunder.

Harold knew well of the approaching storm, but William and his bands did not come until autumn, when a considerable number of Harold's troops had dispersed for the harvest season. Meanwhile there had been trouble in the north. Harold's own brother Tostig, whom Edward had deposed as Earl of Northumberland with Harold's consent, owing to his harsh treatment of the people of that province, joined with the King of Norway in raids on the Yorkshire coast. Harold, when he heard the news, at once marched to the aid of the two northern earls, Edwin and Morkere, who were his brothers-in-law, but arrived near Stamford only to learn that York had submitted to the enemy. However, he came on the Norsemen and surprised them at Stamford Bridge, winning a victory in which both his own brother, Tostig, and the Norse King were slain.

At the very moment when he was celebrating this feat, a messenger arrived with news that the Normans under William had landed at Pevensey on the channel coast. Harold at once hurried southward to meet the new foe but without the troops who should have followed him. At this critical moment the weakness of the old English system of dividing the administration of the kingdom into a few great earldoms made itself fatally felt. We have noted that the country had come to be governed by practically two great families, those of the descendants of Godwin and their adherents, and those of the descendants of Leofric and such followers as adhered to them.

In their danger, Harold had gone to the aid of the latter in the north as King of all England, but when danger threatened England in the south, they refused to help England by aiding Harold. Some of the troops did follow him, and, of course, his own "house carls." He gathered others on the way, but it was with an inadequate force that he finally faced William at Hastings.[1] He was to fight only with infantry, of whom a large part, those of the "fyrd," were without armor. Their weapons were chiefly the old battle axes which were to be wielded effectively but were not to win the day. We do not know how many men Harold had but the number was certainly much less than that of the Norman host.

The latter, although no exact figures can be had, seems to have been composed of about 12,000, somewhat less than half of them cavalry. They were a mixed crew of adventurers and, although there were many of the Duke's feudal retainers, the army was not a feudal levy but made up of those who sought their fortunes in the chance to plunder England. There were feudal nobles and knights from provinces which owed no allegiance to William, and the best description of the invading host is that of Trevelyan, who calls it "a joint-stock enterprise for the sharing out of English lands." And they got them, though the amazing part is not the loss of this first battle by the English but that a force of not more than 12,000 should have been able to subdue and rob a nation of perhaps 1,500,000 to 2,000,000. The fact is that England was not yet a nation, but was now at last to be made into one, and the Norman was the final invasion of the country by foreigners, as the landing of the later William in 1689, by invitation, does not deserve that name.

In the centuries that have followed, the wild English landscape of the earlier day has changed almost beyond recognition into that parklike aspect in general that so strikes all foreigners, and it is hard to realize as one stands today at the top of the steep slope at Hastings and looks downward over the lush lawn to the

---

[1] A certain school of historians now call this the battle of Senlac but I prefer the more usual and familiar name.

44

winding brook at the bottom, now seeming like a haunt of ancient peace, that here one of the decisive battles of the world was fought. If the aspect has changed, the lay of the land remains the same, and it is easy to note how well Harold chose his ground at the top of the slope so that the Norman cavalry would have to charge up it before they could come in contact with the British.

Twice they charged and were forced back, but a feigned flight of the Norman left wing lured some of the English down the hill. When the enemy unexpectedly turned back to the attack the defenders on the slope had been thrown into some confusion, yet they stood their ground, behind a barrier of locked shields. Then William ordered his bowmen to shoot their arrows into the air to fall on those behind the improvised defense. When the deadly rain of shafts had ceased, Harold and all his house carls lay dead, and such survivors as there were among the ordinary troops fled into the dark of night.

King and army were no more. Such leaders as were in London chose Edgar, the grandson of Edmund Ironside, as a new king, but there was no united action against the invaders. The northern earls, thinking only of defending their own earldoms, fled to the north. William's victorious army harried Kent and Sussex, and isolated London. On Christmas Day of this same year, 1066, the election of Edgar was reversed and William was proclaimed king in London, being crowned in the same abbey where Harold had received the crown a year before. It is one of the odd facts of English history that England was never again to have a royal family of purely English blood. There were to be the Norman and Angevin lines, the Welsh Tudors, the Scotch Stuarts, and the German Hanoverians of the present House of Windsor, but no more English. Yet England was now to be united as never before, and with the last important infusion of foreign blood of the conquering Norman army and those who came after them, the English race was to be welded into its present form.

CHAPTER III

THE RULE OF THE NORMANS

CIVILIZATION IN BRITAIN always advanced more rapidly in the rich lands of the south and east of England than in the mountains of Wales or Scotland, and it was one of the unfortunate effects of the topography of the island and of its geographical relation to the Continent that it was always precisely the most civilized regions which were most open to attack. Moreover, when the barbarians overran those regions they also cut off the culture of the west and north from European influences. The Saxon and Danish invasions had linked England not to the culture of the Continent but to its barbarism. The coming of the Normans, for the first time since the passing of the Romans, was once more to bring Britain within the orbit of the most advanced culture of the time, and in this respect, as well as in welding England into a unified nation, the conquest by William was both necessary and eventually beneficent.

But the land had been gained by conquest in spite of William's specious claim to be merely the lawful successor of Edward; and its owners and dwellers were promptly made to feel the reality of that fact. The Conqueror's task was colossal. He had to control a native population of perhaps well on to 2,000,000. He had also to control his own followers, numbering only some thousands, but all bent on plunder, and on them his own power had primarily to rest. Unlike the followers of Canute, who could be sent home loaded with Danegeld, those of William had come to stay. Having assumed that he was the successor of Edward, he asserted that Harold had been a usurper who had kept him from his throne, and proclaimed the forfeiture of his estates and those of all his followers. This wholesale confiscation of English land and wealth for the benefit of himself and his Norman barons and knights was but the beginning. Further fighting as a result of uprisings gave him the excuse for confiscations on an even greater scale.

The whole south, including the great estates of Earl Godwin in Wessex, was soon in his hands. In Mercia and Northumbria, however, the Earls Edwin and Morkere rebelled, assisted by the Welsh and the sons of the King of Denmark. William's vengeance was swift and savage. In his "harrying of the north," as it is called, between York and Durham, he left no house standing and no human being living. A considerable part of the population of Yorkshire was massacred. The countryside there and in Durham and other sections was left waste, without buildings, crops or cattle. The Danelaw submitted to his rule and it was as useless as it was gallant for a man like Hereward "the Wake" to make a last stand in the fen district. The English, without leaders, were beaten to their knees, and the whole country was subject to such unification as William's despotism or statesmanship might bring about.

But it was not enough to conquer the English. The Normans must also be controlled, and both races governed. William had sworn to maintain the old laws of Edward, but his power must evidently rest upon some form of the feudal system to which his followers were accustomed. Great fortresses, such as the Tower of London, from which the Norman barons could maintain control, were built throughout the country. But just as the loosely organized English kingdoms had tended toward anarchy and weakness, so the feudal system on the Continent had become wholly anarchic. To understand the situation in the eleventh century, which Vinogradoff has well called "the water shed" of English history, we must forget our modern ideas of government. No government or king was then all powerful, nor had our conception of "the State" yet arisen. What William did, though we cannot describe all his policies in detail, was to fuse to some extent the old English ideas with those of feudalism, making a new form and starting on their long history such fundamental factors in English life as the monarchy, the landed aristocracy, local government, and the Church.

The feudal theory on the Continent had been logically perfect. At the head was the duke or other leader. In a descending scale came the lower ranks, each owing service to those above it in return for use of land. We have already noted the theory in the more attenuated form it had obtained in England. But, on the Continent, in practice, the greater barons and others in their castles had become so powerful as frequently to defy the head of all, and to fight or combine among themselves. William wished to avoid this situation in his new kingdom. He destroyed the great earldoms of Saxon times, and in parcelling out lands to his Norman followers took care to distribute their holdings in various sections of the country so that though their estates might be huge they would be so scattered and broken as to afford their lords less power to fight one another or the king, though the latter could command the allegiance and service of all the scattered domains of each.

Moreover, with the exception of three counties on the Scotch border, it was the King and not the barons who ruled locally. William did this in part through his feudal followers but also through new officers, especially the sheriffs, who were directly responsible to the Crown. The smallest feudal unit was the manor, of which we shall speak presently, and it was the lords of the manors who were made directly responsible for the collection of taxes. On the whole, with the exception of setting aside huge tracts for his hunting, such as what is still called the New Forest, William governed well, and he could count on support from the English, so that he had no great difficulty in suppressing a rising of the barons against him in 1075, which was a result of their dissatisfaction over the curbing of their powers. The fact that the claws of the vassals had been cut made for peace in the realm, and the ordinary man wanted peace.

William did not rule entirely without advice, although it may be assumed that he usually took his own. He had the feudal council made up of his tenants-in-chief, that is of those who held their lands directly from him, though such holdings might be enormous or a mere manor. As a rule he probably consulted only those who were easily accessible, but in 1086, the year he completed the Domesday Book and the year before he died, he held a great Council at Salisbury at which not only tenants-in-chief but sub-tenants also attended in large numbers, all being forced to take an oath that they would be faithful to him personally against all other men. This was another break with continental feudalism, for though every man had his lord, he had now sworn to be faithful not to the lord but to the King if there were conflict between the two.

The Domesday Book, just mentioned, illustrates both the power and the careful administration of the King. It is a record of the lands and certain other property, including all cattle, swine, etc., of every feudal tenant and sub-tenant in all England, down to the lords of the manors. As the theory was that the king owned all the land, all others holding only from him directly or indirectly, it was a complete survey of Crown property. Those below the lord of the manor owned him as lord and the manor now replaced the town as a political unit.

The lord held his own court of justice and, as we have just seen, was responsible for the collection of all taxes due from his tenants. There were also other courts, such as that of the Shire or County, and of the higher feudal nobility, but as yet the only royal court was that for crimes against the atrocious forest laws. These were cruel in the extreme and it has been stated that under William the royal forests came to cover one-third of the entire territory of the kingdom. The King, however, took a long step forward in his separation of the ecclesiastical from the lay courts. This move was to enable Church and State each to develop on its own lines, an extremely important point, for the English common law would not have developed as it did had it been tied to the growth of the Canon Law of the Church instead of being left free to grow up in its own way. Rome did not rule England because

49

William insisted on his right to appoint the bishops and abbots, who were as important as many of his lay feudatories.

We may now turn to consider a little the life of the people in the Norman period, that is the reign of William and his immediate successors. We have already spoken of the barons in their castles. Nothing like these huge stone fortresses had been seen in England before, and it seems to be a question whether they had existed in Normandy either. Such ruins as those of the castles of Rochester, Guilford and others are well known to all familiar with the English countryside, whereas the waste which their owners all too often created around them has disappeared. Of the tangible effects of the Conquest nothing is left more striking than its architecture with its characteristic round arch, and many of the most beautiful buildings in England remain to us from this period. The castles are all in ruins but William was a generous patron of the Church, and where he placed a powerful lay lord he was likely also to establish an equally important ecclesiastic, and many of the abbeys, and particularly the cathedrals, have fared better down the centuries than the castles. Religious worship continued and needed the old buildings whereas changed methods of war made the castles useless.

We may think of England as first dominated by the invincible spirit and vast ability of William. Below him came the great lay barons and the leading bishops and abbots. But perhaps even more important than these, though less conspicuous, were the innumerable lords of the manors and the great mass of common folk. The great castles, though numerous, were fortresses, and in their gloomy and often vast interiors the life led was apart from that of the rest of the nation.

There was much less difference between the manor house and the earlier Saxon hall than between the castle and anything that had appeared before. Although the hall of the manor house was often of stone, the rest of the building was usually of wood as in earlier days. The furnishing and use of the hall remained also much as before, except that the manor Court of Justice was held in it. Furniture was simple and plain, but beside the hall we now find a sitting and bed room for the lord and lady and distinguished guests. In addition to them the house was inhabited by pages, squires and girls of good birth, who there served and learned their manners and duties somewhat in the fashion of a modern "finishing school." Besides these there were the many servants and attendants of various sorts, and all of these slept together in the hall, there being no other separate bedrooms than that of the lord, and it may be added, no night clothes of any sort for any one. Light was scant both day and night, the windows being without glass and artificial light being limited to candles or torches. Although there were hunting, games, dances, minstrels and music, life must have been a rather dull affair. The poorer people had merely hovels, with no light, and often even fires were hard to come by. It is no wonder that heavy drinking was general among all classes. Although the villeins and free tenants occupied a position between the lords of the manor and the boors or serfs, it was to be some generations before what we now call the middle class began even slightly to emerge.

Much has been made, as in Scott's *Ivanhoe*, of the fact that the two races, Norman and Saxon, lived separate lives side by side. This is true only in part. The deep gulf which separated the upper class from the laboring was rather feudal in nature than racial. It was to a great extent also linguistic, as the upper class spoke French for some three centuries while the lower was developing English as a spoken and not a written language. French was also the language of the law courts, and the majority of our law terms today are of French origin. From their social life and dealing with their dependents, at least most of the upper class must have been bi-lingual. Indeed, many, tri-lingual, for Latin was the language of the Church, and almost all of those who were "learned," that is, who could read and write, were clerics and not laymen. Out of this medley, our modern English slowly developed. The Conquest was to create not only a nation but a language and literature.

There was one other result which we may mention here although its full effect was not felt for a century or more. Under the Saxons an estate was generally inherited by the several sons. This, however, did not fit into the military-feudal system, and with the Conquest was introduced the law or rule of primogeniture by which only the eldest son inherited, so that both ownership of the estate and its attendant duties should not be successively sub-divided. One of the most notable features of the English aristocratic system is that it forms no closed caste as on the Continent, a point we alluded to in the Introduction. On the Continent the son of a noble was a noble himself by virtue of birth, whereas, in England, the younger sons, instead of being sheltered as nobles, although with perhaps very small or no patrimonies, are not only thrown out on the world to make their own way by their own energy and ability but also to become commoners. In spite of the obvious objections which may be brought against the system, it enables great families to continue for generations and at the same time makes an elastic social structure. On the whole I think history shows that it has been for the good of the Empire, but whether so or not it has certainly been one of the great molding forces which has given British life its present form, and it came from the Norman kings.

The monarchs both of that line and of the later Angevins, all French, who were now to govern England were, as a rule, men of very marked ability. This did not apply, however, to William's immediate successor, William Rufus, who might have undone his father's work had the foundations not been so firmly laid. The first William had left three sons, Robert the eldest who inherited Normandy; Rufus, nicknamed the "Red King," who inherited England; and Henry who inherited merely money. Rufus was a man of shameless immorality even for that age, wholly untrustworthy and unfit to be a king, but of great energy.

Within a year of his accession the barons revolted in favor of the claims of Robert, who they thought would be easier to control, but Rufus with the help of the English suppressed the rising, making promises which he broke as soon as his power was restored. Through his chief minister, Ranulf Flambard, who became Bishop of Durham, he so increased feudal dues of various sorts as to ruin innumerable families and estates, accumulating wealth while he impoverished his subjects. He put down insurrections on the Scottish border and in 1096 took Normandy in pawn when Robert went to the East on a crusade. The latter's rule had been as despicable, though not as strong, as that of Rufus in England, and the landless Henry had established himself as a ruler of a small part of his brother's domain at the request of the oppressed inhabitants. In 1100, Rufus, while hunting in the New Forest, was killed by an arrow shot from an unknown hand. His death, whether intentional, which is probable, or not, was a blessing for England.

When the news reached Normandy, Henry at once hurried across the channel to Winchester, then the royal capital, and was proclaimed king by such of the nobles as chanced to be there. He then went on to London where he was crowned in Westminster, pledging himself to restore justice. Unlike his brother he kept his pledges, and placed Flambard in the Tower as prisoner.

We may pass over the reign of this "Lion of Justice" and merely note that he managed to control the rebellious barons who rose against him because they felt their powers curbed by the strength with which he maintained the law; and that with the peace and order established by him trade flourished and the country developed. The control over the barons, begun by William the Conqueror himself, was to prove of great influence on later history, and in his struggle with the Roman Church, as represented by Anselm, he anticipated the still greater struggle to come under Henry VIII. It should also be noted that to please the English he married Eadgyth who became known as Matilda or Maud, because at the Court English names were considered barbaric. By this marriage, however, the blood of Alfred and the earlier English kings was transmitted to the later line.

Following the death of Henry, whose only surviving legitimate heir was a daughter, Matilda, there ensued a period of anarchy during which the great barons revolted, and it appeared for a time as though such civilization as England had attained would be drowned in a sea of blood. Indeed in the war which ensued between Matilda, Stephen (another descendant of the Conqueror), and the barons it was said that "Christ and his saints were asleep," so savage were the methods of fighting and the tortures inflicted. Eventually, however, following Stephen's death, the throne went to Henry, a son of Matilda and her husband Geoffrey of Anjou, or Geoffrey Plantagenet as he was called, and a new line of kings began.

The young Plantagenet, or Angevin, Henry II, who although only twenty-two years of age had seen much fighting in England, had inherited from his father the great provinces of Normandy and Anjou and by his marriage had acquired Aquitaine as well. When he undertook the difficult task of restoring order out of anarchy, he was thus possessed of the largest realm any King of England had yet been called upon to govern—all of England and Wales, most of the western half of present France, with claims on Scotland. From the King of the latter he regained the counties of Northumberland and Cumberland which Stephen had surrendered. So young when he came to so great power, he was singularly free from vices, and possessed a clear mind, strength of will and tireless energy. His empire which extended from the Scotch border to the Pyrenees might well have tempted him to overweening ambition, but he wisely made no effort to conquer further territory on the Continent, and devoted himself to the consolidation and administration of what he already possessed.

Desirous of governing well he realized that he must have the good will of those below the rank of the great barons, the latter being the chief enemies of a stable order. He destroyed many of the castles which they had built in defiance of the royal will, and, this done, set himself to strengthen the Crown and bring peace and content by changes and improvements in the administration of law and justice. He consulted the Great Council more often than his predecessors, but it was a Council in which he saw to it that not only the great barons but also the lesser landholders were called to give advice and learn the art of governing.

He also made a change, which was to have far-reaching consequences, in the military system. The fighters raised in the old

Saxon "fyrd" could not be called upon to leave England, and those raised under the system of feudal levy could not be made to serve for more than forty days. Although Henry was not aggressive, the wide extent of his domains demanded a better system and army. For that reason and also to lessen the power of the feudal nobility, he came to an agreement with the knights that instead of military service, each should pay annually a sum of money called scutage (shield money), which released him from a burdensome duty and gave the king funds with which to employ mercenary troops where and as he would. From this we may trace the gradual rise of that very characteristic and valuable factor in English life—the country gentleman, with public duties, and a strong sense of them, but duties which were now to become of a civil and not a military nature.

Peace in the land after the long anarchy of Stephen and the barons brought prosperity and opportunities to increase wealth, both on the landed estates and in the growing towns. In the latter, although the day of the yeoman farmer had not yet dawned in the country, a middle class, which is the balance wheel and main strength of any government, began to develop. Henry was thus building up classes whose desire for peace and order might be even more important to him in holding the barons in check than any mere fighting force.

At the extreme opposite end of the social scale from the barons whom Henry was trying to tame into submission for the sake of civilization, were the serfs or villeins. These were forever bound to the soil on which they were born and were as much a physical part of an estate as the trees which grew upon it. They were bought and sold with the acres, were subject to many unjust taxes by their lord, and in some respects were mere slaves, although they never sank to such misery as the French peasants. Each had a little land of his own and shared in the use of the "common" land. Even more important, they had certain legal rights, and in so far as Henry ameliorated their position at all it was by the improvement in the administration of justice.

Although it is true that the serf could not plead in the "King's

Courts," nevertheless, as all justice improved and the sense of it and of law increased, the villein did gain access to the Manor Courts and was not a mere slave or chattel but could plead against his lord in open court. The lord could not do with him as he would. It is said that the villein even had the right of sitting as a judge with freemen in his lord's court, and his services, wrongs, taxes, and right to his own little land and a part of his own time were settled not by the whim of one man but by the "custom of the Manor." Hard as his life was, brutishly narrow and impossible to rise from, here were checks on his exploitation which the continental peasant did not possess.

One of the great advances made by Henry was his double system of juries. The old system of arriving at the guilt or fraud of a man by making him walk on red hot iron or by other "ordeals," and the earlier system of compurgation or the later trial by battle had none of them anything to do with essential truth or justice of any case, and it is impossible to estimate the amount of suffering and injustice through centuries that they must have caused. Henry provided for two jury systems. One jury was made up of twelve men called Recognitors who were witnesses to the facts in a case, if such men could be found, and if not they were to make all possible enquiry. They had to come to a unanimous verdict and if they did not, others were added until some twelve could agree. Here is certainly the germ of our modern jury system, different as it is in important particulars, and it was an immense advance over the former barbarous and illogical ways of reaching a verdict.

The other form of jury he instituted is nearer to our modern Grand Jury. In each county he provided for a body of twelve men from the hundred and of four from each township, whose duty it was to "present" a person accused of crime. If they "indicted" him as we might say today, he had to go through the ordeal and even if he succeeded in this if they decided he was of notorious bad character he was banished from England. This was bad enough but it was an improvement upon the earlier methods of justice— so-called.

As we shall see in a moment, the new King's Courts and justice had their bad points, but there was one great gain, unseen perhaps by Henry himself. Because they were improvements they became popular, and in addition the Crown wanted to get as many cases tried in them as possible for the sake of the fines and other perquisites. Henry renewed the system of itinerant justices, and little by little throughout the country for many cases the King's Courts replaced those of the county and manor. This permitted the growth of a uniform body of law which belonged, however, to neither of the two great systems which had grown up on the Continent, namely the Canon and the Civil laws of Rome. The Canon law had been relegated to the ecclesiastical courts when they were separated from the lay courts; and English lawyers, though they studied the Roman Civil law, preferred to settle cases by custom and precedent rather than by cut and dried rules. Thus developed a great mass of case law and precedents, which owing to the universality of the King's Courts gradually came to be the "common law" of England, which has run on wholly different lines from the codes of the continent. Henry thus laid the foundations of the modern English legal system.

The King's Courts, however, were connected also with the Exchequer, and could be and were used to increase taxation and the royal revenue, particularly under his successors. Later, what was known as the General Eyre became notoriously a means of raising money, often unjustly. A special commissioner would be sent to a county to examine every transaction of the sheriff and freemen for years past, exacting fines for every error they could discover. The possibilities of extortion on behalf of a needy monarch in such a system are obvious.

Before we leave the question of Henry's reform of the law we must notice one seed, unwittingly planted by him, which grew into an evil of huge proportions in the next few centuries. In general, the King was a good judge of men to serve him, but he made one irretrievable error. When he came to the throne as a young man he had made Bishop Thomas of London, afterwards known as Thomas Becket, his Chancellor, and later unfortunately made him Archbishop of Canterbury, and so head of the English Church.

57

Becket at once said he could not serve two masters, chose the Church and resigned the Chancellorship in which he had done good work.

Various causes of contention arose between the King and the Archbishop, among them the acquittal by an ecclesiastical court of a clerk, or cleric, who had committed rape. At a Great Council held at Clarendon, the King secured the drawing up and approval of what became known as the Constitutions of Clarendon. Among the sixteen points ruled on was one providing that a criminal clerk if convicted by an ecclesiastical court or pleading guilty should be deprived of his clerical immunity and then turned over to the civil courts for punishment. It must be recalled that, as we have said before, the term clerk included practically every one who could read and write even if he were not in holy orders and a priest of the Church. Becket strongly objected, and other matters also came between the King and his former official.

Becket fled to France and Henry banished four hundred of his adherents. Becket did not receive the aid he had hoped from France or either of the two Popes who were then rivals. However, he could still consider himself Archbishop, and Henry made no move to try to appoint a successor. Some six years after Becket's flight, Henry in an effort to secure the royal succession to his eldest son had him crowned by the Archbishop of York, others taking part in the ceremony. At once Becket sent a notice of excommunication to all the bishops involved on the ground that the Archbishop of Canterbury only could crown a monarch. Henry then allowed Becket to return on a vague understanding that the past would be forgotten and a *modus vivendi* arranged. Becket, however, refused when home to remove the excommunication, and in a moment of irritation Henry exclaimed that there was none to avenge him on an "upstart clerk."

Four knights at once started for Canterbury and after an altercation with the Archbishop assassinated him in the cathedral. The catastrophe had come from the Archbishop's pride and unyielding temper and a fit of anger on the part of the King. Becket, among other acts, had refused assent to the Constitutions of Clarendon, and owing to the popular indignation over his murder, which made his tomb one of the most noted places of pilgrimage in England, the advance which had been made in the Constitutions was lost. All who could claim to be clerks or who could obtain minor orders once more came under only the ecclesiastical and not the civil courts, with gross legal abuses which lasted well into the Middle Ages.

Henry himself immediately had recognized the full nature of the catastrophe to his policies which the foolish knights had brought down on him. He was on the Continent at Agentan when the news reached him and for three days he neither spoke nor ate. The whole clergy of England were forced into hostility to him. The populace talked of the miracles being performed at the martyr's tomb. The barons felt themselves strengthened, and the King of France took a hostile stand, while the Pope was prevented from excommunicating the English monarch only by the unauthorized promise on the part of his messengers to the Pontiff of unconditional submission. England was in turmoil, and scarcely a safe refuge to which the King could return for the moment, and so Henry turned to Ireland, which was in a condition of anarchy.

There Danes warred against the Irish, and the Irish warred among themselves, but in 1154, Adrian IV, the only Englishman who ever became Pope, had given the country to Henry on the grounds that he had the disposal of it as all islands belonged to the Holy See. Thither Henry now turned, and for twenty weeks violent storms prevented all news reaching him from England. Although he was unable to conquer and pacify the island he did do much to prevent the growth there of a feudal baronage which would have strengthened the English barons against him. In spite of this, the latter revolted and there was practically civil war by 1174, the younger Henry taking their side against his father, the ungrateful heir claiming that his coronation, and a second one in France, had made him king. Henry put down the rising with the help of his mercenary troops, whom he employed in England for the only time on this occasion. When once more in power he reorganized the service of the old English "fyrd," and showed that he meant to govern with the help and consent of the English, and to preserve them against both the anarchy that feudal baronage meant and a royal despotism on the part of a king, in so far as he could. It was perhaps the greatest of his achievements that he showed the way for England, first of European nations, to emerge from the necessity of such a choice. His last years were embittered however by quarrels among his sons. Although Henry and Richard were both pledged to go on a crusade to the east, they took to fighting between themselves, with Philip II of France now on one side and now the other, and the King's best-loved son, John, undertook to support Richard against his father.

On the King's death, 1189, Richard was acclaimed as inheritor of all his father's English and Continental domains. Called the "Lion Hearted," he was a generous and chivalrous warrior but not a statesman. He was a typical knight errant, the man with his own code of chivalry, and restless for adventure. His reign is an odd interlude in English history. He was not an administrator like his father, and preferred life in his Continental possessions to England. His first wish was to go on a crusade, and while he was away his disloyal and unpopular brother John plotted against him.

As compared with the luxurious East, Europe was still crude and semi-barbarous. Moreover, not only had the holy places of the Christian religion, including Jerusalem, fallen into the hands of the infidels, but there had long been danger lest the East overrun and conquer the nascent civilization of the West. In this period, however, due to various changes such as the Christianizing of the Hungarians, there appeared to be opportunity of reversing the tide, of carrying conquest eastward and of recovering the Holy Land for Christendom. The effort, represented in successive crusades, was characteristic of both the chivalric and religious ideas of the time. Although the crusades were of very varying degrees of success and importance, and did not gain their object, nevertheless they were of large influence on the life of both Europe and England. The Saracens and Byzantines had both much to contribute to the commercial, social and intellectual lives of the peoples of the West. What was striven for was lost, but what was not striven for and even despised—science, commerce, art, a higher standard of living—was gained.

The reign of Richard, except in so far as it paved the way for the succession of the hated John, and so to revolt and Magna Carta, made little impress on England. Before he left that country at the beginning of his rule, to return only once for a short period, he made such careless arrangements for its government as to throw open the road to John.

On his way back from his unsuccessful crusade in 1192, Richard was seized by the Duke of Austria and turned over to the Emperor, Henry VI, who demanded the enormous ransom of £100,-000, a sum vastly greater in those days than now. The taxes necessarily levied to pay this ransom of the King were correspondingly heavy, and took various forms, including 25 per cent of the value of all movable goods. Nevertheless, they were paid and when Richard landed, John felt it best to submit. As soon as he could gather all the money possible, however, Richard left the country for the last time for his beloved Aquitaine and to defend his Continental possessions against the attacks of his other brother, Philip. He was soon to end his days in the magnificent fortress, "Saucy Castle," as he called it, the Château Gaillard on the banks of the Seine, dying from blood poisoning a few days after being shot with an arrow by a man whose father and two brothers had been killed by the King. Although Richard had ordered the man set at liberty when he heard his story, the King's followers tortured him to death, an example of the combination of chivalry and barbarism which was the character of the age.

Richard had no children and on his death the only surviving male heirs of Henry II were Richard's brother John and his nephew Arthur. The election of a king was still in vogue, and the barons in meeting chose the grown man rather than the youth, but few worse kings were ever chosen than John proved himself to be. His reign, however, was to be notable as including among its events one of the great landmarks in the history of English liberty, although there is much misunderstanding about it.

We must turn first to John's affairs on the Continent and his relations with the Church. On his accession Normandy and Aquitaine accepted him but Anjou declared for his nephew Arthur, who was supported by Philip of France. War followed, but Philip and Arthur fell out, and John gained a respite. He used it only to enrage the nobles of Poitou and to raise fresh enemies against himself. Tired of his wife, he got some Aquitanian bishops to pronounce a decree of divorce, and then married the betrothed bride of one of the Poitevin noblemen. Philip again joined John's enemies, and, although during the ensuing war John captured the young Arthur and is said to have murdered him with his own hands, the struggle ended with the loss of all Normandy, Maine, Anjou, Touraine, and part of Poitou. Only a portion of that latter province, and Aquitaine, remained of all the Continental empire of Henry II.

In 1205 John had a quarrel with the monks of Christ Church, Canterbury, who nominally had the choice of the Archbishop, over the selection of one to succeed Hubert Walter, who had died, and the next year the Pope settled the matter by naming Stephen Langton to the office. This, it is true, was a deviation from custom, but John was no diplomat and could not work out the difficult situation as Henry would have been able to. In anger he sent the monks into exile, and in return the Pope, Innocent III, pronounced, 1208, an interdict against the kingdom. All the churches were closed and no sacraments could be administered except those of baptism and extreme unction. Not even burial services could be read.

There are two interesting points about this affair. One is that whereas two centuries earlier a Gregory would have struck directly at the king, now a Pope felt he had first to work upon the people and to create, so to say, a back-fire before he made a full frontal attack. The second point is that John had made himself so unpopular that both people and clergy stood for the Pope against him. With a folly fortunate, perhaps, for the cause of eventual freedom, John with reckless heedlessness paid no attention and not only seized the property of the clergy who obeyed the Pope, but also demanded as hostages the eldest sons of the barons. He thus arrayed baronage, Church and people against him.

In 1209 the Pope felt that he could take the next step and excommunicated the King, the action, in spite of John's attempt to suppress the news, soon becoming known to the nation. The King had already laid terrible taxes, but in his need for money he now, by imprisonment and torture, squeezed some £40,000 from the Jews, and forced the abbots and Cistercian monasteries to contribute about £127,000 more. When some of the barons revolted, their hostage sons were murdered. The Pope's next and final step was to threaten to depose John if he would not come to terms, and to give the crown to Philip who prepared to invade England.

John knew he could not trust the army he had raised, and at last made submission to Innocent. He agreed to tribute and became the vassal of the Pope, no longer a free king. He now conceived the idea of reconquering his lost possessions on the Continent but the barons refused to engage in the enterprise. In ill-advised anger John turned on them, but Langton, the Archbishop, threatened to excommunicate all who might fight against the recalcitrant baronage. Although the King did cross the Channel with some of the barons he gained nothing by the battle of Bouvines, 1214, and returned with heavy debts to face his people.

The stage was now set for the final struggle of John and the barons. In reply to the demand for exorbitant payments by all who had not followed him to Normandy, the barons met at Bury St. Edmunds, and swore to force the King to rule according to the charter of Henry I, which Langton had produced for them to read the year before. John resorted to the bringing over of foreign mercenary troops, to which the barons retorted by raising an army, which was admitted within the walls of London. England was becoming more and more English in outlook. It was no longer merely part of an Anglo-French empire, for the remaining Continental possessions of Gascony and the city of Bordeaux exerted none of that intellectual and political "drag" which the former Channel to Pyrenees possessions had done.

The story which now runs to Runnymede requires some comment. There are two schools of historians: one which finds the spring of events in individual leaders, good and bad—the "great man school"; the other finds the springs in general social forces and believes that the course of history would be the same regardless of individuals. The truth, as so often happens, lies, in my opinion, in a middle position. Both social forces and great men bring about events, and both are essential in the proper combination of time and place. In the case now being considered, John was the individual factor. But there had also been social forces at work to bring on the crisis.

Given the character of the races which inhabited England, and the danger of anarchy from weakness of the central government on the one hand, and the danger of despotism on the other, it had been necessary to develop a strong monarchy which could control the baronage and the people, and yet this, in turn, had to be controlled if it were not to run into sheer dictatorship. The best of the Norman and Angevin kings, after England had been welded into unity by the after-results of the Conquest, had achieved the first end; but the reigns of Richard and John had exposed the second danger. The monarchic principle had stood for order; and the fairly constant resistance of the barons had stood for local autonomy and a check on tyranny, even though both originated largely in selfishness. The later history of England will to a great extent be the swinging of the pendulum from one side to the other in this struggle. As McKechnie, the leading authority on Magna Carta, well said, "the main plot of early English history centers in the attempt to found a strong monarchy, and yet to set limits to its strength."

The earlier Norman and Angevin kings had won the battle for order. Henry II had been an autocrat but not a tyrant. From his death, however, and under Richard and John the interest of the struggle shifts from the establishment of order to the preservation of freedom. It had openly begun with the rebellion of the barons in 1173, who were fighting the battle of liberty, though unwittingly, in striving to preserve their own privileges. They could not win then because Henry in spite of difficulties had retained the allegiance of the Church and people. In 1215 the situation was wholly different. John had not given good government in return for power, and had alienated both the Church with which he quarrelled and the people whom he had oppressed. The barons could thus count on the sympathy and co-operation of the Church which even furnished a leader in Langton, and of all classes of ordinary people.

The King's position was so untenable that he was forced to meet Langton and the barons in conference at Runnymede in June, 1215. None of the barons were remarkable men, though Langton was, but behind them was the public opinion of most of the baronage of the whole kingdom and of its freemen. The great charter, or Magna Carta, which after a few days John was forced to sign, has been one of the most influential and at the same time misunderstood documents in history.

It was an agreement wrung from the King to remedy certain evils in his administration by certain specific guarantees. Of all nations the English are least given to rhetoric and generalizing. They plant their feet solidly on the ground of a specific fact or situation. In this they differ markedly from both the French and the Americans, and it is one of the odd points in the later expansion of the Empire and the history of America that the American-English should become so different from the English-English, as we shall again have to note in the final chapter of this volume. The Englishman does not believe any generalized political truth to "be self-evident" or to hold good everywhere and at all times. What he does know, or rather senses with his whole organism, is a trespass on his property, a denial of an ancient right of way across a field, or other interferences with his accustomed ways of doing things or his accustomed relations to government, taxation and so on, which he has come to consider his personal "right."

That was what happened in 1215. The barons felt that for a long time their rights, or what were called their "liberties" in the sense of specific rights and not of a generalized ideal of liberty as such, had been increasingly interfered with. They objected to extraordinary levies for taxation and to such other things as the steady withdrawal of legal cases from their own courts to the King's Courts. They knew, moreover, two other things, first that in their fight against John they would have to have the support of the Church and the freemen, and second that they could not establish in England a feudal system of the old Continental sort. The work of the centralizing, order-bringing kings from William I to Henry II had been too well done for that.

The consequence was that in the extremely technical document of Magna Carta no generalizations were made as to liberty, which no one at that time would have understood or cared about, but specific abuses were promised cure for all the three classes mentioned above. The document can in truth be understood only by those versed in the social and legal conditions of the time, but, as these changed in later centuries, expressions which had one meaning in 1215 came to be interpreted much more broadly and differently. For example, Magna Carta did not, as came to be said, guarantee the right to a trial by jury to every one, but only to the "freemen" and those above them. This did not touch the great mass of serfs or villeins, but when serfdom came to be abolished and all became free, the meaning of this clause automatically became extended. Nor was a Parliament established or the principle of no taxation without representation, and many other things attributed to the great charter.

The seeds of these things, however, were contained in it, and a king had been brought to book by all classes, except the lowest, working together toward a dimly visualized constitutional monarchy. What was perhaps of even more importance, Magna Carta, whether historically correct or not, was to become by tradition and misinterpretation a palladium of later liberties. The Englishman always looks to the past for a precedent, and the value of, even falsely, basing the demand for wider and wider rights on the part of all classes on this ancient compact between sovereign and people was immense. As for its immediate effect, the Church was to have its privileges respected; the tenants-in-chief on the lands were to pay only certain taxes other than which none could be levied on them without consent of the Great Council; the towns of London and others were assured of their charter privileges; and the ordinary freemen guaranteed against unusual fines or imprisonment.

John refused to accept defeat, secured from the Pope a release from his oath, and opposed the barons with his mercenary troops. For a time there was again civil war, the barons having invited the son of the King of France to accept the English throne. The forces were more or less evenly balanced but in October, 1216, John died, and the way was opened for a peaceful succession. The Pope likewise died, and the new one proved less troublesome to English liberties than Innocent had done. John's eldest son, Henry III, was only nine years of age, but in spite of his minority it was decided that a boy-king was preferable to a foreign one, which is indicative of the growth of English nationality, considering not only the prejudice against but the real dangers of a minor on the throne.

The French were expelled and twice, in 1216 and 1217, Magna Carta was renewed by the young King, who was to prove weak and untrustworthy. However, perhaps owing to growing distrust of the barons and the fear of a return of feudal anarchy, more power was granted to him and the approval of the Great Council to additional taxation was avoided in the charter renewals. Henry, however, entrusted his powers to unworthy favorites, mostly foreigners, especially after his marriage to Eleanor of Provence. By odd chance, the man who was to become the leader of the English barons and chief enemy of Henry was himself a foreigner, Simon de Montfort of Normandy, who was also, however, Earl of Leicester in England. It was only some years after he inherited the latter title and estates that he came over from the Continent and married the King's sister. Not only, however, did the barons turn against him, but soon the fickle King did so also, and an outward reconciliation proved but hollow.

The next few years were of great importance for the development of modern England. When the King insisted on engaging in war to recover some of the lost possessions on the Continent, the

Great Council spoke its mind freely, and flatly refused to grant any money. Henry failed in his attempt, but brought back more foreigners, to the disgust of the English. The Church was becoming equally restive under the demands of the Pope, and disaffection was rapidly growing. In 1244 the Church and the baronage joined in remonstrating with Henry and in a suggestion that the Great Council, which was gradually tending toward a Parliament, should appoint the executive officers of the government instead of allowing the king to do so. This step, which was too advanced for the time, looked ahead to the modern system of Parliamentary government and a responsible ministry. There was still fear of giving too great power to the barons, and such a system required make-weights in other classes of the community. Parliamentary government of that type is practically unthinkable without a strong middle class.

Events, however, were soon to advance that government another step. Among the causes were Henry's continued Continental adventures and constant demands for money; the English churchmen's opposition to the endless exactions of the Pope and diversion of Church money to Henry; and the bad government of the King, which affected all classes. In 1254, while Henry was on the Continent, and his wife and brother had been left as Regents, the Great Council was called together to provide more of the unprecedented sums of money which the King required.

For the first time, there were summoned to it not merely those who had customarily been eligible but in addition four knights from each shire. Although presumably they were merely expected to declare what sums they thought could be raised in their respective counties, this broadening of the base of representation in the Council was of supreme importance for its development into the later Parliaments. When only churchmen and barons were in the Council there was always danger of submitting the country to the control of foreign ecclesiastics or of restoring the old feudal anarchy should the barons become so powerful that they could renew civil wars between themselves. If, however, the important landowners of a lower class from every county, who would certainly be on the side of peace and order, could have a voice in the conduct of affairs, the whole picture might be changed.

We may run rapidly through the events of the next few years leading up to the Parliament of 1265, which is a turning point in our story. The demands of both the King and the Pope increased. For the sake of a war of his own in Italy, the Pope demanded one-tenth of the income of the English clergy, as though it were a crusade. In 1258 Henry, in spite of bad harvests and starvation among his people, demanded one-third of the revenue of all England. Parliament was convened at Westminster and the barons appeared in arms, as did the lesser tenants in chief. The proposals made and passed, which have been called the Provisions of Oxford, reduced the powers of the king but gave too much to the barons, whom they made all powerful. The old Council, or Parliament, was to be abolished and replaced by a body of twelve men, all chosen by the barons, which was to meet thrice a year to discuss affairs with a council of fifteen, controlled by the barons, and without whose consent the king could take no action.

Trouble and danger were at once apparent. De Montfort had gone over to the side of the barons but was mistrusted by them as he was hated by the King. Now he went over to the side of a much broader party and demanded that the people at large must be considered. An arbitration of the situation which was to be accepted from the French King, Louis, did nothing to solve the problem, and 1264 found Montfort at the head of an army made up of barons, citizens of towns, and knights from the shires. At the battle fought at Lewes both the King and his son were captured.

Earl Simon, now in power, appointed three Electors, of whom he was one, to choose nine others who were to name the ministers of state. He also, however, called a Parliament in which sat not only the barons and ecclesiastical lords, but also the knights of the shires and two members from certain towns. This was going too fast and the Parliament of 1265 was ahead of its age. Montfort had for his friend and adviser one of the best and wisest men of his period, Bishop Grossetete of Lincoln, and although Parliament

69

was to develop more slowly, they had together pointed the way to the future. A precedent had been created and an idea had begun to fructify.

Moreover, Henry's son, Edward, who was soon to succeed him, had been taught that a king must rule under law, and although in the battle of Evesham he defeated the forces of Earl Simon, who was slain in the fight, he was to continue Montfort's development of the Parliamentary idea. Opinions differ as to both Montfort's ability and disinterestedness, but there can be little doubt as to the service which he rendered England. It was, perhaps, time for him to leave the scene, for he was a dominating character, and England required for its development a king and not a great noble towering above his fellows. Fortunately it found the man in Edward I. After Evesham, Henry left most of the government to his son, and by the time he died, 1272, England had become so settled that, although Edward was on a crusade to the East, he was quietly accepted as his father's successor in spite of his absence. He returned to an England that was gradually taking on the form of things to come, and from now on we shall have to deal more and more with the growth of modern Britain and the seed pods of the Empire.

CHAPTER IV

EDWARD I: MEDIÆVAL BRITAIN

IN THE PREVIOUS CHAPTERS we have had to trace the story of
England from before the dawn of history through the various conquests of the original British savages or barbarians by
Romans, Anglo-Saxons, Norsemen, Danes and Norman French.
Much that has been told seems far remote from the modern British Empire, though not without its influence. We now enter upon
a period in which we look forward to the future rather than back
to the past. The battles of Crecy and Agincourt, the appearance of
Justices of the Peace, the beginning of serious labor difficulties,
and other items which we shall now encounter from time to time
are living today in practice or tradition in a way that the Roman
occupation or the Gemots of the Saxons or battles of the Vikings
are not.

Considering this work for a moment as a biography of the Empire, we are now passing from the section in which we have described the environment, ancestry and childhood of our subject to
the period of adolescence. Manhood will be achieved later, in the
reigns of the Tudors, and the full fruition of mature efforts must
await still later times, but we are now passing from those events
and circumstances which may seem occasionally to have had little
to do with "the shape of things to come," and yet which sowed
the seeds of character and many institutions. Moreover, just as we
found in the Roman period that debasement of the coinage and
inflation were considerable factors in the downfall of the old civilization, so in this period we shall encounter efforts at the fixing

of wages and prices which have a curiously contemporary ring today.

The period was mediæval, and one of its chief characteristics was the development of the corporate spirit. History has no water-tight compartments, and years, reigns or centuries are mere convenient divisions of time, through which the stream of life flows unceasingly. Everything is connected with what has gone before and what comes after, but the emphasis changes from one period to another, and in this one the coming of the friars, which greatly strengthened the popular hold of the Church, the development of universities, the craft guilds, and Parliament, all helped to increase the feeling of a common and corporate life in the nation.

We have already noted the importance of the Church as an institution. Its dignitaries, however, were almost, sometimes more, statesmen than religious leaders of the people. The monks, although they did much for learning and for the poor, did not greatly influence the religious lives of those among whom their monasteries and rich lands were placed. Nor, so far as we can tell, did a large number of the often ignorant parish priests. The Church was an influential and at times a dominating institution, but it lacked the spirit which would stir and attach to it the common folk.

Both the Dominican and Franciscan Orders had gained a foothold in England early in the thirteenth century, but in the next two the Franciscans in particular ministered to the people and made the Church living. Vowed to poverty, they spent their time close to those whom they served, helping the poor and sick in their humble homes, and preaching everywhere in such fashion as to bring about a genuine and great religious revival. In time they abandoned the vow of poverty, and the priories which they built and the part which they took in developing the growing learning of the day in philosophy and science were both far from the vision of St. Francis. Roger Bacon, Duns Scotus, and others were Franciscans, whether Francis would have considered them as his followers or not, and although with increasing wealth and ease the Order degenerated, it maintained its popularity until the fifteenth century, and unquestionably was immensely influential in creating that religious spirit which is still strong in the British, and, though to mention it is to take a long leap into the future, was one of the factors leading to the abdication of Edward VIII in our own day.

The corporate mediæval life was perhaps most clearly expressed in the universities and guilds. The great Renaissance of the fifteenth century had been preceded by that of the twelfth, which because it occupied itself chiefly with scholastic philosophy and but little with science, literature or art, occupies a much smaller place in modern interest. It was, however, of marked significance, causing a stirring of intellectual curiosity, a sharpening of the mind as a tool, and, above all, the creation of the universities. These, in Padua, Paris, Oxford, Cambridge and elsewhere, were at first mere groupings of young students around teachers without buildings or equipment. Later, colleges, in the English and not the American sense, were built and endowed in order to house and control some of the students, who often attended in quite amazing numbers for what so many still consider as the dark ages.

They came frequently from long distances and foreign countries, the Scotch, for example, preferring the French and Italian universities to those in England; and the mingling together of these ambitious if often rowdy youngsters must have had a stimulating mental effect. For the most part, everywhere, they came from the lower middle class, such as the yeomen farmers and town citizens in England, for whom a stay at the university was the passport to a career such as was not required by the upper classes. It was symptomatic of the age that education should so easily take on the corporate form, which was also assumed by business employers and workmen.

The Guild Merchant had had a long history and it is impossible to trace its origin. It was an association of the merchants in a town to monopolize, regulate and control their business. In the period now being considered, however, it became less important than the many craft guilds that sprang up, which largely split up the former general monopoly. Usually such a guild, called a "mistery" or company, embraced all the artisans or craftsmen in a par-

73

ticular trade or calling within one town. Primarily they were to see to it that the quality of workmanship was maintained, and in addition they regulated the hours and wages for which the journeymen should work. They also had their social and religious aspects such as special church services and festivities of various sorts, including the pageants, which the English still love and which increased in popularity and elaborateness in this period.

In the fourteenth century there was a tendency for the journeymen in some arts or trades to set up guilds of their own separate from those of the masters, but the struggle was not nearly as marked as in Germany, and the workmen's guilds apparently eventually became subordinate to or merged again into those of the masters. The trouble appears to have come from disputes over hours and wages, although these should have been comparatively simple to determine when limited to one trade in one town as contrasted with the experiments we shall encounter later. It is evident, however, from points we have noted, such as the appeal of the Church to the common man, the university which opened opportunity to those who had not known it before, and the guilds in their various forms, that we are passing into a period in which society is more complex and in which the lower classes are to play a more important part than in any earlier day.

Although we have spoken of Wales, Ireland and Scotland in so far as they impinged on the destinies of England, they also from now on will have a larger part in our story, for the relations between them and England become more important and continuous. They were all to contribute elements to the later Empire, particularly perhaps Scotland, but if we have not treated their early histories at length it must be recalled that the Empire after all was the eventual result of the expansion of that "half an island" which was England, and England has remained the heart of Empire as London has remained its capital.

As we have already seen, Henry III's son, Edward, who was to succeed his father, was absent from England at the time of Henry's death, in 1272. Indeed he made a very leisurely progress home and did not arrive there until 1274. The fact that the succession was undisputed in spite of these facts showed how far England was at this time on the road to peace and settled government.

Edward was proclaimed king on the day of his father's funeral, the great nobles swearing fealty to their absent monarch on the high altar of Westminster Abbey, as they still swear fealty at the coronation of each new king even to the present day. Although accepted as king by "hereditary right and the election of the magnates" the fact that the throne went quietly to the absent heir strengthened the principle of hereditary right though that of election did not wholly disappear, as we shall have occasion to note in later periods. Moreover, the dating of his reign from the day of his father's funeral may be considered as the starting point of the theory, though not given definite form until the fourth Edward, that the King never dies, with the consequent distinction between the Crown as a symbol and part of the constitutional machinery, and the person of the monarch as an individual.

The new King was to prove one of the greatest in England's long line. Although of powerful physique, fond of hunting, the tournament and other outdoor sports, and of quick temper, he was chaste in his marital relations which bespoke an unusual character in those days. These qualities were combined with a somewhat marked callousness of feeling, but as statesman, organizer, and lawgiver, few have surpassed him. One of the notable acts on his return was to accept the terms of King John's Charter—which his father had repudiated—requiring that the King would receive scutages and grants only with the consent of the Great Council or Parliament. We shall defer the legal and Parliamentary aspects of his reign to discuss briefly the story of his foreign relations and wars.

As contrasted with the now fairly developed nationalism of England, the organization of Wales, Scotland and Ireland belonged to a far earlier period and was still largely in the clan stage though overlords arose with somewhat shadowy rights and powers. We early pointed out the difference between the fairly level land of much of England, and the mountainous districts of

Wales and Scotland. In both these latter, development of settled ways of living had been slow. Wales had, indeed, been turning to some extent from grazing to agriculture but there were no towns, scarcely villages, and the leaders in the innumerable valleys, largely cut off from one another owing to lack of roads, still carried on local wars and raided their more peaceful neighbors on the borders.

Between the settled English and the wild Welsh lay the estates of the border barons, the Mortimers and others, who were ahead of the Welsh but behind the rest of the English in their advancement. There was practical anarchy in Wales itself and constant forays on the border, with the Welsh always willing to side against the English whether in war or raid. The Welsh princes, although regarded by the English kings as vassals, were in fact largely independent, and after Edward's accession to the throne Llewelyn, Prince of Wales, refused to do homage for four years. Finally, in 1282 he and his brother David made war, and Edward marched against them. Llewelyn was killed and the next year David was captured and executed.

Irregular as was the military organization of the Welsh, they had developed the use of the "long bow," and Edward was wise enough to adopt this new weapon, which was to make the English archer famous and to have, in time, great effect on both war and social life. It has been said, although the statement seems almost incredible, that an arrow from such a bow in Welsh hands had been known "to pin a knight's armored thigh through his saddle to the horse's side." In any case the weapon was a powerful one and made almost as great a change in warfare as gunpowder was to do later. That the English adopted it, while the French did not, accounts for some of the astounding victories we shall soon have to record. It was also employed against the Scotch and against the northern Welsh, who still used the spear, the bow being distinctly southern Welsh in origin.

The new weapon had a profoundly democratizing effect. The English archers who were to mow down the French chivalry, unlike that chivalry, came from all classes, and the yeoman's son might now be more than a match for the armored knight. Edward made another step in increasing the efficiency and democratizing war by introducing the system of regular pay in the army. Feudalism had tended to do away with the foot soldier, and in any case feudal levies could be kept in the field for not more than forty days. There had been in the past paid foreign mercenaries, who had been looked down upon by the ordinary citizen, but Edward by arranging to retain his own English subjects in the army for pay created a new instrument of war, and England was on its way to becoming in that age the strongest military power.

After the deaths of Llewelyn and David, Wales came under the complete power of England, and the great castles at Conway, Caernarvon and elsewhere, which stand today, were built to guard the new possession. The King's second son, who was later to become Edward II owing to the death of the elder, was born in Caernarvon Castle, and on the death of his brother was there formally presented to the Welsh people as the Prince of Wales, a title almost uniformly bestowed since on the eldest son of the reigning sovereign, and it was at the same Caernarvon Castle that the present Duke of Windsor was thus presented and given his best known title as a boy of twelve. Edward I displayed his statesmanship after the conquest by granting to the Welsh their own laws, confirming them in possession of their property, and building up an administrative staff largely of local officials.

He also tried to solve the problem of Ireland, which has always, as if by malign fate, been the great failure in British imperial administration. A century earlier, in the reign of Henry II, a partial conquest had been made though not in the English national interest. It was conducted chiefly by individual adventurers from the Welsh borders of whom we have just spoken. These, as we have indicated, even in the time of Edward formed a social class apart, being more feudal than the English and less anarchic and clannish than the Welsh. But as early as Henry they had also become something of a race apart, with their mingling of Norman, English and Welsh blood.

Ireland likewise was a racial mixture. Mostly pure Celtic, early

British or what you will, in the wilder western portions, in the eastern there was an English settlement around Dublin, called the "Pale," and the remnant traces of Norse and Danish invaders. The Irish themselves were considered as savages and had certainly not carried out the promise of their early period of bloom. They were remote from the main currents of European life and had relapsed into a sort of semi-barbarism.

The adventurers from Wales, led by de Clare, Earl of Pembroke, called "Strongbow," carried with them, long before it was used by the English, that long bow of which we have spoken and from which Pembroke derived his nickname. There was no national feeling in Ireland at that time but neither did the conquerors, nor Henry, who had too much else on his hands, establish a national government which might have been tolerated even though administered by foreigners if it had brought peace and justice. It brought neither, and the various Anglo-Norman-Welsh barons not only fought the Irish, as the Irish fought them, but both groups fought among themselves. It was this chaotic situation that was taken over by Edward. Under his administration there was distinct, but unfortunately for the long unhappy tale of Ireland, only temporary, improvement. Order was better maintained, and towns, agriculture and commerce began to flourish in the doleful land, but it was the promise of a false dawn.

Edward showed less statesmanship in dealing with Scotland, though after some three centuries of warfare that country was to be peacefully and happily united with England as Ireland was never to be. The event almost came about in 1290, but was prevented by one of those accidents which in spite of the theory that history is the resultant only of great social forces and not of the lives of individuals have often deflected its course. Although there was infinite difference between the south of England and the highlands of Scotland, and, as we have pointed out, the two countries were at different stages of development, there were also links between them, which might in time have brought about more than a formal union far sooner than proved the case. There was no great difference between the people of northern England and of the Scottish lowlands. Moreover, the Scottish nobility was almost as Norman in blood as the English, and, just as many of the English had feudal fiefs on the Continent, so in similar fashion the Scots had large estates in England.

Edward was most anxious to unite the two nations, and as a step in that direction to reclaim for the English Crown the obligation of the Scottish kings to do homage which had been sold by Richard when in need of money. The Scots King, Alexander, however, resisted Edward's demand, but after the Scotch monarch met death by accident his only descendant was a young granddaughter born of the marriage of his own daughter and the King of Norway. It was agreed that the child should marry the Prince of Wales, and although the two kingdoms were to remain distinct, they would thus in time probably have come under the rule of a single sovereign. Unluckily, the "Maid of Norway," as she was called, died on her way to Scotland, and the plan for a peaceful union came to naught.

There were now three claimants to the Scotch throne, each with a certain show of right by descent: John Balliol, Robert Bruce and John Hastings. To avoid civil war they appealed to the arbitration of Edward, all agreeing to do homage to him if chosen. The King decided in favor of Balliol and all might have gone well had Edward been content merely with the recognition of his overlordship, but he insisted that legal cases should be appealed from the Scottish courts to Westminster, an obnoxious and costly proceeding which at once set Scotland against him. One of the first effects of this misstep was a conflict between Edward and Philip IV of France, who also formed a league with Scotland which endured for three centuries. This friendship, for it was much more than a mere treaty, between two peoples seemingly so dissimilar as the Scots and the French, was to prove of great importance in the destinies of both British nations and we shall have to refer to it many times in the course of our story.

Edward now decided on war, and in 1296 crossed the Scottish border with an army, Balliol at once renouncing the allegiance which he had sworn when chosen by the English King in preference to Bruce and Hastings. He was, however, decisively defeated at the battle of Dunbar and carried off as a prisoner to England. Edward also took with him the famous stone from Scone on which the Scottish kings had sat when crowned and concerning which ancient legend prophesied that wherever the stone might be, there Scottish kings would rule. It has ever since remained under the seat of the Coronation Chair in Westminster Abbey, though the prophecy was not fulfilled until the Stuarts came to reign over the united kingdoms more than two centuries later.

Edward now acted on the feudal theory that, as he was lord paramount of Scotland and his vassal Balliol had rebelled against him, he could take the fief into his own hands, and he declared himself to be the ruling head of the neighboring kingdom. The nobles accepted him as such, but the country was misgoverned by those whom Edward left as his representatives. Not only did many of the Scots question Edward's feudal claims but, partly under the impact of conquest and oppression, a strong feeling of nationalism had developed which Edward did not take into account.

In 1297 there was a powerful and temporarily successful rising under the hero Wallace, who with his followers defeated the English army near Stirling and descended upon northern England ravaging the countryside. Edward, who had been absent on the Continent fighting the French, patched up a truce and hastily returned to take the field in person against Wallace, whom he defeated at Falkirk, breaking the revolt. The Scotch leader fled to France but returned some years later and, although he took no part in the new uprising of 1304 he was ignobly betrayed into the hands of the English and hung at Tyburn.

Edward having again subdued the rebels, as he considered them, levied heavy fines on all who had opposed him, demanded the surrender of the Scottish castles, and established an English government, though the old Scots laws were to remain in force, and according to his ideas the country was not harshly treated. The feeling of independence and nationality was, however, too strong to permit of foreign dominance, and the Scots found a new leader in Robert Bruce, who had behind him the common people and most of the nobles. Although Bruce was defeated and forced to become a fugitive whose adventures form one of the great romances of Scotland, Edward had to give up his dream of a union of the two kingdoms which, given the character of the two peoples, could not be achieved except willingly.

Had Edward not died in 1307 he might have won greater victories over the French and subjugated Scotland, but these would have been barren fruits compared with the lasting results of his work in England, where he displayed a statesmanship and understanding of conditions and people lacking in his relations with the Scots and Irish.

We have already noted, as Edward did in his youth, the beginnings of Parliament in the days of de Montfort, but it was under Edward and his two successors that that institution advanced rapidly toward its modern form. The King needed money for his French and Scottish wars, but he also had some of the later Tudor instinct for governing his English and realized the increasing power and useful influence of what we may call the emerging middle class. The knights and burgesses, whom we may roughly if not wholly accurately consider as country gentlemen, and the citizens of towns or boroughs were becoming important in the royal eyes.

To have them represented, not occasionally but regularly, in Parliament would serve several useful purposes. Their willing consents would broaden the base for taxation; their meeting together would enable them to understand national policy and its necessities, and spread the knowledge in their localities; their presence would help the king to keep in touch with all sections and classes of the people, except the lowest—the villeins whose day for consideration was yet far off; and they would serve as a useful check or balance to the more powerful baronage. Therefore to his Parliament of 1295, often called the "Model Parliament," Edward summoned not only bishops, abbots and lower representatives of the Church, as well as earls and barons, but also two knights from every shire and two burgesses from every town.

Other peoples and nations, in various periods, have added their special contributions to the world's store of all that goes to advance civilization. That of the English has been particularly the art of government, notably as carried on by the Parliamentary system including the essential invention of the Cabinet. In spite of its drawbacks and shortcomings, no other system has preserved to any such extent personal liberty and self-government for such masses of population for so long a period, or shown itself on the whole so flexible in adjusting itself to changing conditions. It is especially interesting, therefore, to note some of those institutions which started it on its way and differentiated it from other attempts in the same direction. A few of these we have already mentioned but we may pause to gather the threads together. The future will have to mold its own institutions to meet new needs for new times, and it is possible that the Parliamentary system may not endure even in a largely altered form, but we are here writing history and not prophecy, and are speaking of the past half-dozen centuries and more, not of those to come.

We may note first that in England the Church did not care about its representation in what was to become the national legislature, and although some Bishops still sit in the House of Lords, the lower ecclesiastics of the Edwardian period ceased attendance in Parliament, and the number of abbots and priors dropped from about seventy in the Parliament of Edward I to about twenty-seven in the reign of Edward III, the higher Church officials moreover sitting largely in virtue of their lay benefices rather than as representatives of the Church. The latter preferred to levy taxes on itself in its ecclesiastical assemblies called Convocations held at York or Canterbury attended by the clergy only. Of the three "estates," the Church, the nobility and the middle class, the sharp divisions between which were to hamper the development of popular government across the Channel, one, the Church, thus voluntarily withdrew from direct participation in the political life of the English nation almost at the very beginning of Parliamentary government.

But neither did the other two estates develop in England as

separate and often conflicting interests as they did in France and elsewhere. It is true that the interests of the nobles and middle class were often opposed and that the commons greatly augmented their position as they came to hold the balance of power on many occasions between the Crown and the nobility. But the rule of primogeniture, which we have already mentioned as practised in England, prevented any such sharp distinction as existed on the Continent between the *noblesse* and the *bourgeoisie*. There all the sons of a noble were considered as noble, whereas in England the younger sons automatically became commoners. They often entered trade and other pursuits of the middle class, and as members of that class rose into the ranks of the nobility, and as there was also nothing to prevent intermarriage, there was a constant commingling of interests and personnel between the two classes.

Thus, the civil wars in England have never yet been class wars. A. F. Pollard, in his *Evolution of Parliament*, states that there are some thousands of descendants of English kings among the commoners and several hundreds of thousands of descendants of peers. This situation, of course, was just beginning in the period we are now discussing, and peers in the modern sense belong to a much later time, in spite of the fact that it is the law that any one who can prove descent from any member of the Parliament of 1295 who received a special summons to that body and took his seat is entitled to a peerage. The knights and burgesses at that time did not receive a special royal summons but, like some of the lesser barons, merely a general writ from the sheriff of the county. In its modern form the House of Lords dates, in fact, only from the Restoration of the Stuarts in 1660.

Parliament did, however, soon divide into two Houses, though it is impossible to tell just when. At first all members sat in one chamber, the knights and burgesses apparently not taking part in the general debate but giving their voice through one member, their "speaker," from which office later developed that of the "Speaker of the House." The origin of the separate House of Commons appears to have been in their meeting together to discuss matters and reach the decisions which their "speaker" was to deliver to the general body in which they could not speak themselves as individuals. The upper House, however, was not a body of hereditary "peers" sitting by right of descent. Edward might summon an earl or baron to sit in one Parliament and never call him again.

A large part of the business of these early Parliaments, besides taxation, was the receiving and acting on petitions received from individuals or bodies who considered themselves injured or petitions formulated by Parliament itself. Although no sharp distinction can be drawn, the latter may be considered as the origin of bills initiated today by Parliament and the former as cases which would now be dealt with in the various law courts. All this business and discussion, however, enabled the King to obtain knowledge of the state of the kingdom and of public opinion, though he had no intention of turning over to Parliament his own powers.

These were, indeed, essential for the peace of the realm. In spite of the advance made, there was still widespread lawlessness which could be suppressed only by the strong hand of centralized authority, and the turbulent barons were as yet far from desisting from all private wars and peaceably acquiescing in either royal or Parliamentary control. For minor and local disorders, the King initiated a policy which has lasted to the present day and has had profound effects on English life and character. By proclamation he ordered that all persons above the age of fifteen should swear, according to the old law of Canute, that they would be neither thieves nor robbers, nor harbor the same, and would join in the hue and cry in pursuit when called upon. Knights in each shire were appointed to see that the law was enforced, and these "Conservators of the Peace" developed in a short time under Edward III into the Justices of the Peace, who still later had to hold their local courts four times a year in "Quarter Sessions."

With the new mode of warfare, the knight had mostly lost his old military and feudal character and become a country gentleman, and we have here the beginning of that responsibility for

84

unpaid service in local government which has become such an important feature of English life. These Justices may not have been learned in the law but on the whole they rendered justice among their neighbors who knew them and looked up to them, and it has been said that much of that respect for law which is characteristic of all classes today was largely fostered by this system, in addition to the development of public spirit on the part of the country gentry.

These knights, or country gentlemen, were also increasing in wealth and importance during Edward's reign, and the King encouraged this process just as he did the political rise of the citizens and burgesses in order to strengthen himself in his struggle with the barons, a struggle which was to last for generations and to end in the Wars of the Roses. The number of barons appears to have been decreasing, but this did not diminish their power because of the combination of baronies by marriage. In fact, as their numbers decreased, their individual influence grew greater. Marriages became of great political and social influence whether we consider them vertically, so to speak, as reaching up and down between the baronage and the middle class, or horizontally between the members of the baronage only.

All powerful classes, whether aristocratic or plutocratic, tend to increase their wealth or power by this means, and the King himself used the method by arranging for members of the royal family to make the most important marriages available. In this way his brother Edmund, Earl of Lancaster, became almost as wealthy and powerful as the King himself, and founded that House of Lancaster of which we shall hear much a century later.

In spite of his Model Parliament, Edward considered himself, as the kings did for long after, master of the nation, and was practically, as the kings are yet,—but only in theory and by legal fiction,—the legislature, the executive and the judiciary. To maintain this position he had to control the baronage, the Commons and the Church, and for the most part he did so, though now and then he had to make concessions, as in the crisis of 1294–97, when he fought against all three. Powerful as the barons were, they had to combine with the Commons, and the latter had a grievance in the enormous increase in the taxes the King laid on wool without consulting Parliament. Owing to the combined pressure brought against him, however, he had to agree to a clause in the "Confirmation of Charters" promising not to lay any excessive duties of that sort in the future, but he still retained the right to lay such duties on imports as he pleased by agreement with the foreign merchants only and not with Parliament.

The cost of the French and Scottish wars, which had led him into this difficulty with the Commons, which the barons used for their own purposes, also led him to defy the Church. His Statute of Mortmain naturally greatly antagonized that body which had been absorbing more and more of English land. For one reason and another, whether from genuine piety or not, individuals had been constantly making grants to the Church, which, unlike individuals, did not die, so that the land once in its hands remained there forever. Edward by his statute forbade any more grants. In addition, however, his financial need led him to defy the Pope, who had forbidden the clergy to make any contribution to the cost of the French war. Three years earlier, 1294, the King had already forced the clergy to give him one-half of their total revenues for his immediate need, and he now threatened them all with outlawry, that is, denial of protection in any court, unless they would make the grant demanded in spite of the Pope, and the clergy had to agree.

We may conveniently here speak also of a great change which had been going on since the Norman Conquest a century before. That was the alteration in the English language. Anglo-Saxon, after the earlier conquest, had practically replaced the speech of the tribes which had been conquered, with certain additions to the vocabulary in the sections where the Danes had settled. There is no more fascinating story than that of how our modern English language, the richest and most flexible in the world today, gradually developed as one conquest followed another, each leaving its impress on our speech. Saxon had been an inflected language and those who study such ancient or modern languages in which complicated inflections have to be mastered may well be grateful that the system disappeared from our own. This process, as well as simplifications in the grammar, had been well under way before the Normanizing of England made French the language of all the upper classes, but that change probably hastened the other.

The greater influence of the Conquest, however, was in the vocabulary. Owing to the decline of literature before William landed, Saxon had almost ceased to be a written language, and in any society the vocabulary of a written, literary language is far larger than that of every-day spoken conversation. In fact, the vocabulary needed for the uses of ordinary life is remarkably small. Such words as Saxon had possessed for purposes of higher thought or expression had already disappeared to a surprising extent before the cultivated classes adopted French, so that there was a linguistic vacuum to be filled. It was not so much that French or Latin words displaced Saxon as that they provided a vocabulary for the expression of ideas which had already been lost, especially those of a complex or abstract sort, or which stood for acts, objects or institutions in a higher and more refined civilization.

The lower classes, with need for only a small vocabulary, continued to speak Saxon, but as the two languages gradually merged, and when, as we shall note in the next chapter, the national feeling of England and hostility to France developed, the combination of Saxon, French and Latin, with small admixtures of Danish and other languages, had given to the new nation a medium of expression which was to follow its own independent growth into the marvellous literature of the Elizabethan and later periods, and to become the predominant tongue among all peoples who inherited the culture of all Western civilization.

One more point in Edward's reign and services must be noted. He was a great lawmaker, and in some respects fundamentally altered the basis of law which in the great statutes passed by him through Parliament effected a transition from the old feudal and other laws to the legal conceptions of our own day. Some of these statutes are still necessary for reference, especially in the field of land law, and were of such effect as greatly to hasten the change of society, as well as mere law, from feudal to modern.

Moreover, it was under him that the profession of law became secularized and its leaders ceased to be churchmen. The courts as we know them today also began to take separate shape, such as those of Common Pleas, the Exchequer and the King's Bench. The rise of the legal profession opened new roads to advancement, and like the universities, the new methods of warfare, and the rise of trade, assisted the democratic process, running counter to ecclesiastical and feudal monopolies of opportunity, for those who would be leaders in learning or in state. Although the barons were still powerful enough to balk the King in his effort to decrease or suppress private courts, this was later to be accomplished by the growing preference of the people for the King's justice.

If Edward was at times, from his own ability and temper as well as the circumstances of the time, led perilously near to trying to be a dictator, he was essentially a national leader, and the nation rallied behind him. In spite of his French war his chief interest was in England and the hope of making Great Britain one. Perhaps nothing shows more clearly the national spirit which he had fostered among his subjects than the result of his second encounter with the Pope. When that prelate, Boniface VIII, claimed that Scotland belonged to the Papal See and ordered Edward to cease from attacking it, the King left the answer to Parliament which replied that even should Edward yield to this claim, the English people would not allow him to do so.

CHAPTER V

THE FOURTEENTH CENTURY: THE ENDING
OF THE OLD ORDER

IN OUR STORY we have already almost imperceptibly advanced
a long distance from that day when Cæsar landed on
the shore and secured his first glimpse of a barbarian and
native Briton. The centuries of peaceful Roman civilization with
its cities, their forums, baths and great municipal buildings, as
well as the villas in the country, have become a dream from a
forgotten past. The fall of Rome and the horrors of the barbarian
invasions, the burnings, plunderings and massacres by Saxons and
Danes, even the conquest by the Normans, have become of slight
interest, if known at all, to the ordinary people who have gradually been building the England we have now reached in this
chapter. Life had gone on in spite of all, and England was
steadily developing, partly under the conscious guidance of leaders and largely under the unconscious influence of the wills
of millions who within the little circle of light which each life
casts around itself had been striving to better their own positions
and to increase their freedom, now in one direction, now in another, following the urge, which is another essential English trait,
to be one's self and do as one chooses.

The fourteenth century was not marked, as the preceding two
had been, by any startling constitutional changes but this does not
mean that there were none. If there was no Magna Carta or
Model Parliament, nevertheless there was distinct advance in
both the form and power of Parliament. By the end of the period

we find the legislature definitely divided into upper and lower Houses, sitting apart, with a greatly enlarged control over the voting of public money in the form of taxes, and the emergence of the Commons as the more influential of the two chambers. To a large extent these developments were due to foreign wars, otherwise uninteresting and unimportant, and to the character and ages of the kings.

Of the latter there were three during the century, two of whom ascended the throne at the ages of fifteen and ten, respectively. In our own day, the dividing of a historical narrative into reigns is largely a matter of convenience but in earlier times, when the power of the monarchs was far greater in controlling and guiding events, their characters and abilities become of prime importance.

The century was one of extreme disturbance. The beginning of the Hundred Years' War with France, the Black Death which reduced the population by nearly one-half, and the threat of total destruction of the social order in Wat Tyler's rebellion, all changed the face of social and political England as completely as a succession of floods, fires and hurricanes might have altered the physical landscape. The course of history lunges and plunges, and at the end we begin to glimpse the forces making for the creation of the Tudor period and modern England.

The unhappy reign of Edward II (1307–27) well exemplifies what we have just said of the importance of the personality of the king. His father, Edward I, had been able, owing to his own character and ability, greatly to extend his authority and was the real founder of Parliament. He had conquered Wales and almost conquered Scotland. Had he lived he might have defeated the Bruce, ruled the whole of Britain, and become too strong for the new forces of law and Parliament which he had put in motion. The weakness and incapacity of his son served England well. Lazy, frivolous and obstinate, he relied upon favorites, who were naturally, and to a large extent justly, blamed for the bad government which marked the whole reign. First there was the young foreigner, the witty and impudent young Gascon knight,

Piers Gaveston, who after he had been banished three times and recalled by the King was murdered by the barons at Warwick. Next came the Despensers, son and father, who were English and of the baronial class which, however, hated both of them.

We may pause a moment to look at the change which had been occurring in that class, including both earls and the greater barons, soon to be mentioned legally in official documents for the first time as peers. It was much the same change which we have noted in the transition of the feudal knight into the country gentleman. The nobles had been passing through a similar transition. The feudal bonds had long been slowly loosening through all society from king to serf, and although the nobles were as restless as ever they had had to adapt themselves to the growing centralization of the nation. They now strove for power through attempting to influence or control the central government with the king at its head rather than by building up local power as had the earlier great feudatories. They also counted less on their own feudal vassals than they did on bands of paid retainers who wore their livery and were in fact small, private military forces.

Moreover, London was becoming more and more that center of national life which it has ever since remained. The royal court which had in former days moved about from place to place was now fairly steadily in residence, and London had also become the usual, almost permanent, seat of Parliament, and the location of the most important law courts. The new class of lawyers, who hoped to rise to power and influence, had taken over the Temple after the Knights Templars had been suppressed, and made it their headquarters. The increase in trade meant a like increase in wealth and luxury, and the nobles were beginning to build palaces in town, and in spite of their armed opposition to Edward were tending in the direction of the more modern courtier and away from the old feudal relationship.

They had, however, no able leader, and the Earl of Lancaster, who headed the opposition to the King, had only narrow and selfish views. They made the mistake, moreover, of not aligning the commons with them, and so, to the benefit of England, led the King to patronize the commons at the expense of the nobles. In 1311 the latter presented Edward with a set of Ordinances ostensibly for the reform of the kingdom but which in fact would merely have placed him under the control of a baronial oligarchy. Edward refused, and the barons took up arms.

Meanwhile, Bruce had increased his power in Scotland and two years later captured Stirling, the only remaining English fortress of importance in his kingdom. Marching against him, with only partial support from the baronage and other English, Edward suffered a severe defeat at Bannockburn, and, although fighting continued until the truce made ten years later, Scotland had been definitely lost, and Edward had to struggle against the Lancastrian faction at home, until in the battle of Boroughbridge in 1322 Lancaster was defeated, seized and executed.

Meanwhile the King had been forced to accept the Ordinances, but immediately after ridding himself of Lancaster, he assembled a Parliament at York and had them declared invalid. His later government was no better than before but by his action in this matter Parliament had taken a great step forward. As a counterweight to the nobles Edward needed the Commons, and the declaration which he had Parliament pass included the vastly important statement that thereafter matters concerning king, kingdom and people should be considered and passed on only "by the consent of the prelates, earls and barons, and the commonalty of the realm, according as hath been hitherto accustomed." We have seen how in the Model Parliament of his father in 1295 the knights of the shire and burgesses had been included, but the custom had been for a short period only, and there was nothing to prevent a king from not following it. Now, however, it had become law of the land, and no future law could be passed without the consent of the commons.

Before the end of this weak and unhappy ruler, Parliament was to take another notable step forward. Four years later, Edward's wife, who had been conspiring against him in France, returned with her lover, Roger Mortimer, and her son, another

Edward, and together with the barons defeated the King, and hanged the two Despensers. In 1327, Parliament, meeting again in London, forced the King to abdicate, and proclaimed his fifteen-year-old son King in his stead. It was a bold assumption of power, accepted by Edward, who was murdered at Berkeley Castle eight months later.

Although probably the result of scheming by selfish nobles, an unfaithful wife and her despicable paramour, it was a not inappropriate end to twenty years of misrule of which practically nothing good can be said, except the accidental increase of the powers of Parliament and people against both monarch and nobility, and the creation of significant precedents.

There are times when a succession of strong and able kings is of benefit but such a succession also involves dangers to growing liberty. Had the successors of Edward I been as strong and able as himself the development of self-government might have taken a far less favorable direction than it did under his incompetent descendants; and we may here note that it is characteristic of the entire long evolution of the British Constitution, as of the later Empire, that at no time has any all-embracing declaration of principles been laid down. The Constitution has developed, as we have already seen thus far in our story, by applying to each grievance or crisis its own particular remedy at the time. There has never been any effort, as Arthur Young said of the French, to make a Constitution "as though a Constitution were a pudding to be made from a receipt." There has been one step at a time, and each step has followed naturally from some preceding one. For that reason, as a Frenchman has pointed out, the British Constitution has preserved those "happy incoherences, the useful incongruities, the protecting contradictions" which can be likened to the similar ones which exist in the universe and man's life. Obviously such a Constitution cannot be improvised by any nation starting an independent life at some given date, as we in the United States had to do. Nor can it fit, or be operated by, peoples of all characters and temperaments.

The British have developed their Constitution continuously

for some fourteen hundred years. Moreover, such a Constitution can flourish, as Bryce said, only among nations "of a conservative temper, nations which respected antiquity, which valued precedents, which liked to go on doing a thing in the way their fathers had done it before them." We may add also that it can flourish only among a people which cares little about abstract logic but much for compromise; which does not indulge in generalities or wishful thinking but faces each concrete problem as it is forced on its immediate attention.

We in the United States have neither the fourteen centuries which the British have, so to say, "banked," nor have we their temperament. For such nations as do not possess a considerable measure of both these things, their molding influence has to be replaced by a written Constitution which to some extent trains people to act toward hasty and unwise legislation in the same way as history and character cause the British electorate to act instinctively, though no one can predict what changes of temperament or character the future may hold even for them.

The reign of Edward III was a long series of disasters, touched here and there with the flash of brilliant military victories which fired the patriotism and imagination of his people. For three years after the boy of fifteen came to the throne, at which age he was married, power rested in the hands of his mother's lover, Mortimer. He was, however, no match even for the aging and ill Bruce, who was harrying the north of England, and Mortimer was forced to make a treaty acknowledging the independence of Scotland. The boy-King, who had been kept almost a prisoner, was accepted as leader by the discontented barons. Mortimer was seized in the castle of Nottingham and hanged in spite of the frantic entreaties of the Queen Mother, Isabella. From that time Edward assumed the reins of power, which he unfortunately used to carry on almost endless and quite futile foreign wars, the sole advantage of which was not anticipated by the King or evident in his lifetime.

Scotland, which, happily, was never to be forced into union with England by conquest, was the first object of his attack. In

1329, Bruce, who had leprosy—then and for long after a fairly common disease—died and left the throne to his son David, a child of five. Edward and the barons who thought they saw their opportunity endeavored to set the son of Balliol on the throne, but although the war dragged on for some years it resulted in nothing except an alliance between the French King, Philip VI, and the young Bruce, and the plundering of the Isle of Wight by the French.

Of far more importance was the beginning in 1337 of that long contest with France which is known as the Hundred Years' War, which brought untold misery to both nations, though, as in the case of the wars against Scotland, it was an important factor in developing the spirit of nationality in all three.

France, which had been but a petty kingdom, had by 1300, under a succession of three able kings, become the greatest power in Europe by the subjugation of the great vassals and the conquering of almost all those lands which had been English under Henry II. Now, however, the country was ruled by a king who could not claim descent in the male line, and although Edward had been sent to France by Mortimer as a boy to render homage for the remaining English possessions in Aquitaine and had acknowledged Philip as king, he decided upon fighting for the throne himself. It was a wholly unstatesmanlike venture, for even if military success should be on his side for a while, it would be impossible to merge the two States into one or to hold France permanently in bondage. War, however, was popular at first, and although foreign policy was in the hands of the King, a war which seems the height of folly could not have continued, with occasional truces, for a century between two neighboring powerful nations unless the peoples themselves had been willing to carry on.

On the English side there were various considerations. The traditional friendship between France and Scotland, which we noted earlier, made the desired conquest of the northern kingdom more difficult if not impossible. The road to the unifying of the island of Great Britain lay through the crippling of England's Continental foe and Scotland's friend. Moreover, the rapidly expanding France was threatening England's last remaining Continental possession in Aquitaine. In addition, there was the question of wool.

As we have noted, English trade and wealth had been expanding, and the most important staple was raw wool which was exported to Flanders, the center of the cloth industry. In England itself this had served to bring the country gentlemen, who raised the sheep on their estates, and the merchants who marketed the shearings for them, into close alliance. Unlike in much of their outlook as a knight of the shire and a burgher might be, they were bound together by this economic tie, a fact which was of vast importance in its influence upon their working together in Parliament and the strengthening of the House of Commons.

Two-thirds of the annual wool crop was sold to the Flemish cities of Ghent, Ypres and Bruges, and when these were threatened with subjugation by France, they appealed to Edward for their defense. Moreover, war with France had become somewhat of a tradition and the normal relationship between the two nations. It offered prospects of plunder and adventure, and there were plenty of English besides the barons anxious for both. A sort of neo-feudalism had also grown up, giving birth to a bastard chivalry which needed feats of arms to satisfy its adherents.

Edward, however, was no greater leader in war than in peace, and the struggle dragged out its first three years in ineffective invasions and no victory until the battle of Sluys in 1340. Until then the French navy had held the Channel and even burned Southampton but when the King called into play every vessel he could find, though mostly merchantmen, the French fleet was almost totally destroyed by the deadly archery of the English.

In spite of the success no use was made of it, and after a brief truce, the war again continued for six years before the English gained one of the most famous victories in the long roll of those to come in future centuries. Edward had taken his forces on an unwise expedition into France, almost as far as Paris, only to find bridges down and a great host advancing against him. Following the river Somme down almost to its mouth he was at last saved from fighting a losing battle, with his back against the uncrossable stream, by finding a ford, over which his troops passed and took stand on a bit of rising ground near Crecy. There they were attacked by the French host.

The two armies well exemplified the differences in the two nations. France was yet in the earlier feudal stage with almost no class between the *noblesse* and the despised and down-trodden peasantry. The former were present in large numbers in armor or shirts of mail, and exhibited to the full that lack of discipline which was characteristic of feudal levies. In addition there were foreign auxiliaries, including Genoese crossbowmen variously estimated in numbers from six to fifteen thousand. On the other hand, England had not only developed new classes unknown to feudal society, among them the yeoman, burgess, and country gentleman, but also that longbow which in the hands of trained archers was for long yet to give her supremacy in war when properly used. Moreover, there was a unity among the different classes and a practicality of mind among the English lacking in the French. This was best shown in the course of the battle by the dismounting of the English armored knights on horseback to fight side by side with the archers between whom they thrust their long lances. All ranks fought together on foot with good discipline, whereas the French mounted knights pressed forward pell mell, each thinking only of winning personal glory.

The Genoese were also of little use. Not only was the longbow a far more powerful weapon than the crossbow, but there had been a heavy rain which the mercenaries had allowed to wet the strings of their bows, thus rendering them practically useless while the English had kept theirs dry. Under the lead of the Black Prince

> Whiles his most mighty father on a hill
> Stood smiling to behold his lion's whelp
> Forage in blood of French nobility

as Shakespeare wrote, the slaughter inflicted on the enemy was terrific, and it is said that the number slain far exceeded the total of the much smaller English force. Among those killed on the French side was the blind King of Bohemia, who had joined the force in the spirit of knight-errantry, and his crest and motto, the famous three ostrich feathers and "Ich Dien," were adopted by the young English Prince and have been retained by the Princes of Wales ever since.

Both sides fought with conspicuous bravery but the extent of the victory was in large part owing to the mistakes of the French. The lesson, however, was not learned nor, later, when they attempted to use the longbow did the Continental peoples ever achieve the skill with it which the English always showed. The weapon and tactics, which were not the invention of Edward but had been gradually developing, had the weak point that the formation could be broken by flank attacks of cavalry, but this the French did not attempt, and the dazzling series of individual victories during the long war, even though nothing was accomplished in the end, did much to build in the English nation the belief in their own superiority and invincibility.

After Crecy, Edward hurried to the siege of Calais, which surrendered to him and seemed to promise both military strength by the occupation of a fortified port on the French coast and the opening of new Continental markets. Meanwhile, the old French-Scottish friendship came into play, and the Scotch King, David, invaded England but was taken prisoner in a severe defeat at Nevill's Cross. In spite, however, of these resounding victories, Edward made truce with France and practically nothing further was done for eight years. One reason for the cessation of major hostilities was the Black Death, which was sweeping Europe and reached England about 1348, and which we shall speak of presently, passing it for the moment to complete the story of the French war under Edward.

The struggle began again in 1355, the King leading an expedition based on Calais, while the Black Prince moved far to the south. A rebellion in Scotland forced Edward home without accomplishing anything, but the Prince pushed on and in the brilliant victory of Poitiers, fought against terrific odds, he not only won the fight but captured the French King and brought him back to England, which could now boast of two captive monarchs at once, to be held for vast ransoms. Four years later, in 1360, Edward again crossed the channel with the hope of being crowned King of France at Rheims, but the raid ended disastrously, and he was forced to consent to the Treaty of Bretigny, by which he gave up all claim to the French throne but retained Calais and Ponthieu, and added considerably to the English possessions toward the south. The war, however, was far from over, and revolts in Guienne resulted in carrying on the fighting even into Spain.

By another fourteen years the English had lost all their French possessions except Calais, and in addition the English fleet had been all but annihilated by the Spaniards. Edward, broken and ill, had returned to England, as had also the Black Prince, after a ferocious attack on the town of Limoges in which he put the entire population to death. It was the equivalent of our modern air raids, such as that on Barcelona, but in thinking of chivalry we must make place in our thoughts for such cruel acts as this massacre of every man, woman and child in a surrendered city. The Prince, like his father, fell ill, and, for a while, his brother, John of Gaunt, Duke of Lancaster, continued the fighting, but his efforts ended in complete disaster.

After nearly half a century, with yet another half century of warfare to come, England had been burdened with heavy taxation, and her attention and energies had been diverted from their proper sphere, the British Isles, to the Continent, with the result that she possessed less there than when the war started. Only a portion of her strength could be exerted against Scotland, and Ireland was left to herself until by the Statute of Kilkenny in 1367 Edward established a local Parliament for the English within the Pale and abandoned the rest of the country. But the drain of the continued French war prevented even the defense of the Pale itself, which was plundered by the Irish.

In his last years the King, who was suffering from softening of the brain, allowed himself to be controlled wholly by his mistress, Alice Perrers, who shared her power with the Duke of Lancaster, whose elder brother, the Black Prince, was usually too ill to exert himself. There was, however, a flicker of his old energy at the end. Lancaster had allied himself to the baronial party which the Commons had long learned to mistrust, and it was rumored that when the Prince died his young son Richard would be set aside so that Lancaster might proclaim himself King.

In what is known as "the Good Parliament" of 1376, the Prince put himself at the head of the Commons, now sitting as a separate House. Not only was Lancaster excluded from the new Council of State, and Alice Perrers driven from Court, but the Commons refused to vote new taxes until previous accounts of expenses had been laid before them. Parliament also, for the first time, impeached, if we may use a modern term, two royal officials for embezzling the King's money.

During the session, however, the Black Prince died, and although Richard was recognized as heir of the dying Edward, Lancaster regained his influence over his imbecile father, and was able to obtain a reversal of the acts of the Good Parliament by one elected under his own packing, and which levied a poll tax on the heads of all except beggars, of which tax we shall hear more later. The same year the King ended his inglorious life, dying deserted by all, even his mistress who remained by his side only long enough to steal the rings from his fingers. Sluys, Crecy, Poitiers and two captive kings could not redeem the fifty years of an otherwise disastrous reign.

One thing, however, of great importance which had occurred during the half century and as a result of the wars, was the development of nationality on both sides of the Channel. France had suffered most from the presence not merely of foreign armies but of the marauding and undisciplined bands of adventurers bent only on plunder whom even Edward and the Prince could not control. Much of the country had been left waste, and famine stalked among the miserable peasantry. But though France had not learned the art of the new warfare, it had been hammered into shape and consolidated into one of the two leading powers of

Europe, as England had become the other. The two nascent nations had marked each other as eternal rivals and enemies, and the long duel between them which was to last until into the nineteenth century had begun in earnest.

Moreover, the victory of Crecy, like that of Agincourt in the next century, and others, all served to build up a tradition of patriotism, invincibility and duty to the past, in the English. In *King Henry V*, Shakespeare makes the Bishop of Ely say to the King before the battle of Agincourt, carrying his memory back to Crecy,

> Awake remembrance of these valiant dead,
> And with your puissant arm renew their feats:
> You are their heir; you sit upon their throne;
> The blood and courage that renownéd them
> Runs in your veins. . . .

Historians shift from theory to theory, and interest to interest. The school of a generation back which would have us believe, as a few still insist, that the economic motive governs all, is happily passing. Innumerable other motives have moved mankind and changed the course of events. There has also been an intense reaction against the old "drum and trumpet" school which delighted in long and detailed narratives of wars. Yet we must not forget that we cannot understand the character of a people and the deep springs of their being without understanding what the memory of a Crecy or an Agincourt or the last fight of the *Revenge* by a Grenville does to them in their racial memory. To understand a nation we have to know more than such facts, for example, as the rise of their trade unions, even though they, also, may help to complete the picture.

So, in our narrative, we may note here that owing to the French war England had gained enormously in its sense of distinct nationhood. Even before it, while the English nobles had been steadily losing their Continental fiefs and estates, they had been becoming less French, and it is notable that a few years after Poitiers the French language was officially abandoned by statute, and English, described as our "moder tunge," became the language of Parliament and the law courts. It seems certain that hostility to France and things French, engendered by the rancors of the war, hastened this process, which was to be of vast importance not only to the formation of English literature, but to the growth of English feeling. The French which had been spoken by the upper classes had become uncouth enough, but, however it may have sounded in Paris, so long as it had remained the official language and that of the higher ranks, it had served as a barrier to the unity and development of the new nation.

Another event which was also to have profound influence was the introduction into England of the Black Death, already mentioned. In any case a disease which suddenly wiped out from a half to two-thirds of the entire population would have had enormous effects on the economic and social life of the people, but it also came at a time when important changes had been in silent operation for several generations, changes which it was greatly to emphasize. Apparently it was of the same nature as the plague which was to continue to appear for more than three centuries until the great plague in London in 1665. It was characterized by swellings, carbuncles and boils, vomiting of blood, and delirium, acting in this earlier period particularly with great swiftness, and attacking all classes from the Archbishop of Canterbury to the lowliest laborer. It is thought to have originated in China, and to have been spread through Europe by traders engaged in traffic with the Orient. Accompanied by famine and starvation the change it wrought in England was appalling.

To understand the part it played in giving birth to a more modern civilization we must turn again to that transition from feudalism which we have already had to note several times. There had been many forces at work breaking down the old system, such, among others, as the changed method of raising troops for war and the rise of the archers. To these we must add the change to a new money economy. The feudal lord, on his manor or great estate worked by serfs bound to the soil, had as a rule little need of cash. It was not necessary for wages, and taxes were largely paid to him in the produce of the soil.

Gradually, however, the landowners came to require money, for the new luxuries coming into use, for their houses in London and other purposes. The merchants of the trading towns were becoming rich and setting new standards of living. The constant wars required financing, first by the Jews, who had been expelled by Edward I, then by the great Italian banking houses of the Bardi and Peruzzi, and when they crashed in 1345, by English financiers who had risen to a new position, the chief of whom was one Walter de Cheriton. Times were clearly changing, and the old feudal aristocracy and the country gentlemen changed with them.

This alteration affected the relations of the lord to his serfs in various ways, but all tending to transform serfdom into freedom. Instead of so many days' labor, the owner of land in many cases preferred to accept a small money payment. The amount was fixed on the records of the manor or estate, and, so long as it was paid, the former serf or villein could not be dispossessed of the small holding allotted to him, becoming practically a free proprietor himself. Portions of the lord's land might also be rented by him to farmers who hired their own labor. Those who still remained in their old position of serfs bound to the soil naturally looked with envy on these classes which arose from the freedom evolving from the lord's preference of money to produce. They became restless, imbued with a new hope. To the increasing numbers of yeomen farmers and free laborers working for wages were added those soldiers returning from the wars who naturally did not become serfs. In the towns also the breakdown of the old merchant guilds and the rise of the craftsmen guilds were giving labor a new sense of its possible status.

The old feudal and medieval systems were passing into the modern system of a money and wage economy. The growth of the wool trade was also exerting influence on both town and country. The great importance of this trade was exemplified by the "woolsack" on which the Lord Chancellor still sits in the House of Lords, a custom said to date from this period. The export of raw wool was the largest source of trade revenue to the kingdom, but

Edward's export duties had also tended to build up the cloth industry at home, giving employment to a new branch of free labor in the towns. In the country, landowners, anxious to increase their money income, turned farm land into grazing pastures for sheep, and the farm laborers thus displaced were free to wander as no longer needed by the lord.

When, however, the Black Death swept away half or more of all the labor of England, both landowners and town employers found themselves in a terrible predicament. Considering the position of the landowners, we may note that they were hurt on every side. They had lost, we may estimate, half of their remaining serfs and of their hired laborers. In addition, their incomes were heavily reduced by the wiping out of many of the tenants whom they had placed on lands on a rental basis. Lands lay idle for want of hands to cultivate them.

Not only did the remaining laborers take natural advantage of this situation by demanding high wages, but likewise the serfs, seeing wages going up among their friends, refused to work on the old basis of so many days for their lords, and ran away. There is no doubt that the change already in progress combined with the sudden disaster of the plague brought on an economic crisis of the first magnitude, unparalleled since in its sudden severity. The fact that prices of agricultural produce not only did not advance materially but rather tended to decline made the position even worse. There were no additional profits which could be tapped to meet the higher costs.

The laboring class was not represented in the House of Commons, which was largely made up of town and rural employers. These naturally looked at the situation from their own standpoint, and to prevent what they considered amounted almost to a revolution in the established order of things, they passed the Statute of Laborers, 1351, which was re-enacted from time to time. Briefly this attempted to bridle the economic movement by forcing all, bond and free, who did not have land or money of their own to work for any employer who demanded his or her services and at the rate of wages prevailing before the plague. The prices of products were also fixed at those formerly prevailing to restore, if possible, the old equilibrium. There were heavy penalties for both workers and employers who broke the law, which was chiefly enforced by the Justices of the Peace, who belonged to the employer class.

Nevertheless, the movement could not be stopped, for a population could not be wholly subjugated, and so great was the real need for labor at any price that many employers themselves infringed the Act. Great bitterness was caused, and the rise in wages was probably retarded but like all legislation running counter to economic laws the Statute failed of its object. In the end, with other causes, it came near to plunging all England into complete anarchy. The peoples of the Continent also suffered from the plague, but there it did not come at the same corresponding moment in social advance, and in spite of it society remained in the feudal lord-and-serf stage, whereas by the end of the century in England probably by far the major part of all labor had become free, a process to be completed in the next century. It was a free nation that was later to be molded by the Tudors in the great period of expansion and the beginning of overseas empire, a fact of vast significance to both England and the world.

The fourteenth century, in spite of its continuous wars and successive plagues, was far from being the period of darkness which it is sometimes painted. Indeed, much of its remarkable intellectual ferment was far in advance of the times and was to be followed by another century of decline. There was a marked change about 1350.

At the beginning of the century the most popular book among the educated classes was the French *Roman de la Rose*, but in 1356 the reputed Sir John Mandeville returned from thirty-four years of world wanderings, as claimed, and soon every one was reading his *Travels*. This was the first genuinely imaginative work in English prose and had great influence on the development of English style, though the book, which purported to be an account of his travels in the Near East, India and China, appears to have been a compilation from many other works, some in French. It breaks, however, with both feudal and Church interests, and marks the beginning of the travel literature and that love of travel which is so marked an English characteristic.

The work of Richard Rolle was religious but struck the democratic note which was a feature of this period. He condemned much in the religious and social life of his day, and again we get a glimpse of a continuing trait in the better Englishmen of all ranks in his emphasis on the three things needful—honesty in work, freedom of spirit in doing it, and honesty and fairness in all one's dealings with others.

Particularly notable, from the standpoint of the rise of the laborer is Langland's *Vision of Piers Plowman*, a long allegory, possibly retouched by other hands in its several versions and many editions. Langland did not wish to change the order of society but rather to improve it by the improvement of the individual. Nevertheless his work constitutes the beginning of the literature of social reform in England, and is notable as having come from the ranks of the common people themselves. In an age when reading was a rare accomplishment it is a little difficult to understand how the poem attained the wide popularity and influence which it did and which made it a living force in its own day and not a mere item of interest to the later antiquarian or chronicler of literature. The work describes a pilgrimage to the shrine of Truth, and the author mingles human and allegorical figures, but the chief point of interest is that the leader, who later rises to the type of Christ himself, is not a churchman or learned man but a poor plowman. Here, indeed, is a change of center from which to view and criticize the world and the times!

We shall speak in a moment of the religious activities of Wyclif, but before leaving the topic of the common man, we may note that author's contribution to the new ideas. It is going too far, I think, to call Wyclif communistic in his doctrine of property, but his doctrine did run counter again to those of both the Church and feudalism, though he used the idea of over-lordship of the latter. Wyclif's over-lord, however, was God, from whom, he taught, all individuals held directly and not, as in feudalism, through a hierarchy descending from king to serf. As only the righteous could hold from God, it followed from Wyclif's doctrine that personal property and political power over others could properly belong only to those who obeyed the law of the Gospel and rendered that service to their fellows which alone could justify their possessions or position. As righteousness could not be bequeathed from father to son or handed down, neither, he argued, could property or power.

The subversive effect of such ideas is obvious, even though Wyclif was careful to add that no man had a right to seize the possessions of other persons because he might consider them unrighteous. However, it was probably his theories in this regard that for a time secured him the powerful support of such men as Lancaster and others who were hungering to despoil the Church and secure some of her enormous property for themselves. In contrast to such selfish interest on the part of a few, the appearance of two such men as Langland and Wyclif simultaneously, and the influence which they had on the masses of the poor and despised, mark the rise of a new element in English life and thought.

The Church itself had fallen in popular regard, especially during the half century during which two rival Popes held their courts and made their claims in Rome and Avignon. The English objected to the imposition upon them of nominees of foreigners who had no claim to ecclesiastical positions except that they were Papal favorites. They also objected to the carrying of appeals from English law courts to the Pope at Avignon as well as to Papal financial exactions, especially the payment of 1000 marks a year which John had agreed to as a sign of his vassalage. Edward had not paid this since 1333, and Wyclif's doctrine sustained him.

In causing the Bible for the first time to be translated into English, much of which work he did himself, Wyclif also laid the cornerstone of later Protestantism and democracy. By means of the "Poor Priests," who attached themselves to him and went through the country teaching his beliefs, it has been estimated that a third of the population became his followers, or "Lollards" as they were called. Some of his later theological doctrines, notably his denial of transubstantiation, and his opposition to the sale of pardons and the saying of masses for the dead, lessened his following and brought him into direct opposition to the Church, but in spite of persecution the Lollards were not crushed out, and the movement lasted on to join with the more general one of the Reformation.

When that time came, the effort to free the English Church of Papal domination was to be no new or sudden impulse. In the reign of Edward the anti-Papal movement received a considerable impetus. Statutes were passed to prevent the system of Papal nominations to benefices, and of appeals to any foreign court, meaning that of the Pope, while bishops were declared unfit to hold state offices. Anti-clerical and Papal feeling was increased by the decadence of the Church, by the desire of others for its wealth, by its no longer serving the community, and by the dislike of the laboring class for the laziness and luxury of the churchmen, while the strong anti-French feeling engendered by the war was naturally extended to the French Pope living in France and who supported the French against English interests.

New ideas were fermenting like yeast in the social structure which was not yet sufficiently firmly built and established to withstand too great and sudden a strain. These ideas, combining with other causes, were to produce such a strain as not only to threaten England with complete chaos but also to bring about a long reaction, as too rapid advances are ever likely to do.

Richard II (1377–99), a boy of ten, was acknowledged as King on Edward's death, and a Council was formed to govern in the young King's name, as his uncle, Lancaster, was too unpopular to serve as Regent. Although there was far less chance of winning the war against France and of regaining any of the possessions Edward had lost than there had been in his day, the war was renewed, with no success. There was not even a Crecy or Poitiers to give a false brilliancy to otherwise unrelieved disaster and useless waste of the national resources. Heavier and heavier taxes had to be brought before an ever more reluctant Parliament to be voted by them. Those who knew something of national affairs wanted efficiency for the heavy drains on their purses, and realized they were not getting it, while the vast mass of Englishmen who only knew that years of lack of success were costing them more and more money grew increasingly critical and restless. The entire nation was responsible for continuing the hopeless war, but looked less at impossible conditions than for scapegoats in the succession of ministers whom they considered as mismanaging it.

In 1380 the revenue from customs was much diminished owing to civil war in Flanders which interfered with the purchase of English wool, and the pay of the army was months in arrears. The King's jewels were in pawn and would be forfeited if not redeemed. Parliament asked what was the lowest sum required, as "the Commons were poor," and were told £160,000, which was perhaps in purchasing power twelve times the same sum today.

For several years there had been a poll tax, graduated in 1379, though the scale was cruelly absurd, ranging from 4d. from a peasant to only £6 13s. 4d. from the Duke of Lancaster, the richest man in the kingdom and possessed of enormous wealth. In 1380 the tax on the peasant was not only increased threefold, but was also exacted from him for each unmarried child above fifteen years of age. In 1381, however, a still more disastrous levy was laid. Parliament met the demands of the Chancellor by agreeing to raise £100,000 by a poll tax if the clergy, who, as they said, "occupy the third part of the lands of the realm," would make up the rest. Perhaps to avoid the worse evil of confiscation, the clergy somewhat unexpectedly agreed, and Parliament proceeded to lay the poll tax. The law was incredibly unjust, and false returns were made all over England, which if true would have shown that in five years the adult population had dropped from over 1,355,000 persons to less than 900,000.

But grievances of various sorts had been accumulating for a long time. We have already noted the effects of the Black Death a generation earlier. In every section of the country there had been constant bickering and hard feelings between landowners and their villeins, hired labor, and tenants. A bitter struggle, growing out of the exceptional economic conditions, had, in fact, been in progress, the details varying from section to section, and even from one manor to another. Though several times amended and re-enacted, the Statute of Laborers, with its barbarous possible penalties and its attempted control of wage scales and prices, was ineffective.

Each side to the dispute believed itself in the right. The landlords thought they were fighting for the cause of law, order and social stability, while the other classes believed that they were demanding only their just dues. There were also many causes of discontent in the towns. In some, where the lord was a churchman, the inhabitants felt that they were not enjoying the privileges of those in other towns with lay lords, the churchmen being extremely slow in granting the changes the times required. In others, there was bitter feeling between the ordinary citizens and the small oligarchies of rich families who had got control of the local government. In yet other, and mostly larger towns, such as London, there had been going on a struggle between the employers and employed in the guild system. There was also the antagonism against the foreign merchants who were thought to be sucking cash out of the kingdom, making money scarce and keeping wages low. Religious discontent, although earlier historians laid stress upon it, seems to have been more or less negligible in the revolt about to break out.

Although there were many uprisings and much violence throughout England apparently there was no central organization or concerted action. The revolt, taking different forms in different places, was the result of the varied causes noted above, all together suddenly touched off by the new and unbearable poll tax which weighed so heavily on the whole of the toiling masses alike. "Wat Tyler's Rebellion," as it is called from the most notable of its local leaders, was one of the shortest and most dramatic of the really important episodes in English history. It was not so much a fire sweeping the whole nation as a vast number of separate fires springing up simultaneously. It is impossible to chronicle them all, and we will confine ourselves to narrating briefly the happenings in London.

Tyler appeared in Kent, where he at once established his ascendancy over the mobs of that shire, which sacked manor houses, collected blackmail, and captured Canterbury, though with little bloodshed. Immediately after, they moved on to London, being joined on the way by the itinerant socialist preacher John Ball and many additional recruits. The local authorities, who realized that the city proletariat was in sympathy with the rebels, as were also several of the aldermen, seemed powerless, and the King's Council, who had shut themselves in the Tower, seemed equally unprepared and helpless. The invading mobs from Kent and Essex had camped on Blackheath, where on June 13 Ball preached his famous sermon to the multitude, taking as his text the popular jingle

> When Adam delved, and Eve span,
> Who was then a gentleman?

He declared that all men had been created equal, and that only injustice and wickedness had created differences in rank and wealth, urging his followers to do away with lords and lawyers. The young King had decided to leave the Tower and to meet the rebels in person to enquire into their grievances, but when his boat neared the place of assembly of the mob of over 10,000, it was clearly too unsafe for him to land, and he was rowed back amid curses. That afternoon the mob was admitted within the gates of London by one of the aldermen, and a reign of terror began.

Lambeth Palace had been pillaged and now the mob moved on the most magnificent mansion in all England, the Savoy, just finished for the enormously rich Duke of Lancaster and filled with costly treasures. These were carried off and the building burned to the ground. Many others were sacked and given to the flames, and the two prisons of Newgate and the Fleet were destroyed, their freed occupants adding a worse element to the mob.

The King from the Tower tried to negotiate, and finally, a day or so later, rode out with a band of followers to confer with the insurgents, and meeting with them, Tyler at their head, he agreed to many reforms. The negotiations, however, broke down, and Tyler with some of his followers reached the Tower and entered unhindered. There they beheaded the Archbishop, Hales, the royal treasurer and others hated by the common people. The young King Richard had escaped to join his mother in the small palace known as the Wardrobe. The Tower murders were followed by general killings and burnings, including the beheading of about 150 or more foreigners. The next day the King decided again to try negotiation by meeting the mob in person, and met Tyler at their head. In a sudden scuffle following an attempt to kill the King, Tyler was himself mortally wounded in sight of the whole mob, and the most critical moment of the revolt had come. The King told the mob to follow him to the open fields a little to the north of where they were, and rode off at a walk, none daring to hinder him. There he talked with them for a half hour in instant danger of his life.

At last, however, the loyalists and men of standing in London had roused themselves for that united action which if undertaken sooner would have saved the situation in the beginning. Some 7000 men marched out to defend the King, and surrounded the insurgents, whom they wished to massacre. Richard, however, gave the rebels leave to depart unharmed, which they instantly did. As the King sat on his horse, the head of Tyler was brought to him, and the boy of fourteen knew that he had conquered, and, as he told his mother, had recovered his heritage and the realm of England. There could be no greater contrast than between the able and courageous boy of that day's work and the wreck of his later career. What he had said was true. For thirty days the entire social fabric of England had been in imminent danger of complete destruction, and the child King had saved it. Great clemency was shown by the government, and probably less than 200 of the rebels met death at the hands of justice, and later, at the request of the House of Commons, a general amnesty, with some exceptions, was proclaimed.

Under duress, the King had agreed with the rebels that serfdom should be abolished in all England; that villein tenants were to become free, paying 4d. an acre rent a year to the lord; restrictions on prices in buying and selling were to be removed; and other grievances remedied. These charters were afterwards cancelled, but in many places the laboring classes kept copies of them, serving as ideals for which to strive. The revolution, however, did not accomplish any of the results aimed at, and when villeinage and other abuses died out in the next century or so, it was due to slow and natural economic causes working themselves out. The immediate effect of the great shock which the propertied classes had received made them rather less than more lenient with those below them. Bad as the rising had been, it was noteworthy for two characteristics which we shall find increasingly English. Unlike similar risings on the Continent, there was, outside of the short-lived ferocity and comparatively small loss of life in London, where the worst elements were gathered, little bloodshed anywhere, even in the loneliest country districts where risings occurred. Moreover, there was shown the great English trait of compromise and the willingness to talk things over. The boy King talking with Wat Tyler was symbolic of what has made England possible. There was no unleashing of troops to mow the rebels down. There was no stifling of freedom of speech. There was talk between man and man.

The year following, the King was married and the war with France renewed. Not only was an expedition into that country a total failure, but Flanders fell into French hands, endangering the greatest export market of England, and a French fleet threatened the English coast and invasion of the island. An attack on Scotland, in which Edinburgh was burned, produced no other result than increased hostility. The King also created a large number of new peers and gave the Dukedoms of York and Gloucester to his two younger uncles. Things were not going well, and the people demanded change.

Lancaster had sailed for Spain to press a claim to that throne, but Gloucester put himself at the head of all those opposed to the young nephew who had raised him in rank and power, and a Parliament controlled by him demanded the impeachment of

Richard's Ministers and the creation of a Regency Commission to govern the country for a year. During that period a fine naval victory was won over the combined Spaniards, French and Flemings, but Richard, fearful lest the Commission might try to keep him permanently in tutelage, made an effort to free himself. His uncle Gloucester, however, and the Earls of Arundel, Nottingham, Warwick and Derby, the last being his cousin, the son of Lancaster, brought against the King an overwhelming force. Five of his leading Councillors were condemned to death by Parliament, though three escaped, and Gloucester retained the power, though Richard was allowed the Crown.

A second effort was more successful. Richard had submitted to the "Lords Appellant," as Gloucester and the four earls were called, but the people were, from long experience, even more afraid of too great power on the part of a few leading feudal lords than of a despotic king. Perhaps the lords sensed this, because, when in full Council in May, 1389, Richard suddenly asked his own age from his uncle Gloucester and, on being told twenty-two, replied that then he was old enough to manage his own affairs, no opposition was made. Richard at once took over the government and dismissed the entire Council. For the next seven years he ruled constitutionally with Parliament and made no effort to revenge himself on any one, even Gloucester. He at once made a truce with France, which was renewed for twenty-eight years in 1396, a wise but unpopular policy.

Suddenly there came that change in the King which has made his character so difficult to understand. Gloucester, rich, restless and ambitious, had apparently again been plotting against his nephew. In any case, Richard had him arrested, together with Warwick and Arundel, who were also suspected, and accused before Parliament. Warwick was banished, Arundel executed, and Gloucester sent to prison in Calais, where he was murdered, apparently at Richard's command.

His next step was to summon a Parliament to meet at Shrewsbury instead of London, and he succeeded in completely packing it with his own adherents. This extraordinary Parliament declared void all Acts of the Merciless Parliament, as it was called, which had set up the Lords Appellant to rule the King, and further declared that no legal restraint could be put upon him. Not only that but it practically abdicated by delegating all its own power to a committee of eighteen of the King's friends, twelve lords and six commoners. Richard was now free of every constitutional restraint and changed Parliamentary government into a personal dictatorship.

Whether or not he was insane, as has been claimed, he acted as though he were. He banished Derby, whom he had created Duke of Hereford, and Nottingham, whom he had made Duke of Norfolk. He extorted money right and left from others and even made subjects give promises to pay in blank, for him to fill up for whatever amounts he chose. One of the growing dangers to the peace of the times had been the custom we have already alluded to of livery, that is, of the nobles gathering about them large bands of retainers. Richard now did the same. He also threatened the Percys, father and son, and exiled this powerful Earl of Northumberland and his heir to their estates on the Scottish border to brood over their treatment and possible future. When Lancaster died, the King confiscated his vast property, taking it from the legal heir, Hereford.

The clergy had also been becoming more and more uneasy. The Lollard priests had been going up and down the country preaching the confiscation of Church property for the good of the State, and although the laity generally did not endorse this they had been becoming more anxious to break with the Pope on all points except theological doctrine. The Church was thus becoming alienated from the King because he took no steps to check what it naturally considered as doctrines fatal to itself.

Richard had thus put himself into opposition to almost every element in his realm. The most powerful nobles, with the examples before them, feared lest their turn at banishment, execution or confiscation might come. The knights objected to the suppression of Parliament, and the local government of England was chiefly in their hands. The Church was fearful and increasingly hostile.

The witless King, having alienated almost every one except a few favorites built up by him, chose this time to set off on an unsuccessful expedition to Ireland, leaving his uncle, the Duke of York, behind as Regent.

The exiled and despoiled Hereford, now since his father's death Duke of Lancaster, landed on the coast of Yorkshire, and was soon joined by the Percys and others, including the Regent himself, the King's uncle. Richard after a hurried return to Wales found himself, almost without followers, alone in Conway Castle with the whole of his kingdom against him. Lancaster induced him to place himself in his power on pretence that he would help him to govern. The mask was soon thrown aside and the former King found himself a prisoner in the Tower.

There, in 1399, he signed his abdication as King, and Parliament, assembled once more, formally deposed him in addition and proclaimed Lancaster as Henry IV, passing over the claims of young Edmund Mortimer, who was the legitimate successor as much nearer in blood. Henry endeavored to dispute this claim by pretending that his great-grandfather Edmund, second son of Henry III, had in reality been the elder son instead of Edward I, from whom Mortimer was descended.

The claim was absurdly false but is interesting as showing the hold that the hereditary principle was gaining although in reality the new King owed his throne wholly to election by Parliament. For a short time, Richard, though a prisoner, remained a center for plots, and having been transferred to the castle of Pontefract he died in 1400 after a small and unsuccessful rising in his favor. There seems little doubt that he was murdered by order of Henry. The country was stirred and many claimed that he was not dead in reality, a rumor that clearly might prove so troublesome to his successor as to induce him to have the corpse exhibited for two days in St. Paul's Cathedral, the face alone, however, being visible. How death was met was never known.

In the same year in which the despotic King met his mysterious end there also died a man who in his day occupied but a modest place as contrasted with the monarch, but whose name is known today to many to whom Richard II is but a shadow or a character in Shakespearean drama. Geoffrey Chaucer was the son of a London wine merchant, and so of the middle class. Except for his immortal work as poet his life would not be of special interest, save in so far as it exemplifies what might be the experiences of a man of his position. We first find him receiving his suit of livery as a member of the household of Lionel, son of Edward III, and save for a while, when the ascendancy of Gloucester served him an ill turn, he seems to have been in the good graces of both Richard II and Henry IV, receiving offices and pensions from both of them, though he was poor in his later years until the latter King came to his rescue. He fought with the army in France, served on missions to Italy and elsewhere, and touched life at many points.

His poetry, even in his own time, was immensely popular, and was to influence English writing in generations to come, though none so great as himself again appeared in the field of letters for some two centuries, until the glorious days of Elizabeth. The history of literature of any nation is naturally full of the names of men who influenced their own period or who are mentioned merely because, of no great importance themselves, they rise above the still lesser men of their period. Chaucer was not of these, and in spite of the archaism of much of his vocabulary he is yet read after nearly six centuries for delight in his work and not in the spirit of antiquarianism.

Difficult for many as his language may be in part, it is in direct line with the English tongue which we speak today. We have noted that French was being superseded by the native English, the "moder tunge," but of this there were many dialects, as there have since remained among country folk. It was that of the East Midlands, however, that was to be the ancestor of the language of Shakespeare and of today, and it became so not only because it was spoken in London and the university towns of Oxford and Cambridge but also because it was the one in which Chaucer wrote, into which Wyclif translated the Bible, and which Caxton was later to use in printing. It thus became set as the standard of pure English whereas the others became mere rustic and provincial variants. In Chaucer's work we may discern three periods of influence, including those of the French and Italian before he became so thoroughly English in his later poems. The imaginative literary medium of the day was the tale in verse but so great were Chaucer's qualities of character delineation, of love of nature and beauty, his robustness, his interest in all sorts of human types, and his all-pervasive humor, that it is likely that he might have become as great a dramatist in the Elizabethan period or novelist in the Victorian as he was poet at the end of his own.

Of all his works that which is still most popular is the long poem or collection of stories in verse of the *Canterbury Tales* in which the poet takes us with a very mixed company, of whom each tells a story in turn to while away the tedium of the journey, on a religious pilgrimage from London, where the travellers have met, to Becket's shrine at Canterbury. In the Prologue we meet the pilgrims who are described with inimitable touches, "the verray parfit gentil knight," the squire who "was as fresh as is the month of May," the Prioress who "all was conscience and tendre herte," the clerk, or scholar, who "gladly wolde he lerne, and gladly teche," the poor country parson who of "Cristes lore, and his apostles twelve, He taughte, but first he folwed it himselve," and others whom the poet makes pass before us like a pageant of social life at the end of the medieval period. It was indeed the end of a period, to be followed by an unhappy three generations of transition into the age of the Tudors and the beginning of the modern world.

It had almost seemed as though that modern world were already in bud, with the rise in the power of Parliament, even if wrongly used when packed; the false dawn of the Reformation and the break with Rome; the beginning of modern literature with Chaucer. But the nation, like a precocious child, had been developing too rapidly, and there were still dangerous factors to be eliminated, and a more ordered growth required before a sound and healthy maturity could be attained.

CHAPTER VI

THE FIFTEENTH CENTURY: THE THRESHOLD
OF THE NEW WORLD

THE FIFTEENTH CENTURY is assuredly not a glorious one in English history. The continuance of the war with France, futile and hopeless as ever, though to be lit by the great victory at Agincourt; the relations between Parliament and Crown; the struggles to secure the throne; the smaller war against Wales; the risings of nobles and the fighting of these magnates among themselves; all give a sense of a confused period, and most of these brawls, except that the leaders in them have great names and dress in armor or velvets and jewels, become as tiresome and seemingly of as little importance as those of angry fishwives in Billingsgate. However, the results did prove of great importance, though, as often happens in life and history, they were not those aimed at by the actors themselves. In addition there were other movements, such as the rise of the business man, the development of architecture, the secularizing of life and thought, and others that are far more significant for us today than the French war and the Wars of the Roses viewed simply in themselves.

There was one outstanding difference between England and the Continent. On the latter, powerful monarchs were coming to the fore, and governments, large and small, were becoming dictatorships, as we should say now, a condition lasting for the most part well into the nineteenth century, and which in the twentieth was to relapse again in many important cases into one-man rule. In

England, on the other hand, the central power had become weak. The usurping King, Henry IV, as we saw at the end of the last chapter, in spite of fictions, held his title and power by Parliamentary election, and though the fact might be glossed over it could not be concealed. If a Parliament could make a king, there was no logical reason why it could not unmake him and make another. A disputed succession was always a disaster for the people as it meant uncertainty, turmoil, confusion and often war.

The theory of the divine right of kings lay in the future, to be propounded by the Stuarts two centuries later. Hereditary right, with all its chances of personality and character, was the best solution for the problem under the conditions, and had developed because of its practical use in maintaining continuity and giving the least disturbance to peace and property. The times required a strong central authority to keep both people and nobles in order, although it was of the utmost importance for the growth of liberty and self-government that such an authority should be tempered by public opinion with legal means of expression. This it was to lack on the Continent, and freedom in England, which was later to be extended in varying proportions, to the entire Empire, got a head start of other nations by some centuries. England later was also to get a similar head start over certain other modern nations in the acquisition of territory throughout the world, so that, by the time they desired to do the same, conditions had changed for them.

It is less often considered, however, that she also got the same start in learning the lessons of self-control, government and freedom. A national character permitting these cannot be built up or called into existence overnight, and England was happy in unconsciously taking advantage, during some centuries, of conditions which allowed of such development when they either did not exist or were not used by other nations.

The process, however, as we have already pointed out, was not a conscious one. England has never "planned" her institutions or her future. It largely "just happened," as we say, though it did so because of the various traits of the people, good and bad, as they reacted to conditions in the past and molded institutions. If feudalism took a different course in England from that on the Continent, if the yeoman farmer became a very different person from the French peasant, if Parliamentary government became a success in England and nowhere on the Continent, and so on with other "ifs," it was not all accident. It was because of the English character and the way in which it handled historical accidents. But the uncharted course has not run straight. There have been zig-zags, too hasty advances and needed retreats, backings and fillings, but ever with a driving force toward freedom and stability.

For those goals it was needful in the fifteenth century that the claws of the great nobles should be well cut and their powers shorn; that the road to royal despotism should be blocked by a Parliament; and additional precedents created for a constitutional monarchy. These things were not planned, but they came to pass. Indeed, they happened too rapidly, so that in the next century the people welcomed a semi-despotism under the Tudor Henrys and Elizabeth, but great as were to be the powers of the Tudor monarchs they well knew that such powers rested on the willing consent of their subjects and had to be exercised for their benefit if they were to be retained—an outlook very different from that of Continental rulers.

During his short reign of only fourteen years, Henry realized that his chief reliance must be on Parliament, which had made him king. There were other claimants to the throne nearer in blood, even after he had murdered Richard. The great nobles were ready to use their bands of retainers against him for their individual advantage whenever opportunity might arise. The rebellion of 1400 was but one of several; and wars with the French, Welsh and Scotch required money. The rising of the Welsh found a leader in Owen Glendower, who, although he was finally suppressed, became the most popular of Welsh heroes and an almost legendary figure, even the English believing in his magic powers. The words attributed to him by Shakespeare,

I can call spirits from the vasty deep,

and the rest of the well-known passages were believed by many when the campaign against him in 1402 was wrecked by the unusual rains and snows of that season.

The same year, the Scots taking advantage of a divided England also made an incursion from the north but were defeated by the Percys, who had been largely instrumental in making Henry king. This enormously rich and powerful family, headed by the Earls of Northumberland and Worcester, held estates which covered a great part of northern England, and as border lords they maintained retinues that might as readily overturn a king as set one up.

The following year they turned against Henry but the southern English had no wish to have these magnates lord it over them, and defeated their forces at Shrewsbury, the Earl of Worcester being captured and beheaded, and his nephew, Henry Percy, known as Harry Hotspur, being killed. Northumberland was first imprisoned, then pardoned, to become a wanderer in Wales, where he was later slain. The French also attacked the coast but internal dissensions in France saved the English from that quarter, while their lucky capture of the young Scottish prince, later James I of Scotland, gave them a hostage to keep his countrymen quiet.

If during these troubles Parliament was more or less the master of the King, it does not mean that the people were masters in Parliament. The Commons, it is true, held the purse strings, but the powers that controlled the upper House also largely packed the lower. The main point was the relation between Parliament as a whole and the monarchy it had created. The better control of Parliament itself by the people was a matter for later development. Whatever controls passed to Parliament would in time pass to the more powerful chamber in it. Henry, however, like others we have noted, had to balance the yeomen and burgesses against the nobles, and that game, played intermittently from reign to reign, slowly developed the power of the people, though the military power of the magnates had first to be broken. The House of Commons made a stand against being packed, and in this reign they also attempted to meet the increasing financial demands of the Crown by asking for the confiscation of the revenues of the higher clergy, which amounted, it was said, and as Shakespeare phrased it, to

> As much as would maintain, to the king's honour,
> Full fifteen earls and fifteen hundred knights,
> Six thousand and two hundred good esquires,

and two hundred almshouses. The King refused, not because he wanted more troublesome nobles, but because in his struggle against those already existing he had had to make an ally of the Church as well as the yeomen and others of the Commons. Its property was therefore saved, but we have had another glimpse of things to come. What was to happen under Henry VIII was no sudden whim but had a long history behind it.

Although the Commons would gladly have had some of their financial burden lifted from their own shoulders to those of rich abbots and bishops, they had no love of heresy, and when the Church called on the King for a law providing for the burning of those denounced as heretics by the ecclesiastical courts both Houses of Parliament assented. Perhaps no English monarch, save Mary Tudor, has ever cared for religious persecution, and Henry IV was no persecutor. He did, indeed, set out to extirpate Lollardry, but there were comparatively few executions.

Sir John Oldcastle was looked upon as the head of the Lollards and was tried and excommunicated. Before anything further was done he escaped, and a band of his followers formed a plot against the life of the new King. A crowd of them were attacked in St. Giles's Fields, and though most escaped some were taken and hanged or burned. Oldcastle himself some years later was also captured and burned and that ended the historic importance of the movement, though a law was passed that any books written by any of the sect were to be confiscated.

The tale of the short reign of Henry V, less than a decade, may be briefly told. As Prince of Wales he had shown military ability but had been estranged from his father in the last two

years of the latter's life, a period which is known to the world in
Shakespeare's *Henry IV*, with the immortal counter-foil of Fal-
staff. The Prince's wildness is probably exaggerated. At any rate
it was a serious man who came to the throne, though still young.
His attitude toward the Lollards was but one aspect of a religious
nature which desired to restore the Church of the old days. He
also harked back to the past in his desire for the throne of France.
He had, indeed, no title to it unless, somewhat oddly, the Crown
of France could be conceived of as vesting in the Crown of England regardless of descent. His only title to the Crown of England, through his father, was a Parliamentary one, and it may
have been that he wished to make his position at home more secure by a brilliant foreign war, a move with which we are all but
too well acquainted on the part of rulers in various countries
today.

The situation in France appeared promising for the venture.
The French King was insane and the entire country was torn between the factions of the Count of Armagnac and the Duke of
Burgundy. Even so it was a desperate throw of the dice. No
Frenchman accepted Henry's title as King of France and, even
if he could win temporary victories by playing one faction against
another, Frenchmen would not be content to be ruled permanently from England. There could be no lasting success, and an
early failure would endanger his throne at home. Even the night
before he sailed from Southampton he had to execute three leaders in a plot to make the Earl of March, who had a better hereditary claim to the throne than Henry, king in his stead.

Crossing the Channel he captured the port of Harfleur and
opened the way to Paris up the Seine valley. He dared not make
the advance, however, for he had lost by dysentery and fever
about 30,000 of his 45,000 troops, soon to be reduced by another
5000. To return to England after such a disaster might be to lose
the throne. Deciding to move on Calais he found the way blocked
at Agincourt by an Armagnac army of about 50,000. Despite the
odds, he gladly offered battle, rightly counting on the fact that
the enemy was a feudal mob of the sort that had lost the day at

Crecy. Using the same tactics as of that famous day against a foe who had learned nothing he gained one of the most famous victories in history. It was the last of such in which the longbow was supreme, and was won by that weapon against the outmoded chivalry of France. Thousands of the flower of that country were mowed down as they sat on their horses, bogged in the deep mud of a ploughed field soaked by rain, or attempting to fight on foot encased in heavy armor. The year 1415 marks the end of a period in which the English had the advantage of a new weapon, and in a generation the French were to excel in the firearms which were to change the balance of power between them.

All England acclaimed the stunning victory, and Henry returned to London to receive the plaudits of the crowds in a procession through the city amid the gorgeous mediæval pageantry which the English still love. We get some idea of the color and gayety of the period when we read of the mayor and aldermen in scarlet robes, of bands of citizens in red with red-and-white hoods, of figures of giants, of St. George and of angels rejoicing, of the windows all along the route hung with brilliant cloths and tapestries, and of beautiful maidens gayly arrayed, singing "Welcome to Henry V, King of England and of France." Henry was at least safe on his English throne.

The rest of the war in Henry's time may be briefly told. He conquered all of Normandy, and won the support of the new Duke of Burgundy whose father had been murdered by the Armagnacs in the presence of the French King's son, the Dauphin. With his aid a treaty, that of Troyes, was negotiated with the mad King, by which the Dauphin was disinherited, Henry was made Regent of France to become King on the King's death, and received the monarch's daughter as wife. Owing to their bitter internal quarrel the French had in a moment of anger and desperation accepted a ruler from the hated English but it was too impossible a situation to last. There was nothing to unite the nations in heart and everything to divide them. Henry never ruled even from the beginning, and soon died at only thirty-five, leaving for his heir an infant son, tainted by the insanity inherited through the child's French mother from old Charles. France was soon to be wholly lost, and the throne of England to pass from the House of Lancaster.

"Woe to the land when the king is a child" was an old saying, and was to prove all too true. The nine-months-old baby was proclaimed king, as Henry VI, and in the same year, owing to the death of his grandfather Charles, was also proclaimed King of France, though only in that portion north of the Loire not under control of the Dauphin, who claimed the whole. The dead Henry had appointed his eldest brother, the Duke of Bedford, regent in France, and his youngest brother, Duke of Gloucester, regent in England for their infant nephew.

The House of Lancaster seemed firmly on the throne, owing in large part to the French conquests of the late King, which the English nation were determined to retain regardless of the realities of the position. It is interesting to note, however, that although there was no opposition to the accession of the new Lancastrian, both the Privy Council and Parliament insisted on retaining control, denying the right of Henry to have settled the regency by his will, and made their own disposition of the matter. Bedford was allowed to remain in France but unfortunately Gloucester was made Protector at home, with various limitations on his authority.

Bedford had ability and was a good general. Gloucester was ambitious but foolish and undependable. The young King was to grow up religious, well-meaning but weak. The nation was to remain insensately intent on retaining France. The tragedy of the next two decades was woven around these elements.

Bedford advanced shrewdly to his work in France. He married the sister of the Duke of Burgundy, hoping to cement that alliance permanently. He then heeded the old saying that

> If you will France win,
> Then with Scotland begin,

by releasing the captive James I with the promise of his neutrality. A military success against the French seemed to indicate that all his plans were going well when Gloucester showed his folly by invading Hainault and partially alienating the friendship of the Duke of Burgundy in consequence. Bedford continued, however, and laid siege to Orleans which, if taken, might end the war and the prospects of the Dauphin now calling himself Charles VII. The easy-going young French King, inefficient and a lover of pleasure, was no man to save his country, but what he could not do was accomplished by the young peasant girl of Domremi who became known to the English as Joan of Arc.

Her well-known story does not need repeating in detail. Believing in her divine mission to save both the nation and the King, riding in battle as a man with sword and armor, this girl of eighteen inspired a patriotism and courage in the French troops which proved the salvation of France and turned the tide of war. There is no question that it was due to her that the English were driven from Orleans and Charles was crowned king at Rheims. Charles, however, was too indolent to follow up the opportunity, and frightened by the French success, the Duke of Burgundy now aided Bedford and the English.

Moreover, his forces captured the Maid who had been betrayed and deserted by the craven King who owed his throne to her, and the Duke of Burgundy, to his eternal disgrace, sold her to the English for 10,000 francs in gold. Each for their own selfish interests, the military leaders, courtiers, and churchmen, were all against her. No individual and neither nation concerned in her death can avoid the obloquy of it. The trial, a travesty, was managed chiefly by the English Cardinal Beaufort of Winchester and the Frenchman Cauchon, the ejected Bishop of Beauvais. The charge was heresy and sorcery, and not a Frenchman from the King down raised a voice for her who was later to become the glorious symbol of France and to be made a saint by the Pope.

Burned at the stake in Rouen she passed into national immortality, her service fulfilled and the ignominy of those she had rescued completed. By one of those odd coincidents in history, it had been the Duc de la Tremouille, the evil genius of the French King, who had been most instrumental in restraining the King from any effort to save his own savior from the flames. From that day down to about four years ago no Duc de la Tremouille had ever set foot in England, until the last male survivor of his line, the premier Duke of France, crossed the channel and was burned to death on his first night in England by a fire in the country house where he was visiting.

The crime of martyring the Maid availed the English nothing. In the same year in which she met death with entire courage and the cry of Jesus on her lips, Bedford brought the young English Henry, a boy of ten who had been crowned in London, to be crowned King of France in Paris. But he dared not keep him there, and the French were hostile both to his followers and to a French King who dared not remain in the land he claimed. The fortunes of the English steadily declined. Bedford died, the ablest Englishman engaged in the French venture. If he could not win, none could, and the Duke of Burgundy deserted the sinking cause. The Duke of York, now nearest claimant by blood to the English throne, was sent to France, to be succeeded by other commanders, but little by little the English possessions there shrank, until by 1451 Calais alone remained of all the vast pretensions.

Unable to defend herself abroad, England was also sinking into misrule and anarchy at home. The difficulties of the landlords, largely dating from the Black Death, had been increasing and had led them to inclose for their own use more and more of the lands formerly the common right of the groups of tenants or village freeholders as well as to lessen the need of labor by turning more to grazing and less to farming.

The rich were growing richer, the poor were suffering increasing distress, and the nobles with their bands of retainers were becoming more arrogant. The King was weak and was soon to become subject to fits of insanity. The oft-repeated complaint of the people was the "want of governance," and in 1450 an Irishman, Jack Cade, who claimed to be an illegitimate son of the late Earl of March, led a rebellion backed by 30,000 men and demanded that the government should be turned over to the Duke of York. The great families throughout England had been plundering their neighbors of lands and goods, and the poorer rebels now plundered London, to which they had won admission.

Although the rebellion collapsed and Cade was killed, the confused period known as the Wars of the Roses had been inaugurated. They were so called because a red rose was the symbol of the House of Lancaster and a white one of the House of York. Twice the Duke of York became Protector and twice the King recovered from his insanity and the Duke had to retire. With a half-insane monarch and a direct heir who was only an infant and who might well inherit the family taint, there was every likelihood that the dynasty would change, and York become king. The great House of Lancaster, however, had its own ambitions, and the struggle for power which ensued was one between rival claimants for the throne, with their followers among the nobility and other classes, rather than a civil war.

Among the Yorkists were the Earls of Warwick, Salisbury, and March, who defeated the royal army and took the King prisoner at Northampton. York himself, who had been in Ireland, claimed the throne on his return, and when Parliament met it was decided that Henry should remain King for life but that on his death York, and not the baby Prince of Wales, should succeed him. The various battles are without interest, except that in the fight at Wakefield, York was slain and the Yorkist leadership passed to his son Edward, who, although only nineteen, had proved his qualities. Finally at Towton, the Queen and the Lancastrian forces were defeated, Margaret with her husband, the unfortunate Henry, escaping to Scotland, while young York was crowned King at Westminster as Edward IV.

During the struggles, the people-at-large had for the most part kept aloof, even London remaining neutral. Locally there was much marauding and damage to property but the loss of life to ordinary people was very small, and even business went on much as usual. The case was different, however, among the nobles, and the chief result was the destruction of a large part of the class which had long ceased to be useful to the State and who had become merely pernicious nuisances, working their selfish wills on lesser folk and preventing that consolidation of royal power which alone in that period could bring peace and safety to a distracted kingdom. The overthrow of the old order had happily been brought about not by a bloody revolution by the people but by insane suicide on its own part, although the work was as yet far from finished.

On the whole, the more civilized parts of England, the south and east, together with the citizens of the towns and other middle-class persons, had favored the Yorkists as offering the best prospects for peace and good order, and at the end of his first session of Parliament Edward addressed the Commons in person, making a new precedent, thanking them for their support and promising them protection. The change of dynasty from Lancastrian to Yorkist thus augured well with so many of the troublesome nobles slain and the King looking not only to Parliament but to the Commons as his best support.

The hopes raised, however, were false. Edward proved himself dissolute and weak. The Lancastrians took up the fight afresh and the Earl of Warwick shifted to their side. Others turned against the King and he was forced to flee to the Continent while, for a few months, the now imbecile Henry was again placed on the throne. Edward managed to recover it and ended his inglorious days in peace, but there was yet to be no peace for the land. He left two sons, the little Edward V, who was only twelve, and his younger brother, the Duke of York.

The King had also left, unhappily, a younger brother of himself, Richard, Duke of Gloucester, who now started on his infamous career. Claiming the throne by declaring that his mother had committed adultery and that he was her only legitimate son, he secured the deposition of the young Edward and placed both the little princes in the Tower. Parliament, which had agreed to the deposition, proclaimed Gloucester King with the title of Richard III, but he had never been popular, and, when it became known that he had had his two little nephews murdered in their prison, and that he himself desired to marry his own niece, the people turned against him. He had also alienated his supporters among the nobility, none of whom felt safe from his vindictive fury.

The Duke of Buckingham was the first to lead a rebellion but was captured and beheaded. The Earl of Richmond, however, was more successful. He was the grandson of a Welsh gentleman who had married Catherine of France, the widow of Henry V of England. All the descendants of Henry IV had died and as there were no heirs in the male line of John of Gaunt, the young exiled Duke had the best claim to the disputed throne.

This Tudor heir of the House of Lancaster, soon to be Henry VII, landing in England from France, was quickly joined by great numbers of followers and defeated the King at Bosworth Field, where Richard, wearing his crown, rushed into the thick of the fight and met the death he courted. He had been abandoned in the fight by Stanley, Northumberland and other former supporters, and when the victory was won Stanley placed the crown, which had been found in a bush, on the head of Richmond, while the crowd huzzaed for "King Henry." The line of the Tudors had begun and one of the most glorious centuries in English history, which was also to see the earliest beginnings of the overseas empire instead of the idle dreams of Continental expansion.

If, however, the sixteenth century was to be so different in quality and events from the fifteenth, we must realize that great changes in national life do not happen suddenly but are the result of forces long at work though they may be obscured to the eyes of contemporaries and even of later historians by matters of seemingly greater importance or interest. Each event, drab or dazzling, has its own type and sphere of influence. Crecy, Poitiers and Agincourt as battles did not change the destinies of France or the British Empire, but they did have an abiding effect on England psychologically.

Such victories, as we have noted, bred pride and self-confidence and, recalled in song and story even to those who never read history, they were still present in the minds of thousands in the recent World War when at Mons the British soldiers thought they saw the archers of Crecy streaming across the sky and leading them to victory. Such events have another measure than of territory lost or won. The Wars of the Roses gained nothing for almost all those concerned in them, but they did clear England of the decadent remnants of a feudal nobility which had ceased to perform useful functions, placed at last a strong line of rulers descended from a Welsh country gentleman on the throne, and enabled them to build up by a happy understanding of the new classes and conditions in England the firm foundations of the modern Empire.

These classes were those which we have seen getting a start even before the fifteenth century, for, as we cannot point out too often, history knows no neat compartments of time but is a continuous process. They were the middle class, the country gentlemen, the yeoman farmers, the merchants and other town business men and the higher ranks of craftsmen, who if they did not strut the center of the stage were to be all-important from the days of the Tudors.

Every one is agreed that the fifteenth century marked the end of the mediæval period and the real beginning of the modern. Various causes combined to this result. Feudalism, as a form of governing, had long been disintegrating for many reasons, some of which we have touched on in passing. Chivalry, much overrated by romantic writers, even in its prime, had passed through the stage of decadent neo-chivalry, and as many episodes of the French wars and those of the Roses show, had descended to a sheer brutality much below the ideals and manners of the new "lower" classes. The old order of the State, in which there had been a gradation of rights and duties from the king down through the several classes to the serf, had usefully served its day and belonged with the discarded lumber in the attic of the past. Moreover, a new idea of the State was arising in which the powerful noble who could make war on his own account was a mere disturbing factor.

The mediæval idea of civilized Europe, which then meant the world, had had one noble aspect to which in some way we must yet return if the peoples are to be saved from destruction, though in different form as history does not retrace its steps. That was the conception of the unity of all Christian, which then meant civilized, peoples. The world had been unified under the old pagan Roman Empire, and that idea of unity, under new dispensations, had endured down to about 1250 when the "Emperor" of the "Holy Roman Empire" ceased to be the leading power in Europe. His place had been taken by the Popes and for a couple of centuries or so the states of the world had acknowledged, however vaguely at times, the obligations of a general moral law to be laid down from Rome. There had, however, been in progress not only a secularizing of thought, to which we shall again allude presently, but a decline in respect for the Papacy which had in large part come from the decline in Papal morality and ability. The Christian European world was still mainly Roman Catholic but the central authority and unity were fast passing. A new theory or practice was arising of the State if not as amoral at least as subject to no power of any sort superior to itself.

The Reformation was still in the future but from now on we find the great modern political independent states forming, and again get a foreglimpse of the complete break under Henry VIII. This new type of State at its best called for a strong ruler working in harmony with his subjects as a whole, unhampered by the old semi-royal powers of great feudal nobles or by outside control of any power, even spiritual. England was the first to lead on this new road, and in what was to prove a race of nations toward the combination of both empire and liberty she was greatly assisted by the luck of the Tudor dynasty and the rise of her middle class. No other country was equally blessed at a time of critical transition by such a succession of strong but understanding rulers and such an easy development from the feudal to the modern stratification of the social classes.

Until the middle of the fourteenth century, England commercially had been almost wholly a mere producer of raw materials. She could not finance herself; and her kings, when hard pressed, made their loans not from English bankers but from those in

Italy and the Low Countries. Her overseas trade, such as it was, was mostly carried not in her own but in foreign vessels. Even the profits from the sale of her wool went largely to foreign merchants. We have seen that a beginning was made in the fourteenth century in the export of cloth instead of raw wool but it was in the fifteenth that the great change occurred which turned England from a rural country occupying toward the Continent almost the colonial status of her own later colonies, such as Australia, into one of the most active centers of trade and manufacture, no longer dependent on others in finance and commerce.

The century, indeed, is like a page in a book which has illustrations on both sides. On one, we see the highly born or placed, with great names, struggling in the wars or political intrigues already sketched in this chapter. On the other, we see all sorts of obscure persons, whose names are almost wholly lost to history, at their everyday tasks in their shops and counting rooms; tending sheep or bending over looms; on English vessels in storms at sea, and trafficking in foreign ports. Although dimmer and without the false romantic glamour of the other picture this is the more important one. It illustrates the beginning, as the other does the end, of an era, and it was to be the ordinary folk here shown who were, with the help of the painstaking, almost commercial Tudor sovereigns, the two Henrys and Elizabeth, to lay the foundations of empire broad and deep.

Great changes in trade routes or such alterations in economic life as made the industrial revolutions of the fifteenth and nineteenth centuries cannot be effected without suffering to many, and changes in both the domestic and foreign relations of peoples to one another. England had for some time made coarse cloth, but this did not much interfere with the finer manufacture of the great centers of Flanders.

It was when the English turned to the weaving of broadcloths that the full effects were felt. The merchants of the Staple, who had held a monopoly of the export of raw wool, were almost ruined by the decrease in export to only about one-fifth of the former amount. English wool was now being used on English looms and for a century the Flemish towns suffered a lingering death. Ypres, for example, which in 1408 had a population of from 80,000 to 100,000, dropped to around 5000 in less than eighty years, while Bruges, Ghent and the others fared no better. There was fierce competition not only for manufacturing but for markets. The fine English cloths, which have ever since maintained their reputation, were being sold in the Levant and around the Black Sea; at the great fair at Novgorod in Russia; and in the nearer markets of the Continent.

The change in England was not a domestic affair but threatened the lives not merely of foreign trades but of whole populations, as we have just noticed in the case of the Flemish towns. The English merchant whose trade had been welcomed when he had sold merely raw materials for other peoples to make up into finished products soon found himself engaged in fierce strife, and we find rising the barriers to international trade with which we have again grown so familiar in recent years. Flanders shut out English cloth by government decree, and England rejoined by shutting out the cloths from Flemish looms.

The powerful commercial Hanseatic League drove the English from Denmark as the Teutonic Order did from Prussia. In the Mediterranean, ships of the growing English merchant marine fought with those of Genoa and Venice for the carrying trade to southern and eastern ports. We must think of these, moreover, not as the mere cities of today whose grandeur has faded but as powerful states, the Venetian Republic having at that time a population larger than all England.

We have spoken at length of the cloth trade because that was the most important in its effects, but the rising class of English business men was developing enterprises on every side. They were building ships for foreigners as well as for themselves; they were taking the lead in the manufacture of guns and cannon which the new mode of warfare called for; they had captured the copper trade from Dinant in France; they were using English iron ore and coal to build up an iron industry that could not supply the ever-increasing demand even though the price doubled. When there was trouble at one mining center it is said that ten thousand miners came together in one meeting.

We could make a long catalogue of developing industries— lace, bricks, glass, ribbons, linen and so on. Wherever possible, and it seemed to be so in almost every direction, raw material ceased to be exported and was worked up at home, as in the case of leather. Many of the industries for which England is yet most noted were now being founded. The effect on foreigners was often no less marked than in the case of cloth, and the kind of linen called Holland from the country of its first manufacture was being exported thither from England. At the beginning of the century England had been importing its beer from Prussia; by the end it was exporting it to the Continent, and so the story went. It is in odd contrast to the constant wars and brawls, which formed our first picture of the century.

Not the least important effect of all this commercial activity was the altered attitude toward war and diplomacy of the men who were fast growing rich in business. This new and extremely important class had no interest in war to further dynastic ambitions, to afford plunder for armies, leaders and led, or to acquire territory. They had uncertainties enough to encounter without those of warfare being added, and they preferred ways of spending their gains which would be more profitable or redound more to their honor than paying taxes to support armies.

In fact, they were carrying on a sort of warfare themselves, a war which was to have more sound and lasting results for England than the whole hundred years of the old war against France. It was a warfare in which they got little direct or acknowledged aid from the government, as was to be the case all through the Tudor period, although the government had perforce had to change its attitude toward English business and money getting. In the days of the export of raw materials, especially of the great Staple for wool, a large part of the royal revenue came from taxes collected in one form and another from the export monopolists, and this income depended more on the prosperity of foreign manufacturers than upon those of the English themselves.

The English export trade was organized by the government in such a way as to make taxes and duties easily collectible. That was one reason for the Staples, located at various places in England and on the Continent. Even the roads by which the raw export products were to be moved in England were determined by government regulations, and much of the whole mediæval guild structure of industry fitted into this royal or local government control. When, however, owing to the growth of cloth manufacturing at home the export of wool fell by four-fifths, the royal income also fell.

It became obvious, especially to the hard-headed business Tudors, that even from the standpoint of getting taxes out of their subjects it would be more profitable to build up the wealth of Englishmen at home, in whatever way they could make it, than to depend upon the prosperity of foreign manufacturers, or to wage wars which drained resources and led nowhere.

Thus we see the beginning in the fifteenth century of that system which was to reach its highest point under Elizabeth in the next, of making England powerful by making her rich, and letting the subject take the risk of war without involving the nation in costly armaments and supplies. In 1406 the exporters of cloth had been incorporated by Henry IV as the Merchant Adventurers, an outgrowth of the Mercers' Guild, and the new title marks the change which was coming over England. The members of the old guilds had been bound about with all the regulations which in looking back make so close an organization of mediæval society. The men now coming to the fore were in a true sense "adventurers," whatever rules their organizations might make, though the word then meant merely those who shared in a business enterprise. Wherever men joined for such purpose, however, they called themselves by this name, and its more modern connotation gives the real flavor of the period and the nature of their enterprise.

The rest of the world was clearly not going to allow this upstart England to ruin all its established ways of making money without a contest. The new English business men, who by the time of Henry VII formed nearly three-quarters of the House of Commons, did indeed get help at home from the government which protected them to the extent of legislating that not a single article which could be made in England might be imported from abroad, and that none of the materials used in making these could be exported even in a half-manufactured state. But for the most part the Adventurers dealing abroad had to fight their own way to their markets, which they were stubbornly persistent in seeking out.

The government, especially from the time of Henry VII, did work for trade advantages with foreign powers but where not successful the Adventurers of one sort and another took matters into their own hands. On one occasion, for example, we read of the English seizing a fleet of 108 vessels belonging to the Hanseatic League, the Hanse retaliating by capturing English prizes.

In the Mediterranean, whose commerce had long been considered as a monopoly by the Italians, they and the English fought many a battle, as when Sturmys, a rich merchant of Bristol, captured a Genoese ship and confiscated her cargo only to have his own seized and robbed of its cargo of spices on the way home. Sturmys, however, was fortunate, for the English government threw all the Genoese merchants in London into prison and held them until they gave bonds for the repayment of the value of the spices! Such was the new commerce, which was nurtured by smuggling, piracy, and bloody fighting from the eastern bounds of European seas to Iceland, with governmental interferences which often seemed to threaten war but somehow avoided it.

Bristol was in the van in the new trade and her leading merchants, such as Sturmys and Canynges, were accumulating enormous riches. They were shrewd, daring, hard-bitten men, these new business men of all sorts who were piling up wealth all over England, and in the development of maritime commerce, whether from smuggling ports such as those of Devon and Cornwall or ports like Bristol and London. The officers and sailors who were pushing English trade, legitimate or otherwise, into every possible market, taking and giving blows and cargoes, were building up the traditions and methods of the sea dogs of the greater Elizabethan period to come. They were of the breed who were to "singe the King of Spain's beard" and determine to a great extent the destiny of the world.

In the development of this private enterprise the weakness of the State was an advantage which was to have very great influence on the future of the Empire. In the early days of empire building it would have been a catastrophe for liberty had the empire been extended under a strongly centralized government, such as that of France, or under such modern despotisms as those of Italy or Germany. In England at this period, because of the very weakness and comparative poverty of the State, it was essential that the individual should be given the largest amount possible of freedom to increase the national wealth and resources by, in myriad instances, increasing his own. As we shall note later in many parts of the world, it was not only private initiative but to a great extent private commercial trading which built up the imperial structure, and liberty for such enterprises meant also political liberty.

But the century was not all wars, brawls and business. It is true that, until at its end we come to Henry VII, there was no outstanding figure in statesmanship, learning or religion. All, in fact, declined, although learning was later to benefit by the gifts bestowed by the rich of this time. In religion the intense national spirit being developed by the work of business men, and even the half-pirates who manned the merchant ships, was to become effective in determining the course of the Church in the next century.

Life in general was rather coarse and brutal, partly because civilization had not reached beyond that stage, and partly because of the demoralizing effects of the long wars. To a large extent the vaunted chivalry of the mediæval period had always been a veneer which scarcely covered the animal life of earlier barbarism under its artificial manners and codes of honor. The Church, which in so many ways aided the movement toward a more refined and humane life, was also in no slight measure responsible for the crude relations between men and women. Earthly love, when considered as lust and a sin, could not but feel the brutalizing effect of its ostracism from the realm of a higher morality, and men and women in the largely separate lives which they led both lost the better influences which each was later to exert.

We get many a glimpse of the life and manners of the more common people in the Miracle Plays which given under Church auspices became immensely popular. In one of them, for example, on the story of Noah, his wife refuses to enter the ark because she will not leave her "gossips" behind, and insists upon having a drink with them instead of being saved. When finally forced into the vessel by Shem, she gives her husband a resounding slap in the face, which was undoubtedly hugely enjoyed by the audience. In another play on the same theme, the argument between her and Noah resolves itself into a fist fight, which was equally acceptable to the spectators. There was heavy drinking among both sexes, and the sports were chiefly of a brutal sort, such as bear-baiting, bull fighting and others, as they were to remain for some centuries to come. In fact, among the many elements in the British character which we have to note from time to time, we cannot overlook the continuance of a certain coarseness and lack of humane feeling. It is, for example, one of the innumerable contradictions in the English that, although perhaps no other race cares so much for animals, no other gets so much enjoyment out of killing them.

Unlike the Civil Wars in the Stuart period, the constant disturbances of the fifteenth century had a demoralizing effect upon the universities and the intellectual life as a whole. There was little support in England, as contrasted with Italy, for the humanistic side of the Renaissance, and it was only at the very end of the century that the first chair in Greek was founded at Oxford, and among the intellectuals learning was still rather the servant of religion than an aid to a broadly cultured, humane life. Taking the nation as a whole, however, the century was essentially secular in thought and practical in activity rather than religious or intellectual.

In spite of this, it has left us a noble legacy in both ecclesiastical and domestic architecture, one of the noteworthy features of which was its wide distribution. Town life, even quite small-town and village life, was then much more vigorous and alive than today when the great city centers drain the countryside and provinces. The men who were making money in the fifteenth century were widely scattered, and wealth came to many communities which now exhibit little of their former population and prosperity other than the buildings which the fifteenth-century new-rich were erecting. If these merchants were hard bargainers and had no respect for the rights of others, especially foreigners, they were also magnificent spenders for both their own glorification and that of their town. It is not alone in such thriving, bustling centers of trade as Bristol that we find a Canynges rebuilding the great church of St. Mary Redcliffe in which stands his own alabaster tomb with the hard, delicately chiselled shrewd features of the old merchant who almost monopolized the Scandinavian and Icelandic trades, had sixty ships at sea, and entertained King Edward IV in his sumptuous house.

Other business magnates were also building Bristol churches, but in innumerable smaller towns these were likewise arising, especially in such districts as East Anglia, where in Suffolk and Norfolk today great churches stand scattered about the landscape, giving it its characteristic feature. Many times larger than needful for their present congregations, these parish churches are mute witnesses to the change from the fifteenth-century population thriving on the cloth trade to the far smaller agricultural one of today.

The style through the century was changing from the Gothic to the Perpendicular, which if artistically inferior in its abandonment of curves for straight lines, has a beauty of its own, particularly notable in the remarkable towers for which the period is famous. Among the greater of these are the "Bell Harry" tower of Canterbury Cathedral, the central tower of York, and such others as those of Gloucester Cathedral or Magdalen College, Oxford. The catalogue of the greater towers could be much extended, but we owe also to this period large numbers of the lesser ones which form, for example, the chief architectural glory of such a county as Somersetshire. Instinctively we think of a church tower, whether rising from cathedral or country parish church with its surrounding green of cathedral close or rural farming lands as peculiarly "English." At least a foreign tourist does, and it is surprising how much that we think of as English architecturally dates from this century.

Whether the Perpendicular style is inferior to the Gothic may be left to the critics to decide but there is no doubt that it is more distinctively English, for it was a native development whereas the Gothic was always an exotic and no English example of that style can vie with such great French cathedrals as Amiens or Chartres or Rheims. What has been called the "swan song" of Gothic was also of this century and in this case peculiarly English. This was the famous fan vaulting, best known from Henry VII's Chapel in Westminster Abbey but found at Gloucester and elsewhere. As in the case of this type of vaulting much of the architecture of the period seems a *tour de force*, and an exhibition of the power of swelling wealth rather than of artistic instinct or spiritual aspiration. The enormous windows, and the bright light and confusion of color of a King's Chapel at Cambridge produce emotions which for want of better distinction may be called secular rather than religious, but that chapel is more essentially English than a French cathedral or a Romanesque Italian church.

In domestic architecture also the century produced the type that we still think of as English. The Norman castles with their gradual modification do not seem to belong especially to England as do the manor houses being built at this time for the new-rich in the Perpendicular, soon to merge into the Tudor, style. We are not merely reaching into the beginning of the modern period but into that of a new England which feels her strength and her individuality, and, although both belong to the same period, such a manor house as Compton Wynyates in Warwickshire seems much more English than Hurstmonceaux, which harks back to the feudal castle. Largely from this century also dates much of the notable architecture connected with business and the corporate life of the towns, such as the characteristic markets and market crosses in small-town squares, and the Guildhall in London begun about 1411.

It is notable that although the Guildhall was chiefly for the use of the merchant class, the library now there was founded only a dozen years later, and if the century added no glory to English literature and little directly or immediately to education it did make a contribution to the intellectual life of all classes that has been unequalled.

Printing from movable type was an invention of the Continent, but in the fifteenth century, William Caxton, who it is well to note had been most of his life a prosperous merchant, set up the first press in England, in Westminster, near the Abbey, which was followed within the century by others in Oxford, London, and at St. Albans. Caxton, however, was more than a mere printer. He was also corrector and editor of English works and translator of foreign, and his influence on the development of the English language is perhaps second only to that of Chaucer himself, whose works, among many others, Caxton printed, as well as the great *Morte d'Arthur* of Sir Thomas Malory which "set" the Arthurian legends for all time.

Manuscripts had been rare and costly, but now the day of the printed book had come, and that in itself would have greatly helped to fix the language by increasing the number of readers. But in addition Caxton exerted his own pressure by editing. Recognizing the spread of reading that would come from printing, and the fact that the English spoken in the several shires so varied as not to be understandable from place to place by common folk, he set his own standard, which was to be that for all. Clearly he took that of London but avoiding the advice of some scholars that he should employ "the most curyous termes that I coude fynde" he decided that "in my Judgemente, the comyn termes that be dayli used ben lyghter to understonde than the old and auncyent Englysshe."

The task begun by Chaucer was carried on by Caxton with all

the new power of the printed word. When we lament the lack of literature in this century we must not forget its tremendous influence on the literature of the next, and if we today can read Shakespeare and the other glories of the Elizabethan period with an ease which is lacking in the works of Chaucer, the great father of modern English, it is in no small measure due to Caxton, merchant and printer, rather than to any author in the intervening period.

One other art may be briefly mentioned, that of music. Painting and sculpture were negligible, but in the middle of the fifteenth century this England of merchant adventurers, of avid seekers after markets and profits, was leading the world in music as well as trade, and at the same time that men like Canynges were laying the foundations of commercial empire John Dunstable was practically discovering a new art of sound, so great were the advances that he was making in musical composition.

By the end of the century Lollardism had come into the open again and it was evident that if freedom of thought had for a time been suppressed at Oxford, when Wyclif had been silenced, what we may call the Protestant movement had not been, and remained alive among a large part of the ordinary people. The Church had shown no intellectual or spiritual leadership, though it retained its wealth and offices. But the worship of mammon, strong as it was, had not rooted out that of God in the cottages and small homes of English men and women who were becoming more and more important in the State, and both the Church and the Tudors would have to reckon with the growth of Puritanism and nationalism in religious matters.

In 1485 Henry Tudor had been crowned on Bosworth Field and it was his lot to try to bring peace and order to a nation bursting with energy but harassed by violence and disorder on every hand. His features, particularly the eyes, in the portrait in the National Portrait Gallery, are inscrutable, and it has been said no man or woman knew his heart, and the opinions of historians vary greatly as to his character. It may be said, however, that he gave to England and her people precisely the help they needed at this critical stage. Tudor-Lancastrian as he was, he strengthened his hold on the Crown by marrying the Yorkist heiress Elizabeth. Even so there were others with a better hereditary right, and Henry had no army at his back nor was he a great soldier. That he maintained his position and founded the greatest dynasty in English history was due to other qualities.

He recognized, as did his descendants, the need of close alliance with the people at large and especially the rising middle merchant class. The ground swell of the Wars of the Roses had not yet subsided, and the King had to suppress not only the insurrection under Lord Lovel and his followers but also those in which the impostors, Lambert Simnel and Perkin Warbeck, were put forward as impersonators of claimants to the throne. It throws a light on the King's mind that Simnel when captured was made a turnspit in the royal kitchen. There was also a brief war with France, which Henry would gladly have avoided but which he ended characteristically by making a goodly sum of money out of it.

Peace, money and the extension of English trade were the desires not only of the King but of his people, except the great nobles who were still living in the dreams of the past, and the bands of "sturdy beggars" who roamed the roads and were in part the result of the wars and disturbances of the century, and in part, as they were to continue to be in the next century, of economic change. Slowly, however, the King made headway, for courage and patience were among his virtues. Increasingly he made use of the country gentlemen as Justices of the Peace to put down the beggars and bands of the Robin Hood type, while he himself reduced the nobles to order.

Indeed, it may almost be said that the country was governed by the monarch and the Justices, for, during the whole Tudor period, Parliament exercised but a minor influence. The people wanted order and progress, and so long as the close alliance between themselves and the monarchs secured this they were content. It was not, however, abdication to dictators, for all the Tudors had a keen sense of the necessity always of carrying public opinion with them in whatever they attempted. They ruled not by usurpation but by a sort of tacit agreement with their subjects, especially of that middle class which was most largely represented in Parliament, and Parliament under their management, especially after Henry VIII had broken with Wolsey, formed an essential factor in their scheme of government.

More and more they looked to the people rather than the nobles, not only for general support but for ministers of state and other officials. Political careers as well as commercial, with their great prizes, were increasingly open to the talents. The King's Council became more and more an important organ of government, but whereas it had formerly been made up almost wholly of the great nobles who practically forced their way in for their protection, the Tudors were strong enough to choose only such members as they would.

Henry was not a man to endear himself by personal charm to either the populace or favorites, of whom he had none, but worked patiently, slowly, and much as Canynges or other great merchants might in their counting rooms. He secured trade advantages as far as possible for his people with foreign nations, such as the agreement with the Netherlands known as the *Intercursus Magnus*. He himself piled up wealth, often it must be admitted by tyrannical methods, two of his agents being the notorious Empson and Dudley, and the hoard which he transmitted to his successor was estimated at £1,800,000. For the most part, however, he levied fines and "benevolences" on the rich instead of taxing the people at large. The nobles, however, had had their own time of riot and plunder, and the people were not sorry to see them shorn, especially when their power for harm was reduced in the process.

Livery and maintenance, the maintaining of bands of followers who wore their master's uniform and badge, had long been a source of public disorder, and when the King made the Earl of Oxford, whom he had been visiting, pay a fine of £15,000 (say £180,000 today) because on the royal leave-taking Oxford had had drawn up a large band of retainers to do the King honor, the public reaction must have been in favor of Henry. His profit had been great but also the law had been maintained, albeit over-severely, and the ordinary folk drew easier breaths as they realized that here was a master who left them alone while he called the great to heel.

At the very close of the century, 1497, an event little regarded at the time occurred under the royal patronage. The men of Bristol had early driven their trade to Iceland, as we have seen, having discovered the way, probably in 1424, by the use of the compass, the first time we find it mentioned in English navigation. Columbus, venturing further, had found the island outposts of the New World in 1492 and five years later Henry gave assistance, frugal as was his wont, to John Cabot to voyage thither, although he had no intention of disputing the Spanish claims confirmed by the Papal Bull dividing the western or New World between Spain and Portugal.

Cabot, sailing far to the north, discovered the New-found-land, now the oldest Dominion of the British Empire, although more than a century was to elapse before Englishmen were to attempt to colonize the unknown continent of North America. But when Henry died and the throne descended to his son, Henry VIII, we have definitely passed from the history of England as an island kingdom off the shore of Europe to a nation that will before long be fighting not only for trade but empire across many a sea and be matching itself with the mightiest powers of the then known world. The two pictures we have described of the fifteenth century are but the frontispieces to the great story now to come. Under Henry's son, England cut the painter that bound her to the Papacy and the Continent, and under Elizabeth the nation launched out across the seas of all the world.

CHAPTER VII

HENRY VIII AND A NEW COURSE FOR ENGLAND

As we saw in the preceding chapter, historic periods and personalities may receive different interpretations depending in large part on what points or events may be stressed. The two pictures of the fifteenth century which we have called the frontispieces of the story now to come were not only quite different but under ordinary circumstances might seem to be essentially contradictory. This is equally true of both the reign and character of Henry VIII. As one reads both Roman Catholic and Protestant historians, and even different ones among the two groups, one almost despairs of the existence of historic truth.

Without criticizing or defending any of the many positions taken we may try to examine some of the most important changes wrought during his reign and how far they were the result of Henry's changing character and circumstances. One of the strongest personalities who has sat on the English throne, he cannot, I think, be considered a mere puppet, and many of the changes in England must be attributed to him. The second problem—of what motives influenced him—is more difficult and we can point only to what seems a possible explanation.

We may suggest four important points in which the England he left differed from that which he was called on to rule as a youth.

One of these is the distinct progress made in the unification of the four countries, England, Wales, Ireland and Scotland, which were to become the "Great Britain and Ireland" of later days. Another was the completion of the long process we have followed of the modern nationalization of England itself by the elimination of the great nobles as possible military dangers in the government of the nation. Claimants to the throne there might be, as we shall see, in default of lawful heirs of Henry himself, but the will and power of that monarch brooked no opposition, and with him armed oppression or the disturbance of the peace by a War of the Roses on the part of the nobility ceased in England. The nation was henceforth to be ruled by King and Parliament, however much the latter might be "managed" by the former. At any rate the way was made clear for the full development of constitutional monarchy and of Parliamentary control when the people might so desire.

Moreover, nationalism was greatly advanced in two other ways, which by cutting England loose from both Continental ambitions and controls kept the nation from concentrating its gaze across the narrow seas and prepared it to pursue its destiny upon those of all the world. Separated from the continent of Europe by only twenty miles of water at the straits of Dover it could not neglect its dangerous neighbors entirely but there was an immense difference between the old ambition of territorial conquest on the mainland and the new requirement of using force and influence to maintain a balance of power there which would permit England to go her own way unafraid. From the days of Henry onward, although British armies had frequently to fight on European battlefields, it was never to be again with the thought of establishing any wide Continental dominion.

Whatever one's religious view or opinions of Henry's motives may be, it must be conceded that his break with the Pope and his establishment of the Church of England likewise did much to sever old bonds with the Continent and to give an impetus to the independent career of the English people. It also contributed greatly, on account of the untenable half-way house position which Henry assumed, toward forwarding the Protestant revolution and that strong feeling against the Papacy which was perhaps the most potent element in the later war with Spain and the beginnings of empire.

These were all historic factors of prime importance and, even allowing for the often devious ways by which destiny achieves its ends, they were evidently not the work of either a weak voluptuary or a bloodthirsty tyrant. It is hard to reconcile the real achievements of Henry's reign with the pictures drawn of him by many historians. The answer to the enigma may perhaps be found by adopting the common-sense view that a man's character may change with changing circumstances. Henry's appears to have passed through three phases. Reaching the throne at only eighteen, he inherited not only a firmly established monarchy but for those days the almost unprecedented hoard of wealth which his father had left.

That father had been a frugal, parsimonious ruler, and, to put it mildly, by no means a brilliant or dazzling figure in his court. The young prince seemed to have been showered with all the gifts the fairies could give him. All who saw him agree as to his unusually handsome face and figure. He was full-blooded, active and strong, delighting in all athletic exercise on the tennis court, in the hunting field and in the tourney. He was also artistic, a skilled musician, with a keen and trained mind that could find pleasure in the subtleties of theology as well as the new literature of the Renaissance, and a linguist, speaking French, Latin and a little Italian in addition to English. That a son, especially of different type, often reacts against the ways and character of a father is an occurrence too common to call for comment.

In his earlier period Henry spent his father's money, loved the luxury which his father had despised and which also the Renaissance was bringing in, and longed to display himself as, which he was, one of the most dazzling monarchs of his day. Relying largely on Wolsey for affairs of state, he watched carefully with his shrewd intelligence but did not bother himself overmuch with business. After Wolsey's fall came the second phase, when he took the reins himself through harassed years of events peculiarly irritating to a man of his temper and position. Then came the final period, in which he gave full vent to the despotism and worst traits in his nature.

Before passing on to the details of Henry's reign and of the points mentioned above, we must speak of one topic of importance not only to the Tudor dynasty but to England, which may help us to understand much that is to come. In spite of the various efforts to interpret history in the light of one factor, such as the economic, and the vague talk about great social forces, the destinies of nations as of families are frequently deflected, as we cannot too often recall, not only by the influence of personalities but by physical events or conditions which seem wholly out of proportion to the effects they may produce.

The point we have here to consider is the peculiarity of the Tudors in the begetting of children. It cannot be said that the family was sterile but there was a physical defect, whatever it may have been, that was to have extraordinary historic repercussions. Although there were frequently children, though not as many as we should expect for the times, they had a surprising way of being still-born or of dying in infancy. Nor, as the leading student of Henry VIII, A. F. Pollard, says, can this be attributed to the medical science, or lack of it, in the period, for "Yorkist babies clung to life with a tenacity which was quite as inconvenient as the readiness with which Tudor infants relinquished it."[1]

We have already had ample opportunity to realize the havoc wrought in the entire nation by a disputed succession. As the conditions called for a strong ruler, the succession was practically bound to be disputed if there were no direct male heir or if such heir was yet only a child. The objection to a woman ruler was not based on any lack of respect for a woman's abilities, for women had exerted much influence in both State and Church, but on the fact that so long as she remained unmarried the problem of succession remained a disturbing one, and whether she married either a native or a foreigner equally disturbing complications of one sort or another were practically certain to arise. These are the facts that made the problem of Tudor children of such far-reaching effect.

[1] A. F. Pollard, *Henry VIII*, London, 1934, p. 13.

Henry VII had tried to ensure the throne for his family, and peace for the nation, by uniting the Houses of Lancaster and York in marrying the Yorkist princess Elizabeth, eldest daughter of Edward IV, and through that line heiress to the throne. However, the Tudor infirmity came near to making his plan of no avail, and did have an important influence on the fortunes of both his House and of England. Of his three sons, two predeceased him, one at fifteen months of age and one at fifteen years; of his four daughters two died in infancy and the youngest cost her mother's life in child birth. The eldest son, Arthur, was married at fifteen to Catherine, daughter of Ferdinand and Isabella of Spain. Against the advice of the Council, Henry sent the young couple to live as man and wife at Ludlow Castle, and in less than six months Arthur was dead. The child widow was to become the wife of Arthur's younger brother, Henry VIII, with consequences that we shall see.

Henry VIII, although he had six wives, had only three lawful children who survived, Edward VI who died at sixteen, Mary who never had a child, and Elizabeth who remained unmarried. The record of his first wife, the Catherine mentioned above, is interesting. Seven months after marriage she gave birth to a still-born daughter; eight months later to a son who died in three days. Another son was still-born or died immediately. Yet another survived only his christening, and a fourth was born prematurely and died. Then Mary was born and survived, after which there were various miscarriages and another still-born child.

In spite of his marital record, Henry was not sexually licentious according to the standards of his day and position. Indeed, except for the number of his wives and his methods of getting rid of them, he compares very favorably with other monarchs of his time and after. He had two known mistresses, and may have had more, though of that there is no evidence, and king's mistresses were not hidden under a bushel. By his two acknowledged mistresses, however, he had only one child, a boy who became Duke of Richmond and was brought up openly at court with high honors, possibly with the idea that in absence of other heirs he might succeed in spite of the bar sinister. But this child died at eleven. Without going into further family detail we may note that Henry's two sisters were no more fortunate.

Henry VII, as we have said, had tried to ensure the succession by joining the rival Houses which claimed the throne; Henry VIII by trying, with increasing recklessness, a half dozen wives; Mary married but remained childless; Elizabeth gave up the problem, remaining unmarried, and ending the Tudor line, to the misfortune of England, because the Tudors were incomparably better rulers than the Stuarts who followed. It would seem as though there can be no doubt that the Tudor curse, if we may so call it, had a profound effect on Henry's marital course and, later, on the disintegration of his character. For that reason we have had to discuss the matter as an influence on English history.

There were, of course, other causes at work, and, in time, England might have broken with Rome and founded an empire but Henry's acts hastened the process and gave it a different direction and especially a different timing from those which might otherwise have been expected. In history both direction and timing are of enormous importance. It was in no small measure due to Henry and the Tudor curse that England became rabidly anti-Spanish and anti-Catholic under Elizabeth, and so gained control of the seas and the path to empire when the nation might not have been able to do so at another time and with a different international set-up of powers. To realize the importance of timing we have only to consider the unpredictable difference to the world if Germany had become united and imperially minded in the sixteenth or seventeenth centuries instead of in the nineteenth. We may now pass on to consider Henry's reign in more detail.

We note first the clearer drawing of the outline of Great Britain and Ireland, which was to mean much in the reign of Elizabeth. Relations with Wales had greatly improved under Henry VII who had the advantage of being a Welshman educated in Wales, understanding and loving its literature and past. His marriage had also united the border lordships of the Houses of both Lancaster and York so that some fifty or more were bound to him.

It was reserved for Henry VIII, however, to bring about the complete union of the two countries by the first Act of Union in the history of the Empire. By methods which may have been harsh enough he brought peace and order to a land that had never known it, but, more important, he incorporated it with England on terms that were wholly satisfying to the high-spirited Welsh people. The former political divisions were abolished, including the Marcher Lordships, and the country was divided into twelve counties, like the English sub-divisions, with counties and boroughs sending their representatives to the Parliament at Westminster.

In fact Wales became as much a part of England as any other section of the greater kingdom. This was done on Henry's own initiative and against advice, but proved successful, in large part because the reigning House was itself Welsh and so called forth the loyalty of the Welsh people. This was well, because both the changes in Church and the substitution of the English language for the Welsh in the law courts, put a considerable strain upon the new relationship of the peoples. Local government, however, was placed in the hands of Welsh gentlemen and not English, as in Ireland, and the Welsh upper classes were thus not only closely bound to the new order but formed a cement between the English government and the still Celtic-speaking general population. From the time of Henry onward, the island south of the Scottish border was a united kingdom.

Unfortunately Henry was less happy in his dealings with Scotland and Ireland. War with the neighbor on the north was traditional, as was also the alliance between Scotland and France. Henry's war with the latter country, which we shall note later and which began soon after his accession, involved Scotland on the side of her ally, and the Scottish King, James IV, invaded Northumberland with his whole strength, only, however, to be completely beaten at Flodden, the worst defeat in the entire history of the northern nation, a day of bitter mourning never to be forgotten. The King himself, thirteen earls, and many other of the great notables of the kingdom lay dead on the field, and it has been said that "there is scarcely a family of rank in the Lowlands but

counts an ancestor slain in this terrible slaughter." In the words
of what is possibly the earliest ballad on the battle,

> To tell you plain, twelve thousand were slain
> That to the fight did stand,
> And many a prisoner took that day,
> The best in all Scotland.

The dead James had married Henry's sister Margaret, daughter of Henry VII, but the traditional French friendship had been deeper than an English family alliance, and there was once more war with the Scots from 1532 to 1534, which was renewed a few years later after the Welsh question had been peacefully settled. Union between the two northern and southern kingdoms on the island had often been sought by English kings, either by marriage or conquest. Both methods had failed. Henry now tried both at once and again failed, owing partly to his too great ambition. Had it not been for the overwhelming English victory in the battle of Solway Moss, 1542, he might have been more politic and brought about eventual union by the proposed marriage of his young son Edward and the week-old Mary, Queen of Scots. Her father, James V, Henry's nephew, had died on hearing of the disaster to his arms, and when told of the birth of a daughter had murmured that "it came with a lass and it will go with a lass."

The Scots agreed to the betrothal of their infant queen and the heir to the English throne, but Henry then renewed his own claim to the Scottish throne and was not content to wait upon events. In addition he demanded that the Scots give up their old ally France upon whom their strength depended. These demands were too much, the marriage agreement was broken off, and although peace was made successively with both Scotland and France, which latter had gone to the aid of her old friend, there was to be for the time no union of the two British peoples by either war or marriage.

Nevertheless Henry did unwittingly make the way easier for the union of the future by carrying England out of the Roman fold. Scotland, which was to become so strongly Protestant, would never have willingly united with a Catholic England, and the fact that the sister kingdoms on the same island were both to tread the path of the Protestant Reformation created a spiritual bond which was to ease the way to political union.

It is true that the Reformation followed different lines in the two countries. In England it was guided largely by the King and was to a great extent political in character with the desire for complete national independence playing a leading role. In Scotland it was a popular movement, strongly opposed by the monarchy, and with the leading role played by theology as studied and disputed among the ordinary people. In Scotland, this democratic tendency was fostered and maintained by the Presbyterian form of church government, whereas in England the Church tended to become a department of the State. In Ireland the movement took yet another form and, like almost all that has been done in that unhappy isle, a most unfortunate one. Reformation and Protestantism were there imposed upon the people by force, and were never congenial to the people themselves.

Although Henry was thoroughly English, his Welsh descent had facilitated both his understanding of the Welsh and their willingness to unite with the English under him, as we have noted. No such understanding or feeling existed on either side in the case of Ireland, yet conditions there called for action. There was no united Irish nation and no central authority. The Celtic chiefs of the clans fought among themselves, and the Anglo-Norman lords were even worse in their oppression and constant brawls.

The English "Pale," over which alone the Irish Parliament exerted authority, was in a precarious position. The King's deputy, the Anglo-Norman Earl of Kildare, shamefully abused his authority and the King's name in pursuit of his private ends. Henry was not only masterful but he genuinely desired order, and in addition there was the fatal geographical location of Ireland. If the island had been more distant, England might never have disturbed her, or if she had she might have retired as she has from Egypt. But Ireland is like a spear, poised and aimed at England's flank. To change the metaphor, she is a stepping stone from the

Continent from which the Continental enemies whom England has always faced can attack her from the rear. If Ireland has been England's chief failure in administration, nevertheless England's belief that she must maintain control is at least understandable.

Henry decided to exert that control, and as a preliminary step he called Kildare to London and imprisoned him in the Tower. Believing that he had been put to death, his son, Lord Thomas Fitzgerald, renounced his allegiance, and the rebellion of the "Geraldines," as the Fitzgeralds were sometimes called, began. By the time it was suppressed every male of the family, except one boy, had been killed in one way or another. It was one of the bloody episodes which were characteristic of the government or lack of government.

Henry's hope was to treat Ireland in much the same fashion as he had Wales, and to make it over on the English plan. England had for some centuries been able to prevent the Irish from governing themselves, if indeed their warring clans could have done so, without being able to govern her herself. The result had been a steady retrogression from the days when Ireland had been a land of learning. Intellectual life and genuine religion were largely dead, and both clergy and laymen were untouched by the Renaissance. Almost alone of the countries which had been great, Ireland had no university and few places of learning of any sort. When Henry destroyed the monasteries simultaneously with the English ones, the loss was far more severely felt by the Irish, for there were no other institutions in their island to take their place and carry on their work.

Henry appears to have been honest in his efforts to unify the two islands with a large degree of home rule for the subject one, but in trying to make the Irish adopt the English language, dress and manners, in giving preferment in both Church and State only to those who spoke English, and in attempting to introduce the English form of land tenures, he could not but fail. He tried to conciliate the chiefs and to bring them in to the English system by giving them English titles of nobility, and among many others, "The O'Neill" became the Earl of Tyrone and "The O'Brien" the Earl of Thomond, but the people remained unchanged. He did, indeed, bring about peace, especially while the chiefs were allowed to fatten on the spoils of the monasteries, but there was no settlement of the perpetual "Irish question," as Elizabeth and later sovereigns were to find to their cost, and Ireland's.

The Irish appear at that time not to have been the ardent Romanists that they were to become later under the teaching of the Jesuits, and they might have accepted Henry as the Head of the Church as easily as the English did, had he not in other ways attempted to change too radically and generally the ways of life which they had always followed. The Irish Parliament, which was now to function for all Ireland, was attended for a while by the chiefs with their new titles, and Henry was probably surprised that the effort at reorganization of the country did not succeed as well as his efforts in Wales. To some extent, however, he did bring peace and order, and the Irish Parliament bestowed on him the title of King of Ireland which marked a stage in political relations. Hitherto he had been merely "Lord," a Papal title which indicated that he held the island only as a fief from the Pope and not in his own right.

Thus under Henry, England and Wales became permanently and happily merged; Ireland was united directly to the English Crown; and the way was smoothed for the peaceful combining of England and Scotland under one King little more than a generation later. We may now turn to other aspects of his reign which are best considered together.

When Henry, a youth of eighteen, of handsome presence and evidently of high ability, ascended the throne, he was rapturously received by the English people. Both his brothers had died and he alone stood between the nation and another civil war or anarchy. When we add his personal qualities it is little wonder that the monarch won almost adoration from the people. The nobility had largely cleared themselves out of the picture, and there were but one Duke and one Marquess left in England. Henry himself chose his greatest servants not from the great families of the past but from the new or, like Wolsey, persons of comparatively humble birth, and of the sixteen peers named as regents of his will not one title was a dozen years' old. Never have the monarchy and the people worked in closer harmony than under the Tudors but it was a direct relationship. If the nobility was discarded, so also to a great extent was Parliament, which having made too rapid a growth under the Lancastrians had shown itself inadequate to express the real will of the nation.

What has been called the Tudor despotism was in reality a fortunate combination of royal will with popular desires and aspirations, which combination tided over a dangerous period in constitutional development. Both Henry and Elizabeth may have seemed at times omnipotent, but they both had an extraordinary ability to understand the people and the trend of popular opinion and to guide the nation along the paths which the people wished to be followed. As Trevelyan has well said, speaking of the religious aspect of Henry's reign more particularly, "the nation could do nothing against the will of the Crown, and the Crown nothing against the will of the nation, but the two together could do anything they chose." The modern means of mass appeal—the press, cinema and radio—did not exist and "wills" were real wills, not to be created but to be reckoned with as existing.

Such a government was as far removed from early despotisms as from modern dictatorships. It is a mistake to think that the English have consistently and always thought in the same terms of liberty and parliamentary government. No other people have more persistently, as individuals, wanted to have and go their own way but, practically minded, they have never sacrificed reality to theory. The English had had enough of the troubles of weak government, and they were quite willing to relinquish much into the hands of the Tudors provided, however, and it was an important proviso, they got good government, which they did under the two Henrys and Elizabeth. But neither party to the implicit compact ever lost sight of its own rights or power, and if Parliament was somewhat eclipsed it remained with its precedents ready to be used by the people whenever that weapon should be required.

The Renaissance had reached England in quite a different form from that in which it flowered in Italy. Painting and the other arts came to no such bloom, nor on the other hand did the theory of politics descend to that of a Machiavelli as exhibited in his *Prince*. The freeing of the individual from moral law and restraints was more pervasive, and in considering the whole later Tudor period we have to allow for the tremendous impetus given to individualism, both for better and worse, in escaping from the controls and ideals of medievalism. The lowest examples of the change may be found perhaps in the lives of the petty rulers of Italy but the sea dogs of Elizabeth owed their adventurous daring to the same powerful release, and it is only fair to Henry to consider both the political problems he inherited and the intellectual and moral climate of his period.

On the whole, and in its best manifestations, the Renaissance had a practical and serious side in England which was largely lacking in those countries in which its influence was exhibited more in art and personal license. The highest point it touched in England may be said to be in the *Utopia* of Sir Thomas More, one of the finest spirits of the movement, and for long an intimate of Henry. This book, which still has interest, was an effort to think out the plan for an ideal state. It was ahead of its time but it is noteworthy that the best fruit of the Renaissance in England should be the contemplation of an ideal country in which the poor were not oppressed by the rich, and the motive governing men, all of whom had sufficient, should no longer be the desire for possessions; in which complete toleration prevailed; and in which all children should be well taught and trained at public cost.

Two of the first acts of Henry on becoming King were to imprison the hated Dudley and Empson, the unpopular gatherers of money for his father, in the Tower, and to marry his young brother's widow, the Spanish Catherine. The latter event, for which a special dispensation had been got from the Pope, involved Henry closely in the new situation now developing on the Continent.

France, under Charles VIII and Louis XII, had been attacking Italy to extend her domains there. Spain, the Pope and the German Emperor had joined her in a sordid effort to dismember the Republic of Venice, but France's growing strength alarmed them, and in 1511 the Pope, the Emperor, Spain, and leading Italian states joined to force her out of the Italian peninsula. The theory of the balance of power of the rising modern states, which may be said to date from the first French foray into Italy in 1494, was now beginning to take shape, and Henry decided to join his Spanish father-in-law and the others against France. He planned to attack that country in both the north and the south, and the former expedition, in which Wolsey's organizing ability first won him the King's favor, was to some extent successful.

In fact Henry was in danger of dreaming again the last time in history the old dream of French possessions. Fortunately as soon as his allies had got what they wanted by breaking French power in Italy, the Alliance broke up and Henry, sore and angry at his father-in-law, was left alone. It was part of his education in *real politik* and he never forgot the lesson. He made a new alliance with France, gave his sister as bride to the worn-out French King, and the English policy of balance of power on the Continent and not conquest became established in England although hostility to France remained a tradition.

International affairs now began to move with dramatic swiftness, and the scythe of fate cut a wide swathe. In 1515 the old King of France died and was succeeded by his son Francis I. The next year Ferdinand of Spain died, and his grandson Charles, already in possession of the Netherlands, so important to England for trade, inherited the Spanish dominions. Less than two years later his other grandfather, the Emperor Maximilian, died and the boy of sixteen inherited all the domain of the Habsburgs.

The title of Emperor and its powers could be acquired, however, only by the vote of the German electors. Although Henry and Francis were also candidates, Charles was elected as expected, thus becoming by various accidents ruler of the Netherlands, Spain, the American possessions of that country, southern Italy, Austria, and parts of Germany, while the rulers of other German states were nominally subject to him. The world seemed to be mostly divided between the three young men, Henry twenty-eight, Francis twenty-six, and Charles nineteen.

For the next ten years Henry with his Chancellor Wolsey, who had also become Cardinal, struggled with the problem of alliances and the balance of power. The balance between Francis and the Emperor was not so unequal as mere territory might make it appear. The Spanish Empire was a hodge-podge of peoples and states, scattered, unwieldy, and much of it disloyal. Its different races, with various languages, outlooks and traditions, had no cohesion, and the solid block of France was in its center. Moreover, as far as England was concerned, Charles as master of the Netherlands, within short sailing distance of the English coast, was a traditional foe. England's strength lay chiefly in her wealth, largely laid up by Henry VII, which both the King and Wolsey were now to use lavishly to bring England almost to the position of arbiter of Europe, though it was not to prove enough.

These were the years in which Wolsey was to reach the highest pinnacle of his power before his fall. The Venetian Ambassador reported that when he first came to London, Wolsey used to say "His Majesty will do so and so," which gradually became "We shall do so and so," and by 1519 had become "I shall do so and so." The Cardinal was to be the last, as he was the ablest, of great ecclesiastical statesmen in England, and he was notable as a wily diplomat but his policies as well as his personal career were to end in failure, and there is little to admire in the man himself.

His arrogance, on which the Venetian commented, like his ambition and greed, knew no bounds, and the springs of all his actions appear to have been the desire for unlimited power and wealth. His accumulation of bishoprics and other church benefices in his own hands, the use of his position to pile up wealth from foreign foes and allies as well as from his fellow countrymen at home, and the ostentation which he displayed in sumptuous living, all brought him unpopularity and even rebukes from the King when continuing to employ him. It was an age of display which was to reach its highest point in the meeting of Francis and Henry, but we can understand in part what led to the fall of the over-reaching Cardinal when we learn that although the splendor-loving and royal Henry allowed those who waited on him at table to keep on the caps which were customarily worn, Wolsey insisted not only on their removal but on being served on bended knee.

It was clear that peace in Europe could not long be maintained between the two young rivals, Francis and Charles, for there were too many questions, Italian and other, between them. Which side would England take? For the next eight or nine years Henry apparently followed the lead of the Cardinal-Chancellor, whose capacity for work was colossal. Henry was, in time, to "drop the pilot," and the important influence which the King was to exert on English history was to be felt chiefly thereafter, whereas little of lasting value was done for England by the Cardinal in the ten years or so of his rule, if we may call it such.

England's interests were more or less divided between an alliance with Charles and one with Francis, and the first moves were cautiously made. In 1520 the French and English Kings met not far from Calais, and so great was the expense and luxury which marked their meeting that it has ever since been known as the Field of the Cloth of Gold. It was, however, a field of deception, as those of diplomacy are apt to be. Henry and Wolsey had already decided to throw their weight on the side of Charles. As usual, Wolsey had interests of his own at stake and the advancing of his own ambitions, so that the decision in the Emperor's favor appears to have been made in part because of his promise to support Wolsey for Pope in the next Papal election. The impression left on Francis, however, from the events and conversations on the Field of the Cloth of Gold, was that England would at the least take a neutral stand as between him and the boyish Emperor.

When war broke out in another two years, however, England invaded France, with the usual result of having to suffer an invasion from the Scots herself. The English military operations were not important. Charles indeed did not need help, for his own forces were overwhelmingly successful. At Pavia in 1525 he crushed the French and captured Francis himself. With the Duchy of Milan lost to France, and her King a prisoner in the hands of the Emperor, it appeared that Charles might become all-powerful on the Continent, which did not suit English purposes. Moreover, in the same year in which Charles captured Francis, a new Pope, Clement VII, had been elected and the Emperor had done nothing to redeem his promise and forward the aspirations of Wolsey for the highest office in Christendom. The Cardinal and Henry now reversed their policy and allied England to France, as the weaker party.

It is impossible to determine just how far Wolsey's personal motives may have influenced international relations but in any case England had been definitely carried over from the old period of Continental conquest to the new one of playing the part of makeweight in the balance of power. That is perhaps Wolsey's chief claim to remembrance. Otherwise his diplomacy had been a failure. France was humbled, with her King in the hands of the enemy. So far from maintaining the balance of power, Charles threatened universal empire, and England by playing fast and loose with both sides had no claim to spoils of war and no influence in the councils of the new dictator.

In addition she had spent vast sums and the Crown had grown poor while the Chancellor had heaped up riches. England's position, which had seemed brilliant a few years before, had rapidly declined, and there was to be trouble at home. The throne was indeed secure and had been made more so by the execution of the Duke of Buckingham, who had claims to it and had talked too freely about them in the event of Henry's death. But money had to be had. Wolsey had ruled for eight years without summoning Parliament but between diplomacy and extravagance the hoard of Henry VII had been exhausted, and in 1523, before peace had been arranged, the representatives of the people had to be called together. Wolsey asked them to grant the unprecedented sum of £800,000, equal perhaps to £12,000,000 today. When he found that the Commons did not comply at once, he personally appeared before them to argue with his customary arrogance. Thomas More, who was Speaker, informed him coldly that such action was against the privilege of the House and he had to leave defeated.

He was in fact a broken man, though he did not realize it as yet. Money was voted, though a far less sum than had been asked, and two years later more was needed. The plan of an "Amicable Loan," which was in fact a demand from citizens under threat of retaliation if not paid, was put on foot, historians disagreeing as to whether the plan was Henry's or Wolsey's. In any case the Chancellor had to take the blame and his unpopularity was greatly increased. After the peace noted above had been made and alliance shifted to France, the French King had been released by the Emperor on condition of large cessions of territory, but once safe home Francis repudiated the agreement.

Henry was not the only one who had grown fearful of the swollen power of Charles; and an Italian league, headed by the Pope, was formed against him. The consequences were the sack of Rome by the Emperor's troops and the capture of the Pope himself, a fact of importance for our story.

Meanwhile, events of another order had also been happening on the Continent. A figure far different from the Emperor or the two Kings, the Cardinal-Chancellor, or such English humanists as More or Dean Colet, had begun in Germany that Protestant movement which was to be of such vast influence in politics as well as in religion. Martin Luther, starting with his opposition to the sale of indulgences by the Church, went on to teach the doctrine of man's direct relation to God and to deny the need of any human intervention between them.

The doctrine was not new, but the time was ripe for a man who could preach it as Luther did. In 1521, Henry, always fond of theology, published a book in which he attacked Luther, and was rewarded by the Pope with the title, which still forms part of that of the British Kings, "Defender of the Faith." To understand Henry's often misconstrued attitude toward the Church we must realize not only the close connection between religion and politics but also that there were two distinct religious movements at work in the world of his day.

There was the doctrinal movement of Protestantism, in which Henry had no part. In spite of the anomalies of his character

Henry remained not only a sincerely religious person but devoted to the old doctrines. The other movement may be described as institutional and anti-clerical. This was the more general of the two, for vast numbers of people who were not Protestant in religious dogma were yet strongly opposed to the abuses and interferences of both the Papacy and the clergy. This was a movement which could obviously, as it did, operate both within the Catholic and later in the Protestant churches.

It was the opposition of the layman to what he considered the unwarranted and exorbitant demands for authority over him by clerics, whether by the Pope, who in addition to claiming headship of the Church had also become a territorial ruler like any other, or by Anglican bishops. It was this second movement of the modern age that Henry did so much to forward, but when he finally substituted himself for the Pope as head of the Church of England it was with no intention of changing the dogmas of that Church, which explains why he attacked both Protestants who did wish to change the doctrines and Catholics who wished to halt the institutional anti-clerical movement which the King considered essential. Henry wished to free England from foreign domination and ecclesiastical control but to keep it doctrinally unaltered. When the Protestant movement took firmer hold of the English people and doctrinal disputes became bitter, the position of the English sovereign as head of the Church brought the more complex problem that Elizabeth had to face. Henry had built for a time a half-way house but the religious contentions of its inhabitants were to threaten to destroy the house entire under his daughter.

When Rome was sacked Henry was thirty-six years of age and had reached maturity after a rather slow development. From about this time he began to take over the reins from Wolsey, who had failed both at home and abroad. Henry had decided to be master though the Cardinal's fall was yet delayed. How masterful the monarch could be was to be shown in the matter of the divorce from Catherine, though the unhappy drama unrolled slowly.

At what date Henry first began to consider the matter cannot be known, but if we accept Gardiner, an historian very hostile to

Henry, it had been in 1521, a year before he met Anne Boleyn. It was by chance the same year in which a group of Cambridge students, including Tyndale, Coverdale, Cranmer, Latimer and others, began to meet at a tavern to discuss the doctrine of Luther. The coincidence is suggestive.

In dealing with the problem of the divorce we have to consider an extremely complex web of motives and forces which cannot be certainly unravelled and which, in a paragraph or so, cannot even be described. In brief the chief actors are Henry, who morally as a husband was much above the royal average of the time; Catherine, loyal and spotless and one of the most pathetic figures in English history; the Emperor, who was Catherine's nephew and whose power in Italy the Pope dared not defy; the Pope, Clement VII, who had none of the great qualities of a Gregory VII, and whose position as a temporal ruler like other heads of states was even more jeopardized by his dilemma than his position as head of the Church.

For further background we have Henry's coming to maturity, his ambition to have both England and himself play leading roles, and his desire for an heir contrasted with the maternal record of his wife. Of all his children the Princess Mary alone survived. We have already spoken of the danger both to a dynasty and the nation of a woman as queen. In this web the part played by Anne Boleyn has, I think, been often much overrated.

Gardiner, for example, speaks of Henry's lust after her as the leading motive in his divorce. This is utterly inadequate. If that had been all there was to the matter the affair would have been simple. Henry had apparently been considering divorce for five or six years before there is any indication that his love letters to Anne began, though she had been at Court for most of that time. She was not beautiful, except for her eyes, and was a little flirt without much mind. Daughter of a rich London merchant, her elder sister had been one of Henry's two known mistresses, and she herself likewise became so before her marriage to Henry. There is nothing in her light character known to us that would indicate that she would have the tenacity to hold off the King for

years, and at the same time the ability to hold him while insisting
that the only way to possession was marriage, preceded by the
difficult and long process of divorce dragged out for years. Such a
reading of the case is indeed incredible.

Henry must always remain something of an enigma, and the age
was a curious blend of superstition, religion, freethinking and
hard self-seeking egoism. Fully admitting the King's excessive
share of the last quality, allowance must also be made for the other
factors. But here we come to a yet more tangled web of conscience
and scruple.

Although six years older than the King, Catherine had made his
interests and those of her adopted country wholly her own, and
there is nothing to indicate that the marriage was unhappy. But
there was no male heir, and now at last no hope of more children
of either sex. The importance of royal marriages in those days was
political rather than religious, and Popes had usually proved themselves very compliant in breaking the rules of the Church.

It had been a Papal dispensation that had first allowed the
young King to marry his brother's widow, a sin in the eyes of the
Church. Was the tale of still-born, short-lived babies and miscarriages a judgment of Heaven? Henry's mind, dwelling on this
idea, on the need of a male heir for the sake of family and nation,
perhaps on his infatuation for the worthless Anne, gradually
shaped his intent.

But there was more. Strictly speaking, having had Anne's sister
as a mistress, he was as inhibited from marrying the younger
Boleyn as he had been, without Papal dispensation, from marrying his brother Arthur's widow. Popes had usually been willing
to arrange such matters for important sovereigns, but Clement
could not. He was in the hands of the Emperor, and although
policy and not sympathy played its part, Charles was unwilling
to have Henry divorce his aunt. There was plenty which ordi-
narily, in such a quandary as Henry was in, Popes could do and
had done to help. Henry suggested that the original dispensation
be declared invalid, which would have made the marriage void
and the one surviving child, Mary, illegitimate. The King also

toyed with the idea of a dispensation for bigamy, using Old Testament examples. In fact in 1437 the Pope had given a dispensation to Henry IV of Castile to take a second wife for a given time to see if she could produce children, and Clement now offered Henry the bigamy exit from the difficulty, but the King decided against it.

There was then the divorce method. His sister Margaret and both the husbands of his other sister had obtained Papal divorces. Why not he? Clement was even willing to grant a dispensation for the Princess Mary to marry her half-brother, Henry's illegitimate son the Duke of Richmond. The Pope also suggested to Henry that he settle the matter himself, marry Anne, and then the case would come before him only as to the validity of the second marriage. But Henry wanted neither indefinite delay nor question as to the legitimacy of his heirs. If the Emperor and not he pulled the strings with the Papacy, what might not happen if he trusted only to an English court to declare his marriage with Catherine void and then had to trust the Pope to declare his second one valid?

If the Pope was in a tight hole, so was Wolsey. If he could not win the divorce for the King his career was finished, but if he did win it and Henry married Anne it was equally so, for her relations, who would come into power, including the Duke of Norfolk, were all his enemies. One cannot withhold a certain amount of sympathy from all concerned, above all from Catherine.

Finally the Pope appointed Wolsey and another Cardinal to open a Legatine Court in London and try the case, though no decision should be valid until it had his approval. Henry demanded now that the marriage should be declared null from the start. In open Court the Queen knelt before Henry and asked that after being a faithful wife for twenty years she should not be put away in shame.

This was in 1529 and delay followed delay, which was what the Pope was playing for. Clement's various offers had shown that he had no moral scruples in the matter whatsoever. The fact became plain that he was acting not as Pope but as temporal sovereign who feared to offend his over-lord the Emperor. The religious question in England, which had centered in the problem of the marriage, was evidently to be decided for the English King, not by the Pope, as head of the Church, but by a rival monarch as Emperor and Lord of Italy. Henry decided to settle the affair among the English themselves.

Wolsey, whose fall had been only a question of a short time in any case, was dismissed and stripped of his wealth and most of his offices, though the King allowed him to retain the Archbishopric of York, a certain amount of his possessions, and some other lucrative posts. When, however, Wolsey entered into correspondence with the French he was charged with treason, and would have suffered on the scaffold had he not fortunately died at Leicester Abbey on his way to meet his fate at London. The remarks of the dying are not infrequently dressed up for posterity and we cannot take those attributed to the fallen Minister too seriously. If the words he is reputed to have said are true: "If I had served my God as diligently as I have done my King, He would not have given me over in my gray hairs," the comment is that the Cardinal had always thought first of himself rather than of either his God or his King.

The rest of the story, though it was to drag out nearly four years more, can be told more briefly. In 1529 Henry called Parliament to assemble and this Reformation Parliament sat for seven years. What it did was of great significance in English history, and most significant was Henry's use of it. Parliament had been dwindling in importance, and if Wolsey had continued to have his way, it would have been called as infrequently as possible, and English constitutional development might have gone the way of the Continental nations.

The Cardinal, with all his energy and ability, did not understand his own people. It was the happy gift of the Tudors, with all their faults, to understand them and to forward the main stream of their history. It was to be Parliament, and not the Church, meeting in Convocation, that was to bring about the independence of the Church of England, and decide the religious future of the English people.

The following year, Henry made another effort to induce the Pope to permit his marriage by placing the question before the universities of Europe. Where the King's influence dominated, opinions were given in his favor, and where the Emperor's dominated opinions were the reverse. Nothing had been gained and another year had passed. The next year, Henry declared that the entire body of English clergy had become liable under the Statute of Premunire by having accepted the Legatine powers conferred upon Wolsey, and although they offered to buy pardon by grants of some £120,000 in money of that day, Henry refused unless they would accept him as Supreme Head. This they agreed to do, with the vague phrase added "so far as allowed by the law of Christ."

Henry was not yet ready to break with the Pope, and his claim to headship was to make him supreme only in the relations between clergy and laity in England, but it was another threat of what might come. Another year went by, and Henry through Parliament passed an Act denying Convocation the right to meet without being summoned by him. This would prevent their taking any action as to his divorce or marriage without his consent. This "submission of the clergy," as it was called, forced the resignation of Sir Thomas More, whom the King had made Chancellor after Wolsey, and who feared for the doctrines of the Church. Indeed, gentle as he was, and approving of toleration in Utopia, he had not hesitated to burn heretics in England, which helps us better to understand other characters of the age. The Chancellor probably saw what was coming and did not wish to take part in the break with Rome.

Henry himself still did not wish to break with the Pope but to force him to yield, or rather the Emperor who pulled the strings that made the Papal marionette dance. In 1532 Parliament passed the Act of Annates by which the first year's incomes from Church benefices, which had previously been paid to the Pope, should be withheld. The Pope still could not be moved, and the year and Henry's patience came to an end together. January 24, 1533, he married Anne Boleyn, who seven months later gave birth to Elizabeth.

Parliament next passed the Act of Appeals which declared that the King was head of all temporal and spiritual courts in the realm and that no appeals to other courts should be valid. Thomas Cranmer was appointed Archbishop of Canterbury, and a few months later pronounced sentence against Catherine after Convocation had declared her marriage to be void. Although Henry had appealed over the head of the Pope to a General Council of the Church, none was held, and Clement himself decided in favor of Catherine. In the next two years the break was made complete, chiefly by financial measures in Parliament which transferred payments formerly made to the Pope to the English Crown.

The problem had now been solved. England, which had been long growing into a nation, had cut loose from Europe. The balance of power on the Continent was to remain important, but the English no longer had territorial aspirations which would lead them into wars of conquest nor was there left any power which could claim moral or legal control over any aspect of English life. If England could defend herself, she was free and independent of any other power, temporal or spiritual. Whatever the tangled motives had been behind it all, what Henry and Parliament working together had wrought was a Declaration of Independence which left England free to work out her own destiny spiritually, intellectually and materially, in that new world which was soon to emerge. The tremendous outburst of energy, bodily and mental, which was to come in the days of Elizabeth cannot be understood without considering the work of her father.

It is impossible to attribute the slow but persistent efforts of Henry for a dozen years or so, from his first thoughts of annulling the marriage with Catherine to his marriage with Anne and the break with Rome, to a mere animal lust which would normally have worked off long before that period in a man with the world —and its women—at his feet. But the long struggle or strain, or both, had told on Henry, and a degeneration in his character had set in, which was to become more and more notable.

It was fortunate, however, that the first stage of the Protestant revolution came under Henry, who was strong enough to maintain peace and order even if he were ruthless on occasion. The Reformation was sweeping across Europe, and England could not have remained unaffected. There were victims to Henry's policy but they were scattered individuals, and the country was not to go through the agonies of civil religious war or wholesale massacres as did many nations on the Continent. This was due to the strength of Henry and in part to the acquiescence of his people in the new order of things.

As we have noted from time to time, the islanders had often objected to interference with their affairs by the Pope, and in that respect the final break with him was in accord with a strong strain in national sentiment. Moreover, England had never been bound to Rome by ties other than official. She had not had, so to say, her share in the Papacy, and of the long line of Popes only one has ever been an Englishman. The Pope was always a "foreigner" and usually of the Latin race, for which the English have the least liking and sympathy. It is true that the "divorce" (really annulment) of the marriage with Catherine was unpopular at first, and sympathy went out freely to the woman who was the victim of both physical circumstances and the forces of the time, and there was nothing about Anne Boleyn which could win popular affection or respect as an offset.

But looking at the question in its larger aspect, Henry's policy did become popular, as is evidenced by the fact that it was carried through from start to finish by him without any armed force to rely upon and with no popular disorder save for the abortive and not serious Pilgrimage of Grace, a small rising in the north. This general sentiment in favor of making the English Church independent was cemented in important ways by Henry's suppression of the religious order of monks and friars, and the confiscation of much of their property. The orders had for long been degenerating and had mostly ceased to perform the useful social functions which they once had done in learning, education and charity. The immorality charged against them was unquestionably grossly exaggerated, but they had become easy-going and they possessed a large fraction of the land and wealth of England.

When a considerable part of this was taken from them it should, perhaps, according to modern ideas, have been devoted to the social functions which the orders had once performed and which could then have been better performed by others, instead of being given to individuals. The passing of it into private hands from the "dead hand" of the Church had two results. Better use of the land and more active employment of the wealth acted as stimulants to the business activity of the nation, and also created in both cities and countryside a large class which having received its property by the destruction of the old order would be staunchly on the side of the new.

There were, however, other results. Three alternatives were presented with reference to the Church lands. They might be left in the hands of the Church; given, after confiscation, to private owners; or become the property of the Crown. It is probable that the people suffered somewhat by the rejection of the first in favor of the second, as, whatever faults the Church may have had, it did do more in many ways for its tenants or neighbors than the more hard-fisted private owners rising into a new-rich class. Moreover, in spite of the advantage of attaching a new group to the interest of the King and the changes he was bringing about, it paved the way for the later poverty of the Crown, which had no small part to play in subsequent reigns. That Elizabeth was not a wealthy monarch was much to the advantage of her policy and people. The Stuarts, however, were to have neither her tact nor her popularity, and the fact that they were also always short of money certainly had a large influence in bringing about the constitutional crisis and may also well have prevented the creation of a complete despotism.

Henry, however, in his ecclesiastical policy, had also appealed to the intelligence of the people at large. In the promulgation of what were called the Ten Articles, drawn up by Convocation and

sent out with his approval, the object was to make the old doctrines of the Church more easily understood and acceptable to the
ordinary layman. Such an appeal to the intelligence of the individual was again made in the authorization by the King and Cromwell
of the publication of a new translation of the Bible. The version
had been made by Miles Coverdale and presumably had a much
greater circulation than the earlier one by Tyndale. Although the
effect of trying to make men think for themselves, in spite of the
simultaneous policy of persecution, was to be far wider-reaching
than Henry expected, it was something new to appeal to the mind
of the nation in matters of State or Church.

There had also been a change in the position of Parliament,
which, it has been said, doubled its power by the passage of all the
Acts which the fundamental alterations in the relations of Church
and State called for. Henry spoke of himself and Parliament as
"conjoined and knit together in one body politic," and if he and
Elizabeth "managed" Parliament, nevertheless they relied upon
it. If they were despotic they gave the people the feeling that
all were working together, a feeling that was to overthrow the
throne in the next century when Stuarts sat on it who opposed,
instead of forwarding, the trend of popular evolution.

Under Henry, Parliament was usually, though not always,
amenable to his wishes. The Acts of Treason and Supremacy,
passed in 1534, conferred the title of Supreme Head on earth of
the Church of England on the King, and made it high treason for
any one to wish harm to him or his heirs or to call him a heretic,
tyrant, schismatic or usurper. These Acts gave tremendous power
to Henry, which was freely used by him and Thomas Cromwell,
now become his chief agent. More and Fisher, the Bishop of
Rochester, were both beheaded for denying the King's supremacy
in the Church, and other lesser men suffered the more horrible
deaths of traitors.

The year after, the Queen herself was to come to the block.
The unhappy Catherine had died earlier in the year, and there
had been much talk of Henry's divorcing Anne. The reasons for
the final tragedy cannot be certainly known. Henry had probably

tired of her, and he had now entered upon the more brutal period of his life. Most of his acts up to this year 1536 could have been motivated by needs of state, and in each case, by happy fortune or otherwise, they had redounded to the good of the people, but this cannot be said of what was now to follow. How low Henry had fallen was indicated in January, when he celebrated the death of Catherine by a state ball in which he appeared joyously clad in bright yellow. Since the birth of Elizabeth, Anne had had two miscarriages and no more children. An ecclesiastical court, headed by Archbishop Cranmer, declared the marriage illegal, on what grounds we do not know. But at the same time she was on trial for incest with her brother and criminal intercourse with four other men.

Her judges, at the head of whom was her own uncle, the Duke of Norfolk, unanimously found her guilty, and on the 19th of May she was beheaded in the Tower. Four of the five men named also suffered death for treason. One only, to save his life, had confessed, and the truth remains unknown. However, as Pollard points out, if Henry had merely wished to rid himself of the Queen, who in any case had been divorced two days before her execution, there was no need to kill four men with her, and the Duke of Norfolk and the twenty-six other peers who sat in judgment must have found some grounds of justification for their unanimous verdict against all the six accused, counting in Anne herself.

Within ten days after Anne's head rolled from the block, Henry married Jane Seymour. As Catherine and Anne were both dead there could be no doubt of the legitimacy of any children the new Queen might have by Henry but to settle the question Parliament passed a new Act of Succession. It had already declared Catherine's daughter Mary illegitimate, and now added Elizabeth, settling the succession on the descendants of Jane, who died the next year a few days after giving birth to the boy who was to become Edward VI.

In 1539 Henry married Anne of Cleves, a German princess he had never seen and with whose looks he was greatly disappointed when she arrived, although he went through with the ceremony. Cromwell, who had arranged the marriage with "the Flemish mare," as Henry is said to have called her, paid some months later with his head, and Anne, with her own consent, was divorced. In 1540 Henry next married Catherine Howard, another niece of the Duke of Norfolk, but, having discovered that she had been incontinent before marriage, had her beheaded in 1542, the next year marrying Catherine Parr, who survived him and nursed him tenderly in his last illness.

Such was Henry's marital story and its effect upon the nation. We have already mentioned that Henry had had no intention of changing the doctrines of the Church, and in 1539 he had secured the consent of Parliament to the Statute of the Six Articles, which declared the real presence of the body and blood of Christ in the Lord's Supper; communion in one kind; clerical celibacy; perpetual obligation of vows of chastity; private masses; and auricular confession. Whoever denied the first was to be burnt to death; and hanged on the second offense of speaking against any of the others.

If we have to smile somewhat cynically as we contrast Henry's life and doctrine, we must recall that in the latter he was taking a needed reef in the sail of the ship of state. The English do not take readily to new ideas but cling to the old. The storms of religious differences were tossing all states in the sixteenth century. The nation was ready for the break with Rome, but to have allowed schismatics to go further and to fight over religious dogmas would have been to bring on the orgies of bloodshed which the continent witnessed. By moving as far as he did and then knowing when to stop, Henry showed how completely he understood the task and his people.

In one other important respect the same knowledge, or the uncanny Tudor ability, unfortunately to be lacking in Mary, was displayed by her father. More had happened in his reign than the mere snapping of Continental ties and the abandonment of Continental ambitions. England was unconsciously preparing for her island destiny, and Henry, still one with his people, was the real founder of the Royal Navy. From the launching of the *Great Harry* in 1515 his interest never ceased, and thirty years later it was to be the navy he had created that was to save England from the threatened invasion by France. He established the Navy Office, built the royal dock yards at Woolwich and Deptford, and himself designed new and better types of ships, more efficient than any of the English merchantmen or the war vessels of other nations. In nothing did the King, great or often unlovely as he was, show himself more in line with the England that was to come than in turning his back on Europe and preparing for the conquest of the seas.

CHAPTER VIII

THE TUDOR INTERLUDE

BY THE END of 1546 the days of the King were coming to their end. He had held in check both the forces of reaction and those of too rapid change. But now he would soon be gone, and his only son, a child of nine, would sit upon the throne, delicate and immature. Henry, in his will, had arranged the order of succession: Edward, Mary, Elizabeth—an infant and two women. A child monarch had always meant confusion and disaster to the realm, which feared a woman ruler as much. Who, when Edward should be king, would really rule?

That problem had employed every one, the dying King himself, the nobles, and among the commons all thinking men with property and conscience at stake. Henry had provided for a Council of Regency during his son's minority made up of both parties, but there were already intrigues among the great families. The balance carefully planned by Henry was suddenly upset. The Duke of Norfolk, whom he had made one of the Councillors in his will, quartered the royal arms with his own, although forbidden to do so by the Herald's College. He had in the past been accused of ambitions leading to the throne, and now his son, the Earl of Surrey, "the most foolish proud boy in England," was asking who but his father should become Protector of England?

In January 1547 both were sentenced. On the 20th, Surrey, the young poet who first introduced the sonnet into England, was beheaded, and on the 27th orders were given for the execution next morning of the Duke, who was in the Tower, awaiting his fate a few hours off. No more dramatic reprieve was ever given to a condemned traitor. During the dark vigil which the Duke was keeping, the King died in his palace at Westminster, clasping the hand of Archbishop Cranmer.

The Duke's life was saved but his power was gone, and it was to be not a Howard but a Seymour who was to become Protector and practical ruler. The King had died about two in the morning of the 28th but no announcement of the momentous fact was made until the 31st. Meanwhile much was going on in haste behind the scenes, and when the curtain rose with the young Edward VI as king, the power in the Council his father planned had been won by the innovators, with Edward Seymour, Earl of Hertford, Henry's brother-in-law, at their head. Those who had won immediately bestowed new honors upon themselves, Hertford becoming Duke of Somerset, Dudley taking the title of Earl of Warwick, and Parr, another brother-in-law, that of Earl of Northampton.

In order to understand the events of the two brief reigns which we have to chronicle in this chapter, we must consider two aspects of English life when Henry died. One was the economic condition. Especially during the latter half of his reign Henry had lacked an able financial adviser and he himself was far from being the business-minded King his father had been. Both Henry and Wolsey had provided the example of luxury and extravagance, and this pervaded all the higher ranks, aided by the enormous property taken over by private individuals from the Church.

On the other hand, the lower classes were faced by changing conditions in both business and agriculture, as all were also by that most insidious and dangerous of poisons in the economic body, an unsound and depreciating currency. Ostentation and wars both cost money, and the new-rich were becoming wealthy by spoliation rather than by expansion of commerce or industry. Henry's interests and preoccupations did not include, like those of his father and his daughter Elizabeth, building up the economic life of the nation. When the stream of taxation dried so far as to make financing of the monarch and nation first difficult and then impossible, in spite of large foreign loans, Henry had taken what has seemed to so many rulers and governments, before and since, the easiest or only way and had debased the coinage. The lowered values of the coins caused prices to rise, and the rapid increase in the cost of living and dislocation of prices in the whole national economy merely made it yet more difficult to raise revenue by taxation. In addition, the gold and silver which were being received in huge quantities by Spain from America were also beginning to have their disturbing effect on the price level and economy of all Europe. English conditions went from bad to worse, and Henry continued to debase his coinage more and more until by 1551 the silver coin minted had only one-quarter the amount of silver in it that it had had in 1506.

The wages of agricultural and other labor failed to keep pace with the rise in prices ensuing on the above causes, and there was consequently much hardship and discontent. In addition, the increase in the practice of enclosing common lands by grasping landlords, and the use of land for sheep rather than for farming, threw large numbers of laborers out of work, who could not find other employment in any expansion of business or industry. There was also much dislocation of labor due to the change of ownership of the Church properties, and a considerable diminution in charitable aid. The country swarmed with "sturdy beggars," and there was a large increase in petty crime. The problems of business, the currency, and the poor all had to await their partial solution until the reign of Elizabeth.

The religious situation at the death of Henry was also a delicate one. The half-way house he had tried to erect was by no means firm on its foundations. On the one hand, the break with Rome had been fairly recent and the new Church of England had no long tradition behind it to ensure affection and loyalty, and there were many, especially among the old nobility and other upper classes, who were still attached to the former order. On the other hand, the ordinary people in the towns and in the south and east of England were becoming more and more devoted to a

Protestantism of the type preached by Zwingli in Switzerland, which was radical according to the Church of England, although milder than the Calvinism that was to become predominant in Scotland. This problem, like the economic one, was to have to await Elizabeth, but the confusion, ignominy, horrors and dangers of the short reigns of her brother and sister were to do much to prepare Englishmen to accept with fervor the magnificent leadership which the greatest Queen in history was to display.

We need not discuss the character of the apparently rather precocious and vain boy who for about six years was to occupy the throne as Edward VI, dying of tuberculosis at the age of sixteen. Somerset, who seized the real reins of power on the death of Henry, was an odd combination of a man who could often see clearly the right ends to be aimed at without the slightest comprehension of the proper means to attain them or of the difficulties in the way. For example, he dreamed again the dream of uniting England and Scotland, this time by marrying Edward to the young Queen of Scots, Mary, a few years younger.

Possibly the object might have been attained peaceably but Somerset undertook to forward his scheme and the English claim to the Scottish throne by force of arms, a method bound to arouse the Scots and foil the end aimed at. Although in the battle of Pinkie Cleugh ten thousand Scots were slain with little loss to the English, even the military victory was not followed up. The only result was to bring the French once more into alliance against the English, and further to embitter the feeling of Scotland for England.

But this was not all. The young Scottish Queen was sent to the Court of France to be educated with the French royal children as a devout Catholic and to become the bride of the Dauphin, Francis, in the year of Elizabeth's accession, a secret marriage treaty providing that in case there should be no child the throne of Scotland should pass to France. Again a possible chance of peaceable union had been lost only to prolong the bitterness between the two nations.

In the economic and religious fields Somerset displayed the

same ineptitude. Although he was as anxious for spoils as any of the other nobles of his day, building his magnificent palace of Somerset House from his loot, he appears to have been democratic and sympathetic with the troubles of the laborers and other lower classes. He did not, however, improve their position, but rather the reverse, as the landlords resented his taking them to task, just as the owners of the spoliated Church lands resented his attacks on them when he himself was one of the worst offenders. In the religious field he was equally unsuccessful. In his desire for toleration he was in advance of his age, and as usual did not realize the conditions under which he had to work.

Not only is toleration a plant of slow growth and one easily killed, as Europe has learned in our own day, but it cannot grow in all soils. In the new nations emerging from the mediæval period one of the most essential duties of government was to govern and to maintain order. What Henry and Elizabeth both realized was that the nation could not advance too far in one direction without endangering the orderly advance in others. Politics and religion were closely intertwined, and a degree of toleration of differences of opinion in either which was quite possible for Englishmen in their strong, law-abiding social organization of the nineteenth century was quite impossible in the sixteenth.

Nothing is more misleading in history than to believe that an ideal can be achieved as readily or successfully under one set of conditions as under another. The greatest achievement of the British race has been the steady growth of liberty within the law, steering a course from century to century between the Scylla and Charybdis of anarchy and tyranny, and between freedom and dangerous license of thought and speech.

In the sixteenth century government was advancing from the medieval to the modern forms, and in the spheres of spiritual and intellectual life the currents of new ideas were rushing fast and tumultuously. It was a delicate question just how rapidly England could take or be given her own head along the new course she was to travel. The decision called for statesmanship of the highest order, and in the Tudor interlude covered by this chapter there was no statesmanship. Somerset was too tolerant; Mary too intolerant. Both missed the middle way, which is the English way, and which had to be found.

The Protector influenced Parliament to permit the marriage of the clergy and to repeal some of the most oppressive of the laws of Henry, such as the Statute of Treason, the Acts against the Lollards, and others. There was also, however, under government orders much smashing of images and stained-glass windows with the pictures of saints, and the abolition of many church practices to which the people were accustomed and attached. There was so much objection to some of the innovations that sermons were prohibited except by clergymen who received special licenses, and Bishops Gardiner and Bonner, because of their objections to doctrinal and other changes, were placed in the Tower. Parliament also authorized the use of the first English Prayer Book (1549), mostly written by Cranmer, to whom we owe the larger part of its solemn and beautiful phrasing.

Although the Church was advancing rapidly on the Protestant road, Somerset not only engaged in no persecution but allowed complete freedom of religious discussion. Catholics and Protestants of varying shades of opinion, however, too often turned freedom of speech and opinion into the license to brawl and fight among themselves, and so violent did the disturbances become in Oxfordshire that they had to be put down by government and some priests were hanged.

In Cornwall and Devon disorder developed into a serious revolt. In the former the farmers and laborers still to a large extent spoke Celtic and objected to having the Church service in English, which they could not understand. They could understand no better the Latin of the old service but they were accustomed to it and in order to retain it rebelled against the government. Joined by the Devonshire men who had been stirred up by their priests, the insurgents besieged Exeter, and it was only after some months and desperate fighting, including the use by the government of foreign mercenary troops, that the insurrection was put down. Evidently the forward movement both in

Protestant doctrinal innovation and attempted toleration was proceeding too fast.

Meanwhile, there was also a serious rising in the eastern counties which was due to economic and not religious causes. Somerset had posed as a friend of the people, and was inclined to leniency, but action had to be taken when many thousand peasants under the leadership of one Ket, a tanner, formed a camp near Norwich. The basis of the trouble was the old one of increasing enclosures by the landlords, which question was being considered by Parliament.

The grievances had much foundation, and the insurgents, if we may call them so, were offered a free pardon if they would disperse. Ket declined to accept the terms, was declared a traitor, and his forces then captured Norwich. Order was eventually restored, but only with the use of the same Italian and German mercenaries who had been used in the West. That such were being used at all, for the first time since King John, was one indication of the chaotic conditions threatening. Another rising in Yorkshire was more readily suppressed locally.

The international situation was also serious. By the terms of the French Treaty of 1546 Boulogne had been given to the English for eight years as a financial pledge, but it was a sore point with the French. England was considered so weakened internally that the French not only threatened to regain their port but made a naval attack on the English island of Jersey. War was declared, but Somerset's fall was now imminent and a few weeks later he was arrested and sent to the Tower.

Warwick, soon to be made Duke of Northumberland by the boy King, now took the lead. Again the question arose as to whether the all-powerful nobleman, who had not however been made Protector, would favor the old religion or the advanced Puritans. Caring little himself, he chose the party of the latter for political reasons. The King himself was taking a decided interest in the matter, and, young as he was, had become an ardent Protestant. In 1552 Parliament authorized a revised version of the Prayer Book, which with slight changes is that in use today, and the following year adopted forty-two articles of faith, changed to thirty-nine in Elizabeth's reign. The more advanced Reformers recognized that their power would flow from the King, and Northumberland that his would also.

Meanwhile, however, the Duke had had to make an inglorious peace with France and to give up Boulogne before the date set. The currency had again been debased, and an effort by Northumberland to improve it by coining large quantities of sound gold and silver money of the old standard of 1543 had no effect because the baser coins were still allowed to circulate and so drove out the new for hoarding. Business conditions continued to get worse, and the Duke was thoroughly unpopular.

Somerset, who had been released from the Tower, was reported to have suggested that he might return to power, and was tried and beheaded with the approval of his nephew, the young King. Worthless as Northumberland was he had gained an ascendancy over the boy's mind, but in doing so had had to make his choice of boldly leading the advanced religious party instead of compromising with the old. The result was that if the King's elder sister, Mary, an ardent Catholic, should come to the throne the Duke would certainly forfeit power and probably his head. And now it was becoming evident that the boy's illness was progressing so rapidly that the end could not be far off.

Only a daring play could save the situation, if anything could. Henry VIII had left the throne in his will to Mary and Elizabeth after Edward. Northumberland played on the boy's vanity and fears for the Church. He was King, and if his father could settle the succession by will why could not he, and if Mary should succeed him Protestantism would be lost.

What was not observed was that Henry's will had been sanctioned by an Act of Parliament and Edward's would not be. Northumberland suggested as heir the Lady Jane Grey, granddaughter of a younger sister of Henry VIII, and a Protestant. The Duke tried to secure himself still further by marrying Lady Jane to his own son, Lord Guilford Dudley. To ensure, as he thought, the welfare of both Church and nation, Edward made the will and obtained, with much difficulty, the signatures of his Councillors, who expressed their belief that it was unconstitutional for a king to set aside an Act of Parliament.

The judges, when consulted, took the same stand, but finally signed on condition that instructions and a pardon would be granted them under the Great Seal. It was not a very courageous stand for leaders of the kingdom to take, but that they did actually object so strongly shows how far the authority of Parliament had reached even in the eyes of courtiers who wished to do the King's bidding.

Mary and Elizabeth were both excluded from the succession on the ground that they had both been solemnly declared illegitimate and therefore that no later contrary decision would be valid as against an unquestioned legitimate descendant of Henry VII.

Immediately on Edward's death Lady Jane Grey was proclaimed Queen in London but passed through streets that were ominously silent. Not a shout went up. Rumors had been abroad for some time that the hated Northumberland was hatching some plot, though it was not known what it might be. The nation was prepared for the accession of Mary. Had she not been named by Henry, his Council and Parliament as his lawful heir after Edward? She had been quiet and dignified during her brother's reign, and, although it was known that she belonged to the old Church, the full course that she was to pursue was not realized. Lady Jane Grey was a beautiful, retiring and highly educated girl of sixteen, but had been so little in the public eye that people scarcely knew who she was. They did know, however, that though there might be great danger in a woman as Queen, there was even more in a succession disputed between two women, and yet more in having Northumberland rule with his daughter-in-law as puppet on the throne.

There is no more pathetic figure in English history than the child—she was scarcely more—who had just been proclaimed Queen riding through the silent capital. But the people had judged rightly. The throne could not be willed away by a boy of sixteen or seized by a plotting nobleman against the people's will embodied in an Act of Parliament. Throughout England there was no support for Lady Jane, and a few days after she had been proclaimed in London Mary was at the head of an army of 30,000 men in spite of an effort on the part of Northumberland to have her captured. His own army deserted him. The fleet compelled its officers to declare for Mary. Quickly the whole plot fell to pieces. Within nine days Mary became Queen, showing extraordinary leniency toward the plotters. Lady Jane Grey, her husband and a few others were imprisoned, and it was only after being urged unanimously by all her advisers that the new Queen consented to the execution of Northumberland himself and two companions.

But if Mary continued to show clemency and to hesitate to shed the blood of even her most dangerous personal foes, she was to show herself capable of shedding it in rivers when it came to the foes of her faith, and her short five years on the throne were to prove almost unrelieved tragedy, not only for the nation but for herself. Important as they were to prove in their influence, the persecution, the marriage, and the war with France can be quickly detailed.

Mary had all the driving will of the Tudors and was at once more obstinate than her father without his fine tact in discerning the hair line which often divided the possible from the impossible. She also lacked that understanding of the people and that desire to work along the essential line of English development which were at once the foundation stones and the saving graces of the so-called Tudor despotism. Owing her throne to the good will of the people at large, she knew before the end that she was hated; craving love she found herself abandoned by the husband to whom she had been faithful and for whom she had sacrificed much; wishing above all to forward the cause of the Church to which she was whole-heartedly devoted, she knew she had irretrievably ruined it. History has on the whole been no kinder to her than her contemporaries, and it is one of the many ironies of her life that the ruler who up to her time in England had shown the greatest clemency of all to her enemies should come down to us as "Bloody Mary," because of her religious persecution.

The English people were longing for peace, for restoration of economic well-being, for business expansion, and if Mary had given them these things or even had been known to be striving for them, it is quite possible that she might have re-established the religious half-way house of Henry. Her first Parliament made no difficulty about restoring the Mass in the Church service and repealing the Act permitting the clergy to marry, but it flatly refused to acknowledge the Pope or restore the confiscated Church property. Mary should have known that submitting the English Church again to Rome would run counter to the swelling current of English nationality and offend the deepest feelings of the Protestant population, while restoring Church property would make enemies of the multitudes, high and low, who in one way and another had profited by the spoliations.

From the same Parliament Mary also vainly attempted to get consent to her marriage with a foreigner. The foreigner whom she designated was Philip of Spain, not only a hated Spaniard but by many feared as a Catholic. Mary, who was twelve years older than her chosen husband, was to dote on him, and the nation which had felt the pride of independence of the Continent and other powers, temporal and spiritual, dreaded the thought of being tied through the subservience of a doting wife to the destinies of the greatest Catholic power in the world. Moreover, Mary had asked for the renewal of the old laws for the persecution of heretics.

The result of the discontent produced by these various designs was a rebellion led by the Duke of Suffolk, who was the father of Lady Jane Grey, and by Sir Thomas Wyatt. Mary, however, had been on the throne less than a year. She had been placed there by the Parliament and the people, and though her plans were alarming to many, the nation was not ready either for civil war or to overthrow a legitimate sovereign. The rebellion failed completely, and Suffolk and Wyatt were executed. The former had not intended to place his daughter on the throne but Mary's own sister, Elizabeth.

The projected marriage, the plot and rebellion, all showed the dangers which Henry had tried to guard against and which were involved in having a woman at the head of the nation and also those of a disputed succession. Elizabeth, who had had nothing to do with the plot and had wisely abstained from being connected with it in any way, was placed temporarily in the Tower but was soon allowed to go to Woodstock and then to Hatfield under mild surveillance. The problem of Lady Jane Grey was different. As a result of the former plot she had been crowned Queen, and her husband had demanded to be made King. Now her father had hatched a new plot and rebelled a second time. Lady Jane, however, had not been implicated nor had the plot been in her favor.

In the next reign, Elizabeth was to hesitate years before sending to death a far more dangerous figure, the Queen of Scots, whose plotting against her was notorious. In spite of the case made out in Mary's favor by some historians, the execution of Lady Jane and her husband would appear to be the one blot on the humanity of the Queen other than the religious persecution to which she felt herself compelled by religious and not personal or political motives.

The next Parliament finally gave consent to the marriage to Philip, who became King of England and not merely the Queen's Consort. Another Parliament proved even more compliant. It agreed that the Church should again become subservient to Rome but that the new owners of the confiscated Church property should not be molested in their possessions, a distinctly sordid compromise. In addition, the Queen, King, and both Houses of Parliament knelt before the Papal Legate, Cardinal Pole, confessing their sin in that the nation had ever severed itself from Papal supremacy, and receiving absolution. The old Statutes for the burning of heretics were also re-enacted, and the stage was set for what followed. Although the blame has all been laid on the Queen, who was certainly the prime mover in the entire series of events, nevertheless the Parliament which so supinely abased itself before her and the Pope must share the responsibility. Had it shown but a tithe of the concern about the nation which it did about property, the course of Mary's reign might have been different.

Soon the persecution began. Bishop Hooper and others went to the stake, followed by Bishops Ridley and Latimer, who were burned at Oxford together. Latimer encouraged his companion in the terrible ordeal. "Be of good comfort," he said, "we shall this day light such a candle, by God's grace, in England, as I trust shall never be put out." The turn of Cranmer, the author of the Prayer Book, came later. Having recanted without avail and then having repented of his recantation, when the fire around him started, he held the offending hand, which had signed the document, in the flames until it was consumed.

In all, the persecution lasted for less than four years, and between three and four hundred persons met their deaths for their faith. Such a loss of life for such a purpose was small in comparison with what happened at times in many countries on the Continent, and the great impression which the persecution made on contemporary England, as well as the horror with which it has ever since been recalled, are indicative of English character. Brutal and coarse as it has often shown itself, it has never been bloodthirsty or vindictive, and has in general preferred compromise and reasonable tolerance to the imposing of opinion by force and violence. The horrors of a French Revolution, of the present regime in Russia, or other historic episodes would be unthinkable in English history at almost any period. As it was, Mary's persecutions struck home to the hearts of men, but instead of strengthening the Catholic cause they strengthened the Protestant, and the Queen knew before her death that she had defeated her own object.

Her marriage was equally a failure. Her husband had never cared for her but only for the throne and aid of England. On the abdication of his father he had become ruler of the vast Spanish possessions in both Europe and America, including Spain, part of France, Italy, all the Netherlands, and the incredibly rich gold and silver resources of the New World. Most of his time was spent on the Continent away from the wife who cared only for him and the Catholic Church, but on several occasions she had thought herself with child by him. At last she realized that the time had passed and that she could bear no heir and that the Protestant Elizabeth would inherit the throne. Deserted by her husband, she nevertheless drew England into war with France on his behalf, only to lose Calais, which had been English for well over two centuries and was England's last foothold on the Continent. The loss was fortunate but stung English pride.

Public opinion had almost wholly turned against Mary. The persecution, the hated Spanish marriage, the unsuccessful war were too much. Even business had languished, and, above all, the Spanish alliance, with Spain the more powerful partner claiming the seas and the New World, had kept the English mariner and merchant on leash. They strained at it, and all England had come to yearn for independence, for some settlement of religion consonant with English character and nationality, however opinions might differ, and for a chance to act and expand. In every way the forces of the nation had been tightly bound in resented chains which only awaited the death of the Queen to be broken. Suffering from dropsy, she died in November 1558, the Papal Legate, Pole, following her in death two days later. The bonds were burst and a glorious epoch opened. Elizabeth was Queen.

CHAPTER IX

THE GLORY OF ELIZABETH

ELIZABETH must be regarded as one of the greatest if not the very greatest of women rulers in history. The period which takes its name from her does so with unusual justification, for she was not merely the sovereign reigning at the time but in a very real sense she was the creator of the new glory of the nation and of the qualities which were to come into play in the founding of the Empire. Social forces, wholly impersonal, were of course also at work and must be taken into account, but they were confusing and conflicting, and it was the peculiar mind and understanding of the Queen which fused them into the character of empire-building England.

Twenty-five years of age when the death of her sister brought her to the throne and reversed the course of history, she was comely but not beautiful. She had, however, all the flair for magnificence and pageantry which had characterized her father, and the legend of Gloriana, to be hymned by Spenser, sprang from the devotion of the people, the glory which they won under her as a symbol, and the pageants in which she figured and which she delighted to witness. Her "progresses" through the country were more than mere show, and helped to impress on the people her resounding magnificence and commanding position.

She had less foreign blood than any other monarch since the alien William of Normandy, and although there was much more of Henry VIII in her character and temper than of her English mother Anne, she prided herself on being purely English and at one with her people. Unmarried through her long reign, few sovereigns have ever more completely subordinated their personal lives to the upbuilding of the nation, and to an extent before unknown the Crown became the symbol of that nation's character and aspirations.

Her education and experience had been well fitted to prepare her for the arduous and difficult task which lay ahead of her when, sitting under a tree in the grounds of Hatfield House, she was told of Mary's death and of the new life opening before herself and the nation. In an age when, thanks to the influence of the Renaissance, the nobility counted many learned and cultured women in its ranks, Elizabeth stood high among them. She could speak French and Italian as fluently as English, and Latin and Greek fairly well. If she owed much to books and to her tutor, Roger Ascham, she owed still more to experience.

When Elizabeth was less than three, her mother had been beheaded, and since then the young princess had seen much of life and death, of sudden rises to fortune and equally sudden falls from it, of plots and counter plots. Suspicion of complicity in one of these had placed her in the Tower where she had expected to be executed. She had learned to walk warily and to give her trust to few. Without force to back her, she had had to use her woman's wit and charms to the utmost, and she continued to do so all her career. She could play on men's love or ambitions, twist and turn and lie, stretch out dangerous situations until she saw her way, although at times capable of bold and quick decisions. After an early episode in childhood, in which, if a little unsavory by modern standards, there was nothing essentially wrong, she held her womanly emotions firmly in check, and though she suffered from them it was not they but her cool brain which guided her course.

Above all, she had to the full that Tudor instinct, which Mary had so completely lacked, of understanding and trusting her people and making their interest one with her own. Besides the instinct, she deeply admired her father and undoubtedly had been well schooled in his ideas and policy. In addition, when in danger in the Tower from Mary, it had been Parliament and the people who had protected her, a lesson she never forgot. It was true that as the power and wealth of England might grow, so would her own, but it was no narrow ambition which led her to seek above all things the independence, strength and welfare of the nation, and as during her long life the nation came to realize this, it repaid her with its devotion.

She asked much from those who served her and she had to walk so warily among the many pitfalls that often she might seem cruel or niggardly in requital. But it was not only a personal devotion but devotion to the ideals of the nation itself, which seemed to have acquired a renewal of youth, that made all willing to serve her on such terms, taking the hazards upon themselves. She could be despotic in the Tudor sense, and also rate Parliament soundly, but she always sensed the genuine national will and aim, and bent herself to it, so that at the end of her life she could truly say to the Commons that "Though God hath raised me high, yet this I count the glory of my Crown, that I have reigned with your loves."

There was, indeed, another point to note which will have much to do with the story. Both Mary and Elizabeth had been declared illegitimate by English courts. If the succession should follow the lines of legitimacy then Mary Stuart, Queen of Scots and wife of the Dauphin of France, was entitled to the throne and not Elizabeth, who succeeded by virtue of her father's will and a Parliamentary Act, to be followed in the new Queen's first Parliament by another Act legitimating her and accepting her as lawful sovereign by blood. If Parliament were supreme, Elizabeth's right could not be questioned, but, unlike Mary, Elizabeth's legitimacy had never been recognized by the Pope, and so ran counter to Catholic doctrine, as Parliamentary supremacy also did to the Stuart doctrine of divine right of Kings. Elizabeth's title to Queen was thus wholly Parliamentary, something more which she never forgot. During almost all of her life the threads winding around her own succession and the succession of the person who might follow in case of her death, had to be woven into a web of

195

The laity had thus controlled the Church, and religious matters came more and more to be determined by the Crown and Parliament, a system which has lasted to the present, with increasing toleration granted from time to time. Even today in such countries as the United States, where there is no state Church and all religions are constitutionally tolerated, it cannot be said that politics are not influenced in part by religious considerations. Such toleration in Elizabeth's day would have meant political chaos, as the next century was to show.

Many of the English Protestants who had been in exile during Mary's persecutions now returned. Those who had come to believe that the ceremonies and vestments of the Church were Popish and un-Christian made difficulty for Elizabeth in her effort to unite her people, but those who came back convinced Calvinists were even more dangerous to a settlement of the religious-political question. John Calvin had organized a rigid form of Church government which was to be as independent of the political state as was the Papacy. The Presbyterian system, however, was essentially democratic in that its power rose from the members of each congregation, however humble. There were no bishops, but in some countries as in France the congregations elected representatives to meet in a General Synod, which might become a nation-wide body with its roots among the common people in opposition to the political government which was anything but democratic.

In Scotland, the leading defender of the Calvinistic order was John Knox, and there an organization was formed, including many of the nobility who wished to overturn and seize the property of the bishops of the old order, although the chief strength of the whole movement lay in the peasantry and ordinary people among whom Calvinism took far deeper hold than in England. This may have been in part due to the political outlook of the two peoples, for in Tudor and later England a state Church suited the mass of the citizens better than an independent Church whether ruled by the Pope from above or from democratic laymen in congregations from below.

It also came, in probably larger part, from the discipline of

198

Calvinism which was as austere and rigid as the Church organization itself. Each local church elected lay elders who exercised the most strict supervision over the private lives and morals of the members of the congregation, with power of excommunication for such sins as card playing, singing songs, or profaning the Sabbath with any amusements. This system suited the "dour" character of the Scots but could not possibly have been accepted by the mass of Elizabethan Englishmen whose general nature we shall mention later. The fact, however, that in the same year England returned to Protestantism, and Scotland became deeply Protestant also, although the forms were different, was to be of immense significance in the relations of the two countries so long hostile.

The struggle between Protestantism and Catholicism had become European in scope. To the old political alignments of the Continental powers had been added the religious, though the former retained predominance. In the uneasy balance of powers at the time of the accession of Elizabeth, Scotland by an odd chance was the pivot on which the general situation hung. Spain was still the greatest empire, but Mary Stuart was Queen of Scotland, and soon to become Queen of France by the death of her father-in-law. As we have already said, when she married the Dauphin a secret treaty had been made transferring Scotland to France in case she had no children.

She laid claim also to the throne of England, and when she became Queen of France had quartered the English arms with hers. The age-old danger to England from a Scottish-French alliance was now to be intensified by the union of the two states under one monarch. England seemed to occupy the position of a nut between the two jaws of a cracker. Also she was faced by the two great Catholic powers on the Continent, Spain and France, the latter only twenty miles away across the straits of Dover, the former but sixty because of her possessions in the Netherlands. In fact, however, England had one element of strength which Elizabeth was quick to seize.

Philip of Spain, the husband of the dead Queen Mary of Eng-

land, was Catholic but also he was the most powerful ruler in
Europe, though his domains were scattered. His position would
be lost if the thrones of France, Scotland and England were all
occupied by one ruler. It was therefore to his interest to keep
England independent if he could not win her for himself. Although Elizabeth's brother-in-law, he had offered to marry her
but she well knew from Mary's example and the temper of the
people the danger of a Spanish marriage, though she kept him
dangling as suited her. She also knew that although neither he
nor Henry II of France wished her well neither would allow if
possible the other to gain control of her island kingdom.

Moreover, events were to move with dramatic swiftness. Henry
II was suddenly killed by accident, and it was then that Mary
Queen of Scots became Queen of France as wife of his son, Francis II. Meanwhile, Elizabeth had ended by treaty the war with
France which had been started by her sister, and that country and
Spain made peace soon after. Scotland had been governed by the
young Mary's mother, Mary of Guise as Regent, an ardent Catholic and wholly unsympathetic with the Scotch people. The Lords
of the Congregation, with their peasant followers, had risen
against her, and fearing defeat had called on Elizabeth for aid.

She hesitated for a year but when Mary of Guise gathered a
French army in Scotland and her daughter Mary claimed to be
not only Queen of Scotland and France but of England as well,
Elizabeth sent armed forces by land and sea and captured Leith.
The Scots although willing and grateful allies of the French for
centuries had no wish to become a mere appanage of France, and
Calvinism had also introduced a splitting wedge into the former
union of hearts.

The French, indeed, had become almost as unpopular in Scotland as the Spaniards were in England. At the end of 1560 Francis II died in France, and Catherine de Medicis became Regent
for her young son, the new King Charles IX. As the Regent was
opposed to the Guise faction and jealous of Mary, the young
Queen who had claimed three kingdoms now had to retreat to
the protection of her subjects at Edinburgh. She had lost the

French crown, and the French, after the capture of Leith, had acknowledged Elizabeth's rightful claim to the English one. Mary herself had refused to do so, and therefore had had to make the passage to Scotland by sea as Elizabeth naturally would not allow a claimant to the throne to land in England.

There could be no greater contrast than the two Queens who were now to be in opposition for almost a lifetime. Mary probably had the more delicate nature of the two as she certainly had the more emotional. She could plot and scheme and was even capable of far-reaching plans but could ruin all on one moment's impulse. Elizabeth was harder, although also very womanly. Just about the time of Mary's return to Scotland Elizabeth, indeed, had been guilty of her only real folly over a man. She had allowed the worthless Lord Robert Dudley, son of the hated Earl of Northumberland, to become subject of common gossip in connection with herself. It was even rumored that he would poison his wife, Amy Robsart, and marry Elizabeth.

Whether the Queen really had any intention of marrying him as an English subject should he ever become free to do so it is impossible to say, but when his wife was found dead under suspicious circumstances, Elizabeth at once realized the impossibility of the situation and drew back. If folly there had been, it was the last, and thenceforth Elizabeth used rumors of possible marriage only to serve the purposes of statecraft, though she enjoyed the company of men and possibly was genuinely in love with both Leicester and Essex, in spite of various medical surmises, never proved, as to physical impediments to marriage. Apparently, however, her refusal to marry was based on policy and for the good of the nation.

No such self-denial, however, could control Mary. For the pleasure-loving girl who had not seen Scotland since earliest childhood, the change from Versailles to Holyrood must have been chilling. The moment, whether so chosen or not, for her return was a wise one. Elizabeth had just antagonized a powerful party in Scotland by refusing marriage with the Earl of Arran, and although she had saved the Reformation in that country it was now ready to welcome its own Queen who had ceased not only to be Queen of France but even a factor of importance there. Scottish independence no longer seemed in danger from accepting her, and she apparently readily agreed to the maintenance of the Calvinistic order, although she angered Knox by insisting upon having Mass in her own chapel, and by her love of dancing and other pleasures.

She soon won over most of the nobles to her support in spite of the diatribes of Knox against her, and there was at that time practically no class between the nobility and the peasantry. But she wished to marry again, and having declined Elizabeth's advice, she took as her husband Henry Stuart, Lord Darnley, a man of no intellect and of coarse fiber, a fool in many ways but who was to be the head of the Stuart line in England. Elizabeth urged rebellion, and Mary's illegitimate brother, the Earl of Murray, raised forces but was defeated, and fled to England. Meanwhile Darnley had become suspicious of the relations between his wife and her Italian secretary, David Rizzio. As a relief from her husband and the general life of her court, the Queen may well have found pleasure in the company of the musical and cultivated Latin but it is impossible to say whether Darnley's belief in her infidelity was justified or not.

In any case, the jealous husband entered into a plot and Rizzio was murdered after having sought safety at the Queen's knees. About three months later, Mary had a son, who was to become James VI of Scotland and James I of England. Mary was now in love with the Earl of Bothwell, a coarse, brutal man who would stop at nothing whether his motive was love of the Queen or the desire for power. Both were married, but Mary's husband, Darnley, was got out of the way by being blown up by gunpowder in a lonely house to which he had been enticed, and Bothwell then divorced his wife, and carried Mary off from the palace and married her.

As in the case of many other points in the life of the tragic Queen opinion is divided and it is impossible to say whether she was an accomplice in her husband's murder or not. In any event,

she had no party left in her favor, and when the worthless Bothwell fled to Denmark as an exile she was forced to abdicate, and
having escaped from her captors sought refuge in England
where she threw herself on the protection of Elizabeth, whose
throne she claimed! What to do with her was a problem. She obviously could not be set back on the Scotch throne by force or
allowed to return to France to be the center of intrigue there,
though Elizabeth had no wish to acknowledge the right of subjects to depose their ruler. Mary's case was placed in the hands
of Commissioners who examined the evidence in the Darnley
murder, including the famous "Casket Letters," which form one
of the most noted puzzles in history but which were accepted as
genuine then, and proved the Queen's guilt as an accomplice to
her husband's death. For the rest of her life Mary remained a
prisoner, to make ample trouble.

Meanwhile there had been civil war in France between the
Catholic and Protestant parties, in which England had taken part,
though peace had to be made in 1564 with no gain, and for about
a quarter of a century Elizabeth was to avoid any further military operations on the Continent.

The Queen, as we have said, had tried to find a *via media* in
religion and Church organization which would hold together the
great bulk of her subjects, but she was to encounter difficulty
from both sides. The north of England and the lowlands of Scotland merged into one another, and the great nobles of that section, more particularly the Earls of Westmoreland and Northumberland, held to the old faith and would have been glad to have
replaced Elizabeth by the deposed Mary, whom it was planned
to marry to the Catholic Duke of Norfolk. A rebellion, known to
history as "the rising of the North," occurred in 1569 but was
easily suppressed with the flight of the earls and the execution
of many of their followers.

The earls had taken the road to Scotland, and there, after the
murder of Murray, who had become Regent for the young James,
some of the nobles again conspired to restore Mary to the throne.
The danger to Elizabeth was considerable, for the Catholics of

each country would favor Mary for both thrones, and also as a woman with a son she appeared to others as a safer assurance of peaceable succession than the unmarried and childless Elizabeth. In 1570 the Catholic Church dealt another blow at the English Queen when the Pope, Pius V, excommunicated her and absolved all her subjects from any allegiance.

The question was posed clearly as to who was to rule England: the Pope from Rome or the sovereign named by Parliament. How deadly the struggle was to be was shown even ten years later when Pope Gregory XIII declared in writing to certain conspirators that they would commit no sin if they should assassinate Elizabeth. The letter written in December 1580 by the Cardinal Secretary to the Papal Nuncio in Madrid shows the extent to which the Papacy was and had been willing to go.

Meanwhile, there had been other dangers. France and Spain were stalemated for different reasons. Spain was trying under Alva to destroy the Protestants in the Netherlands by methods so cruel as to rouse the citizens of both religions against her, and had her hands full. In France civil war between Protestants and Catholics had again broken out and although peace was made, even the sovereign did not wish for a Catholic England which might unite with the French Catholic party.

The English Catholics therefore turned to Spain, and through an Italian banker named Ridolfi, in London, corresponded with Alva with the hope that he would send troops to England to head a rebellion which they claimed would be successful. It was planned first to murder the Queen, and Philip of Spain consented to the arrangement. Aware of some but not all of the plot, Elizabeth had been toying with France with the suggestion of marriage with the Duke of Anjou though she had no idea of carrying it through. When her secret service unravelled the details of the conspiracy, the Duke of Norfolk, who had been proposed as Mary's husband, was found implicated and was sent to the block, Parliament calling also for the head of Mary.

The events of these and the immediately succeeding years were pregnant with results of the greatest importance for England and the growth of the Empire. In France, Catherine de Medicis induced her immature and unstable son, Charles IX, who was in favor of the Huguenots, to believe that they were forming a conspiracy against him. The punishment, suddenly let loose, was the terrible massacre of St. Bartholomew, in which Admiral Coligny was one of the many victims. The rank and file of the Huguenots were among the ablest and most industrious craftsmen in many lines in France, and a host of them emigrated to England. This was important in itself, but probably far more so was the fact that they formed to a considerable extent the best seafaring population in France with Coligny at their head. Had he and they been spared to France, that country would have run a far closer naval race with England, which had been slow in starting on the seas. Drake and the other "sea dogs," of whom we shall speak more particularly in the next chapter, might not have pushed England so rapidly on the way to empire had it not been for the massacre of 1572. Another civil war following the death of Charles was also to tie the hands of the French.

These years witnessed the rise of the Dutch Republic and the decrease of Spanish and Catholic power across the sixty miles of the North Sea from England's shores. Spain had largely wasted her seemingly inexhaustible wealth derived from the mines of Mexico and Peru in her vain and brutally stupid oppression of the Netherlands with the result that she was driven out of the whole seventeen provinces. Although the eleven southern and Catholic provinces submitted to the Duke of Parma, the seven northern ones, coastal and chiefly Protestant, united in a republic under the rule of the Prince of Orange, reducing the danger to the Protestant island so near across the water, and influencing English Continental policies in the future.

Danger also threatened England, however, from Ireland. The evil fate which has always hung over Anglo-Irish relations had continued under Mary, who had sent English colonists to take up lands in the Irish counties of Kings and Queens. For long to come, indeed, Ireland, which, like Italy in the nineteenth century, was a "geographical expression" but not a nation, was to be considered as a barbarous land open for colonization much as America was to be, and with the same result that colonists and natives fought each other in wars of extermination. The native chiefs continued also to fight among themselves, and Elizabeth, like preceding sovereigns, had not the resources to complete the conquest or even to maintain order. On the other hand, Ireland was, as always, not only herself an enemy of England but offered a convenient place for the landing and concentration of other enemies who might plan an English invasion.

This danger was increased by the religious situation. The attempt to reform and consolidate the Catholic Church, notable in the proceedings of the Council of Trent (1562–3), had been followed by the formation of the Order of the Jesuits by the Spanish knight, Ignatius Loyola. The primary object of the Order was to gain recruits for the Church, and both the iron discipline maintained and the extraordinary adaptability of its membership to all grades of humanity, from the utter savage to the most cultured, were to give it enormous power and influence. The Irish had been traditionally Catholic though the strength of that faith had declined with the semi-barbarism into which the population of the island had fallen. The coming of the Jesuits, however, marked a great change, and the native Irish tended to become militantly Catholic and were counted upon as allies by the English Catholics in any trouble that might be stirring.

In 1580 the Jesuits also began coming to England, headed by Campion and Parsons, bringing new hope to the Catholic cause there. In the same year Spain was winning against Holland; Philip annexed Portugal and its colonies; and an Italian and Spanish force landed in Ireland. The year before, a smaller force had also landed under authority of the Pope, and although both of these were defeated there was great alarm in England. It was the same year in which the Pope had authorized the assassination of Elizabeth, as now proved by documents but not known then except by the later confessions of the conspirators Tyrrell and Parry, who confessed on the rack and were executed. Two years before, a college had been established at Douai in France for the training of priests, especially for work in England, and these now began to arrive in considerable numbers.

The close relation at that time of religion to politics and the stability of the State was obvious. In England Parliament passed the first of the "Recusancy Laws" which, among other things, laid penalties on those who did not go to services in the Church of England. Campion was tortured and executed while Parsons escaped to plot against the Queen's life, with Philip in Spain and the Duke of Guise in France. In Ireland there was an insurrection under the Earl of Desmond, who was defeated and slain, and it is said that 30,000 Irish died in 1582. In Scotland the Catholic Duke of Lennox had become Regent and influenced the mind of the King, still a child. By 1583 Parma had conquered much of the Dutch Republic for Spain, including important ports on the coast, and an invasion of England by France, Spain and Scotland was planned.

The plot was discovered; the Spanish Ambassador was dismissed from England; and some months later the Prince of Orange was assassinated by orders of the same group who sought the life of Elizabeth. Amid the manifold dangers which surrounded her, the Queen had for some time been using the old device of her possible marriage to divide her enemies, this time the suitor being the French Duc d'Alençon. However, in 1584, he died and the Huguenot Henry of Navarre became heir to the throne of France. As an effect, religious civil war again broke out in that country and it looked as though Philip might dispose of its fate and add its weight to his Spanish empire. The threatened Spanish invasion of England appeared more imminent than ever.

In 1586 a new plot against Elizabeth's life was discovered among a number of young Catholics at her Court, whom she had allowed to remain there, headed by Anthony Babington. The chain of evidence implicated, or appeared to, the Queen of Scots as one of the conspirators. Brought to trial, she was condemned to death and Parliament petitioned Elizabeth to sign the warrant. In spite of real or assumed hesitation she finally did so, and Mary was executed at the castle of Fotheringay in February of the following year. As Mary's Protestant son, James of Scotland, was now next in line of succession to the English throne, England could not be made Catholic by the simple method of assassinating Elizabeth to make way for the Catholic Mary. It could be done only by conquest or revolution and a change of dynasty.

Thus although the danger to Elizabeth's life was lessened, that of invasion increased. There was, however, no fear of revolution. Her own character, hatred of the Spaniards, and detestation of the constant plots against their Queen had all created an intense loyalty to her on the part of the great mass of her subjects. Her chief reliance, as she well knew, would be not only on her people but on their extraordinary power of individual initiative and daring which had grown up during her reign and which she herself had done much to foster. She had never had much money at her disposal and on one occasion had even returned to Parliament a grant which had been made. There was no national army and scarcely a navy but there was a nation full of adventurous men devoted to her and to England and anxious to fight against Spain and the Pope.

At the end of 1584 great numbers had voluntarily joined in an association bound both to defend her and to kill any person implicated in her death, which association Parliament confirmed the next year, when it also banished all Jesuits and seminary priests on pain of death. Elizabeth did, indeed, send a small force to aid the Dutch, under the incompetent Earl of Leicester, but it was characteristic of the period that the glory was won by swarms of young Englishmen, such as Sir Philip Sidney, who went over as independent volunteers.

To a far greater extent this had been notable on the sea, where an undeclared war against Spain had been carried on by individuals, with the connivance and often high approval of the Queen. Drake and others had preyed upon Spanish commerce, especially the rich galleons bringing over the gold and silver from Philip's American possessions, as well as on the Spanish ships passing through the Channel between Spain and the Spanish Netherlands. Various incidents had nearly led to declared war but neither side was ready for that, and according to the customs and international law of the day it was difficult to draw the line between piracy, or private wars between individuals, and acts which could be considered as national, a situation of which other peoples, such as the Dutch, took advantage as well as Elizabeth's English sea rovers.

At last Spain was ready. Philip had claimed the English throne after Mary's death and prepared a fleet for the invasion of England in 1587 which had to be delayed because Drake ran his vessels into Spanish ports destroying so many of the store-ships which were to have accompanied the fleet that it could not sail. The next year, however, what the Spaniards grandly called the Invincible Armada set sail with the plan of going first through the Channel to Flanders where it was to take on Parma's army in addition to the soldiers already on board, who far outnumbered the sailors, and then descend on the English coast to invade the country.

The odds seemed heavily against England although in reality they were far less so than appeared, or as they have often been considered. It is true that the Armada, after many delays, finally put to sea with 130 ships and that the Royal Navy had only 34 which had been increased to 197 by volunteers. Even so the tonnage of the Spanish fleet was nearly double that of the combined English, and the number of men and guns also about double. But the Spanish commander, the Duke of Medina Sidonia, was incompetent, knew it, and was serving against his will.

On the other hand, the English were commanded by Lord Howard of Effingham with such able subordinates as Drake, Hawkins and Frobisher. Both the Spanish ships and tactics belonged to the old style of warfare whereas the English had learned at sea very much the same new methods which they had learned a century and more before in the French wars on land and which had given them the victories of Crecy and Agincourt. The seamanship of the English was also much better and their morale higher.

The English fleet had collected at Plymouth and from there

espied the Armada coming into sight in the Channel on July 19. From that date until August 2 when the last English vessels, short of ammunition, drew off from the Spaniards then in full flight to the north, off the east coast of England, the manœuvring and fighting were constant. On one occasion the Spaniards took refuge in the harbor of Dunkirk but were forced out so suddenly by fire-ships sent among them by the English that they cut their cables and fled, leaving their anchors behind, a loss that was to cost many of them dear. In the flight the formation of the Spanish fleet was lost and it was engaged at one time by all of the English, who carefully avoided getting to such close quarters that they could be grappled and so give the Spaniards the only advantage they possessed. The gunnery of the English was excellent and the carnage on the decks of the Spanish ships crowded with useless soldiers was terrific.

Driven out of the Channel and into the North Sea, they dared not return and attempted to sail back around the north of Scotland. Heavily damaged and without anchors, a violent storm completed the destruction, and the Scottish and west Irish coasts were strewn with wrecks. The disaster was complete although estimates vary as to the number of Spanish vessels eventually reaching their home ports, the figures running all the way from 34 to 60. The island went wild with a joy blended of relief and of an immense increase of national pride and self-reliance. Although the storm had had much to do with the vastness of the destruction, the defeat had been primarily owing to the superiority of the English over the Spaniards at sea, a superiority of which they had already been becoming well aware in the many fights of the earlier undeclared warfare. Henceforth British sailors were to believe in their own invincibility and that Britannia ruled the waves.

In spite of another effort, Spain was in fact beaten, and was also to lose the hope of aid from France. The successive murders of the Duc de Guise and of the King brought Henry of Navarre to the throne, after he had nominally turned Catholic to please the Parisians, and when Philip had tried to intervene the French had clearly shown that they resented Spanish interference almost as much as the English did. Elizabeth had helped Henry with both men and money, and France became the ally of England as against Spain. But if the gravest danger to England from both Spain and Rome was now past there were still difficulties at home, in the religious and Irish problems, which may be touched on briefly before passing to the next chapter in which we have to discuss many aspects of this extraordinary reign which lie outside of the more purely political narrative.

Although the Catholics had taken part in the plots against Elizabeth many had shown their loyalty during the Armada crisis, and indeed Effingham, the head of the fleet, was himself a Catholic. Unfortunately in spite of this the Spanish-Papal record had made so profound an impression on the people at large that the laws against Catholics instead of being softened in the last years of the reign were made more stringent.

The Catholics, however, gave little further trouble, the difficulties arising rather from the more advanced Puritans. Many of these made points of conscience of such matters as vestments and ceremonies which Whitgift considered of slight importance. He believed that the Queen, as Head of the Church, might well decide regarding them, but as there were objectors, and as it was decided that there must be uniformity, the Court of High Commission was erected to deal with those who wished to remain in the Church without conforming. Only clergymen were brought before it but many were deprived of their livings or imprisoned for their refusal to conform.

Although many of the Puritans objected to conformity most of them desired a state Church, and there was therefore less opposition to the steps taken against the new sect of the Separatists or Brownists, as they were also called from their leader, a clergyman named Robert Browne. These Separatists, whom we shall encounter again as an important factor in founding the British Empire in America in the next reign, believed in separating entirely from the national Church instead of trying to reform or alter it, and to govern themselves in their own congregations to which only those should be admitted who met their standards of godliness. Their view was advocated with some violence in the Marprelate Tracts, and the government felt called upon to act against those who advanced the belief that the State had no right to interfere in any way with the religious conscience of the individual.

The world advances slowly, and however true the doctrine might be it could result only, under the conditions of the time, in political and social anarchy rather than in complete religious freedom. This was also the opinion of most contemporary Englishmen, and as the Separatists grew somewhat in numbers and much in their violent denunciation of those who did not agree with them, as is the way of reformers, Parliament passed an Act designed to punish those who should attend private religious meetings instead of the services of the Church, and three of the leading Separatists were even hanged.

The problem of Ireland meanwhile remained as insoluble as ever. The attempt to colonize it had failed for lack of sufficient numbers of English willing to go there, and the Irish themselves at last united under a single leader, Hugh O'Neill, the Earl of Tyrone, to drive the English out. Spain promised aid, but Philip died and it was not until later that his son actually sent troops. In the meantime O'Neill had routed an English army, and it began to look as though Ireland might be lost and become a Spanish-Catholic outpost of Philip III. The Earl of Essex, a favorite of Elizabeth, was despatched to retrieve the situation but failed utterly and, having deserted his post, returned to England leaving the remnants of his army to care for themselves and trusting to Elizabeth's fondness for him to save his own position. It was the Queen and not the woman who confronted him as he rushed into her presence in his soiled travelling clothes without waiting to change, and his dereliction of duty was too serious to be condoned. Imprisoned for some months and then released but not allowed to return to Court he foolishly put himself at the head of a rising against the Queen's ministers rather than the Queen, in his own mind, but with the idea of forcing his own reinstatement. At his trial it was shown that in addition he had been in a treasonable correspondence with James VI of Scotland, and the Queen refusing to be swayed by former affection consented to his execution.

The same year, 1601, Spanish troops at last arrived in Ireland but Lord Mountjoy, who had replaced Essex, was of a different breed and defeated the Spaniards. By 1603, O'Neill and his forces also surrendered, and Ireland was left desolated but thoroughly conquered for the time.

The great Queen, however, was also near her end. All her generation had gone, including her chief dependence, Cecil, who had long since been made Lord Burghley. Friends as well as old foes had gone before her—Philip of Spain, the French Kings, the Queen of Scots, and of late Essex, whose ring she still wore. Thanks to her, the star of England had risen while those of France and Spain had been dimming. England possessed not a town or foot of land on the Continent, but Wales had become fully incorporated, Ireland was conquered, and England and Scotland were but waiting to be at long last peacefully combined under the same monarch, for the Queen had made the Scotch King her heir.

At the beginning of her reign when pressed to marry she had declared that she would have none but the English nation for a husband, living and dying a virgin for its sake. In spite of her marriage projects for policy's sake she had kept her word, and no sovereign had ever served her people more faithfully. The beginnings of overseas empire and the flowering of the rich English life during her long reign must be left for the next chapter, but that reign was almost at its end. As though to symbolize her mystic marriage to her people she had never once removed the coronation ring from her finger but now it had to be sawed off on her dying bed, because, again symbolic, it had grown into her flesh.

Early in the morning of March 24, 1603, the great Queen breathed her last, and the couriers, who had been posted for the purpose along the great North Road, started post haste for Edinburgh to inform King James VI of Scotland that he was also proclaimed King James I of England. The dynasty of the Tudors had ended; that of the Stuarts was to begin. The first had started amid civil war and confusion but had left England at one of its highest pinnacles of glory; the second came peacefully to the throne of a united kingdom but was to end in disaster and disgraceful flight.

CHAPTER X

THE ELIZABETHAN PERIOD

I N SPITE of the fear of a woman monarch it is odd that the two periods of history in which the whole life of the nation soared to higher levels and in which new and glorious prospects were opened, were both periods in which great Queens, Elizabeth and Victoria, sat upon the throne. They were both periods in which, in the main, politics were subordinated to other national activities, and in which from new discoveries and the free play of mind infinite vistas seemed opened for the future of mankind. They were periods of abounding energy and optimism, and of great changes in daily life.

These were the leading characteristics of the "spacious days" of Elizabeth in which England appeared suddenly to have acquired many of the qualities attributed to youth—a dare-devil courage, a spirit of adventure, idealism, love of poetry, and a vast gusto for life itself. As in similar periods of unusual activity and enterprise, there was a seamy side in increasing differences of wealth between rich and poor, in speculation, financial abuses, and unemployment owing to maladjustments in a shifting economic order.

It was not a period, as we have said, of great political interests. It was the Queen herself, with her Councillors, who led the nation into its wider life. During the forty-four and a half years of her reign Parliament was in session only about thirty-five months in all. Yet Elizabeth and her people were one, and if

Parliament did not meet often, its constitutional position was largely maintained, including liberty of speech, freedom of its members from arrest, and other points which had already been gained. There were occasional sharp clashes between the sovereign and the legislature but, on the one hand, the Queen knew when to yield, and on the other there was no serious constitutional crisis because Elizabeth moved steadily in the direction in which both the people and its representatives wished in the main to go. It is difficult to quarrel long or seriously with a person who is helping you to get what you want.

In religious disputes there was also a lull. If the *via media* of Elizabeth's religious settlement could not satisfy the extremists on either fringe, it did satisfy the nation as a whole temporarily, and it was not until well into the next century that the religious storm threatened to wreck the political fabric of government. Men's minds were thus unusually free to turn to the non-political and non-religious concerns of their daily life, and the outburst of energy in other fields was remarkable.

Changes came swiftly, and were not welcomed by all. Those who live in such periods are often ill judges of it, and looking back on it now some of the contemporary estimates seem strangely lacking in both truth and judgment. To us the period is especially notable for the strong personalities it produced, and the height to which personal achievement reached. The roll of the famous is too long to be called, but, to mention only a few names, what a gap would be left in the glory and tradition of England if we had not the Queen herself, Drake, Hawkins, Grenville, Gilbert, Frobisher, Spenser, Raleigh, Francis Bacon, Philip Sidney, Marlowe, Shakespeare, and a host of others!

Yet because oak began to be used in the building of private houses, Harrison, living in the midst of those stirring times, could write of this innovation: "yet see the change, for when our houses were builded of willow, then we had oaken men; but now that our houses are come to be made of oke, our men are not only become willow, but a great manie through Persian delicacie crept in among us altogether of straw, which is a sore alteration." And this but a short time before Drake's famous voyage, and the defeat of the Armada with the humbling of the power of Spain!

The governance of the Tudors, with the exception of the brief Mary-Edward interlude, had been steadily building up the wealth, power and pride of Englishmen, but there had also been other than national influences at work. New discoveries are great liberators of the spirit when times are ripe, and discoveries had come fast both of a forgotten world of mind and art, and of a new world of dazzling material possibilities. The first was due to the Renaissance and its resurrection of the buried civilizations of Greece and Rome. Europe was suddenly—speaking in historical terms of time—brought into direct contact with a world of thought which had been practically unknown to it before, and the mental effect was profound in stirring into life aspects of man's nature which had long been suppressed. The second was due to the exploration and scientific work of such men as Columbus, Magellan, Copernicus and others. Europe ceased to be the known world, and the earth ceased to be the center of the universe. The effect of these discoveries was as profound on men's minds as was that of the classical thought and art and way of life. All together, these things achieved a liberation of spirit, a production of energy, and an optimism unknown before and not to be paralleled until the scientific era of the nineteenth and twentieth centuries.

Englishmen for a while had not taken part in exploration, and for sixty years or so after Henry VII had sent Cabot on his voyage to the new lands in the West nothing important had been undertaken. Englishmen, always in many ways insular even to this day, when they control a quarter of the globe, had been largely outside the main stream of European life. Moreover, although under the fostering care of the Tudors, trade had increased and extended, England had been a small and relatively poor country. Economically her great assets were the cloth and woolen industries, which alone accounted for well over 80 per cent of her total exports of something over £1,000,000. Her merchants were not rich, though steadily growing more so, and the capital of the greatest, estimated by the Venetian Ambassador as some £50,000, compared but shabbily with that of a firm like the Fuggers of Augsburg, who controlled about £875,000, and who possessed a remarkable private news service between the principal commercial centers of Europe.

Capital, however, had been increasing as well as the desire for luxury and wealth, and the importance, as we have pointed out, of the middle class. It was this class, which had always been the special care of the Tudors, that was to make the glory of the Elizabethan period, in trade, war, and literature. By the reign of Elizabeth these people were ready to express themselves and were afforded the opportunity. For England the world suddenly opened and expanded. We may take note first of the explorers, whose object was not scientific but partly curiosity and chiefly trade.

Columbus had discovered the New World in 1492; twenty-seven years later Magellan had passed through the straits which bear his name, and, although he himself died in the Philippines, one of his ships circumnavigated the globe and got back to Spain by way of the Cape of Good Hope. Other explorations had also been in progress, and the Portuguese had rounded Africa and reached India, the East Indies, and even Japan. The Italians likewise had been to the far ends of the earth, but unlike the Spanish and Portuguese made no permanent settlements and established no trading posts. The latter two nations not only made discoveries but claimed all lands found as exclusively their own, though, in fact, with the exception of Japan they did not make use of their discoveries in the East or West north of the latitude of northern Africa. In all this activity the English had taken no part, and had actually been driven even from their Mediterranean trade by pirates. Like Germany some centuries later, England came into the race for markets and colonies only after a large portion of the then known world had already been staked out by others.

The northern part of the globe, however, although in part claimed, was in fact open to discovery and trade, and with the general outburst of English energy from the mid-sixteenth century onward, merchants and explorers turned their attention to that field. Sir Hugh Willoughby, Chancellor, and others rounded the North Cape, Chancellor leaving his ship and travelling overland south to Moscow. Trade was opened, and in the first year of Elizabeth's reign Jenkinson had pushed down the Volga to the Caspian Sea, reaching Khiva and Bokhara. On a later trip he opened relations with Persia, the English thus by this new route getting behind the Hanseatic League merchants in the Russian trade and the Italians in their Persian commerce. The northern Russian trade with the Lapps and others was a valuable one in fish, furs, and oil, though it soon had to be shared with French and Dutch.

New markets whetted the appetite of merchants and adventurers, and men were found who dared the Spanish and Portuguese claims to the south. In 1562 John Hawkins sailed to Portuguese Africa, picked up a cargo of slaves, and sold them in the Spanish West Indies. The African coast was too long to be patrolled by Portuguese ships, and, on the other hand, Spanish island planters were so in need of slaves that in spite of prohibitions they were willing to buy from the English. The voyages were repeated and in 1567 Francis Drake accompanied Hawkins, but the vessels were caught by a Spanish fleet in the harbor of Ulloa and only two escaped, reaching England with famished crews and a lasting hatred of the Spaniards on account of the cruelties the English had seen inflicted.

But Hawkins and Drake had not confined themselves to carrying slaves from prohibited coasts into prohibited harbors. They had attacked and plundered Spanish settlements in the New World. In the previous chapter we noted the relations of England to Spain and the danger in which both Elizabeth and her people stood. Both Protestantism and English independence were threatened. If Spain could not be beaten in open war it was nevertheless important that she be wounded and harassed wherever possible. This was being accomplished by men like Hawkins, Drake and others on the seas and in distant lands where acts of violence did not yet spell declarations of war. They were not pirates nor were they yet quite, as some writers prefer to call them, privateers.

They had no protection from the government and carried their lives in their hands.

Sir Francis Walsingham, whose daring was a balance to Cecil's caution, was in favor of allowing them to do all they could, as was the Queen herself, who shared in the political benefits as well as the plunder. In 1577 a greater coup was planned in which Elizabeth gladly acquiesced. The plan was as novel as it was venturesome. In the Pacific, where no enemy vessels had ever appeared, the Spaniards carried the vast treasures from Peru to the western side of the Isthmus of Panama, whence they were transported by land, and then shipped to Spain.

Drake, with a few ships, was to sail into the forbidden ocean by way of the Straits of Magellan, and to plunder the practically unarmed treasure ships of Spain. This he did, although his own vessel, the *Pelican*, renamed the *Golden Hind*, was the only one to get through the treacherous straits. With less than a hundred men he attacked ports and vessels all up the west coast, and then, loaded down with untold treasure in gold, silver and jewels, he set out for home by circumnavigating the globe. When he rounded the Cape of Good Hope he had but fifty-seven men and three casks of water left, but arrived safely at Plymouth nearly three years from his time of starting. Word of his depredations among the Spaniards had come over the Atlantic long before, and Spain had made loud protests. Had he come back empty-handed, the Queen, to avoid complications, might well have condemned him, but, as it was, after some hesitation she went down to Deptford, whither he had brought his ship, dined on board, and cast defiance at Spain by knighting him on the deck.

Both in the Atlantic and the Pacific the war of the "sea dogs" against the Spaniards continued. Ports and treasure galleons rich with spoil were attacked and looted, and in 1586–88 a Thomas Candish or Cavendish repeated Drake's exploit along the American west coast and of circumnavigation, returning with enormous booty, to be shared with the Queen as usual. With such dazzling successes and the defeat of the Armada, the English spirit rose and England became irrevocably wedded to the sea. After open war had been proclaimed the English continued in more regular fashion to attack Spanish ports in Europe as well as America, and the great "plate fleets" as they sailed to Spain with the products of the American mines. On one occasion, in 1591, about twenty vessels, including six of the Queen's, were lying in wait for the treasure galleons off the Azores when instead of expected galleons the Spanish naval fleet, which had located the English, was suddenly reported as coming with enormous superiority of ships and men. The English were in no condition to fight. Their ships had been damaged in a storm, they were short of provisions and water, and a large part of the crews were ill.

All wisely fled to sea except Sir Richard Grenville on the *Revenge,* who remained to engage the entire force of the Spaniards with but his one vessel and a crew of 190, of whom 90 were incapacitated by sickness, against an estimated 10,000 in the enemy fleet. Grappled by two of the largest Spanish war-ships, he and his men fought through the late afternoon, night, and next morning until the ship was a wreck and her decks shambles covered with blood and dead. Grenville, who had wanted to blow up the vessel rather than surrender, was mortally wounded, and although the Spaniards at last got possession of his ship it was so badly damaged that it sank in a storm which came on. We may say that it was magnificent but that it was not war. Neverthless, it was woven of the stuff of the Elizabethan period, and Grenville became one of the legendary heroes of the British Navy for all time. In the spirit which it helped to foster, the last fight of the *Revenge* has been worth more to England than many a well-planned and glorious victory.

In reading of the exploits of these, the sea-dogs of Elizabeth, our minds instinctively go back to the days of the raids on the coast of England herself of the Danes and Vikings, and we glimpse again that continuity which, in spite of multitudes of varied details, runs throughout the story of the Empire.

Closely interwoven with the Spanish struggle, which was eventually to bring England mastery of the seas and of which we have been able to recount but a few episodes, was the beginning of her empire as contrasted with mere foreign trade. The overland route to India was impracticable for the latter, though several Englishmen traversed it. In the spirit of the age, however, while some men were fighting Spanish monopoly in the West, others were attacking that of Portugal in the Far East, and Sir James Lancaster and Benjamin Wood had both made more or less plundering expeditions round the Cape to Portuguese East Africa and Malacca. In 1600 Lancaster with others received a charter for the first English East India Company and led an expedition to the East India islands, and on a third voyage, 1608, left a factor, or agent, at Surat in India itself. The permanent connection with that country, which was to have such vast results, had begun.

Exploration had also been going on in the extreme north of America in the Arctic wastes which were penetrated by Martin Frobisher, John Davis, and (1610–11) Henry Hudson. As early as 1583 Humphrey Gilbert had taken out a colony to Newfoundland, but was forced to return with all the colonists, he and many of the others being lost in a storm on the way home. Sir Walter Raleigh also essayed colonizing in spite of Spanish claims, but the efforts in Virginia were a failure, and the first permanent settlement there had to wait until 1607. A wild scheme of his to plant a colony in Guiana was also abortive, but if Gilbert and Raleigh both failed for the moment their spirit had shown what Englishmen were soon to attempt successfully. Speaking of planting English colonies in the New World, Gilbert had said that "he is not worthy to live at all that, for fear of danger or death, shunneth his country's service and his own honor," and shortly before his death, with his mind still on America, Raleigh muttered "I shall yet see it an English nation."

By the end of Elizabeth's reign England may have had a population of somewhat less than 5,000,000, and her resources, though increasing, were not yet great enough for her to wrest empire from Spain, which was fortunate. Had she been able to secure the riches of Central and South America, thus diverting her energies from the task now lying directly ahead, the story of the British Empire and perhaps of the British peoples would have been a very different one. It was her great good luck that she was able to save herself from Spain without acquiring its curse of gold.

At home the scene was a busy and picturesque one. Agriculture had deteriorated and a farming village would appear very poor by modern standards. There were no winter crops, practically no effort at drainage, no chemical fertilizers, and no attempt to improve livestock. In many ways the old system of three fields and common lands for grazing and wood worked badly from the standpoint of any agricultural improvement. The manure was scattered over the wide extent of commons and had to be carried by each villager to his own fields. Moreover, the promiscuous mixing of the animals of all the villagers prevented any one individual from trying to improve his own breed. The cow was much smaller than our present ones and not worth as much as a sow. Oxen were more generally used than horses though not fattened for eating. Sheep also were valued for their wool and hides and not as mutton for the table, in spite of the fact that diet consisted largely of meat, with fish legally enforced three days a week, with but few vegetables.

Both farms and villages, often isolated, were largely self-supporting, and the village farmer required almost no cash. Food, clothes and household utensils were chiefly raised or made by each family. An agricultural revolution, however, was under way with disastrous results for many. There was, indeed, something of the same conflict which has been occurring in America, and which we describe as that between farming as a way of life and farming as a business. The old form of village farming with its common land and communal management was unquestionably uneconomic and retarded improved methods. One man or a small group could veto any suggestion of progress.

On the other hand, its common ownership and comparatively simple economy had undoubtedly kept men on the land and protected them from some of the dangers of individual ownership and risk. By this time the old feudal system, with its ties and responsibilities, had gone almost completely. New classes had arisen of free farm laborers, small tenant farmers, and the rich middle class who looked to the land only for money and prestige. Better methods of farming led to improvement but also squeezed those who had not the capital or ability to employ them, and as the tendency became steadily stronger to enlarge and consolidate holdings, as well as to reduce the demand for labor by improved and altered methods, many laborers and small holders were thrown out of employment or turned off of their properties.

The result was a great increase in poverty and unemployment, and the rapid growth of the "sturdy rogues and vagabonds" who infested the countryside. Highwaymen plied their trade on lonely roads or near the larger towns. Whether, as Shakespeare makes him in *Henry IV*, the young heir to the throne of that day had joined in these adventurous if criminal doings is not known, but probably many a young man of good family but scant fortune now did so, and from the great mass of men thrown out of the ordinary functioning of sober society in one way and another—sufferers from what we would call, in current jargon, "technological unemployment"—were recruited many of the men who helped to build the Empire by sea and land, and the colonists of a few years later. Criminal law was severe, and by the close of Elizabeth's reign all felonies, except the theft of less than 12 pence value, were punishable with death, and in a population of less than 5,000,000 some 800 persons were hanged each year. As felony involved forfeiture of property, many refused to plead, thus escaping trial, sentence and loss of estate for their families, but under penalty of being pressed to death under heavy weights.

In 1569 a search was made for "masterless men," which may be considered as a first census of the unemployed as we would call it, and over 13,000 were apprehended. Various poor laws were passed, and much of the legislation remained on the Statute books for nearly two and a half centuries. It is impossible to detail all such legislation of Elizabeth's long reign, but we may note the spirit of it in part by such items as that "vagabonds" were to be "grievously whipped" and burned through the right ear unless they could find some one to keep them in employment for a year; and that among "vagabonds" were included, with many others, all able-bodied persons having no employer or land, or practising no trade or craft, and also those laborers who refused to work at such wages as were customarily given in the places where they lived.

The last point was particularly important as being part of the general official effort to fix both prices and wages, a hang-over from medieval theory and practice which has again become popular in our own day as a new discovery, but which is hoary with age, and has ever in time broken down of its own clumsiness and weight. The children of the poor were cared for by being bound out as apprentices, and some effort was made by levying local taxes to care in other ways for the older poor who could not be quite classified as vagabonds. It is worth noting that usually the House of Lords showed more compassion for the poor than did the Commons, which was to a greater extent made up of the new rich of the middle class.

Although England was still chiefly agricultural, trade and commerce were rapidly expanding, and much of the new wealth, which was building up the luxury of towns and cities and overflowing into the "gentlemen's seats" in the countryside, came from far corners of the earth. The joint-stock company for trading came into great vogue, and usually involved a monopoly of the trade to certain countries. Thus, the Muscovy Company, managed by fifteen directors and with some 160 members, claimed the whole trade of Russia, Armenia, Persia, the Caspian Sea and other sections, and on one occasion managed to raise the price of cordage by 150 per cent by cornering the market. The East India Company, of which we have already spoken, controlled the trade in spices with the Far East, as the Virginia Company, soon to be organized under James I, was to control that in tobacco from America. The Eastland Company monopolized the important Baltic trade, and the Levant Company that with Turkey.

The monopolistic feature of such companies, which were mostly composed of London merchants, aroused much opposition among both Londoners who were outside them and also merchants of other ports such as Bristol. In some cases there was something to be said for complete control of trade. The Levant Company, for example, claimed that to carry on trade at all with Turkey an ambassador had to be maintained at Constantinople and large bribes given to officials. On the other hand, trade profits were large, even if risks were great, and independent merchants insisted on sending their ships regardless of Company claims here and there. In fact, these "interlopers," as they were called, came to do perhaps the bulk of most trades, and the quarrel between monopoly and "free trade" long troubled the political and business worlds of Elizabeth and the Stuarts.

English merchants in many ports were developing an energy and spirit of adventure that would no more stand for exclusion from markets by other Englishmen than by the Spaniards. If Spain's claim to exclusive trade with America was ignored at the sword's point, it was not to be expected that a London firm like Colthurst would quietly accept exclusion from Turkey because the Levant Company demanded it.

Even more than today there was a spirit in the air of resistance to all monopolies. In studying Elizabeth we must always recall that she was, as a sovereign, financially poor with a dislike of heavy direct taxation for her subjects. If the latter point accounts in part for her popularity, the former also accounts for much of the individual initiative developed by the Englishmen of her period. At no time has there been shown a greater loyalty to the nation, but men had to work for it much on their own. Rewards had also, however, to be given, and one method was to grant monopolies of the sale of certain articles. Resentment against this practice steadily rose, and almost at the end of her reign, in the most popular speech she ever made, the Queen yielded.

Although the badness of the unmetalled roads of the day has been often overstated, many of the smaller towns were in fact largely cut off from a general circulation of commerce, though the excellent Ordnance Survey map of seventeenth-century England shows a network of roads connecting the larger places for at least the southern half of the country almost as would a modern railway map. The popularity of the trade fairs, which still continued, was due chiefly to the belief that they in a sense represented free trade and competition, tending to prevent monopolistic practices by local merchants. Most good-sized towns still had one or two fairs a year and some many more. Some of these fairs were confined largely to a few special commodities whilst others were miniature cities, suddenly set up, at which almost any article could be bought, and at which games and all sorts of side-shows had their place, as depicted by Ben Jonson in his play of *Bartholomew Fair* in London. People, especially of the smaller towns, welcomed them for their merry and social aspects as well as for their limitation on local prices.

The medieval price system was indeed beginning to break down. In such matters as foodstuffs, for example, in the days when transportation was difficult a neighborhood had been chiefly dependent on its own local crops, which might vary all the way from famine to overabundance. Not only did many communities try storing in good years against the bad at public cost, but price-fixing was local and fairly simple, as well as necessary. As roads became better, and there was more interchange of goods among communities which became more specialized, the supply became more national and prices less subject to wild local variation as well as more difficult to regulate by authority.

There was also more travel for pleasure or business as roads improved, and in 1572 a posting system was established on the chief routes and, although the government did not carry letters, the public could make use of the system by hiring post horses at the various stations set for them. When the roads were good, about ten miles an hour could be made, and occasionally we learn of remarkable records, as when Sir Robert Carey, posting to Scotland to carry the news of the Queen's death, made 162 miles in less than twenty-four hours.

Although most travel was still by horse or on foot, wagons and carriages were beginning to come into more general use, and the first road- or guide-book was published in 1577. Many of the inns to accommodate travellers were excellent, and the busy and picturesque life of the road began to assume a modern aspect.

Foreign travel for pleasure as well as business also began in the modern sense, not of the wide exploring we spoke of earlier but of the "grand tour" of Europe for sight-seeing and education. Many travelled to Poland, Germany, Austria, France, the Low Countries and Italy, then a congeries of petty states. The last particularly attracted the English, and perhaps Venice, then in its heyday, was the most popular resort.

At home, London was of course incomparably the largest city and the center of national life, with a population by 1600 of perhaps 200,000. The streets were winding, narrow and medieval as yet and the great highway was the river. All used it, the Queen, the Archbishop and the Mayor, as well as the city Companies, in their barges of state, but ordinary folk did likewise. Many of the theatres were on the bankside, and some of the most notable and luxurious of the private palaces and houses, each with its own landing stage and perhaps "water-gate." Boatmen were numerous and played the part to a large extent of the taxi drivers of today or gondoliers in Venice. Even state funerals sometimes followed the river instead of the streets. There were no coaches in use when Elizabeth began her reign but before the end there was so much congestion of street traffic due to these and other vehicles that complaint was as loud as in our own time. There were crowds and noise, and perhaps the outdoor life was more Continental than before or since, with open-air puppet shows and various exhibitions, venders, itinerant or fixed, of all sorts of goods, making use of the cries which were long to remain characteristic and some of which may be heard even now in the town.

At no other time, unless possibly in the eighteenth century, has the dress, especially of men, been more luxurious or extravagant both in style and cost, and the variety of color and costume from the satins, velvets, laces and brocades of the rich down to the coarse cloth and leather of the workmen, set against the Elizabethan architectural background, must have yielded a kaleidoscopic succession of extraordinarily interesting and often beautiful scenes. The love of such effects is a lasting element in the English character and taste, as we noted in the Introduction, and whereas other nations for the most part, even the Oriental with their former love of color, costume and pageantry, have come to be content with modern motor cars, dark and individually indistinguishable clothes for men, the English still love the gorgeousness of a state procession with the monarch riding in a glass and golden coach, the old costumes, and such shows as are staged on Lord Mayor's day, or the profoundly moving pageant of a coronation in the Abbey. Today such things are loved not only for themselves but also because, as I have said before, they symbolize the unity and history and all the past victories, glories and aspirations of the race, but there was little historical sense in the days of Elizabeth and all these things were then liked and indulged in with a simple and naive pleasure in themselves with no mystical over-tones.

A rather odd exception was in the theatres of the period in which no scenery was used though costume was. In countries where the color and pageantry of daily life have been discarded, the theatre and opera have become their last retreat but in Elizabethan playhouses the stage contained nothing more colorful than sign posts stating where the scene was supposed to be laid. The earlier plays of the period were given in inn yards, open to the air above, and often surrounded by a gallery where spectators could sit, as well as at room windows or in the yard itself. Soon, with the growing popularity of the theatre, many buildings were erected especially for the purpose, among the most famous of a dozen or so being the "Globe." These were patterned largely on the conditions of the former inn yards, and to a great extent the modern theatre has continued the same arrangement, except that the stage of the Elizabethan theatre, instead of forming the groundwork for the making of a picture at which all look from the same front direction through the proscenium, then jutted out into the audience, which surrounded it on at least three sides, an arrangement which may have delayed the use of scenery.

London was also notable for its unusual number of private gardens, as it is still of all great cities the greenest and most rural. The Londoner loves not only his parks, which are kept as rural and as little formal in aspect as possible, but also his own garden. This love of flower gardens largely dates from the Elizabethan period, and during it the flower garden took its permanent and lastingly important place beside the earlier kitchen-garden and orchard. It may be that, as Bacon, one of the characteristic minds of the reigns of Elizabeth and the first Stuart, said in his essay, *Of Gardens:* "God Almightie first Planted a Garden. And indeed, it is the purest of Humane pleasures," but in the sense of flower gardens it was about this time that Englishmen first began to plant them. Just as on the American frontiers there was no time or energy for flowers, so the life of England had not lent itself before to such delight, but the more settled conditions and, for many, increasing wealth and leisure led the way to what soon became a lasting English passion.

These factors also affected the architecture and life in the homes of both town and country. New, and in many cases great, houses sprang up throughout the whole country. There was in general, for those who could afford it, a large increase in both the number and diversified use of rooms which indicated an increase not only in luxury and wealth but also in the refinement of taste. Thus we find the "winter parlor," placed near the kitchen for warmth; the characteristic long gallery; the drawing room; breakfast room; studies and libraries. A definite break was made with the old tradition of fortified or semi-fortified houses or castles, and homes no longer whispered of fear of war and sudden attack.

The "home," which is so essentially English, may almost be said to date from this period, and in fact almost all of the building was domestic in character, scarcely a single church dating from Elizabeth's reign, and the only new large edifice for public use was the Royal Exchange, built for business purposes and opened by the Queen herself, both facts indicating the rise of commerce as one of the leading factors in national life. The mediæval buildings had been very irregular in style and plan, a room or window being placed here or there as internal convenience dictated without regard to outward symmetry, though the effect was often extremely picturesque and what we consider essentially English. During the earlier part of the period this irregularity was continued even in such great places as Knole, Penshurst and Haddon Hall, but in the later years the Italian and classical influence came to be felt, perhaps due in part to the increased travel to Italy.

From the combination of the mediæval, Gothic and classical styles we get magnificent examples of great houses, as well as smaller, which if less indigenously English are no less typically so, for no one can mistake an Elizabethan great house or manor house for anything anywhere on the continent. The general plan became more or less standardized and was usually in the form of the letter H or E, the house following the lines of the letters with open courts between. Outward symmetry was aimed at and the architects had no small task in fitting the rooms called for within into the new and more regular outward framework of these new houses. Some of the largest examples were the royal palace of Nonesuch, Longleat, Hardwick Hall, and Holdenby House. The latter had a frontage of 410 feet, and like all the newer houses was full of windows, which now also became glazed, glass having previously been almost exclusively used only in churches, and stained not clear. Bacon, indeed, complained that houses had become "so full of Glasse, that one cannot tell, where to become, to be out of the Sunne, or Cold." For this reason he advocated bay windows, not only to keep off the wind and sun to some extent from the room but also because "they bee Prettie Retiring Places for Conference."

Another new feature was the broad wooden staircase, often extremely elaborate as to balustrades and carvings, such as that at Hatfield House, and which suddenly replaced at this time, with no intervening adaptation, the inevitable circular and narrow stair, like that in a church tower, of all previous building. The latter had been useful for defense in case of attack, and had lingered on, but for social purposes the change was immense, and the gorgeously dressed company moving up or down one of the new stairs must have been a pageant in itself.

The larger houses were almost bewildering in their size, the plan of Holdenby House, for example, showing nearly sixty rooms on the ground floor alone, while the earlier Knole House, built and rebuilt, with its inner courts, covers several acres. The permanent household establishment, consisting of family, dependents and servants, almost equalled the old feudal Baron's army of retainers, to say nothing of the stream of guests, and of poor at the gates. The cost of maintaining such places must have been very great, especially when the owner was honored by the Queen and her train on her constant "progresses." Lord Burghley, for example, entertained her twelve times at his place, Theobalds, at a cost each time of from £2000 to £3000 or in money value today of from £10,000 to £15,000.

In the life of the day, manners, though they had improved in refinement, were still coarse, and even the Queen herself could spit at a courtier to show her dislike of his clothes, box the ears of another, use vulgar language and whip out tremendous oaths. Her example set the style and for those who are ever railing at the follies of their own generation it may be interesting to note that because the Queen was pale and slim, women, wishing to be like her, ate gravel, ashes and, as a contemporary complained, "to get a straight spagnolised [slim, Spanish-shaped] body what pinching, what girding, what cingling will they not endure?" Sanitary arrangements were extremely crude and bathing infrequent, which accounts for the demand for perfumes. In the larger houses the family and guests had their meals at one table and the servants at a lower one in the same room. There is no record of tooth brushes for another half century. Forks were not used and in Scotland even the knives were often cannily chained to the table. The floors of many of the smaller houses were still covered only with rushes. Soap was a luxury and clothes were washed with cow-dung and other substitutes, in rivers and even in wells. In cities, slops and the refuse from water-closets were often thrown out of the front windows into the streets, already made filthy by the constant horse travel. The plagues which from time to time took their appalling toll of victims came in no small measure from lack of medical knowledge and sanitation. In spite of the enormous growth of luxury and expense, life was still incredibly crude in many ways.

Yet all this motley life, with its sea dogs, its freebooters and merchant adventurers, its rogues and vagabonds, its coarseness and extravagances, brought forth from it all the highest achievements in the entire range of English literature and thought. Before considering this we may note briefly some of the other arts. Somewhat oddly, the new wealth, as well as the rise of the new merchant and middle class, had no such effect on painting as similar developments had in other countries such as Italy and Holland. The English mercantile new-rich preferred to lavish their money on furniture and plate, and cared nothing for pictures except portraits. For the most part even these were painted by such foreigners as Holbein who to some extent became domesticated in England.

The furniture was excellent in type and much of it of almost incredible cost. The "great bed" in larger houses often cost over £1000 in money value of our period, while that at Knole House, specially made for James I some years after Elizabeth's death, hung with embroidered cloth of gold, cost the almost incredible sum of £40,000, our money. The constant stream of gold and silver from America into Europe had made it possible for silver plate to appear even in the houses of some farmers, and in technique and design the plate of all sorts of this period surpasses possibly that of all others. In this art, the English were abreast of the best in Europe.

In music also there suddenly came a rapid advance after the decline of preceding reigns, and especially in secular music England equalled, if it did not in fact surpass, other countries. It was not socially nurtured but a genuine national and folk movement which came upward from the masses of the people, until England came to be called a nest of singing birds. It has been estimated that there are some 420 references to music or song in Shakespeare's plays alone. Among the leading composers were William Byrd and Orlando Gibbons, but there was a host of others, and so excellent and popular did English music become that many English musicians, singly or in companies, appeared in many of the Continental cities, including those of Germany.

But beyond all the other glories of Elizabeth's reign was the sudden and extraordinary development of literature, which marks it forever as one of the great periods in the entire history of man's intellectual and artistic rise. We do not know what brings such periods into being, for any of the arts, but some of the essentials would appear to be abounding energy, the stirring of imagination by new experiences, of ambition, pride and self-confidence developed by engaging in new and high enterprises, and in general a sense of the possible greatness of the individual. Many of these factors, as they had been present and active in the flowering period of Greece, were also present in the England of Elizabeth. They do not explain all, but they help us to understand. The Renaissance and the Reformation were tremendous forces for the liberation of man's mind and spirit in all the countries which they touched, as were the new discoveries which gave views of a new world and a new universe, and seemed to open boundless vistas of opportunity undreamed of before.

But in England there were also other more national forces at work. Largely under the wise guidance of the Queen, the little nation found itself becoming a great one, a chief defender in the world of the new Protestant faith, and able also to stand forth boldly and oppose the whole power of the world's mightiest Empire, Catholic Spain. An intense wave of nationalism and patriotism, of profound love for England, a willingness to sacrifice all for the cause of Queen and country, swept over the nation. Moreover, partly because of policy and partly of necessity, Elizabeth had liberated the people's energies by forcing them to take the risks and win the glories of acting for the nation as individuals, and not merely as officers or men in the great machines of national armies or navies. Great prizes were to be won in both war and trade, and from all these causes individuals suddenly felt stirring in the air about them the wings of a great freedom. With causes to fight for, prizes to win, and encouraged to be themselves to the limit of their ability and daring, life became a high adventure that stirred men's blood and minds, as it never can in a people nursed and coddled by government at every turn.

It is this sense that stamps the greater part of the literature of the period, which is surprisingly little concerned with either politics or religion but with human nature itself and the adventure of living. That is one reason why it is vibrant and belongs to the ages and not to a period. There was action and reaction. English life and character formed the literature, and in turn that has ever since influenced the life and character of the people. It is amazing, with so much forgotten in between, how the words and thoughts of these Elizabethan writers are woven into our everyday speech and thought today even of persons who have no idea of their sources. Many of these writers lived on into the reign of James, but the period is well called by the name of the Queen, as practically all the leaders were born and most had got well started on their work while she was still the living inspiration of the nation.

It is impossible here to detail the richness of the literary output of the last twenty years of Elizabeth and the early years of James, and we can do scarcely more than catalogue the illustrious names. First, however, we may anticipate a few years by speaking of the King James's Version of the Bible, authorized in 1611. Its beautiful, stately and marvellously modulated prose, in addition to the fact that it was the Bible, was to bind the English-speaking peoples throughout all the later Empire and elsewhere together by the subtle influence of deeply felt thought and language. Far below any surface differences, the possession in common of the finest expression of the depths of their spiritual lives was a cementing force beyond computation. Its influence on the language has been equally great. In the *Pilgrim's Progress* of Bunyan, which we shall mention in a later chapter, its phrases were to constitute almost the entire language in which was written the book that in popularity and religious influence has been second only to the Bible itself. And we must also remember the millions of common men who never wrote but whose language and expression have acquired a simple beauty and dignity from their constant reading of the work of the little band of scholars who gave to the English people a version of the most widely read and distributed book in the world, which version was to be the only one used for over three centuries.

Turning back to the earlier part of the period we have to note that in prose we have the great collections of voyages made by Hakluyt and later by Purchas, the former in particular being a great sea saga for the English race, which must have had a profound influence in turning the thoughts of many a youth to gallant adventure. Hakluyt opened the world to them and in a style which occasionally reaches the very highest levels of English prose.

The rather sudden development of prose is, indeed, one of the features of the period. There had been, up to this time, no such thing as good English prose but Thomas Hooker, in his *Ecclesiastical Polity*, and Bacon in his *Essays* gave it rhythm, dignity, and clarity. Bacon, indeed, still had the feeling that he should write in Latin but he did perhaps more for English prose than any one else, and after more than three centuries few volumes of essays can be more widely read than his. This is the more notable because he was the first to introduce the literary form of the essay which in spite of the rise and fall of other forms, such as the drama and novel in various periods, has never lost its special appeal. It is rare indeed, however, that the inventor of a new form retains his popularity through the centuries in competition with later writers who have all the advantages of new topics and a perfected instrument of expression. The fact attests the depth and soundness as well as the universality of Bacon's thought.

A little earlier Ascham had published his *Schoolmaster*, Foxe his *Book of Martyrs*, Lyly his tedious *Euphues*, and Sidney his *Arcadia* and *Defence of Poesie*, but none of these had shown the possibilities of prose as a literary medium. Chroniclers like Holinshed and Stowe were of value only for their historical facts, although it is noteworthy that Holinshed provided the great Elizabethan dramatists with much of the material for their plots.

The especial glory of the period lay in its poetry and drama, which alone seemed capable of allowing the glowing exuberance of the age full expression. Among the poets the greatest was Edmund Spenser, called "the poets' poet." His most notable work, the *Faerie Queene*, an immense allegory, contains some of the finest poetry in the language, but on account of both its length and its allegorical form is probably less generally read now than such shorter pieces as his *Shepherd's Calendar*, *Astrophel*, the *Epithalamium* and some of the sonnets. No other writer, however, not even Chaucer or Shakespeare, has had such a deep and lasting influence on English poetry. This was to be particularly discernible, though it had been continuing, in the revival of his work late in the eighteenth century, which was the immediate cause, to a large extent, of the development of the romantic movement in literature in the next three generations. Few now, except students of literature, read the historical poets such as Warner, Drayton or Daniel, but the songs and lyrics of the period are still a priceless possession, and many of those by Campion, Lyly, Peele, Raleigh, Greene, Ben Jonson and others, with Shakespeare at the head, are still constantly read and sung. Who does not know such a rollicking song as Bishop Still's "I cannot eat but little meat," or Dyer's "My mind to me a kingdom is," or Marlowe's "Come live with me and be my love," or Jonson's "Drink to me only with thine eyes"; and a host of others? We shall speak in a moment of the intense English quality of Shakespeare, the greatest English dramatist of all and perhaps of the world. It is to be noted here, however, that English drama itself, differing profoundly as it does from the Greek, French and others, was a distinctive national development stemming straight from the Miracle Plays of the medieval period already mentioned. Unlike the French Mystery Plays which dealt chiefly with the lives of the Saints, the Miracle Plays, presented in homely language and in a homely way, often with an abundance of rough English humor, were based on stories from the Bible, and were the direct precursors in their technique and character of the later secular plays.

So prolific was the production of notable dramatic works in the

Elizabethan and early Stuart periods that we can scarcely do more than call the partial roll of their authors.

First comes the group known as the "university wits," Kyd, Nash, Lodge, Peele, Greene, and greatest among them Marlowe, most of whom died young, and who used to meet and carouse in the taverns which were then used much like clubs. Marlowe, killed in a brawl at twenty-nine, could write in his *Tamburlaine, Jew of Malta,* or *Edward II* much mere gorgeous bombast but also in such poems as *Hero and Leander* and passages in his dramas, poetry which for sheer beauty and imagination must rank him with Spenser and Shakespeare. Who can ever forget, for example, the impassioned address of his Doctor Faustus to the vision of Helen of Troy when conjured before him?

> Was this the face that launched a thousand ships,
> And burnt the topless towers of Ilium?
> Sweet Helen, make me immortal with a kiss.
> Her lips suck forth my soul: see, where it flies.
>
> O, thou art fairer than the evening air,
> Clad in the beauty of a thousand stars.

Among others who belong to the Elizabethan-Jacobean period may be mentioned Beaumont and Fletcher—who worked so closely together that their names are indissolubly linked—George Chapman, John Marston, Thomas Dekker, John Webster, Cyril Tourneur, Thomas Heywood, Thomas Middleton, and greatest of all, before we come to Shakespeare, "rare Ben Jonson." The last was probably the most learned of all the dramatists but his most popular plays were comedies dealing with the characters and life of the London he knew so well, such as *Every Man in His Humour, The Silent Woman* and *The Alchemist.*

Drama was then the accepted literary form, as the novel was to become in our own day, and certainly few generations could ever claim such a brilliant galaxy of writers in any form as those named above. They also were of their age in that they experimented in every direction, were filled with energy, and had the dash and spirit of adventure characteristic of the period. Even the learned Jonson could carouse and engage with Shakespeare himself in a tavern combat of wits. Without the latter the age would have been one of the great ones in the history of all literatures but with him it became incomparable.

Of the facts of his outward life surprisingly little is known, so little for so great a figure that from time to time lovers of puzzles deny that he was the author of his own works and assign them to Bacon, the Earl of Oxford or others. Born at Stratford in 1564 he came to London where he became gradually actor, a maker-over of old plays, a theatrical manager and owner, and finally the greatest dramatist of all time, retiring to his native village with a comfortable fortune to die there in 1611. There is a larger literature about him in all languages than about any other world author, estimated, I believe, at some 30,000 volumes, and it is not necessary to speak in detail of his work. We may say that it was divided between his miscellaneous poems, his sonnets, and the immortal plays.

No other writer has ever so fully comprehended the entire range of human nature, with the exception of religion, and his plays are a world in themselves. If as he wrote, "All the world's a stage," it is no less true that his stage is almost all the world. Although universal, he is also deeply English, and writing for all time, he also depicts his own as in a mirror. His supreme interest is in human nature in all its manifestations, and his historical plays contain great character studies rather than the details of accurate history. In *King John*, for example, he does not even mention Magna Carta. But his work, shot through with a passionate love for England, has been of incalculable influence in building up the English legend of devotion and glory. It has also been a profound unifier of thought and language for all those throughout the world who speak his tongue. After three centuries his very phrases drop daily from the lips of thousands without even the realization of quotation.

To illustrate the depth and nature of his feeling for his native island, a feeling which his words have transmitted to untold millions of his fellow-countrymen since, we can make but one quotation from the vast abundance available. In *Richard II* he puts the following into the dialogue between Lancaster and York as the former is speaking of England:

> This royal throne of kings, this sceptred isle,
> This earth of majesty, this seat of Mars,
> This other Eden, demi-paradise,
> This fortress built by Nature for herself
> Against infection and the hand of war,
> This happy breed of men, this little world,
> This precious stone set in the silver sea,
> Which serves it in the office of a wall
> Or as a moat defensive to a house,
> Against the envy of less happier lands,
> This blessed plot, this earth, this realm, this England.

In this impassioned apostrophe how many traits we find which have by this time in our story come to be English! "This sceptred isle." History is filled with monarchies but in no other case has the feeling of the nation towards the Crown been what it has been and is in England and the later Empire. Elsewhere kings have been individual rulers, good or bad, but in no other country has the Crown, as symbol, gathered to itself all of which I spoke in the Introduction. The adjective "sceptred" has a subtle sense of rightness in the above lines though it would mean nothing if applied to the other kingdoms of Europe. Again, we have the sense of England as a world apart, happy in being so, and desiring not to mix with others, but to separate and defend itself from war and the "infection" of foreign lands and ways. Its unique position, which lasted for some centuries, as protected by the Channel and the seas, has by Shakespeare's time already sunk deep into the sub-consciousness of its people. Above all, there is the hot glowing love of "this other Eden," the new garden set apart from the rest of the world for happy and contented men to dwell in, a passion which lies deep and usually mute in the breasts of all Englishmen. It is a wholly different feeling from that of the Frenchman for his individual patch of soil or for "la gloire" of the "nation." Impossible to analyze, like so much else that is English, it finds its expression in Shakespeare and the others who have created that priceless treasure of garnered poetry which, with liberty, law and self-government, has been the incomparable gift to the world of the "nation of shop-keepers."

CHAPTER XI

THE FIRST OF THE STUARTS

SHAKESPEARE and many of the others whom we have mentioned in the preceding chapter lived on into the reign of James and some of their finest work may be called Jacobean rather than Elizabethan. However, although not only in literature but in some other aspects life may have seemed to continue to flow for a few years in its accustomed channels following the death of the great Queen, in reality there was a vast chasm in English life between the Tudor and Stuart periods, and between the sixteenth and seventeenth centuries.

The keynote of the latter was rebellion against authority and old ways. As history flows steadily on, every period is in a sense a transitional one. The earlier century had been a transition from the remnants of the feudal period to a more modern outlook, and as instruments of the process strong monarchs had been essential. England was singularly fortunate to have at her head for a large part of the period the two Henrys and Elizabeth who thoroughly understood the needs of the people and the times and who in return received almost king-worship from the Englishmen whom they were leading in the direction in which they wished to go.

The very forces, however, which were in motion and which the Tudors had done not a little to foster, such as the rise of the middle class, could not stop in their course. England was moving on to something different, and although the divine right of kings reached its highest point under Charles and James, the people instinctively felt that that was not and could not be the constitutional settlement of the problem of government. Just as in the field of religion they were to work toward greater toleration, and in the field of thought toward a greater freedom, so in politics they were groping for increased control over their own destinies. The "Tudor despotisms" had worked well and popularly but even a continued line of Tudors might not have been able to settle the constitutional problem without a struggle. The time had gone by for such great extent of personal government as they had wielded, and yet Parliament had not developed into the instrument for popular government which it was in time to become. Nor had the modern idea of a Cabinet, which should be the link to hold together a constitutional monarch and a popular Parliament, been discovered.

The English do not discover political ideas. They grow into them by slow processes, and it was to take a century and a half or more really to solve the problem which faced the Stuarts and their subjects. How strong the popular forces were, more or less blindly working toward a new organization of the Constitution, is shown by the fact that the nation went through civil war, the experiment of a republic, a dictatorship, restoration of monarchy, and a later revolution before even a working basis, on which to build again, slowly was found. Monarchs with the political sagacity and popular understanding of the Tudors would undoubtedly have eased the process, but there is not much use in considering *if's* in history, and with Stuarts on the throne an appeal to force became inevitable.

However, when James made his leisurely journey from the gloom of Holyrood Palace to London the people were inclined to receive him without misgiving. For one thing, it was much that the succession to the throne had passed peacefully to a legitimate heir who in turn had a male heir to continue it. He was learned, though in a pedantic fashion, reasonably good natured, and not, according to his own views, bent on playing the tyrant, but rather on continuing the Elizabethan form of government. Freedom and self-government in the new America about to be founded were to owe not a little to the political liberality of the charters granted by James, as religious toleration was later to be forced on Massachusetts by the second Charles. Unfortunately for the Stuarts and perhaps for England, the constitutional crisis I have mentioned was inevitable in their reigns, and they were not the type of men who could guide the struggle or help the nation to ride out the storm.

James had never lived in England and knew little of the character and motives of Englishmen, while his son, who did live there, knew even less and learned nothing. Trouble started almost immediately on James's arrival but before giving details we may note that there was one continuing source of evil in the Stuart line which was bound to poison all their relations with the nation. That was their belief in Divine Right. James believed that he owed duties to his subjects but that he alone was to judge of what was best and be the fount of law for them. He considered kings as "God's lieutenants on earth," and that their laws and orders should be accepted as implicitly as the revealed word of God Himself. They should not be bound by Parliament or laws but be laws unto themselves. Such a doctrine could not fail to bring on violent collision with the increasing desire for self-government on the part of the people. James, however, despised the people with all the fervor of a man who believed himself a God on earth and had an inordinately vain conceit of his own scanty wisdom.

Above all, James lacked that marvellous tact which Elizabeth had possessed even though she had had to a great extent as exalted an idea of her own position and power as had her successor. She, however, like her father, had always known to a hair's breadth how far she could go in asserting herself and still retain her people's good will and loyalty. James had no such sensitiveness in statesmanship, and also came to the throne with none of that devotion toward his own person or House which the nation had come to feel for the Tudors. The Scots were not popular and the new marriage between monarch and people was one of convenience and not of love. Accepted with a show of good feeling, he would none the less have to walk warily.

One of the first acts of the new King, who had continued Elizabeth's Secretary of State, Sir Robert Cecil, in office, was to make peace with Spain, and to imprison Sir Walter Raleigh, who had been one of the leaders of the war party, in the Tower, instead of imposing the death sentence for treason which had been passed upon him. The peace treaty was unpopular with the people at large on religious grounds and with the mercantile classes on account of business. Spain's ships and her colonial possessions overseas could no longer be profitable and legitimate objects of attack.

In Elizabeth's day even when the government was not technically at war in Europe, the exploits of men like Drake "beyond the line" on or across the Atlantic were looked upon with favor and received a certain amount of support, but this was not so under James, and although individuals continued to wage war the Elizabethan "sea dog" tended, because of his illegal and unrecognized status, to degenerate into a mere freebooter and pirate. Moreover, the first Stuart did not recognize England's destiny on the sea, and, for the most part, neglected the navy. In view of these facts, so different from the attitude of Elizabeth, English seamen felt no loyalty to the new dynasty, which was thwarting instead of forwarding one of the strongest tendencies in the changing life of the nation.

Another tendency was the increasing devotion to Protestantism, which, among many, was devotion to Puritanism. Either there would have to be increasing toleration of those outside the national Church or that Church would have to become broader. An opportunity and a decision were promptly forced upon James. The Millenary Petition, so called because it was intended to be signed by a thousand Puritan clergy, was presented to him asking that they be excused from wearing a surplice and from certain other practices in the Church without having to separate from it entirely.

A conference between some of the bishops and Puritan clergy was called at Hampton Court, with James presiding, to discuss the problem. If the King knew little of England he knew much of Scotland, and he feared the possible setting up of a Presbyterian form of Church government. In the course of the conference he made his famous statement of "No Bishop, no King," and also said in anger that if all the clergy did not conform precisely to the regulations laid down by the bishops and Church he would "harry them out of the land." Before long, some 300 were turned out of their livings, and it was evident that in England there would be no toleration of difference of opinion even on minor matters either within or without the Church. Hence, control of government, but more immediately of the Church, became a matter of prime importance which was certain more and more to involve the passions of the people.

The King also became embroiled with the Roman Catholics. In 1604 he banished the priests from London, and the next year reimposed the fines on the Catholic laity which he had previously remitted. Resentment took the form of a plot, headed by a Robert Catesby, to blow up the House of Parliament at the opening of the session when the King and his two sons would be present. The work of placing the barrels of gunpowder in the cellar was in charge of Guy Fawkes, and all was ready for the perpetration of the horror, November 5, 1605, when the plot was revealed, and all those involved were seized and executed.

The King, nevertheless, became more and more unpopular. His plan for a union of England and Scotland, consisting of more than the mere union of the Crowns and involving the naturalization of all Scotchmen in England, and of free trade between the two countries, aroused much resentment. There were also constant quarrels between James and Parliament over the grants of money. He also increased the hatred of the Irish by trying to alter the customary relations of the chiefs to their tribes, and by ignoring the Irish land laws. When two chiefs, heads of the clans of O'Neill and O'Donnell, fled into exile in Spain, James confiscated six counties, which did not belong to them but to their clans, and peopled them with Scotch and English settlers. The Irish troubles called for more money from the Crown which was already in desperate straits.

In connection with what was at the time a somewhat minor source of revenue, the imposition of import duties on currants, an interesting case arose which may be considered as later leading up to part of the discussion between England and the American colonies before the Revolution in the next century. A merchant, John Bate, denied that the King had the right to levy the duty which could be levied legally only by Parliament. In the Court of Exchequer the judges decided that the duty was levied to regulate trade and that there was a distinction between such a duty and one merely to raise money. As the Crown had complete control of foreign relations, such a duty was part of the prerogative. Although James at once made use of the decision to increase his revenue without recourse to Parliament, his needs required that he ask for more.

There were various causes for this, and we have already mentioned the lavish grants to individuals of the Church lands by Henry VIII. In addition, among difficulties which the King had to face, there had been a large rise in prices, felt universally, which correspondingly reduced the purchasing power of the royal as well as all private incomes. Apart from their own characters, the key to the story of the Stuarts, their troubles with Parliament, their dependence on France, and the other facts we shall have to note, may be found largely in a study of their financial problems, for which they were themselves in considerable part, but not wholly, to blame.

In 1611 negotiations with Parliament for straightening out the royal finances were in progress when James angrily decided to dissolve it, and for three years he ruled without calling another together.

He was no more successful with the so-called "Addled Parliament" of 1614, which he likewise dissolved because it would grant no supplies unless he would restore the clergy ejected in 1604 and make certain reforms. Meanwhile, favoritism and corruption around the Court increased, and the King raised, or allowed money to be raised, by every means while declining to call Parliament. He created the new order of baronets, making each receiving the title pay over £1000 a year for three years. He also sold peerages, and offices. In 1620 the new Lord Treasurer had to pay £20,000 for the post.

Monopolies of all sorts which raised the cost of living were granted in order to support Buckingham and other favorites. James not only did nothing to make himself popular but on the contrary continued to increase the demands of his own prerogative rights, saying that it was presumption for any subject to suggest what a king could or could not do, and even holding, in 1616, that it was his duty, "a thing regal and proper to a king to keep every court within its true bounds," and to see that judges did not break the law as conceived by the monarch.

Moreover, events on the continent leading up to the Thirty Years' War were bringing him to adopt a pro-Spanish policy to protect the lands of his son-in-law in the Palatinate, and he was considering the marriage of his son Charles to the daughter of the King of Spain, both intensely distasteful policies to England. Meanwhile other episodes had added to the King's unpopularity, such as the unsavory murder of Sir Thomas Overbury by the Countess of Essex who had obtained an annulment of her marriage to Essex to marry James's favorite Rochester. Overbury had tried to prevent the marriage, and when both Rochester and his new Countess were convicted of poisoning him James pardoned them, and the popular reverence for royalty was immensely lowered at the very time that James was trying to exalt its godlike nature.

The dismissal from office of Chief Justice Coke, who had done more than any other judge to uphold the common law, because he disagreed with the King also aroused great resentment.

Finally Parliament had to be summoned and met in 1621, at once taking up the question of various abuses. Among these were certain monopolies in favor of Buckingham, which the King had to recall. The Commons next attacked Francis Bacon who had become Lord Chancellor, supported the monopolies, and was now found guilty of having taken what were practically bribes before giving judgment in cases before him. He was dismissed from office, fined and imprisoned. Then the Commons proceeded to petition the King that his son might marry a Protestant, and indicated that they wanted war and not marriage with Spain. When James denied their right to discuss matters on which their advice had not been asked, they entered on their minutes an assertion of their right to discuss any public matter. James tore the passage from the page, and dissolved his third Parliament, which had granted him nothing.

On the other hand, another aspect of the struggle between the King and Parliament has to be considered. The latter was by no means representative of the nation as a whole. That had to wait until the great democratic changes in the nineteenth and even twentieth centuries. It had, in the days of James and Charles, become plutocratic, and to a large extent was working for the selfish interests of its own members. From one standpoint the contest was between prerogative on the part of the King, and privilege on the part of Parliament. Outside the ring in which this fight was taking place stood the great mass of ordinary people who had gladly accepted, and prospered under, the paternalistic rule of the Tudors. Unfortunately, the Stuarts could never bring themselves to consider the people as a whole, as the Tudors had done. They considered their own quarrels with the often too legalistic Parliament as personal and not national, and could never broaden the base of their government beyond the throne on which they sat. Had they been able to take a wider view of the constitutional questions, and relied upon the common people for support against an increasingly grasping upper middle class, as earlier kings had done in their struggles against the barons, the growth of Parliament would have been far more healthy, and many later crises and troubles avoided. But these are "might have beens." There were two despotisms in the making, that of the King and that of Parliament. Neither could lead the people on the path of ordinary English development in the ordinary English way but only along a path of blood.

The foreign policy of James was to break down as completely as his domestic. Except for "voluntary" contributions from those who feared him, James had no money to support his son-in-law, and the Palatinate was overrun and lost. In the hope that if Charles married the Spanish Infanta, Spain would restore that territory, young Charles and the favorite Buckingham set out for Madrid to carry on the wooing and negotiations in person. The fine-spun discussions of the theologians, the intrigues of the statesmen and courtiers, the escapades of the two young men, all set against the background of the Madrid of the day, might well make a dazzling comic opera, but at length it became evident that neither could Charles obtain his bride on any acceptable terms nor would Spain intervene to help his brother-in-law regain his lands.

Charles and Buckingham, angry and crest-fallen young diplomats, returned to England, and for one brief moment were popular because they had failed in a project so hated by the nation. Buckingham came back with the title of Duke, and Charles with a burning desire to beat the Spanish in war. Negotiations were quickly opened for his marriage to the French Princess Henrietta Maria, but although both he and James had promised Parliament, which had again been summoned in 1624, that if Charles married a Catholic no liberty for Catholics would be allowed in England, the characteristic Stuart duplicity and unreliability showed itself, and because the French King insisted on liberty for his co-religionists, both father and son had agreed.

When, before the end of the year, however, a force of 12,000 English troops was sent to aid the Palatinate the French King would not allow them to land and pass through France. They had to go to Holland, and for want of money and supplies, three-quarters of them were soon dead without having met any enemy except Charles's new father-in-law. Buckingham, who since the Madrid episode had become the intimate favorite of Charles, had pledged the nation to heavy financial commitments. He was also soon to rise to the summit of power, for Charles in a few months, March 1635, became king when the old James, with his odd-shapen body, his shuffling gait, his slobbering mouth, and his infinite conceit was stricken by illness, and death carried the first of the Stuarts off the stage.

Before, however, passing from this "wisest fool in Christendom," as Henry IV of France called him, we must take note of one aspect of his reign which was to prove of transcendent constructive importance—the real founding of the British Empire overseas. We have already spoken of the beginnings of trade and even of the locating of permanent "factories" for trade purposes, but what happened under James was far more significant, although it was to follow two widely different courses in India and the New World.

The trade, which we have mentioned as beginning with the Far East, had a number of different branches of which the two more important ones were those with India on the Asiatic mainland and with the Malay Archipelago, including the Spice Islands. The Portuguese had been first on the scene but the temporary union of the Crowns of Spain and Portugal in 1580 had brought the smaller country into the whirlpool of European politics and wars, as a cockboat in the wake of the Spanish galleon. The Portuguese had made themselves masters of the Spice and other islands, and had been able to establish themselves in India. The Portuguese, however, in the course of a century had greatly weakened their position by their extreme cruelty to the natives, their immorality, and their mixed marriages with consequent racial decline.

The Dutch and the English both wanted their shares of these Far Eastern trades, and more or less joined hands in fighting for them against the Portuguese. But by the reign of James several things had happened. For one, although both countries had been at war with Spain, and so all attacks on the Portuguese were warranted as against the two nations' enemies, James, in 1604, made peace with Spain, and so with Portugal, whereas the Dutch remained at war until 1641.

In consequence of this situation, although the ships and representatives of the English East India Company continued private warfare with the Portuguese, the English Government did not back them while the Dutch Government did back *its* citizens.

Moreover, the Dutch East India Company was richer and

stronger, establishing forts on the islands and maintaining troops. The Dutch grew jealous of the English who seemed to be sharing the benefits of the trade without bearing their share of the expense and work; and friendly co-operation changed into practical warfare between the merchants of the two countries. The rivalry ended in the driving out of the English from the islands after a group of English traders had been captured, tortured and killed in what is known as the Amboyna Massacre, an episode the English never forgot and which was one of the causes of the later Anglo-Dutch War under Cromwell.

This expulsion of the English from the island trade is important in that it forced the East India Company to turn its whole attention to continental India. There the situation had greatly altered since the early Portuguese days. Southern India was still divided among a number of hostile states but north of them the great and powerful Mogul Empire had been established under a succession of able rulers, Baber the founder and the later Akbar, Jehangir and Shah Jehan. The last was contemporary with Charles I in England, and built the Taj Mahal, the Pearl Mosque at Agra and many other beautiful buildings.

It was with this powerful and highly cultivated Empire that the English now came into contact, James sending an ambassador to Jehangir asking the privileges of trade. The Great Mogul, as he was called, was, however, somewhat in fear of the Portuguese should he grant privileges to others, and it was evident that the English would have to deal with them first. This they did, and in 1612 and 1614 two and four trading ships of the East India Company, respectively, soundly beat overwhelming Portuguese naval forces. In 1622 the English also captured the Portuguese fort at Ormuz.

The English now had nothing to fear from the Portuguese, and English prestige was high in India. Various "factories," or trading posts, were founded about the coast of the Bay of Bengal, and, looking ahead for a moment into the reign of Charles, in 1639 the East India Company acquired its first territory from a local rajah on which it proceeded to build a fort, named St.

George, which afterward developed into the present city of Madras.

Thus were begun those relations which were to develop into the British Empire in India, and it is to be noted that, like the beginnings of empire in other parts of the world, they were the result of private enterprise, and not of government initiative. The overseas empires of Portugal, Spain, to a large extent the Dutch, and later the French, were government enterprises. While this was an advantage in some respects, it was a distinct disadvantage in others. Such a method lacked the energy and drive of the English haphazard one, and also proved far less flexible. The English one led to immense variety in local government and to much greater freedom for those who ventured out from the home island to trade or live in new settlements.

We shall from time to time touch on the later history of British India but may here note that both the climate and the teeming millions of native population prevented that country from being suitable for colonization. The story of English rule in India is a fascinating one but that rule has always been imposed from without, and India never has been or can be an offshoot of the British race and civilization.

This was not true of other beginnings of empire under James, and we must now turn again to the New World. This, like the Far East, was made up of mainland and islands, but keeping to the north of lands claimed and occupied by Spain, all were suitable in climate for white men and also were sparsely settled by natives. Although it was to be a half century or more before France became a contestant for India, she and England entered the race for this new American empire almost simultaneously.

In 1603 the great French explorer Champlain had sailed up the New England and Canadian coasts, and the following year attempted a settlement at Port Royal, in Nova Scotia. Four years later he established a permanent trading post on a bluff above the St. Lawrence and so founded Quebec. Although the French were to become intrepid explorers and missionaries in all eastern Canada, the Great Lakes section, and the Mississippi Valley,

French Canada was long to be a center for fur trading rather than an agricultural community, and population increased but slowly. This, as well as the French choice of the part of the continent for exploitation, was fortunate for the English. Rivals until the cession of Canada to England in 1763, it meant that during the intervening period the French would always be heavily outnumbered, and also that, with the exceptions of the small colonies of Dutch around New York Harbor and the Hudson River country, and a few Swedes on the Delaware, the whole coast from the French in Canada to the Spaniards in Florida was open to the English.

Virginia was chosen for the first English settlement, although unhappily Sir Walter Raleigh who had prophesied that it would yet be English did not have the chance to assist in the enterprise. Mewed up in the Tower he was not released until he was allowed to sail for Guiana in 1617 in search of a mythical gold mine, and, having failed, after coming into hostile contact with Spaniards, was sacrificed to the complaints of the Spanish Minister and executed.

Meanwhile in 1606 two companies were chartered to plant colonies on the Atlantic coast, one the Virginia Company between the 34th and 41st parallel and the other the Plymouth Company, between the 38th and 45th, with certain restrictions as to the overlapping strip. The efforts of the latter Company in Maine were unsuccessful and may here be ignored, but in 1607 a company of emigrants sent out by the Virginia Company landed on the shore of Chesapeake Bay and a few weeks later at an unfortunate site founded Jamestown, the first permanent English settlement in America. In spite of Indians, famine and mismanagement, the colony pulled through, and we are here not interested in its local history but in some of the broader aspects of the enterprise.

We may first note that the original charter and the several amended ones until 1624 were for the incorporation of a private company, the usual way in which English colonies have started, and it is important to see who took part in financing such

ventures. In the amended charter of 1609 there were represented 56 companies in London and 659 private persons. Of
the latter individuals 21 were peers; 96 knights; 11 doctors,
ministers, etc.; 53 captains; 28 esquires; 58 gentlemen; 110 merchants, and 282 not classified. It is thus evident that the interest,
financial and otherwise, in such ventures was widespread among
all classes. Such companies were entirely private affairs but, as
in the first charter, subject to check by the royal Council. By 1624
the direct control of the private company was ended, and the
Crown, not the Company, secured the right to appoint a royal
governor who could in turn appoint the upper house of the local
legislature although the lower house was to be elected by the
people. The latter, the first popular assembly in the New World
(though another was to follow in Bermuda the next year), had
been provided for in 1619.

In general, with some exceptions, this was the form into which
each colony was to develop, and has developed ever since, a
royal governor, forming a link with the Crown, and popular representation in a legislature, having to a large degree local self-
government, supported by the power of England, and safeguarded by English law.

English constitutional development, as we have said, has been
a slow and steady advance, with only a very rare *impasse* which
has caused the need of settlement by force. Later in this chapter
we shall have to discuss the civil war in England. By the time of
the American Revolution another such *impasse* had been reached
in colonial affairs, but with the latter exception the colonial system has worked extraordinarily well on the whole with local self-
government and imperial unity and protection, developing into
the British Commonwealth of Nations of today, the present British Empire. In considering the fatal faults of the Stuart regime
it is well to recall that at least it originated the system of liberty
within law for the English overseas.

The Virginia enterprise, like the colonization of Bermuda, had
been for profit. With the settlement of Plymouth in 1620 we
come to another factor in the development of the Empire, al-

though that also was primarily considered as commercial, at the time. More than one group of those dissatisfied with Church conditions in England went to Holland. Among these were a congregation of Brownists or Separatists, with their minister, from Scrooby in 1606, and who, after some years, decided that Dutch conditions did not suit them and that they preferred to be in an English community though not in England.

After various suggestions they decided to emigrate to Virginia, and received permission of the Virginia Company. They had little money, and a company was formed in London to finance a new settlement, about a hundred persons being sent out in 1620 on the famous *Mayflower*. By accident the passengers had to be landed on the bleak shores of Cape Cod Bay, which they named Plymouth, and which was outside the boundaries of the Virginia Company's charter.

Although the colony fought through its difficulties and was a lasting one, its interest lies chiefly in two points. One is that though the Pilgrims, as the religious element from Holland was called, amounted to only one-third of the total passenger list, emigration, as represented by them, had begun to America for the sake of freedom to worship as men might choose. The other was that as among the other two-thirds, who were ordinary emigrants of all sorts sent out by the London financial backers, there were a number of undesirable and unruly individuals, the problem of order and government on shore arose for the whole company about to land in a place not covered by any charter. On board ship the captain had been absolute and could maintain discipline. Some peoples then, like some today, would have considered that the same method could have been applied ashore, and a dictator appointed.

The fact that, instead, the "Mayflower Compact" was drawn up, providing that a government should be formed and that all would have to submit to the laws made by the majority, showed how far the English had already gone in the instinct of self-rule. It was not intended to be a historic document or the sudden establishment of a democracy. It was merely the way in which an average Englishman would react to such a situation, and it helps to explain why in England, some years later, Cromwell's dictatorship was doomed before it began.

It is merely another, but very interesting, example of the way that the English have developed their political life and institutions by the simple method of meeting each difficulty, which they rarely ever call a "crisis," as it arises without looking beyond the exigencies of the moment or making any effort to establish general principles. When they have been called upon to settle some problem, they have done so in much the same way as a business man settles one that has arisen in his day's work, without feeling called upon, in doing so, to propound a whole system of theoretical economics.

To the better element on the *Mayflower* that cold December evening, the "Compact" was just a bit of common sense used in a pinch, not the propounding of a new theory of government, and if democracy was steadily to grow and broaden in America it was because of the potent combination of English political instinct and the necessary results of frontier life. Important as the latter factor was, however, it is well to recall that many other peoples have also lived on frontiers without attaining to free self-government, and so we have to lay most stress on the intangible "political instinct." How important that has been, and how rare, may be noted by trying to discover where, outside of the modern British Empire and its offshoot the United States, stable democracies can be found.

Besides the mainland of America, certain islands were also settled under James, Bermuda already mentioned, Barbados in 1625 and St. Kitts in 1623. On the mainland again there were also various more or less isolated settlers on the Massachusetts coast outside of the Plymouth colony, as well as a small group who had moved from Cape Ann to the present Salem. England had definitely passed from the stage of mere foreign trade to that of colonizing and building up new Englands across the seas. It was a momentous change not only for England but for all the world, and which before the process was complete, in spite of the loss of America, was to bring England into possession of a quarter of the world and establish the first and only marine empire on the grand scale ever known to history.

Charles I, who followed his father on the throne, was a stubborn young man without political wisdom or experience and with even higher ideas than James of the divine right of kings. He had a fatal lack of resolution and of self-confidence. He introduced a new refinement, however, into the manners of the Court, was a collector of art, and in some respects and on certain occasions, was to play the role of a great gentleman, but he was also unfortunately to prove, throughout his reign, shifty and thoroughly untrustworthy. These qualities were, indeed, shown at once. Because of the promise made to the King of France that Catholics would be protected if he secured Henrietta Maria as wife, Charles did not dare to have Parliament meet until the marriage, by proxy, was safely performed. Then when it did meet, in order as he hoped to secure a large grant for carrying on a war with Spain, he consented to renew Catholic persecution. In a few months he had thus attempted to deceive and circumvent both Parliament and his father-in-law. The action was unhappily thoroughly characteristic.

Parliament, however, dissatisfied in the above matter and with the disastrous military expedition to the Continent, made only a small grant and refused more unless the King would appoint Ministers in whom it could have confidence. The demand was aimed at Buckingham who was corrupt, rapacious and incapable but who, as favorite, dominated the policy of the King. The latter refused the demand and dissolved Parliament. He not only did not wish to sacrifice Buckingham but saw also that if he could choose only ministers who would be satisfactory to the House of Commons he would lose much of his arbitrary power. That road would lead, as at long length it did, to responsible ministers, the Cabinet system, and a constitutional monarchy. It must not be supposed that this was in the mind of the Commons at the time, who were not at all consciously trying to elaborate a new Constitution.

Charles and Buckingham decided that, if they could gain a great victory with plunder, Parliament might become more complacent, and with what money could be collected a fleet was sent to capture Cadiz and if possible the annual treasure fleet from America. The expedition, badly planned and manned, proved a disgraceful failure. There was no discipline and, when the troops landed, instead of taking Cadiz they all got drunk, and the treasure fleet reached port in safety.

Buckingham, in an effort to build up a Continental alliance, had gone to Amsterdam to negotiate and to raise money by pawning the Crown jewels but the canny Dutch bankers would not lend on them. Parliament had to be called again, and as sheriffs could not leave their counties Charles made the leaders he most feared in the Commons sheriffs so as to prevent their attendance. A new leader was found, however, in Sir John Eliot, and the attacks on Buckingham continued until again the King dissolved the sitting.

Unable to get grants, Charles asked his subjects for free gifts but got practically nothing. It was then suggested to him that although the laws forbade him to confiscate money from his subjects he could force them to make loans, which he might have no intention of repaying. Orders were at once issued to collect such a forced loan, and many of those who refused to pay were put in prison merely on the order of the King and Privy Council.

One cannot avoid the conclusion that at this stage in treating with Charles, Parliament showed itself mean, parsimonious and incapable of realizing the real financial needs of the Crown. Both King and people, however, were in the grip of economic forces they did not understand. The rise in prices, of which we have already spoken, was greatly altering the economic framework of all lives and institutions. Such a fundamental change as a rise in the price of wheat of 250 per cent between 1570 and 1648 could not fail to have resounding repercussions in the national life, as, on a yet greater scale, the economic disorganization of our own day has overthrown established governments, and altered the world almost beyond recognition for those of middle age from what they knew in youth. Not only the King but all men were twisting this way and that to escape from the financial traps in which they found themselves caught because of conditions they could not understand.

Meanwhile, affairs on the Continent had been going badly. There had been a defeat in the war for the Palatinate, and when Buckingham in person led an expedition to the Isle of Ré to relieve the Huguenots of Rochelle he was ruinously defeated by a French fleet and returned to England with less than half the troops he had started with.

Besides the religious and constitutional questions which were to be fought out during the reign of the second Stuart there was also the question of which fundamental idea would prevail in English law. There were two, one, descended from Roman Law, was that the king was the fount of law and could force judges to lay down and administer laws as decided by himself alone. This was done in the so-called Prerogative Courts, including that of the Star Chamber. The other idea was that of the English Common Law, as developed particularly by Coke, which was that laws were above the king as well as his subjects and could be altered only by Parliament when changes in existing law were called for.

Under the Tudors both systems of law had existed peaceably together. Because the Henrys and Elizabeth had not pressed the prerogative too far, and because many cases could be decided more quickly and at less expense in the Prerogative Courts, there was little opposition to them and the Tudor Court of the Star Chamber was even popular.

That situation changed under the Stuarts who not only carried their claims to the prerogative far beyond what Englishmen would allow, but, as Charles packed the Common Law courts with judges of his own way of thinking, it was becoming apparent that *all* might become mere prerogative courts. Among the citizens who had been imprisoned for refusing to make the forced loans were five knights who appealed to the Court of King's Bench for a writ of *habeas corpus*. When they were brought before the court and found that they had been jailed without charges and merely on order of the King and Council, they demanded a trial for cause or release on bail. The Crown lawyers argued that the King had always had the right to imprison without showing cause if he considered the safety of the State endangered, and although the judges did not decide the case they returned the knights to prison. Although Charles soon released them he had forced the English people to think on the matter which was taken up by the Parliament which he was forced to call in 1628.

Both Eliot and Sir Thomas Wentworth had been imprisoned for not paying the loan, and now became leaders of the Commons, but were of very different types. Eliot was a country gentleman with no ambition beyond the public good, whereas Wentworth, later to become Earl of Strafford, was to desert the popular cause and to become a favorite of Charles. Although both were for the moment united as against the greedy mismanagement of Buckingham and the course of the King, it may be noted that even at this time Wentworth did not believe in Parliament and preferred the Stuart theory of government though he thought Charles was making practical errors from the standpoint of his own interests. Both he and the King placed the chief emphasis on efficient administration rather than on any theory of government. The Parliament had shown itself often incapable of providing the former, and Wentworth felt that he had the best interest of the nation at heart, and was best serving it, in carrying on against any obstacles, from any quarter, which seemed to him to be in the way of running government efficiently both at home and abroad. Efficiency and freedom, as the world has too good reason to know today, do not always go together, and there are certain types of mind which prefer the former, and others which prefer the latter even with the confusion which it often breeds. It does not mean that Wentworth was either unpatriotic or, when he finally abandoned Parliament to follow the King, a "lost leader," because his mind was of the first type.

Eliot, on the other hand, believed that the King should be guided by the Commons. That body now proceeded to frame a bill known as the Petition of Right, drawn up largely by Eliot, Coke and Selden, which provided that in England there should be no more martial law, enforced quartering of soldiers on the citizens, forced loans, taxes except as imposed by Parliament, or imprisonment except for shown cause. Charles shuffled but, in need of money, was forced to give way and sign the bill. In return he received a grant large enough to enable him to send out another expedition, to be headed by Buckingham, to relieve Rochelle, but the favorite was assassinated at Portsmouth before sailing.

The problem of finances, however, had not been settled. It had been customary in the past for Parliament to make a grant for the life of each sovereign of certain customs duties known as Tonnage and Poundage, though it had not yet done so in the case of Charles, who had nevertheless been levying the duties. Parliament now proposed to make him the grant only annually and denied that in accordance with the Petition of Right he could levy the duties without Parliamentary consent. It was a moot question whether they were strictly taxes in the sense of the Petition but if the King could levy these duties as he pleased, which already formed a third of the royal revenue, it was possible that he could get along without Parliament.

The religious question had also again come to the fore, Charles having issued a declaration that in future there could be no public discussion of the points in dispute. The Commons were in ugly mood, and when Eliot wished to raise the question of Tonnage and Poundage from the standpoint of Parliamentary privilege, the goods of a member of Parliament having been levied on, John Pym, another country gentleman, urged the House to consider the problem not from this narrow point of view but from that of "the liberties of this kingdom." Eliot's motion was carried but when the officers who had seized the goods in the Custom House were ordered to appear at the bar of the Commons, the King refused to allow it.

The clash between King and Commons was direct, and Charles ordered the House to adjourn. No solution was found during the adjournment and when the members met again, and the Speaker rose to read the royal order for another adjournment he was pushed back into his seat while Eliot read three prepared resolutions. These declared that whoever brought in innovations in religion, levied Tonnage and Poundage without Parliamentary consent, or who paid those duties so levied was an enemy of the country and a betrayer of its liberty. In spite of the tumult the resolutions were again read behind the locked doors of the House and voted with loud "Ayes." The King immediately dissolved Parliament and when the members rushed out of the now opened doors the Commons were not to meet again for eleven years. The struggle between King and people had not been settled but the voice of the latter had been silenced and the King was to rule alone.

CHAPTER XII

PERSONAL GOVERNMENT AND ITS RESULTS

THE KING by removing impartial judges and his refusal to summon Parliament had made himself as absolute as possible. The experiment of personal rule over a people long accustomed to having a voice in their government was to be tried. The spirit in which it would be conducted was exhibited by the King at the start. In spite of their privilege as members of Parliament, Eliot and two other members were imprisoned in the Tower for their actions in the Commons. There Eliot died and the others remained for eleven years until Parliament again met. When the King continued to collect the customs dues without authority, a merchant who complained that he and his fellows were treated worse than in Turkey was imprisoned and fined £2000. Other methods of raising money although upheld by the courts aroused much opposition.

Among these were what was called ship money. In the past, taxes had been laid on port towns for the use of the navy but in 1635 the King demanded such money not only from the ports but from inland towns as well. It might well be that, as the navy was used for the whole country, the whole country should support it but that had not been the custom, and in addition Englishmen complained that in spite of the Petition of Right Charles was laying taxes without consent of Parliament. The judges when consulted upheld the King, stating that he had the right to do what he would for the realm in time of danger as to which he alone could decide.

264

It was evident that if Charles could raise what money he would on one pretext and another without Parliament he could make himself absolute. In 1638 John Hampden, an inland country squire, refused to pay the ship money tax which had been levied on him and the case was argued before twelve judges in London. Although he lost the case, seven judges deciding against him to five in his favor, the opinions of the latter were circulated throughout the country and accepted as the correct ones.

Two of the men upon whom Charles was chiefly to rely in carrying out his policies were Wentworth and Archbishop Laud. The former was sent to Ireland where he inaugurated a ruthless policy, returning to England in 1639 to be made Earl of Strafford and to become chief adviser to the King. Laud equally believed in the policy of "Thorough," as it was called, and made enemies for the King in all parts and among all classes. It was his wish greatly to strengthen both the discipline and power of the Church. All preaching outside it was forbidden and within it the ritual was modified in a direction away from Puritan beliefs. Puritans and Nonconformists were persecuted, and the powers of the Court of the Star Chamber and of the High Commission were freely used until they became hated by the people.

Laud was almost mediæval in his opinion of the rights of the Church and its priests, and haled great numbers of laymen before the spiritual courts to answer for alleged misdoings. The English struggle against clericalism had been a long and bitter one, and it now appeared as if it would have to be waged all over again. Laud's ecclesiastical ideas coincided with the constitutional ones of Charles, and the clergy everywhere preached in favor of the King's prerogative and his divine right. While the persecution of Puritans went on apace, the toleration of Catholics, partly perhaps because of the influence of the Queen and partly because of the leanings of Laud, became notable. We shall have in a moment to note two important developments overseas of these two trends of church policy.

Meanwhile, the business depression and uncertainty which were to increase for twenty years were beginning to be felt. Everything—business, the constitutional quarrel with the King, the new religious persecution—made the future appear black to many of the best men in England of all classes. The consequence was the beginning of the great migration which was solidly to establish the English race in America and the West Indies. In a dozen years or so after Charles dissolved his Parliament it is estimated that about 65,000 persons left for the New World of whom over 27,000 settled in various colonies on the mainland and perhaps 38,000 on the islands, St. Kitts, Bermuda, Barbados, Antigua, Santa Lucia, St. Nevis and others.

In fact, without so intending, Charles and Laud may be said to be the real founders on a large scale of the British Empire across the Atlantic. The emigrants were allowed to go without hindrance, and this new frontier, like so many since for both England and America, acted as a safety valve for local discontents in the old country or settlements.

Not only were no difficulties made about emigration, but charters were freely granted which were liberal in terms, and neither political nor religious persecution followed the colonists over the water. One of the most important of the charters was that granted to the Massachusetts Bay Company, which was controlled by prominent Puritans. Many of these had been considering preparing a refuge in the New World in case affairs grew worse, those discussing the matter among themselves numbering such men as the Earl of Warwick, Hampden as a prisoner in the Tower, Pym, John Winthrop, and others.

The colonial interest of such men lay not only in New England but also in the West Indies. The future importance of New England, however, not only for its own history but for that of the Empire, was greater than that of the islands though its population was for some time to be less. The charter for Massachusetts was in the usual form of that for a trading company, but in this unique case the document was carried over to the colony, and by a series of interpretations by the members of the company became instead of a trading charter the written constitution of a self-governing community.

Partly as offshoots of Massachusetts, owing to persecution or religious differences, there grew up other New England colonies —Rhode Island, Connecticut, New Hampshire and New Haven, the last later merged with Connecticut. All of these developed independency in church organization, and the character of the settlers, the conditions of a frontier life, and the distance from control in England helped to make them democratic and almost independent states. In all cases in which charters were granted they provided for a popularly elected lower legislative House, as already noted in the case of Virginia. This was so even in the case of Maryland, although the charter for that colony in other respects did not take the usual form but erected a County Palatine similar to that of Durham, in England. It had been granted to Lord Baltimore, a Catholic peer, and Catholics were allowed freedom of worship there. It is one of the anomalies of this period when the King and Laud were suppressing political and religious freedom at home, that they were scattering models of popular government and religious toleration through the rest of the now fast-growing Empire.

They may have realized the value of draining overseas such large numbers of those discontented with conditions in England for one reason or another, and the effect must, in fact, have been considerable. In any case, however, it would have been difficult to bring about a rising against the usurped government. It is true that Charles had no army but, on the other hand, there were no longer great vassals with their bands of retainers to raise their banners against him.

England was now accustomed to domestic tranquillity and had become used to seek redress of grievances through peaceable means in Parliament, chiefly by refusing the King money when needed until such redress was obtained. Nor are the English accustomed to seek revolution by means of widespread secret organizations. Leadership was lacking without Parliament, and if the King did not need money and would not summon Parliament, personal rule and a Church prying into private morals, though arousing deep resentment, might last a long time.

It was Charles himself who was to provide the method of his own destruction. Although Scotland had a Parliament, it was of little importance, and Charles thought he could easily extend his personal rule over the border. He forgot that whereas in England the State ruled the Church, in Scotland there was a Church which largely ruled the State. In England he had roused the people by attacking the State. Now he roused the Scotch by attacking their Church. Moreover, when roused, the Scotch could move to war more easily than the English. Although feudalism had to a great extent passed, the clan life persisted, and Scotland had the leaders who could call out troops and move quickly against a foe which peaceful trading England lacked.

There were bishops in Scotland but they were mostly creatures of the King, and the people were intensely Calvinistic and Presbyterian. Had the King not interfered, matters might have slumbered, as the nobles and bishops worked together for the most part to keep things quiet, but the infatuated Charles decided in 1637 to force a modified version of the English Prayer Book on the Scottish Church, and to promote some of the bishops to high office.

The clergy were at once aroused and the nobles went over to the side of the ministers, annoyed at seeing some of their offices go to the bishops and fearing lest Laud might also demand the restoration of lands which they had received from the Church. There was rioting in Edinburgh and at the beginning of the next year all Scotland was signing a Covenant to secure return to the old services they had used before Charles had tried to force the new upon them. During the year, the King attempted to come to terms and even revoked his order for the use of the Prayer Book and made other concessions.

In November a General Assembly sat in Glasgow and, refusing to dissolve when ordered to by the King's Commissioner, deposed all the bishops and established the Presbyterian system. They had practically also deposed the King by paying no attention to his order to dissolve, and Charles marched north with what small army he could gather without asking Parliament for money. He could not keep even such a force together, and when the Assembly and Parliament in Edinburgh confirmed the abolition of episcopacy, he prepared for another attack. Money, however, had to be had, and Strafford, now back from Ireland, suggested calling Parliament, both in Ireland and England.

The Irish Parliament voted supplies at once to fight the Scots, hoping that Charles would allow freedom to the Catholics if they did so. The English Parliament, however, would do nothing until grievances were redressed, and was dissolved within three weeks —which gave it the name of the Short Parliament. So far from having wished to make a grant it had preferred to leave the Scots alone. The position to which the King, who was determined to continue the war, was now reduced was shown by the ignominy of the method to which he had to resort to raise even a small sum of money. He managed to buy a large amount of pepper on credit and then sold it at a low price. This gain did not survive a defeat of the unwilling soldiers who had been forcibly pressed into service when they met the Scots at Newburn. At York Charles called a council of peers, but their only advice proved to be for him to summon Parliament.

This Parliament, known as the Long Parliament, was one of the most important in the history of that institution, in fact such an authority as Professor Trevelyan speaks of it as "the true turning point in the political history of the English-speaking races," and the King, by bringing on the Scottish war, had placed himself at last in its power, unless he were to be financially bankrupt and defied by one of his two kingdoms. The power in the new Parliament was centered in the Commons who carried the Lords in their wake.

In the constitutional struggle with the Stuarts, which had lasted now more than a generation, Parliament had changed much from Tudor times. Under the Tudors business had been presented to them for their decision as prepared by the Privy Council, but the succession of crises which had confronted it since the rule of the Stuarts, with their exalted idea of divine right and their inability to understand either the English Constitution or the English character, had caused Parliament, like a youth passing into manhood, to launch out for itself and to assume the responsibility of initiating instead of merely initialling legislation. It was a mature and stern legislative assembly that now confronted the King, and among its members were some of the ablest men who have ever represented the country. There sat Pym, Hyde, Hampden, Falkland and others.

In history there are certain facts, such as dates and other matters, which may be established in many cases with absolute certainty. In these all historians have to agree. There is much else in the story of the past, however, which is bound always to remain within the field of inference, interpretation, personal opinion. Even, for example, when we find a statesman setting down in writing the precise motives which led him to take a certain action, we still cannot be sure that such were the real ones. He may have desired to deceive posterity or he may, quite honestly and unconsciously, have deceived himself. Often, also, the motives which have led to an important action may have been very complex, and may have ranged all the way from high questions of state and religion to such personal matters as the fact that economic conditions no longer permitted the maintaining of the accustomed seven or eight servants in a household, all of which appear in the list of reasons which induced John Winthrop to emigrate and become one of the founders of Massachusetts. The historian has no godlike capacity to see into the innermost secrets of a human heart, and to weigh true motive against false or even to balance the individual weight of the several true ones.

In other words, there are parts of history which may be "scientific." There are other parts which are bound to reflect not a scientific exactitude but only the interpretation of events by the historian, and this section is, of necessity, colored by his own temperament, views, and ideals. Moreover, current trends of thought are likely to affect views of the past and of the actors in the earlier scenes of the drama which have led up to the living scene in which we ourselves are the actors. Thought has its tides no less than the sea.

We speak of this at this stage in our story because, perhaps, of the waning faith of many in popular as against personal rule, there is at present a noticeable tendency to exalt the Stuarts historically at the expense of the Parliament. It is true that the Long Parliament from its very beginning tended toward revolutionary measures, and a case can be made out legally for the King as upholding the more traditional and constitutional position. A constitution, however, is never static, not even when it is a written instrument, and the time had come to settle certain constitutional questions between the monarch and Parliament, even if we can hardly say between him and the people.

The Stuarts were not Tudors, and the day had passed for even a benevolent despotism. Nor, with their lack of statesmanship and their failure to reckon with the ordinary folk of their kingdom, would it have been likely that their despotism would have been even benevolent. Changes had to come. A constitution has to alter to meet new needs and new stages in national development. An insistence on keeping the old forms and preventing the Constitution from growing with the people's growth may, in truth, be as revolutionary as the taking of steps to bring about a new harmony under new conditions. If the Crown were in some ways more national than the Parliament, Charles failed to recognize that fact. Many of the members of Parliament may have been moved by selfish motives, but even if the development of popular institutions was to receive some setback from the events of the ensuing decades, it cannot, I think, be proved that popular government in the long run would have been better served by a Stuart despotism than by the stormy course of Parliament.

In any case, the courage and temper of the members from whom Charles now had to ask favors was shown at the start by the imprisonment in the Tower of the two men on whom he had relied most, Laud and Strafford, the latter also being impeached. During 1640 and 1641 the Parliament proceeded to strip the King of many of the powers he had claimed, and this work was never undone. He was forced to sign bills providing that Parliament should sit at least every three years whether called into session by the monarch or not, and the less justifiable one that it could not be dissolved except by its own consent, which latter provision might make it a perpetual body without responsibility to either the King or the country. Acts were also passed abolishing the Star Chamber, the Court of High Commission, and certain other prerogative courts; limiting the King's claims to the royal forest lands; prohibiting him from levying fines on those who refused to become knights; declaring ship money illegal; as well as the levying of Tonnage and Poundage or other impositions without the authority of Parliament.

To make more sure of the result it was decided to alter the impeachment of Strafford to attainder for treason, a proceeding in which the Lords would have to agree. Charles and the Queen had already engaged in a plot to overpower Parliament by armed force and to liberate Strafford from the Tower.

This plot being discovered, and both Houses being alarmed lest the great ability of the earl should be again placed at the service of the King to undo the work done to hold him in check, the Attainder was passed. Throughout the sessions of the Long Parliament one of its elements of strength was the constant support given to it by the citizens of London, and crowds of these now gathered before the palace of Whitehall demanding Strafford's death. The King, frightened by the enraged mob, signed the bill, and Strafford was beheaded though Charles had promised him full protection. As the King's ablest supporter placed his head upon the block, waiting for the masked headsman's axe to fall, he murmured the words, which England had also taken to heart: "Put not your trust in Princes." We have already spoken of Strafford's political philosophy. He had taken his stand on it, and the "Prince" on whom the success of that philosophy in practice would have to depend had not only deserted him but by that act had shown himself incapable of playing the role in government which had to be the cornerstone of Strafford's system. He and the King together were necessary to make such a system work, and the King's weakness was, perhaps, the best proof, aside from popular resentment against the policy of both Laud and Strafford, that it could not work. In any case, the latter's execution was a turning point in history, and was to lead directly up through the years until the King's own head was to be placed upon the block.

If the King had been willing to accept his new position of what we would call a constitutional monarch, and if it had not been for the religious question, the constitutional balance reached might have been the basis for the peaceful and more rapid development of the modern British system but Charles would not do so, and the religious problem also raised its head.

Parliament disbanded the small English army and the Scots also retreated within their own borders, but the King went to Edinburgh with intention, it was thought by many, of trying to raise a Scotch army against England, though if that were his object he did not succeed, and returned to London. Meanwhile there was unrest in Ireland, and the Catholic lords there made offers to Charles to send him an Irish army if they should be allowed to take over the government of the island. Impatient at delays in negotiation, the Irish attempted to seize Dublin and also massacred some thousands of English and Scotch settlers. To maintain dominion and order it would be necessary to send an army into Ireland, but who should control it, Parliament or the King? If the latter had such a weapon now placed in his hands he might readily turn it against not the Irish people but the English Parliament.

Meantime the religious question had divided Parliament into two bodies. Both were opposed to the continuance of the changes introduced by Laud; but whereas one party believed that the only salvation lay in the abolition of episcopacy, the other feared that that would lead to Presbyterianism. The so-called Root and Branch Bill, abolishing bishops, failed to pass the Commons, but the religious question was now splitting wide apart those who had stood shoulder to shoulder on the constitutional one. Hampden and Pym, for example, now found themselves in opposition to Hyde and Falkland.

In November, 1641, there was a great debate over the passing of the Grand Remonstrance which detailed the King's errors, demanded that he employ only ministers responsible to Parliament, and that religious matters be settled by an Assembly appointed by Parliament. The party led by Hyde and Falkland believed that this, by giving ecclesiastical control to Parliament, might bring in Presbyterianism in place of the Prayer Book and the Church of England. It also made many hesitate about placing the army under the orders of Parliament rather than of the King. The idea, and indeed the practical political possibility, of tolerating two church systems simultaneously still lay far in the future. Owing to the split between the parties who had been united against him, the King might easily have won peaceably through the adherence of those genuinely devoted to the Church of England and its services had he been patient and wise, but Charles was never either, and merely succeeded in forcing a decision by arms.

The bishops likewise made a mistake. London mobs had shouted against them in the streets, and when one was jostled by a crowd he and eleven others protested that nothing which might be done in the House of Lords without their presence would be legal. This for a moment brought the annoyed peers over to the side of the Commons, who impeached the twelve bishops, and helped to close the ranks again against the King.

Charles then proceeded himself to impeach the leaders in Parliament opposed to him, including Pym, Hampden, Holles, Strode and Hazelrigg in the Commons and Kimbolton in the Lords. January 4, 1642, he personally appeared at the House with 500 armed followers to arrest what he called the five traitors, who meanwhile had taken refuge in the city. Foiled, the King had to leave, his ears ringing with cries of "Privilege" on every side. The city declared for the Commons, and the King left London, fleeing northward, taking up quarters at York. Both he and Parliament now began to raise troops and on August 22 the King erected his standard at Nottingham. The Civil War had begun.

It was neither a sectional conflict like the American in the nineteenth century nor a social one like the French in the eighteenth, but one for religious and constitutional principles. It was to be a merciful war, wholly different from the bloody massacres in Ireland or the horrors of the Thirty Years' War on the Continent. In general the King was strongest in the West and North, among the nobility, Catholics and older landed gentry, whereas the Parliament was in the lead in the towns, the South and East, among the trading classes, and the Puritans. Neither side had an army at first but the King had the ablest commander in his young nephew, Prince Rupert. Parliament, however, had the navy, which had declared for its side, and the city of London with its wealth and financial resources.

Both parties at first had to ask individuals to raise regiments, but throughout the war the deciding arm was to be the cavalry, and in the beginning, indeed until Oliver Cromwell raised and drilled his Ironsides, Prince Rupert's troop of horse was superior to any which could be used against him. It decided the first battle, that of Edgehill, in the King's favor, but when Charles pushed on toward London without Rupert the Royal forces were defeated by the London trainbands at Turnham Green, and Charles retreated to Oxford.

In 1643 the Royalists planned a strategic descent upon the capital again with forces from three directions, but the armies were far apart, and in spite of some minor victories for Charles the plan failed, in part because the soldiers were not regularly paid, were not enlisted for long service, and did not wish to get too far from home and leave their families and properties exposed to attack. In August the King in person laid siege to Gloucester, but it was reinforced from London and he was forced to retreat, as also after the first battle of Newbury,—in the latter case for want of ammunition.

It was of much importance that the Parliamentarians held the ports of Hull in the North and Bristol in the West, and strong defense was now to be built up in five eastern counties by the formation of the Eastern Association, in which Cromwell became the leading spirit. He cared nothing about the social classification of the troops under him nor to what sect they belonged, but everything about their spirit, character and willingness to submit to an iron discipline. They gained their first victories during the late summer at Gainsborough and Winceby, but it was becoming clear that no real decision could be soon won and the country was wearying.

Both sides negotiated for outside help, Charles with Ireland. The Catholics there offered to send him 10,000 troops if he would allow the assembly of an Irish Parliament chiefly composed of those of that faith, but the negotiations lagged. Pym was more fortunate in his effort to enlist Scotland, and a treaty was made, called the Solemn League and Covenant, according to which the members of Parliament, and afterwards supposedly all those on the Parliamentary side, swore to "the reformation of religion in the Church of England according to the example of the best re-formed churches," which the Scots wished to have understood as the Presbyterian; but to this was added "according to the word of God," a difficult phrase to cavil at but which left every man free to decide for himself what it might mean. However, the Scots agreed, and on receipt of money aid from Parliament, which Charles so sorely lacked, a Scottish force under command of an excellent soldier of experience, Alexander Leslie, crossed the Tweed in January, 1644.

Unfortunately, the religious question had again been creating division behind the lines. Although the Westminster Assembly of Divines had come out strongly on the whole for the Presbyterian system, deeply obnoxious to a large part of English laymen, a smaller group in the Assembly were equally desirous of a system in which each church would be independent of any general or-ganization and oversight, thus gaining the name of Independents. This suited Cromwell, who was always tolerant in religious mat-ters, and Sir Henry Vane, who had spent some time in Massachu-setts where such a system prevailed.

Unfortunately Pym, the best statesman in Parliament, died. In consequence of this and the united military operations with the Scots, a Committee of both Kingdoms was set up composed of certain members of Parliament and of Commissioners from Scotland. In spite of the danger of division in the face of the enemy, however, the campaign of 1644 opened in favor of the Parliamentary party, and largely due to Cromwell's generalship and his new troops, it won a brilliant victory over the Royalists at Marston Moor. On the other hand the conduct of Essex and his defeat in Cornwall, as well as the carelessness of Manchester in allowing the King to escape in the second battle of Newbury, brought on discussions in Parliament which revealed clearly the discord between the Presbyterian element which was willing to end the war and the Independents who wished to continue it until victory had been attained.

Cromwell had opposed the Presbyterian general, Manchester, and in the debate it became evident that success could not be reached if leading officers at the front had different views as to the ends of the war and even the wisdom or desirability of continuing it. Parliament, favorable to Cromwell, determined to make a clean sweep of all officers, and by the famous Self-Denying Ordinance secured the resignation of every one. It then chose Sir Thomas Fairfax as Commander-in-Chief with Cromwell as his lieutenant in charge of horse, thus deciding in favor of the Independents and sectaries as against the Presbyterians, at least for the duration of the war.

From a military standpoint no choices could have been better than these two. For the rest, many of the soldiers of fortune and inefficient officers of lower grade were replaced by stern men bent solely on winning the war. In addition Parliament created what it called the New Model Army, one of the chief features being that the men were well and regularly paid, and by Parliament instead of by local districts or organizations. At last Parliament had an army which would serve well and anywhere. Moreover, discipline was well maintained and plundering strictly forbidden. On the other hand, the Royalist forces, ill or unpaid, were steadily degenerating in quality and morale, and becoming increasingly disliked and feared by the people whom they plundered in absence of pay.

The New Army also had a plan, which was to find the King and to defeat the main body of his army wherever it might be located. This proved to be at Naseby, where, chiefly due to Cromwell's horse, a crushing victory was secured, the royal army being practically destroyed though Charles himself escaped. There ensued a series of sieges, and of wanderings for the King who at last in May, 1645, gave himself up to the Scots. The surrender of Oxford and the end of what is called the first war occurred the following month.

Charles was treated practically as a prisoner by the Scots unless he would agree to the establishment of Presbyterianism in England, which he refused. He also strung out negotiations over the terms upon which Parliament insisted, and finally, when the Scots felt that nothing further could be done with him they accepted Parliament's offer to pay the arrears of the army on condition of turning Charles over to its Commissioners, who took him as prisoner to Holmby House, in Northamptonshire.

Unfortunately, as was shown after the World War and others, a government which may be able to wage war efficiently may not be able to make a wise peace, and Parliament was now to enter on a course which was later to lead to dictatorship and the Stuart restoration, but only after a second war with Charles. The country longed for peace, and there was comparatively little bitterness between those who had fought. As often, the trouble came from the legislators. The Presbyterians in Parliament were willing to accept Charles's offer of making the Church Presbyterian for three years, during which time its final form would be decided. The army was largely composed of Independents, and the Presbyterians were now more afraid of it than of the King, though without cause. It is probable it would have disbanded peacefully on being paid but Parliament made the fatal mistake of offering the soldiers only a small part of what was due them. It was a piece of incredible folly.

At once the army was placed in violent opposition to Parliament and its Presbyterian leaders, of whom Holles was head, and refused to disband. Cromwell sympathized with their demand for their just pay and also with that for toleration of the sects but realized the danger threatening the civil government if the army got out of hand.

The Presbyterian leaders next entered into a plot to abduct Charles and to have the Scots invade England on behalf of him and the Presbyterian Church. The plot having been discovered, Cromwell removed the King from Holmby. Parliament then began to raise troops in London, which was largely Presbyterian, but the army demanded the elimination of eleven of the prominent Presbyterian leaders in Parliament, in answer to which a London mob broke into the House and intimidated the Independent members who fled for protection to the army. The remaining Presbyterian members then voted to resist the army by force, in reply to which, in turn, the army marched on London, occupying Westminster and the Tower.

Cromwell was sincerely desirous of arriving at some peaceful and constitutional solution of the difficulty, and was in communication with the King to whom was tendered, in the name of the army, a document called *The Heads of the Proposals* which provided among other points that there should be biennial Parliaments, and complete freedom of worship for all except Catholics. This, however, did not please Parliament, and the army was becoming more restive. The soldiers talked of purging Parliament and even of trying the King. It also prepared a more democratic form of Constitution under the name of *The Agreement of the People*, and threatened to mutiny.

Charles fled to the coast but was caught and imprisoned in Carisbrooke Castle in the Isle of Wight. There, however, while Cromwell was suppressing the mutiny in the army and still working for a solution, the King was negotiating with the Scottish Commissioners for an invasion of England. Parliament had also foolishly confiscated the estates of the Royalists and so antagonized large sections of the people who, when defeated, had laid down their arms with the good will which Englishmen usually show after a fair fight. People were also getting tired of the army and of paying for it.

There were a number of insurrections and the smouldering embers soon broke out into a second war. Both Fairfax and Cromwell had to take the field, and Parliament continued its insane policy of antagonizing every one by passing a law for the suppression of heresy, and then opened negotiations with Charles for his return.

Charles, who all his life had played fast and loose with every one who had tried to work for or negotiate with him, was soon to pay the penalty. The army was tired both of him and of Parliament, and forcibly took the King into its own custody. When the Commons, on December 5, declared a reconciliation with him, Colonel Pride, with a small band of soldiers, entered the House the following day and expelled by force all the Royalist members.

On the first of the following month the remnant of the House remaining after "Pride's Purge" made the proposal to try the King by a High Court of Justice but the Lords would not join. A few days later the few members left in the Commons resolved that they were the supreme power in England as representing the people, and set up the proposed High Court. It was not easy to find men to sit in the tribunal but some sixty to seventy were secured. Charles, brought before the bar of this wholly illegal court, refused to plead, and was condemned. On January 30 on a scaffold in front of his own palace of Whitehall, for the first and only time in English history, a king was executed.

As the axe severed his head a horrified murmur went up from the watching multitude and the English nation was launched violently out upon a perilous and unknown sea. The axe had done more than cleave through the neck of the King. It had cut the English people off from its past, from the laws and institutions to which it was accustomed and to which it had become fitted through centuries. Friends and foes alike that day in London, and day by day after as the news spread through halls and manor houses and cottages throughout all the land, asked themselves anxiously in hushed tones what fate might be in store.

CHAPTER XIII

ENGLAND TRIES A DICTATOR

THE SITUATION for England after the execution of the King was critical in the extreme. The Scots were ready to rise because of the killing of a Scottish King and the throwing over of Presbyterianism. Ireland was unusually united in feeling and, like Scotland, was intriguing with Charles II, the young son of the late monarch. Part of the navy had gone over to the royal cause and English ships under Prince Rupert were preying on other English ships. Colonies in the New World threatened to secede, except New England, which was already semi-independent and mostly Puritan. There was trouble in Maryland, Virginia, Barbados, St. Kitts, Antigua and Bermuda.

While England was thus threatened from many parts of the Empire itself, practically every state on the Continent was also hostile to her, and there seemed a good chance that the young Prince might have foreign backing to regain the throne. Even in England itself there had been a considerable revulsion of feeling after the King's death, and although this has often been over-rated, for the earlier years of the Commonwealth, it and the other factors mentioned at the end of the preceding chapter had their effect in making government difficult.

Moreover, the break with the past, with the old institutions and ways, had been too sudden. Many English did not like it. Above all, not only could the government in no way be considered constitutional, but, even worse—and this was the pith of the matter in the next decade—it could not be considered to rest in any way upon the consent of the governed. The experiment was to end in failure, though not wholly so, as we shall see; but the fact that within three years England had re-established control over other parts of the Empire and had become feared in Europe was due to the efforts of certain leaders, chief among them being Cromwell, and not to Parliament with its fatal flaw of not being representative of public opinion.

One of the most interesting points in the history of the decade is that which has been exemplified in history over and over, and with which we are all too familiar today. This was that once an accustomed and constitutional form of government has been over-thrown it is practically impossible to avoid drifting more and more into a despotism under one man or a small group.

As always, however, we have to reckon with the character of a people, and this whole episode, including especially the execution of the King, was out of character for the English nation, which always prefers the path of compromise and conciliation to that of force and bloodshed which it has entered upon only, and extremely rarely, when the other path has been insuperably blocked, This has occurred only twice in the past three centuries, first in dealing with the Stuarts who could not be dealt with in the accustomed way, and again in the American Revolution. In each case, however, there were large sections of the people who were averse to the method of violence.

When the head of Charles was held up before the horrified crowd by the black-clad and masked executioner, the immediate problem was who or what would govern England, defend her, and restore and maintain order. There was, first, a group of very able men who had supported the revolution, some of them among the greatest in her history. As passions subside, the figure of Cromwell looms ever larger, typically English in his realism and his belief in meeting each situation as it arose by the means nearest to hand. He and the others of the group were far from being mere fanatics, and in addition were sincerely devoted to the public interest.

In the crisis which the shifty, untrustworthy and stubborn

Stuarts had brought on the nation, Cromwell had not hesitated at times to proceed without warrant of law. Particularly in the matter of the trial and execution of the King, for which he was more than any one else responsible, he well realized that he was acting without the shadow of constitutional warrant. Nevertheless, he would have preferred, and constantly strove, to carry on government by constitutional means, though it was to prove impossible. He had, however, more common sense and a firmer grasp on what might be politically feasible than any of the other leaders, and had to use such means as the successive difficulties provided.

Among the others were Blake, a great soldier who was to change his profession and become perhaps the third greatest naval commander in the history of the nation. Also there were Vane, Ireton, Milton and Monk, the last of whom was to play the leading part in the final act of the drama.

As for government, the monarchy was gone, as was practically the House of Lords, while the Commons was represented only by the Rump left after Pride's Purge. Its existence could be considered only as a travesty on parliamentary government. There was also, all important, the army, but that, like the people at large, was divided, and had a strong element of extreme democrats, called Levellers, favoring a form of government for which the nation was not prepared and whom Cromwell would have to suppress. Milton himself was writing, in words that were later to become familiar in many a constitutional struggle, that "all men were naturally born free," and basing government on a contract with the people. Such doctrine, extended and misinterpreted, was strong wine which went to the heads of many in the army and elsewhere, and which in the confusion of the time would lead to anarchy instead of a constitutional monarchy or a democratic and constitutional state.

The first step was taken by the Rump which declared that its membership constituted a Parliament, and that England was thenceforth to be a Commonwealth without King or House of Lords. Owing to the fact that there were no Royalists—still a large party in the nation—among the fifty or more members of the Commons who met, and that even the revolutionists themselves had been purged, the House could not be considered as representative of the country at large. It had, however, the support of the army, except for the Levellers, and proceeded to provide for an executive branch of government by the appointment of a Council of State composed of forty-one persons, many of whom were also members of the Commons.

The government thus became an oligarchy in which the people had no voice and which only the army could influence. Such a form could not continue indefinitely, given the character of the nation and its long experience in parliamentary government, but for a few years it carried on. The members of the Council including Vane and Milton, who was its secretary, were honest and hard-working, and were also faced, on account of the military necessities of which we shall speak presently, with the need of raising a revenue of over £2,000,000 a year, causing, even with sequestrations of the properties of Royalists, heavier taxation than Englishmen had ever before known.

At the same time the so-called Parliament undertook certain reforms both in law and the Church. Religious toleration was established for all who accepted the basic tenets of Christianity, and, even in the Church, ministers were accepted whether moderate Anglican, Presbyterian, Baptist or Independent. It is questionable whether the system would have worked permanently but at least it did enlarge the general understanding and desire for toleration and a broader Church outlook.

Meanwhile, Cromwell had to leave London and undertake the restoration of order and control in both Ireland and Scotland. In the former, the Papal Nuncio had been striving to bring about a Catholic, anti-Protestant and anti-English revolution but without success. Ormond, however, the former King's lieutenant, had united with the Catholics and was threatening to overthrow the Commonwealth government both there and in England, having proclaimed Charles II King.

In the summer of 1649, Cromwell landed at Dublin and at

once started to subdue the island. His view, clearly and fervently expressed in an address, was unhappily that of probably most Englishmen of the time, and of many since. Instead of seeing the real grounds for Irish grievances, past and present, he could see only the turbulence and constant unrest of a native population which he looked down upon as of a lower order, socially and politically, than the English. In September Cromwell stormed Drogheda, a post which refused to surrender when called on to do so. According to the then accepted rules of war, the inhabitants who refused to surrender a place incapable of defense could be put to the sword, and Cromwell slew some 2000, though the gradually increasing humanitarianism of the period is indicated by the fact that even he appears to have considered it necessary to defend his action by reasons other than the old established laws of war. Again there was a similar slaughter at Wexford, and a succession of towns were captured.

In the spring of 1650 Cromwell returned for a brief time to England, leaving Ireton and Ludlow to complete the subjugation, which was accomplished, with savage cruelty long to be remembered. The war had become racial and Catholic rather than Royalist, the upholding of the cause being transferred to Scotland, but Cromwell's policy, which may be called "thorough" quite as much as Laud's or Strafford's, left deep scars. This was especially true of his land policy. He did not, indeed, drive all the native population west of the Shannon as was suggested, but he did confiscate vast amounts of land to pay for both the soldiers and the cost of the expedition, and settled English landlords and the soldiers as farmers on the former Celtic properties.

The plan did prevent any rebellion such as had occurred in the past, but the soldiers merged with the native Catholic population remaining, and the landlord system developed the absenteeism and rack-renting, which were to make trouble down to the nineteenth century. His policy, however, was no worse than that of other English statesmen of before and long after, and with the Irish character and the tenacious racial memory of wrongs, Ireland was to continue the festering sore in the Empire.

Cromwell had but a short stay in England when he was called upon to march to Scotland and suppress the rising there. In the case of Royalist, Catholic Ireland, he had had to choose whether that island should impose its will on England or England should impose its on the Irish. He was now faced by the same problem in Scotland. In June, 1650, the young Prince, later to become Charles II, landed in that kingdom and found the nation at his back after he agreed to become a Presbyterian. The Commonwealth military leader, Fairfax, who had been Cromwell's superior officer in the Civil War, felt that he could not fight the Scots for selecting their own monarch and form of government. Cromwell, with his usual common sense, realized that that was not the question. If Charles, who claimed to be King of England as well as Scotland, could make his position secure across the Tweed, there would be another war, with the possible loss of all that had been gained in the first one.

Therefore he marched north, and after an ineffectual attempt to capture Edinburgh, retreated to Dunbar, with the Scots in possession of his line of retreat into England, A failure would, moreover, mean a rising throughout the southern kingdom, and as he watched events he was rewarded by having the Scots make a premature attack on his position. Recognizing the opportunity immediately, he overwhelmed the Scottish forces and won a victory to be almost immediately followed by the capture of Edinburgh.

Another Scots army, however, marched into England the following year with Charles, hoping to raise an insurrection there. Cromwell, who had kept close behind them, won a complete success at Worcester in which the Scots were practically annihilated, on the anniversary of his first victory at Dunbar. Although the Prince himself escaped, the Scottish problem, like the Irish, was settled for the rest of Cromwell's life, and he could return to London and give his attention to political instead of military matters.

Meanwhile Parliament had been busy with trade affairs. The world was about to enter on a new phase which we shall have to consider on account of its very great effect on the Empire. The year 1648 may be taken to mark the change. In that year Spain at last acknowledged the independence of the Dutch and, although Spain and France remained at war for a while longer, the Peace of Westphalia ended the Thirty Years' War which had involved much of the Continent. It was not merely that peace had come after the disturbances of the long struggle, but that it marked the end of wars of religion in Europe, and from that date the contests between nations were to be based on the struggle for prestige, trade or territory. The medieval period had been finally ended and the modern world ushered in, a world largely given over internationally to fights for colonial empires and business advantages.

The Dutch Republic after the death of the Stadholder William II fell under the control of the great merchants of the province of Holland, an indication of the changes to occur; and the great seaports of Rotterdam and Amsterdam sent out vessels which began to monopolize the sea-carrying trade of much of Europe. Little Holland, as we think of her today, was then a power well in the van in the race for trade and empire. To meet this situation Parliament passed the two Navigation Acts of 1650 and 1651. Most historians concentrate upon the latter, and the great importance of the first has been usually overlooked. It was passed ostensibly with regard to the rebellions, actual or threatened, in the colonies of Barbados, Bermuda, Virginia and Antigua, which had remained Royalist, but enunciated three principles applicable to the entire Empire which were to prove of disastrous importance in the future.

These were that Parliament had supreme power over the colonies; the absolute prohibition of all colonial trade carried on in foreign ships; and the granting to the Council of State the power to nullify any proprietary or company chartered rights. Although the Act remained in force only until the Restoration in 1660 the principles laid down were to remain the political stock in trade of the British Government and eventually, in part, to bring on the American Revolution in the next century.

The second Navigation Act was passed the following year, and although it dealt wholly with trade and shipping its purpose was national defense, and it is a mistake to consider it from any other point of view, as is frequently done. With certain exceptions, it prohibited any trade with England or the rest of the Empire except in vessels belonging to England, Ireland or the colonies, with a majority of English in every crew.

There was nothing new about Acts controlling navigation but the regulations made by Charles I, for instance, had been made to influence trade. This one was enacted solely with the view to building up the shipping of the Empire which, the preamble stated, "is so great a means for the welfare and safety of this Commonwealth." Whether trade, in this or that branch, this or that part of the Empire, might be increased or diminished was not the point, which was the building up of an English merchant marine. How important this was was made all too apparent in 1650 when Ayscue, to whom had been entrusted the task of bringing the revolting West Indian and American colonies to terms, had to delay the operation for an entire year because of lack of ships. The Stuarts had generally neglected the navy, though Charles had begun to build one, as well as merchant shipping, but the Commonwealth government, largely under the influence, as it was, of the mercantile interests of the city, grasped for the first time the idea that, in such an overseas empire as was now developing, a strong navy would be necessary not only to repel foreign foes but to bind the Empire itself together.

The naval committee of the Council of State, with Vane at its head, built up the fleet and got it into good condition, giving command to Blake, noted as a soldier but who had never been to sea until he was over fifty and who knew practically nothing about the different mode of warfare in which he was now called upon to engage. The choice, however, was happily to prove a most fortunate one. Meanwhile, Ayscue had got to sea at last, and although he had to blockade Barbados for three months before he could secure its surrender, he had little or no trouble with the other three colonies which had declared for the King. Thus the

Empire, including Ireland, Scotland and the colonies had all been forced to accept the Commonwealth government before war broke out with the Dutch in 1652.

Meanwhile Blake had been winning a series of victories over the fleet under Prince Rupert, which he had chased into the Mediterranean, the first time the English naval flag had been displayed in that sea, and had shown his ability as a commander. Rupert was a great leader but unfortunately for him he had been called on to face Cromwell on land and Blake at sea. The latter was to find himself, in turn, pitted against one equal in ability to himself, the Dutch Admiral, Tromp.

Feeling between the Dutch and English had been growing in bitterness for a generation, and though not the sole cause of war, Dutch resentment over the Navigation Act, which threatened their hold on ocean commerce, brought matters to a head. Things had changed since the days of Elizabeth, and the Hollanders were now more experienced seamen than the English, although their naval fleets were about the same size. The Dutch trade, however, was far greater than that of England, and although this gave her a certain advantage it also entailed two heavy disadvantages. One was that she had so many rich cargoes afloat that England could wound her to a degree far greater than that in which Holland could injure the English. In fact, it has been estimated that the English took prizes to the value of more than twice of the whole merchant marine of England at the beginning of the war, permanently lessening both the wealth and strength of her rival. The second point was that Holland had been so dependent on her ocean trade that if it were lost or heavily damaged she would be unable to regain her former position in the race for trade and empire.

In a series of eight great battles and other lesser engagements, Blake, and also Monk, won a succession of victories which marked, if not the immediate downfall, certainly the beginning of the permanent decline of Dutch supremacy on the sea, a supremacy which was now to pass to England. In 1654 Holland had to make peace, tacitly acknowledging the Navigation Act with all its consequences for her, and also paying an indemnity for the massacre at Amboyna a generation earlier, which had always rankled in English memory and which was at last avenged.

In spite, however, of success all along the line against rebels and foreign foes, the government, particularly Parliament, had been becoming increasingly unpopular. There was objection to its unjust and inequitable methods of raising money; to the bribery and corruption of certain members; and to its unrepresentative character. Vane had introduced a bill for reform but the difficulty was that Cromwell and the other leaders both in the government and the army believed, probably rightly, that if there should be a really free election the nation would recall the King.

One plan made was that the present members should be members of the next Parliament without standing for election and have the right to reject any elected member. Cromwell objected to this and it was agreed that action would be delayed. The very next day he heard that the Commons were at the moment preparing to pass the measure.

He immediately went to the House and when interrupted in a speech he suddenly cried out, "Come, we have had enough of this. I will put an end to this. It is not fit you should sit here any longer," and calling in the soldiers he cleared the House. Even if the unconstitutional Rump thus passed without regret on the part of any one except themselves, the problem of what to do next remained still to be solved. A free election could not be held, and so Cromwell and some of the other leaders made up an assembly of their own appointees, which became known as the Barebone's Parliament because one of its members had the Puritan name of Praise-God Barebone.

In one point the future was anticipated in the fact that of the hundred and forty who made up the Parliament, five were invited from Scotland and six from Ireland. The "rule of the saints," however, quickly proved a failure. The so-called "Fifth Monarchy Men" in the army, who claimed that the four great monarchies of Assyria, Persia, Macedonia and Rome having fallen, the Fifth should now be erected by the saints—that is themselves—taking over the government, proved no more impractical than the members of Parliament itself. A few of the least so in that body got up early one morning, before the rest knew what was afoot, dissolved the Parliament and placed the supreme power in the hands of Cromwell.

Again the question was what to do with it and how to govern. The problem of establishing some form of constitutional government with the consent of the governed was getting farther from solution all the time, and events were pushing Cromwell forward on the path to dictatorship. Another effort was made, and the Constitution known as the *Instrument of Government* was drawn up and accepted by the leaders. In accordance with its terms, Cromwell was to be Lord Protector with some of the former powers and duties of a king. He was to be assisted by a Privy Council, control of which lay in Parliament and not in the Protector. There was to be a Parliament of one House, to meet at least every three years, with its powers rigidly limited by the *Instrument,* and unable to make any laws that would conflict with that. Whereas the true British Constitution had been the slow growth of centuries, this was a paper one drawn up on a theory and was to prove unworkable.

In electing the members of the new Parliament, new constituencies had been provided for, and also all Royalists had been excluded from the franchise as well as all citizens with property worth less than £200. Even so safeguarded, the new Parliament when it met in 1654 immediately questioned the right of any group of private men to draw up a Constitution. By right of election they claimed power superior to that of the *Instrument* to which alone they owed their election. Cromwell then excluded about one hundred members who would not sign an agreement to accept the form of government, and thus a new purge was made. The remaining members then, with his permission, drew up a new Constitution which possibly might have been agreed to by Cromwell had not a dispute arisen as to whether Parliament or the Protector should control the army, and Cromwell dissolved the House. Circumstances were still pushing him along his destined road.

There were also various minor risings throughout the country and in Scotland, which were easily put down. But Cromwell was, as we have said, faced with the inability to form a government by consent without the almost certainty of the restoration of the King and the probable overthrow of Puritanism. He therefore took advantage of the disturbed conditions to throw over any pretensions to constitutional government for the time, and established a military despotism, dividing the nation into eleven districts, each to be governed autocratically by a Major-General. He himself levied a 10 per cent income tax on the property of all Royalists, and suppressed even the private worship of those who still used the Prayer Book. The Major-Generals, not contenting themselves with merely maintaining order, set about in many cases to reform the population according to the ideas of strict Puritanism in such matters as observance of the entire Sabbath, amusements, drinking, swearing and so forth.

No people can be thought of who are more individualistic and less likely to submit to regimentation or dictation than the English, and it is therefore of special interest to see in Cromwell's course how inevitable it appears to be that when too great power is given to or seized by one man loss of liberty and law inevitably follow.

According to the *Instrument of Government*, the Protector had been given the right to make ordinances when Parliament was not sitting, which would have the validity of laws, and he had done so. Now, however, some of the courts questioned this right, and Cromwell, just as the Stuarts had done, removed judges and imprisoned some of the lawyers in the Tower. Also, as always happens sooner or later in such one-man rule, he reached the point where he believed it necessary to abolish the freedom of the press, and in 1655 he decreed that only two weekly newspapers would be allowed in the nation and that they must be edited by a government agent. How modern all this sounds in the light of recent European history!

Equally familiar was Cromwell's foreign policy which was apparently devised to distract attention from what was going on at home. France and Spain were still at war, and the Protector flirted with each for an alliance, and finally when he could not get what he wanted from Spain he sent out a fleet to capture some valuable island in the West Indies, which proved to be Jamaica, which has remained in English possession ever since, and so added one more stone to the edifice of empire. War, however, was expensive, and Cromwell decided to call another Parliament in 1656 to raise additional funds. It seemed certain that there would be a large opposition in it but the Protector trusted to two things.

First, the Major-Generals were to see to it that the House was packed as far as possible with the right members, and, second, Oliver himself was ready to throw out those he did not want should they arrive. When Parliament assembled, he unceremoniously ejected a hundred or more and proceeded to business with the rest. Parliament was becoming as much of a farce as any legislature is under a dictator. The money was voted, the more readily perhaps as while Parliament was sitting news came that part of the Spanish treasure fleet had been captured, and the loot, in thirty-eight wagons, was soon rumbling through London.

The country, however, was becoming more and more restive. There were plots against Cromwell's life, and even in the fairly friendly, hand-picked Parliament there was an undertone of longing to get back to something more resembling the old form of government. In the *Humble Petition and Advice* which was presented to him by the House, he was asked to alter the Constitution, and himself to become king. He was also to create an Upper House, nominated by him. On the other hand, he was to give up the exercise of the power he had used to expel members from the Commons, retaining nevertheless for himself and his successors the right to exclude any member of the Upper House when he chose, thus building a bulwark for Puritan legislation against any hostile action by the Commons.

In spite of all his arbitrary and unconstitutional acts, Cromwell must be allowed, I believe, to have sincerely preferred some form of constitutional settlement that would have in it the elements of permanency which only consonance with the character

293

of the nation and the main points of the old Constitution could give it. The case of Oliver and England is of very peculiar interest because here we have a nation likely to be the last to submit to a dictatorship, and also a dictator who was steadily groping for some form of government which would not be arbitrary. Several years back he had said to Ludlow that "I am for government by consent as much as any man, but where shall we find that consent?" And now when this new form of government was offered he again said, "It is time to come to a settlement and to lay aside arbitrary proceedings so unacceptable to the nation."

Cromwell was never an ambitious man in the sense that he preferred his own career and advancement to the good of the nation. He had fought for a cause and not for himself. He had won the fight, but only to reach a stalemate, for to return the country to the Stuarts appeared to be sacrificing all that had been gained. His belief was right, as the next forty years or so were to prove that England could not be governed by uncontrolled Stuarts. There was his problem.

He was seeking government by consent but if he got it, the recall of the exiled Charles was inevitable. It is easy to say that he should have bowed to the will of the nation, and stopped his searching for some other form of government which might win consent without a Stuart restoration, but the problem is not so simple. We Americans, for example, praise Washington for his indomitable, stubborn if you choose, will and courage which alone kept up the fight when the country had wearied of it. It is true that he was not a dictator but he did in a real way impose his will on a people and an army, and win through. How far is a leader justified in carrying on when a nation is weary of the cause?

In any case, Cromwell snatched at the chance of establishing the government on a sounder basis of popular approval. Here again was as near an equivalent as could be found of the former King, Lords and Commons without calling in the old ones. No one knows what he thought of the offer to give him the throne but from the man's whole history it is possible he might have accepted, not from ambition but to give the nation its old forms to which it was so deeply attached, had the army not been so obviously opposed to the step. So he declined, but otherwise agreed to the new plan. It was, however, of no use.

When Parliament met in its second session in 1658, the hundred members whom Cromwell had excluded returned to their seats. Also he had had to move many of his supporters in the Commons to the new Upper House, which was now attacked by the Lower. After a fortnight Cromwell dissolved the sitting, saying "The Lord judge between me and you." Abroad there had been certain successes. Blake had won a great victory over the Spanish in the naval battle off Teneriffe; a Spanish army had also been defeated; and Dunkirk had surrendered. England, however, had been helping to kill a dying foe while the star of France was rising, and it was to be that nation and not declining Spain which would be the powerful enemy of the future. Cromwell's foreign policy would seem to have been wrong, and dictated perhaps more by the need of immediate and brilliant results than by insight into the new alignment to come.

Oliver, however, was dying. The strain of the past decade and a half had been too much for even his iron strength and nerve. He was sinking on August 30 when a wild storm passed over all England, and his enemies said that the devil was coming to take his own. On September 3, 1658, he died. One who knew him well said that "A larger soul, I think, hath seldom dwelt in a house of clay."

The remainder of the story of the Commonwealth is short and inglorious. Oliver was peacefully succeeded in the office of Protector by his son Richard, a rather colorless personage in history but who for a moment promised to be more popular than his father as he was not a soldier and little of a Puritan, a large part of the people being heartily tired of both. Not so the army, however, with which Richard soon clashed. His first Parliament met on January 27, and the army forced him to dissolve it on April 22, and himself to abdicate on May 25, ending the period of the Protectorate.

Earlier in the month the army had invited the forty-two re-

maining members of the Rump, the last remnant of the Long
Parliament, to meet but they at once showed both folly and in-
solence, demanding control of the soldiers, declaring all Cromwell's acts illegal, and insisting on the return of all the taxes
raised under his rule. As these had to a large extent been collected by the Major-Generals the result was instantaneous and
what might have been expected. Lambert suggested that the Parliament might as well be at the mercy of the army as the army at
that of Parliament, and as soon as he suppressed a Royalist rising, he sent troops to clear the House.

The soldiers then tried to govern with no Parliament but fell
out among themselves, and recalled the Rump. The situation was
becoming intolerable, and General Monk, who had kept free from
politics and commanded the army in Scotland, decided to end it.
Crossing the border, New Year's Day, 1660, he was joined by
Fairfax, and marched on London. There he found that the Rump
was despised by all and he declared for the free election of a new
Parliament. By pressure but without violence, the Rump voted
its own dissolution, and the extraordinary history of the Long
Parliament came to an end in March.

On April 4, the exiled Prince, Charles, signed what is known
as the Declaration of Breda offering a general pardon to all who
had taken part in the late affairs, save those whom Parliament
might exempt, guaranteeing new owners in possession of confiscated estates, promising arrears of pay to the soldiers, and con-
senting to a law for liberty to "tender consciences," all in accordance with what Parliament should later determine. The new Parliament, composed of two Houses, welcomed the Declaration, and
resolved that "according to the ancient and fundamental laws of
this kingdom, the government is, and ought to be, by King, Lords
and Commons." The ship of state had returned to its home port.
The story of the Restoration, which was now inevitable, belongs
to the next chapter and we have here only to consider briefly
some aspects of the troubled life of England during the war and
the Commonwealth before passing on to a new phase which will
be vastly different, as reaction always is.

Periods of war or even of excessive political disturbance are unfavorable to the development of literature. Even so great a figure as Milton, though he had already written some of his finest shorter poems, such as *Comus, Lycidas* and a few others, was to be for years diverted to the writing of such things as prose political tracts, and to have, as he himself said, the use "but of my left hand." The *Paradise Lost* had to await the Restoration.

There were other conditions tending to alter the course of literature besides those of any war-time period. England had been going through not only a Civil War but a religious revolution, and the rise of Puritanism affected letters in two ways. On the one hand, the intense preoccupation with religious matters made the period rich in religious writings, some of the most noted and lasting dating from these years. Jeremy Taylor was writing his *Holy Living* and *Holy Dying*; Richard Baxter his *Saints' Everlasting Rest*; Thomas Fuller his various religious works as well as his still popular *Worthies of England*; and Ussher and Chillingworth were discussing theology and Church government. On the other hand, the Puritan attitude toward the theatre—all playhouses being closed by law from 1642—undoubtedly helped the decline, already set in, of the drama to end in utter decay.

Naturally, with questions as to government and the Constitution constantly to the fore, there was a large literature dealing with those topics, notably Hobbes's *Leviathan* and Harrington's *Oceana,* but it was curious that, if we except the immensely popular and influential *Eikon Basilike* which described the philosophy and sufferings of Charles I, there was nothing both written and published from 1603 to 1660 in favor of the divine right of kings. There were, however, hundreds of pamphlets of ultra democratic tendency, advocating manhood suffrage, and Milton's belief that man was born free.

In spite of the usual effects of war upon literature, the period of the Civil Wars and the Commonwealth was to form, to a considerable extent, a notable exception, and it is quite surprising how much was written during it that has remained a permanent possession. Izaak Walton's *Compleat Angler,* still one of the popular books in the language, in its love of nature and its peaceful reflections on fishing and on life is far remote from the clash of arms or the political and religious bickerings of the times, as are also the works of Sir Thomas Browne with their quaint or stately prose, still a delight to all who love books. Nor was poetry wholly neglected, and in the lyrics of such men as Herrick, Marvell, Vaughan, Carew and Suckling we have not only some of the finest in English but the last to be written for more than a century and a quarter to come. In fact, no other period of war can show, perhaps, so rich a harvest.

We may also note the beginnings of the modern newspaper. The news sheets proved both numerous and short-lived, 170 having been started, it is said, in the seven years before 1649, when the press was temporarily placed under government control as previously noted. Both the newspapers and the coffee houses, where the former were read and news was exchanged, have continued in varying forms from that time to the present. Hackney coaches also were introduced in London, and there was an improvement in the mail coaches for long and fast travel. Throughout the life of the period there was notable the constant conflict of Cavalier and Puritan ideals. This was to be observed in dress, for example, particularly of men. That of the Cavaliers, although less rich than in Elizabethan days, was still costly and fantastic, with laces, ribbons and bright colors, whereas that of the Puritans was much more sober and simple. Neither architecture nor habits of living had changed in important particulars in the previous generation except for the alterations made by the Puritan legislation and other forms of restriction.

As we have said, the theatres were closed, as were also the bear gardens where the cruel but popular sport of bear baiting had been carried on. Cock fighting was also prohibited, all Maypoles pulled down, and severe fines inflicted for swearing and drunkenness. Such interferences with the ordinary habits and pleasures of the people, as well as the change of Sunday from a day with games and other recreation in the afternoon to the dour Puritan Sabbath, must all be taken into consideration when we read of the joy occasioned by the return of Charles II and of the "good old ways."

The levelling or democratic element had also frightened many. In a contemporary description of London we read that children used to throw mud at the coaches of the rich, calling them "hell-carts," and another writer claims that the ordinary citizens "could scarce endure the sight of a gentleman," and a well-dressed man in the street was likely to be called "French dog" and similar names. It was a time of revolutionary ferment, and as the years passed and there seemed less and less chance of any settlement of government and society except by the re-establishment of King, Lords and Commons, the lure of the old, accustomed, safe and characteristic life appealed to more and more groups and individuals.

But all that had been done and suffered had not been in vain. Even if Cromwell had been unable to form a new government which would suit the nation and win its willing consent, nevertheless the nation never again wished for arbitrary government by a single House of Parliament, for an absolute King, nor for the Laudian system of Church government and control. It had also come to loathe both a dictator and rule by military force.

Tyranny and a standing army became inextricably blended in the minds not only of Englishmen at home but throughout the whole Empire. Should another Stuart forget the lessons Charles I had refused to learn there would be no need for civil war. The nation would be united against him. Not only that, but there were other influences that were henceforth to be of the highest importance in English life which were the results of the trial by fire through which the nation had passed. For one, the old belief that there could be but one Church, one form of faith and worship, had gone for good. However the Church of England might be established and whatever its relation to government might be, it had become clear that somehow, somewhere, in the national life room would have to be found for those who dissented. They might still be persecuted but they were to remain, and they would be there to protest.

Again, the Puritan spirit, even though it narrowed English life and thought in some aspects, added a moral strength to it as well. A considerable part of the people, at least, acquired standards of both personal and political conduct that would be based on something higher than mere expediency. Although there were many Puritans of high rank, the movement was particularly strong in the middle, especially the town and mercantile, classes, and that of the working people. A stiff core of rather severe moral judgment was thus added to the psychology of the nation, and the complex mixture of motives, actions, and opinions in it which in its contradictions so puzzles foreigners is owing in no small measure to the lasting effects of the Puritan Revolution, laid over the earlier "Merrie England" and Elizabeth's "nest of singing birds."

To a considerable extent, it is true that the older England reasserted itself, although the rigors of the Puritan Sabbath remained, but Puritanism, although it came to be the character of a smaller part of the population, remained a force to be reckoned with. Many were to find it too bitter a draught for daily use, and there was to be sharp reaction. In the next century the nation was to be in sore need of the moral regeneration later wrought by the Wesleys and the Methodist movement, but that movement though having points in common with Puritanism was more moral and emotional than theological and intellectual. There is in fact much to distinguish an Evangelical from the earlier Puritan, and it is difficult to think of a Sir Henry Vane, a Colonel Hutchinson or a Milton as Methodist. Both movements, however, have played their great parts in the development of British character and life though originating in different periods and of somewhat different nature.

CHAPTER XIV

THE RESTORATION

AFTER HAVING RECEIVED an invitation on the Continent to ascend the throne of his father, Charles II landed at Dover, May 25, 1660, and in general the country gave itself up to wild rejoicing, especially along the road which the new King travelled from the coast to his palace of Whitehall. Flowers were strewn before him, Maypoles were re-erected, there was dancing on innumerable village greens, and in spite of doubts and misgivings on the part of some, the joy at his reception and return was genuine.

It was indicative of many things which were by now combined in the English character. If one strain in that character responded to the deep seriousness of Puritanism and its stern self-discipline, another strain responded no less instinctively and spontaneously to gaiety, mirth and sports. Also although the people had to a great extent been willing to sacrifice the past for the sake of preserving their liberties as individuals, no less had they felt, almost like a physical wound, the complete break with their past which had been made under the Commonwealth.

The Englishman who wanders over the world for half a lifetime in pursuit of duty, freedom or adventure never ceases to have a yearning for the tight little island which remains "home" in his thoughts, and similarly, the race though it may press on from century to century carries with it a profound sense of its historic continuity. The welcome given to Charles was not accorded to a dissolute though handsome young man but to the return of natural pleasures in life after long repression, and to the recovery of the national history which, even for those who may know nothing of it in detail, forms as much a part of their psychic make-up as the actuality of the present or the vision of the future.

What the thoughts of Charles may have been as he at last reached his palace and looked from the window through which his father had stepped to the scaffold cannot be known, but one thought in those first days and later was fixed and definite—he would not "go on his travels again." He would so govern as, at least, to preclude that. He was, indeed, to die in his bed as king, and it was to be his brother who was to flee back to the Continent as a refugee and deposed monarch, twenty-eight years after the rejoicings with which Charles was welcomed. In order more readily to understand what caused the revulsion of feeling and the final downfall of James, we may follow separately each of the strands of the story of those years to its end rather than treat of the whole chronologically.

Charles was thirty years of age the day he reached London, and had known exile for well on to half of them. His personal immorality shocked many even in the society of the Restoration period in which people, except the Puritans, were not readily shocked by word or deed. He had no principles or sense of honor, and no religious beliefs, though rather inclined to Catholicism as a religion fit for a king and a gentleman. He was lazy, easygoing, and more fond of intrigue than the hard work of government which he left to others. At the same time he was clever, witty, good-humored, ready of access, not given to persecution, and had a grace and ease of manner which helped his popularity. In the earlier years of his reign the burdens of government were shifted to the capable hands of the Earl of Clarendon who had been the chief minister of Charles I and had guided as far as he could the course of the young King in his exile. During the years to come, Charles was, in fact, to be served by and to employ a number of very able men.

This was particularly notable in his development of colonial policy, the most creditable and only successful of the several strands of policy which we shall have to follow. Not only were there to be important additions made to the colonial empire, and for the first time an imperial policy clearly outlined, but the personnel involved, both at home and abroad, was of rather surprisingly high quality. In England Clarendon and later Anthony Ashley Cooper, first Earl of Shaftesbury, were the leaders, but the Colonial Committee of the Privy Council also did good work, and to a considerable degree preserved colonial affairs from the increasing corruption of the times.

In addition, the choice of honest and able governors sent out to the colonies was in striking contrast with many of those in the next century when such offices were given in many cases to political hacks and placemen. This does not mean that no mistakes were made. The Commissioners sent to New England in 1664 to investigate conditions were distinctly unfit, and colonial land grants under Charles to his favorites were scandalous. But, on the whole, the Restoration government took the colonies with deep seriousness.

Americans are apt to concentrate on the peculiar history of New England, of which we shall speak presently, but we have to consider the Empire as a whole, and the criticisms we shall have to make of Charles's reign at home cannot be applied to imperial administration. Such governors as Lord Willoughby in Barbados, Stapleton in the Leeward Islands, Lynch, Atkins and others elsewhere, proved themselves capable, honest and independent, much in the tradition of the present colonial civil service. There seemed to be in general a genuine effort to find the right men, and even in Jamaica, Modyford, who was not a Royalist, was appointed governor.

As most of the colonies had submitted, willingly or not, to the Commonwealth, the situation was difficult when Charles came back, but in no case were there any punitive measures taken, and during his reign not only was every colony supplied with locally elected assemblies with very considerable power over the Royal Governors, but also religious toleration was conferred or forced upon all. What could not be done in England was tried overseas, and Shaftesbury struck a very modern note when he suggested that the colonies be used as experimental laboratories for legislation just as we Americans regard our forty-eight states.

This was all done, moreover, in the face of some danger. Before 1640 the adult colonists had been for the most part English born, and closely tied to the mother country. By 1660, however, a native generation had grown up who had never seen England, together with the addition of non-English stocks, and, which was important, for the preceding twenty years the colonies had been left very largely, when not wholly, to themselves to act as almost independent powers. This had been particularly true of New England, which had taken a very independent attitude from the start when the Massachusetts Bay settlers carried the charter of their company to America with them.

Overseas possessions, however, had been steadily expanding in territory and population. Imperial trade, produce and shipping had become important and England had no idea either of abandoning the Empire or of ceasing to be its center. English colonists in their self-governing institutions and religious freedom possessed advantages which those of no other power did. But because England had advanced far beyond all other nations on these two roads it is unfair to expect that she should do so on all. It is far more striking that she should make innovations in these points than that she should naturally conform to the prevailing ideas of colonial empire in respect to trade which then held sway.

These were embraced in what is called the Mercantile Theory. This, very briefly, contained two errors which are all too prevalent today. One was that as wealth was considered to consist of the precious metals such trades only were believed to be profitable as would bring to each nation an import of gold or silver. The so-called "invisible" balance of trade, consisting of returns from interest, services, and so on, either did not exist or was wholly disregarded. The other point, and this again is unhappily considered in our post-war world of the present as fundamental, was that each empire should be, to the limit of its possibilities, self-sufficient in finance, raw materials and manufacturing.

A certain similarity in the two periods, then and now, accounts for our holding the theory which our ancestors did and which the world, to its great if temporary prosperity, later abandoned and condemned. If nations are to be constantly at war with one another, they must be as self-sufficient as may be. In the earlier period they were constantly or frequently in such a state. Today they are likewise in constant fear of the same state, and a historian of 1938 can understand better than one of, say, 1900, the colonial theory which in between the seventeenth or eighteenth centuries and our own encountered unmitigated criticism as an unwarranted one.

As the various empires developed it happened that, almost universally, though not in New England, the chief products of colonies were raw materials of all sorts—sugar and molasses in the West Indies, tobacco in Virginia, lumber, spices, fish, furs, and other things elsewhere—whereas the home countries were developing manufactures and world trade. It thus came to be considered that each should confine itself to what it could best do or had been accustomed to doing, and colonies were expected to stick to producing the raw materials which the home country needed for either its manufacturing or trade, and not to compete with it in either of the latter.

The Navigation Act of 1651, which like all others had expired with the Restoration, had been aimed at strengthening the naval power of England, but the two Acts of 1660 and 1663 had in view trade and the co-ordination of an empire. In some respects, fairness was intended. Colonial ships, though not Scotch, could carry goods on equal terms with English, but a new point was that a long list of enumerated commodities could no longer be carried to any market except to England.

This was a revival of the medieval idea of the "Staple," of one place only where certain goods could be brought for sale. Some efforts were again made to be fair. For example, although American tobacco could be sold only in England, it was forbidden to raise any tobacco there in competition with the colonial, but nevertheless such legislation in the long run tended to subordinate colo-

305

nial interests to those of the home business man, and unfairly throttled the budding manufactures and international trade of the colonies. Both of these were small in this period but as the colonies should grow and increasingly desire to exploit all their own powers and profits, it was clear that such a system would make for friction and trouble.

Nor would it have been hard for a statesman conversant with all the facts to realize where serious trouble would be likely first to develop. New England, with its harsh climate, its broken topography, and stubborn soil, had no staple crops to raise, and, if it were to buy English manufactures, had to take to trade and manufacturing, including distilling, to get exchange to pay for its English imports. Although some of the colonies made protests, it was not until the next century that these became serious.

The colonial policy of the government under Charles aimed at bringing order out of the somewhat chaotic situation left by the Civil War, and also at tying the bonds of empire closer, but it cannot be considered, either according to the times or in itself, as harsh or unjustified. Massachusetts was the most difficult to deal with but even there the power of the English government was thrown on the side of democracy and increased religious liberty. I have elsewhere described in detail how an oligarchy had largely secured control of the colony, which was aiming at practically complete independence of the mother country while receiving the advantage of her protection. The colony was also entering upon its lowest period intellectually and morally. It had become notoriously intolerant. Not only was the franchise limited to members of the churches organized according to the New England way, but there were also the bloody persecutions of the Baptists and Quakers.

The British Government insisted that the oath of allegiance be taken, that toleration should be allowed to members of the Church of England, the franchise extended to all freeholders "not vicious in conversation and orthodox in religion," and also that the persecution of the Quakers be stopped. Rhode Island, which Massachusetts had tried to overawe, was given a Royal

Charter of its own. The Navigation Acts, as we have said, operated, when enforced, disastrously against New England, and for years bickerings went on as to their avoidance, in which the British agent, Randolph, hated in the colonies, played a biassed part in his difficult position.

The failure to understand the local need for trade in New England was perhaps the one serious mistake in the Restoration colonial policy, and was to end in the high-handed cancellation of the Massachusetts charter in 1683, although the action in the long run was not to prove detrimental to the best interests of the colony.

The Empire under Charles was not only being more carefully administered but was also growing. The days of the Elizabethan sea-dogs had long passed and those of the pirates and buccaneers had come, their exploits reaching their highest point in the sack of Panama by Sir Henry Morgan in 1671, though piracy was long to infest the oceans. These men, however, were in no sense empire builders, and the overseas possessions were henceforth to grow by legitimate warfare or peaceful settlement.

As a result of the Dutch War, the Dutch possessions of New Amsterdam and in Delaware were ceded to the English, the name of the former being changed to New York in honor of the King's brother, the Duke of York, and the English thus came into possession of an unbroken coast line from Maine to Florida with the immensely important river-way of the Hudson into the interior. The year before, Carolina had been granted to Shaftesbury and others, the charter as usual providing for religious liberty and a popular assembly, and after the conquest of the Dutch colonies, which included what is now New Jersey, a grant of that section was made, and in 1681 William Penn was given a charter for his Quaker colony of Pennsylvania. The British colonies along the coast, with the exception of the future Georgia, had now assumed practically the shape which they were to maintain for another century.

North of Canada, in the Arctic region, another imperial venture was undertaken in 1670 by the formation of the Hudson's

Bay Company, which did not attempt to colonize but merely to trade in furs through a series of fortified posts. To pass from the frozen north to the torrid zone, we find another factor in the rapid development of the Empire in the chartering of the Royal Africa Company, 1663 and 1672, to monopolize the trade in slaves. There is no more ghastly chapter in the story of Christian nations than this traffic, and the shrieks and groans and deaths of the poor wretches who suffered the horrors of the "Middle Passage" were to be echoed two centuries later on the battlefields of the American Civil War which was largely brought about by the presence of slavery. One cannot, however, judge one period by the outlook of another, and not only were the leading men and women of England, including the liberal philosopher John Locke, stockholders in the Company, but even the merchants and clergy of godly New England joined in the trade or owned slaves acquired by it.

In the United States, as well as elsewhere, the introduction of alien races for labor has always created serious difficulties in time, but, on the other hand, the system has made for rapid development of population and wealth, which spell power. In the northern colonies, slavery proved economically unprofitable long before it became morally unacceptable, but there can be no question that in the South and in the West India sugar islands, development would have been far slower without it, possibly so slow as to have changed their ownership from the British to some other power, either because of lack of population or of value from the imperial standpoint. In any case, the development of the slave trade under Charles and his successors must be considered one of the factors in the rapid development of the first British Empire. We shall note later the acquisition of Bombay and now return to England to consider the course of affairs there.

We may first discuss the thorny problem of a religious settlement. Charles, like Elizabeth, did not have deep religious convictions or prejudices, and with his easy-going tolerance might have been expected to bring about a compromise, but, unfortunately, he did not possess her statesmanship, and he had what she had not, a leaning toward Roman Catholicism, which gradually grew stronger. In his Declaration of Breda, Charles had promised liberty of tender consciences and that there should be no religious persecution, but in this promise, as in all the others, he had carefully left final decisions to Parliament, and the early difficulties must be ascribed to that body rather than to Charles or his Minister Clarendon.

The Royalists, now back in power, wanted restoration of Episcopacy and the Prayer Book. The Presbyterians were willing to have bishops but controlled by a different method from that of the Church of England. Charles was willing to compromise, wishing also to include Catholics in the general toleration, but both religious parties feared such a measure, and the compromise was rejected by Parliament. The Savoy Conference, so-called because held at the Savoy Palace, between the parties failed to reach an agreement, and the matter was thrown into the next Parliament.

There was more at work than purely religious differences. The Royalists, who had lost property and lands in the late war and under the Commonwealth and Protectorate, were anxious for revenge. It had been the dissenters of all sorts who had inflicted the losses upon them, and thus there was created a new line of religious cleavage. In 1662 Parliament adopted what is known as the Clarendon Code, though Parliament and not Clarendon was its author.

The Act of Uniformity forced out of office every clergyman or schoolmaster who would not accept the Prayer Book entire, and about 2000 clergy were forced to resign. As a result of the various Acts passed, dissenters were also excluded from the universities, which naturally tended to limit their culture and narrow their outlook. Of these other acts we may note the Conventicle Act of 1664 which was ferocious in its penalties, mounting to transportation from the kingdom for seven years depending on the number of times that a person might have attended a religious meeting which was not a service of the Church of England. Charles had asked Parliament to allow him to mitigate the Act of Uniformity by use of the dispensing power of the Crown in individual cases, but the answer had been the Conventicle Act and insistence on the banishment of Catholic priests.

This was followed, in 1665, by the Five Mile Act, which prohibited any clergyman who had been ejected as a result of the Act of Uniformity from coming within five miles of his former parish, unless he would swear never to try to alter the government of either the State or the Church. In all of these acts, hatred and fear of the Catholics, fear of the dissenters, and the desire for revenge played their parts in a way not wholly dissimilar to the political and economic motives at work in the Reconstruction Period in the South after the American Civil War. The dissenters, who were now to undergo persecution, were made up of various sects, such as the Baptists, Independents, the growing body of Quakers, and the Presbyterians. Many of the last accepted the Prayer Book but fought in Parliament for a relaxation of the laws against those who could not do so. Great numbers, however, suffered, and transportation then meant practically being sold into slavery in the West Indies.

In general, the dissenters were found in the lower and middle classes, and in the latter especially in the towns and among those engaged in trade. "Society" and the landed gentry inclined to the Church of England, and the struggle began that distinction between "Church and chapel" which has lasted ever since. Charles several times tried to intervene but by the use of his prerogative which had been denied by Parliament, and in each case, notably in the Declaration of Indulgence of 1672, he included Catholics and dissenters as both having liberty of worship. Both anti-Catholic feeling and that against the use of the prerogative by a Stuart despite Parliament were so strong that even those dissenters who were benefitted received the advantage with sore misgivings. Necessary as it appears to have been to curb the power of the King, the victory of Parliament over Crown was not to be all clear gain. Even if the abler Tudor line had remained on the throne it is unlikely that the nation would have continued in its former relation to its monarchs. The misfortune was that the crisis was precipitated too soon and before the nation was prepared for it. Had Parliament become truly representative of the people by this time, the gain in shifting power from the King to Parliament would have been far clearer. Unfortunately, it seemed essential to take power from Charles before a genuinely representative legislature with the modern form of a quickly responsive Cabinet as executive had developed. If a King who "could do no wrong" had been shown to be a danger to liberty, it remained to be proved that an unrepresentative Parliament might not be equally so.

In religious matters although the King might still retain the title of Defender of the Faith and be considered the head of the Church, it was apparent that the Parliament and not the sovereign had become the real head, and Charles was forced within a year to withdraw the indulgences he had declared. Although his relations with Parliament will be discussed in the next section it may be noted that he here met with a severe defeat at the hands of that body. The people at large, also, even those who suffered from the persecution by Parliament, preferred to leave matters in its hands rather than in those of the King.

The relations of Charles to the Catholic Church, though not known, were feared, the more so as he had no legitimate child, and his brother, James, the Duke of York, who was a Catholic, would be heir to the throne. In 1673 Parliament passed the Test Act to exclude all Catholics from holding office, and Charles was forced to sign it before the Commons would vote him any grant for money.

Although Charles is said to have remarked that his life was safe so long as his heartily disliked brother was his only successor, there were, nevertheless, plots against him, of which the most important in its effects on public opinion was the false one as described by an utterly unreliable scoundrel named Titus Oates, and which came to be called the "Popish Plot." The story was that Charles was to be murdered and James put on the throne as a Catholic with the help of Jesuits. The public uneasiness over the Catholic question had reached a high pitch before the news of this wholly unreal plot was disseminated, and Parliament, in

which some Catholic peers had retained their seats, passed a new
Test Act by which all Catholics were excluded except the Duke
of York, who was specifically named. Five Catholic peers were
imprisoned in the Tower and the secretary of James's wife was
executed.

The affair greatly increased the uneasiness felt over the prospect of James as the next King of England. The religious policy
pursued under Charles was thus that of the people, in so far as
they were represented in Parliament, rather than that of the monarch who both at home and in the colonies fostered toleration.
His motives, however, combined with the other factors at work,
as noted above, were so mistrusted that toleration, which always
included Catholics, was out of the question.

On the other hand, it is suggested by eminent English historians that the management, rather than the settlement, of the
religious problem gave better results than a broader compromise
would have yielded. By keeping out of the national Church not
merely some of the sects but *all*, the numbers outside of the
Church of England, and their importance and wealth, made some
sort of toleration in the future more certain than if the Church
had been broadened sufficiently to take in some while excluding
others. Moreover, as the control of the Church and religious legislation was to lie with Parliament and not with king or bishops,
the way was more open for the pressure of public opinion to make
itself felt in time. Indeed, even in the latter part of Charles's
reign a good many members of the two Houses came to have connections with the Dissenting interest, and a small party, the
"Whigs," came to be favorable to it.

As we have noted, Charles, in his Declaration of Breda, had
promised to support a policy of religious and political ameliora-
tion but had carefully left the decisions as to methods to Parliament, and that body had no intention of allowing him any of the
absolute powers claimed by his father. His hands were in truth
pretty effectually tied. The old Prerogative Courts, such as the
Star Chamber, High Commission, and others, had been abolished, and this action was confirmed by Charles's first Parlia-

ment. Moreover, the King had incurred debts of something like £3,000,000 during his exile, was extravagant in his expenses both for himself and his numerous mistresses, and was always in need of far more money than Parliament would grant.

Although no formula was enunciated making any change in the relations between the sovereign and the legislature, the Restoration in fact resulted in a marked decrease in royal power and an increase in Parliamentary control. It was a milestone in the development of constitutional monarchy, and although in Scotland, where conditions were different, Charles might aim at absolutism, he was far more astute than his father in realizing when to yield in England.

Another step in the direction of the present constitutional operation of government was the definite emergence of a Cabinet, though not so called. England now had a population of well over 5,000,000, and wide-flung colonial and trade interests. The necessary work of the executive branch of the government had become too complex to be carried on by the old Tudor method of the Privy Council directing all affairs. The Council was continued and enlarged, but the work had to be subdivided among committees and boards, the heads or leading members of which would be called upon for reports and meet together for consultation. Although the King attended meetings he was too lazy to act as a modern Prime Minister, and that part may be considered as having been played by Clarendon, who, although holding no office which gave him superior rank to the other Councillors, became the leader owing to his knowledge, ability and capacity for work. The function of the British Cabinet (quite unlike the American) is of enormous importance in the constitution of the Empire of today, and it is interesting to watch it take form in truly British fashion, not as a result of doctrinaire thinking or planning but merely by trying to solve an immediate problem of administration in a practical, hard-headed way. Although we here find the beginnings of the Cabinet and perhaps of the Prime Minister's office, there was to be a long development before they reached their present form. Clarendon, for example, did not realize the need for useful links between the Cabinet and Parliament, and none of the leading Councillors sat in the House of Commons. Indeed, the position of Parliament was still undecided, opinions as to it running all the way from an imitation of the Dutch States General, which met every working day in the year, to the more English one of using the Council (or Cabinet) as the continuous organ of government, with Parliament meeting only occasionally to redress grievances and control taxes.

The first Parliament, called the Convention because the writs for election had not been issued in the name of the King, sat for only a few months. Among other acts it passed that of Indemnity, pardoning, with many exceptions, those who had taken part against the King in the late troubles. Although many were punished by fines or imprisonment, only thirteen were executed, being a small part of even those who had sat in judgment on Charles I. On the whole, the vengeance taken was slight, although the feeling and brutality of the time were shown by the official digging up of the bodies of Cromwell, Ireton and Bradshaw, and hanging the remains on gallows for the public to see. Those of Pym, Admiral Blake and some others were also disinterred from Westminster Abbey and thrown into a pit. The army was paid off and disbanded, and the way was open for the legal election of a new Parliament, and the transition from dictatorship to constitutional government was accomplished with extraordinary ease.

The new Parliament met in the spring of 1661 and was not to be finally dissolved until 1678, from which time Charles was to rule without one. It was in the second year of its history that trouble with the King began. The war with Spain, which was still nominally continuing though there had long been no actual fighting, was ended in 1662, and Dunkirk passed to England by the treaty of peace.

In the autumn, while Parliament was on vacation, Charles sold the city to France for £400,000, and both Parliament and the nation were wild with rage. Suspicion had been aroused the preceding year by the retention by Charles of about 5000 troops, when the army was disbanded, a slight uprising in London hav-

ing afforded him an excuse. He did not, however, have the money
to maintain them and it now appeared that he had put himself in
funds without a Parliamentary grant, as well as sullied the nation's honor.

It is true that Dunkirk might not have great value and also
cost more than £100,000 a year to garrison and maintain, but that
did not alter the fear of the country of the King's high-handed
action and of what he might be planning. He had also issued the
first of his Declarations of Indulgence, spoken of above, which
again put the Commons in a fury as an effort to regain the prerogative and override Parliamentary legislation.

In addition, Charles had acquired a hoard of money by marrying Catherine of Braganza, daughter of the Queen-regent of Portugal, who brought the astounding dowry of £800,000 cash, together with possession of Tangier and Bombay. Tangier might
have been a valuable base in the Mediterranean had England
been able to adopt an aggressive Mediterranean policy, but she
was not, and eventually the garrison there was withdrawn and the
place abandoned. Bombay, which was the first territorial acquisition in India by the Crown, proved to be of little use to Charles
and in 1668 he was glad to turn it over to the East India Company.

The marriage, in its most important object, as far as the people
were concerned, which was the production of a legitimate heir to
the throne other than the detested James, was to prove fruitless,
but it had the important temporary result of aligning England
with France in her war with Spain, which was also at war with
Portugal. Charles was thus drawn more than ever under the influence of his resplendent cousin, Louis XIV, whose rising glory
and absolute government could not but be a cause of envy to the
easy-going young Stuart. The marriage also began that traditional
friendship and close trade relations which were to continue with
Portugal for more than two and a half centuries without break.

In spite, however, of growing friction with the King, Parliament itself in 1664 in the repeal of the Triennial Act was to give
him an opening which he was later to use. The original act had

315

been intended to force holding a session of Parliament at intervals of not less than three years but Parliament, approaching the end of the period, feared that the act might be made an excuse to dissolve it, and so passed another which made clear that it must be called into session each third year at most, but unfortunately failed to provide the machinery for doing so regardless of the King. By this blunder it made it possible for him to rule alone if he could or at any time might at least prefer the attempt to summoning the Houses.

Meanwhile, war again broke out with the Dutch, chiefly on account of trade rivalry, although Charles also had his personal grievance because of the Dutch having deposed his nephew, William of Orange, the former Stadholder, from any office in the Republic. Before war was openly proclaimed the English had captured New Amsterdam, and the Dutch had seized most of the English trading forts for slaves on the African coast. In 1665, however, war was acknowledged and Parliament made the then enormous grant of £2,500,000, and the English navy won a complete victory off Lowestoft. But success was followed by the appearance of the Great Plague, the frightful ravages of which throughout England will be noted later, and the British fleet could no longer defend the sea.

Moreover, Louis XIV was bound by treaty to assist the Dutch, and January 1, 1666, declared war against England, though he did little to prosecute it. In the summer there were several great naval battles between the Dutch and English fleets, but again England was struck by disaster, the calamity of the Great Fire of London being second only to that of the Plague.

The nations were ready for peace but the war continued for another year, during which Louis made a secret treaty with Charles, agreeing to give no aid to the Dutch provided he be given a free hand in the Spanish Netherlands. Philip IV of Spain had died in 1665, and Europe was about to become involved in the question of who should succeed to his vast and scattered empire. Holland quickly agreed to make peace when France advanced her armies toward her border in the Netherlands, and it was thought that the terms of the Treaty of Breda would certainly be arranged without difficulty. Charles, to save money for his pleasures, discharged the sailors and dismantled the fleet, when to the intense mortification and anger of the nation the Dutch sailed up the Medway, captured four English ships and blockaded London. Terms, however, were made, and although England gave up her last foothold in the Spice Islands she retained the far-more-valuable conquered Dutch possessions in America.

The anger of the House of Commons was directed against Clarendon as the King's chief minister for the manner in which the war had been conducted, and the House took another step forward toward modern practice in demanding an account of the way in which the huge sums voted to the Crown had been spent. It had been agreed that a king could not raise money without Parliamentary consent. Now the Commons made the further demand that the money should not be spent without its approval. Clarendon fought against it but was ungallantly deserted by Charles, who owed his throne to him more than to any other man, and the broken statesman fled to lifelong exile in France.

After Clarendon's fall, Charles became his own chief Minister, though he consulted others, particularly Clifford, Arlington, Buckingham, Ashley and Lauderdale, who later became known as the "Cabal" as the initials of their names formed that word, and we now enter upon the most shameful part of his reign.

Louis of France had gone to war with Charles II of Spain, the physically weak and partly imbecile son of Philip, and head of the Spanish Empire for whatever his probable short span of life might be. Other countries became alarmed at the all-grasping amtition of the French King and a triple alliance of Sweden, England and Holland was formed against him to hold him within bounds. A halt was called in the Treaty of Aix la Chapelle, 1668, but the King of England had betrayed the secrets of the allies to Louis, and was soon to sell himself and his country. The next year James openly avowed himself a Catholic, and Charles himself became converted but not publicly. He was already bargaining with Louis but his terms were too high, and in exchange for giving up toleration he secured an annual grant from Parliament of £300,000 for the next eight years, and then prorogued it.

The amount, however, was much too small for his needs, and in spite of all his pledges he wished to free himself from Parliamentary control. At Dover, June 1, 1670, a secret treaty was negotiated between him and Louis by which he pledged England to help France against the Dutch and to forward Louis's ambitions with regard to the Spanish inheritance. Although in case of success certain territorial acquisitions were to be made by England, the chief inducement for Charles was that Louis was to support him against his subjects if needful should he openly declare his conversion as a Catholic, give him £154,000, and the aid of 6000 troops. In addition, during the war, France was to lend him thirty naval ships and give him £230,000 a year.

To cover his tracks, the following year, he made an open treaty with Louis in which no mention was made of his conversion and all the money and aid promised by France was made to appear solely for the purpose of carrying on the war, for which purpose he received another £800,000 from Parliament. His need for money for his own pleasures, was, however, insatiable. His new French mistress, whom Louis had sent over to influence him, was made Duchess of Portsmouth and received an income of £40,000 a year. It is said that in one year Charles gave her no less than £136,000. In 1672 he saved himself from complete bankruptcy by the desperate measure, which bankrupted many of the goldsmiths of London, of cancelling the principal of the loan he had obtained from them of £1,400,000.

Meanwhile, Louis had also bribed the Swedes to desert the Dutch who now faced the greatest power in Europe alone. The sea fights with the English were indecisive, and on land the Dutch defended themselves with heroic courage, led by William of Orange whom they had recalled to public office. The dykes were opened, the land flooded, and the enemy held at bay. Feeling in England was veering in favor of the Dutch and against the French. There were also rumors as to the secret treaty, and

Charles was forced to make peace. The stern, silent William had gained allies on the Continent, and reprieved his country by peace with Louis, though the struggle was only suspended. The French King, now at the height of his power, was determined to make himself master of Europe. In the end the failure of his plans was to be wrought by William and England, but the road to be travelled was long and circuitous.

The English were now given fresh anxiety by the second marriage of the Duke of York. As a Catholic, his possible accession to the throne was greatly feared, but at least his only two legitimate children, the Princesses Mary and Anne, were Protestants and next in succession. These were children of his first wife, Anne Hyde, daughter of the Earl of Clarendon, who had also been a Protestant but Mary of Modena, his second wife, was a Catholic and if he should have a son by her England seemed doomed to revolution or to a line of Catholic Kings. In 1677, James's oldest daughter, Mary, was married to her cousin William of Orange, an event which was to prove of the utmost importance to England.

Meanwhile, the uneasy relations of Charles with Parliament continued. When, in 1676, it refused to grant him money, he prorogued it for fifteen months, and Louis gave him £100,000 a year to make him, if possible, independent of the Commons in which anti-French feeling was strong. The unsatisfactory conduct of Charles all during the war, the enormous excitement and terror created by the Titus Oates plot in 1678, the impeachment of Danby, the King's chief minister, the same year, and the dissolution of Parliament 1679, all caused increasing fear and dissatisfaction.

Acts were proposed from time to time to alter the succession and exclude James. There was even a party in favor of making the King's illegitimate son, the Duke of Monmouth, heir. Opposing parties were formed led by Danby and the Earl of Shaftesbury, and so high was feeling rising that in 1681 Charles summoned Parliament to meet at Oxford instead of London, fearing both Shaftesbury's followers and the city mob. The Whigs,

319

dreading an attack by the Tories, carried arms, and the nation began to fear another civil war. As a result, there was a strong reaction in favor of the King and peace at any price.

Shaftesbury went so far as to propose capturing Charles in order to control him, but finally fled to Holland where he soon died in exile. Violence, indeed, was beginning to mark the times. In order to control elections in favor of the Tories, the King secured the overthrow of the charter of London and many other corporate towns and cities. As the Tories were staunch supporters of the Church of England, persecution of Dissenters began afresh on a considerable scale. Then came the discovery of the unsuccessful Rye House plot, which was a plan of some of the more rash of Shaftesbury's followers to capture the King and James on their way back from Newmarket.

There was also a more dangerous plot which included Monmouth, Russell, Essex, and other notable Whigs, to control the King in some way, though not necessarily by force. Essex committed suicide, Russell and Algernon Sidney were executed, and Monmouth, as the King's son, was sent into exile on the Continent. The three years since the last Parliament had passed but the King would not summon another, again turning to Louis of France for cash to support him. Then a sudden turn of fortune changed the course of history. On February 6, 1685, the King suffered a paralytic stroke and a few days later died after having received the sacraments of the Catholic Church. James came to the throne and England again had an openly avowed Catholic sovereign.

The reign of Charles must be regarded as one of the great formative periods in English history. We have already spoken of the efforts to organize and consolidate the Empire, of the emergence of the Cabinet and Prime Minister, and of the development of the idea of constitutional monarchy. The powers of Parliament had increased materially, and though Ministers were still nominally responsible to the King and not to it, when Parliamentary opposition to them or their policies became strong, they had to be discarded.

The rise of the two great parties, Whig and Tory, which were to dominate British public life for two centuries to come, also date from this period, as do modern electioneering methods, and the idea of party loyalty. The loyalty was not to a set of doctrines but to the party organization and to one or the other of the two great groups into which the nation was divided. On the whole, the Tory party was that of the landowners and of the adherents of the Church of England, whereas the Whigs were made up of the business classes and the Dissenters with some conspicuous members of the aristocracy, though most of the latter were Tories.

The Restoration period had also been marked by a very large increase in trade and business prosperity, in strong contrast to the depression of the Civil War and Commonwealth. Among other enterprises we may note the rise of the East India Company, which declared annual dividends of 20 per cent from 1662 to 1664, and 40 per cent in 1665, and 100 per cent in 1685. From the first date to 1691 it averaged about 22 per cent a year, and this was only one of England's many ventures. More modern methods of banking and finance were introduced, which with company organization helped to mobilize the liquid resources of the nation. Prosperity must have been sound and great, for it had to cope with many adverse factors. There were not only the extravagance and bad handling of the government finances by Charles, together with the Dutch wars, but also two of the great disasters of history.

The Great Plague which raged in 1665 and 1666 was the last and the worst since the Black Death in the fourteenth century. London had become the great center of the nation with a population of well on to 500,000, and naturally the losses were heaviest there. Over 100,000 persons died in the town, and the mortality was great in scattered sections all over the country, though the case of the village of Eyam in Derbyshire, where only 30 persons out of more than 300 were left alive, is exceptional.

The second great disaster was the Fire of London, by which over 13,000 houses, together with all the churches and public buildings in the devastated districts, were destroyed. The property loss, in a day when as yet there was no insurance, was estimated at from £7–10,000,000. The amount was colossal but the cleaning out of such a large part of the old plague-infested buildings and replacing them with new, must have done much to make London a healthier place. A city which in less than seven years could suffer two such losses as the Plague and the Fire, to be followed by the confiscation by Charles of the £1,400,000 from the goldsmiths, evidently must have accumulated very great resources.

The Restoration had caused a marked reaction in morals and social customs from the strictness of the Puritan period. The utter moral laxity of the King himself set an evil example which was readily followed by the young Royalists who came back from exile and by all about the Court. The theatres were at once reopened and became immensely popular, though the Restoration drama, in spite of its wit, pictured mostly the profligacy of the times, even in the works of its leading writers, such as Otway, Congreve, Wycherley, Vanbrugh and Farquhar.

But Puritanism had also left a deep impression. For better or worse, as a social factor, the old Puritan observance of Sunday continued, as it has to a great extent to the present day. Moreover, the period gave us not only the works of Dryden but the most noble of those of Milton, while Bunyan in his *Pilgrim's Progress* gave the nation one of its most widely read religious books. No two figures could be more unlike than those of the two great writers whose genius was so profoundly moved by religion. Bunyan followed his father's trade of itinerant tinker, and it is a fact which casts an unexpected light on this period that a member of an almost vagabond class in society should be able to read and write and get his books published. Bunyan was a genius and one of the greatest writers of English prose. That was accident but the suggestive point remains that the social organization had so developed that a genius so placed could gain an education and reach one of the largest reading publics which any author ever has had. His masterpiece, written in biblical language, became almost as widely known and read as the Bible itself, and this product of a dozen years in jail has been unquestionably the most influential allegory ever written in England and probably in the world. It was intensely earnest, vivid, sincere and natural, and the fact that it came straight from the mind and heart of the common people and was taken back to their heart so universally sheds another light on the nature of the English.

More light is also cast by the greatest figure in the literature of this period, who was also one of the great poets of the world and the ages, for Milton's *Paradise Lost* has but one competitor, Dante's *Divine Comedy*, for the position of the greatest epic since the days of Greece and Rome. His work in the earlier Stuart period had been closely allied to that of the Elizabethans and has already been mentioned. Then came the decades of the Civil War and his own public service when he abandoned poetry entirely and devoted himself to discussion of public affairs in magnificent prose works of which the noblest was his *Areopagitica*, a defense of the liberty of the press which has never been equalled and which is still of profound influence.

Each of the earlier phases of Milton's work had coincided with the general political and social atmosphere of the periods in which they were produced. It shows, however, how difficult it is to make sweeping generalizations about any period when we find the great poet, in the midst of the licentiousness of the Restoration age, writing in his masterpiece the greatest religious poem in English, and possibly any, literature. In the story of the fall of man and, in the lesser *Paradise Regained*, of his redemption, the work is distinguished not only by profound religious and philosophical thought and insight but by the almost unrivalled poetical expression in which it is clothed. In its strength, its loveliness, its solemnity and dignity, its deep religious feeling and tenderness, its earnest seriousness, all robed in a metrical beauty of verse which seems to have all the tones of an organ heard through cathedral aisles, we find, in another masterpiece of the English, qualities which have to be taken into account in trying to understand the race.

The intellectual life of the Restoration was by no means limited to witty if rather obscene drama and great religious works.

Science, also, not only became fashionable but made great advances. The Royal Society was founded and included such names as those of Boyle, Christopher Wren, William Petty, and, greatest of all, Sir Isaac Newton. Such a period must be regarded from many angles other than those of a licentious and untrustworthy King, Parliamentary development, and foreign wars.

In spite of democratic struggles in England and Holland, the age was one which, like the present, tended to worship one-man government in the name of strength and efficiency. Examples were not lacking. In France, Louis had become absolute, and France was the greatest power in Europe. Charles XI in Sweden was to re-establish that nation by making himself equally absolute. Poland could do nothing except under a dictator. Even Holland, to be saved, had had to place herself largely under the domination of William. The question when James came to the throne was whether England would be able to maintain freedom and self-government or whether it, too, would succumb to the prevailing conditions.

The new King, who had Mass openly performed in the chapel at Whitehall, was a far less able man than Charles, and also more stubborn, conceited and unyielding. He would never know, as Charles had, when to yield but would pursue a course to the breaking point. One of his first acts was to get a promise of cash from Louis in case he should have trouble with Parliament, and it boded ill.

The late King had owed much in his last few years to the Tories, and when James summoned his first Parliament it was carefully and heavily packed in the Tory interest. As for the religious question, although he agreed to maintain the Church of England, he was bent on securing toleration for Catholics, while Richard Baxter, one of the ablest of the Dissenters, was imprisoned. The new King began, however, with the feeling in the country in his favor, and the House of Commons, overwhelmingly Tory, voted him the full income Charles had had.

An invasion of Scotland by the exiled Argyle was easily put down and Argyle executed. A far more important incident in the first year was the invasion by James's illegitimate nephew, Monmouth, who was extremely popular in the West. Landing at Lyme he declared himself King, and although none of the gentry joined him on his march to Taunton he was not interfered with. At Sedgemoor he met the royal forces led by James in person, was defeated and fled into the New Forest. Parliament attainted him of treason, and when captured he was promptly executed. Apparently a complete failure, the rebellion of Monmouth was in fact one of the chief factors in the final downfall of James.

Although Monmouth had been a Whig, the actions of James following the rebellion disgusted and terrified the Tories, and did much to bring the members of both parties together as Englishmen who might join on occasion in a struggle for decency and liberty. Judge Jeffreys, notorious for the consistent brutality and coarseness with which he treated the accused before him, was sent to the western counties to hold what have ever since been called the "Bloody Assizes." In all, between 300 and 400 were hanged and 800 to 900 sent to slavery in the West Indies. A shudder of horror went through England.

James also demanded of Parliament the repeal of the Test Act, which would have allowed him to officer with Catholics the army of 30,000 which he had raised in the emergency of the two invasions. In France, Louis had revoked the Edict of Nantes and the Protestants there were given over to a cruel persecution. England did not need the sight of the Huguenots escaping over the Channel to warn her what might come from James. The King, despite the opposition of Parliament, not only placed Catholic officers in the army which he ostentatiously had encamped near London, but brought over shiploads of Irish to swell his forces. He invoked the old theory of the dispensing power, by which kings claimed the right in special cases to dispense with the laws, and when the court disagreed with him, he packed it with his own judges. He also began to appoint Catholics to high office in the Church of England, and established an Ecclesiastical Commission Court, with Jeffreys, whom he had made Lord Chancellor, at its head, which could try any of the clergy in the country.

Spurred on his insane course by the French and Jesuits, he issued in 1687 a Declaration of Indulgence, which gave freedom of worship to Catholics and Dissenters alike, hoping to win over the Dissenting interest to his effort to establish Catholicism. By 1687 his objects had become so plain that all could read them.

At Magdalen College, Oxford, he insisted that the President's office should be filled by a Catholic, and when the Fellows, in whose hand the election lay, refused, they were all turned out. When he had come to the throne, almost all offices in the State, from the Council down to local magistrates, had been High Church Tories, but by 1688 these had been as completely as possible replaced by Catholics. The abolished Court of High Commission was revived, and James began to attack the property and offices of the Anglican clergy.

When in 1688 he issued a new Declaration of Indulgence and required that it be read in every church, seven bishops petitioned him that such clergy as objected might be exempted. James at once called the request a "standard of rebellion," and the bishops were put on trial. When the jury at last brought in a verdict of "Not Guilty" there was shouting for delight all over London, which James could hear out at Hounslow Heath where he was reviewing his troops.

It was thought that James's life might not be long, and next to him were his daughters, the two Protestant Princesses. The nation, in hope of his death, would have put up with him, but on June 10 an event, fatal to him, occurred. A son was born to him, and the nation immediately realized what the prospect of a Catholic heir meant. At first the fact was not believed, and it was said that the child was not James's but had been brought into his wife's room in a warming pan. As, however, the King claimed, what was probably true, that the child was indeed his, the possibility that it was not would make no difference. In fact, the dispute would merely tend to more confusion and the formation of more parties.

Whigs and Tories had been forced to draw together, and for some time, in the face of the growing danger, had been considering inviting William of Orange to come over and assist in placing his wife Mary, James's Protestant daughter, on the throne. During the reign of Charles many had adopted the doctrine of non-resistance and of divine right, but both doctrines melted before the fact of the baby Catholic heir. The object lesson of renewed Catholic persecution in France by Louis was too near English shores. The invitation, signed by seven Whig and Tory leaders, went its way at once.

William was a silent, harsh, unlovely but strong character, the strength of which was seemingly increased rather than diminished by physical infirmities. Unlike most of the Stuart blood, women meant nothing to him. Childless, married for reasons of state, he concentrated his life on the duel with France. Although a Calvinist, religion meant little to him either, but he was a born statesman if not a military leader of the first rank. For some years, the possibility of his being called to England had been before him, but the decision had not been easy. His allies and own people had to be considered, and if the venture should fail, Holland would lie at the feet of Louis. On the other hand, the appearance of England on the Continent in the war against the ambitions of the Grand Monarch was essential to success. William decided to cast the die.

James himself helped toward his success by offending Louis at the very moment when he most needed his help. The French troops offered were not in England, the Channel was clear, the pressure on Holland was diminished for the moment, and William, with his expedition long planned and gathered, landed at Torbay in November, 1688. The concessions offered by James were too late, and as William marched toward London he was joined by the gentry and people along the line, in marked contrast to the abortive invasion by Monmouth. Danby, Devonshire, Seymour, and, above all, Churchill, future Duke of Marlborough in command of James's forces, deserted his cause, brought in additional forces from one county and another and demoralized James's mixed army.

In London the mob rose against him. So widespread had become the doctrine of non-resistance to kings and that of divine right, that civil war might yet have resulted with untold consequences to William and to the history of both England and the Continent, had it not been that James himself fled from the country. On December 10, he sent his wife and young son to France, but attempting to follow next day he was captured and brought back to London. With the connivance of William, he was allowed to escape, and this time reached France in safety.

William had promised a free Parliament elected by the people, and although he could not issue the writs of election, a Convention Parliament was chosen, and assembled in London in January, 1699. The throne was pronounced to be vacant by the abdication of James, and William and Mary were declared joint sovereigns, Mary to have actual power only in the case of the prior death of William. Although James had fled the country, and in doing so had dropped the Great Seal in the Thames, there had been no formal abdication.

Mary was his elder daughter, but her claim to the throne was subject to that of her young half-brother. William's claim by descent was far more remote. The doctrines of hereditary and divine right, as well as of non-resistance, had been dropped overboard as completely as the Great Seal. The new sovereigns owed their throne solely to the action of Parliament, and in the relations in government between Parliament and sovereign, Parliament would henceforth be the superior power. The succession was also arranged for. Mary was to succeed William, and after her their children, if any, in order, males first. If there were none, then Mary's sister, Anne, would, and finally, any children of William if Mary should die and he should have any by a second marriage.

For some years the leading men of England had had to play double roles. It was uncertain whether or not James would so mismanage affairs that he would have to go, or would go. The only alternatives were the baby prince of uncertain parentage and certainly of Catholic faith, and Mary with William as her sword arm. More was at stake for each individual to ponder on than his private fortunes. The interests of the nation transcended those, and the civil wars and the dictatorship of Cromwell were still living memories to many. Those, especially Marlborough, who had to play both sides during those dangerous and anxious years, have been praised or sharply criticized, depending on the party attitude of many, especially of the earlier, historians. The secrets of the conduct and motives of Marlborough and the others lie only in their own hearts, long mouldered into dust.

But if there was much that was inglorious about the "Glorious Revolution," it was glorious in the fact that in a crisis which seemed to portend civil war and a breakdown of government, a transition was managed to a new order with a minimum of illegality and break with the past, practically without violence, and a settlement arrived at which lasted almost without change for nearly two centuries.

Moreover, the way was laid for not only the downfall of the apparently impregnable power of Louis and of France, and the rise of England, but for the salvation of democracy and self-government in spite of the world trend, and in what was to become the dominant power in the world. William and Marlborough were to annihilate the threatened domination of Europe by the Sun God of Versailles, and the Revolution Settlement was to prove a firm foundation for the political genius of the English people and the development of their world power in later generations with such leaders as Walpole, the Pitts and others. If William had "taken England on his way to France," he and those who had perforce had to play shifty parts had saved England herself and set her on the path to world power.

CHAPTER XV

THE REVOLUTION IN ENGLAND

THE RISKS of William's venture had been enormously great and tend to be overlooked by the comparative ease of his success. The fate of Europe and of England depended on the defeat of the vast ambition of Louis, as, a century later, it was to depend on the defeat of Napoleon. No other statesman of the time realized that as clearly as William, the sole passion of whose life was to save his own little Holland and to avert the domination of the Continent by the absolutist French monarch. In the great game that William was playing, and which was eventually to be won, there was no room for the minor ambition to become King of England. In itself that did not count, but he realized that it was essential that he should if possible substitute himself for the Catholic and Francophile James. He calculated the chances to a nicety, won, and changed the history of the world.

But if Louis had not foolishly failed to use his fleet to prevent William's crossing, if the wind had not changed at a critical moment when he had been carried past his landing place, if James had not first offended Louis and later dropped his last card by flight, if the English people had opposed the invasion, if the Tories and Whigs after the bitter strife of years had not held together at the right moment, William would not only not have gained England but would have lost his own country.

Only a few of the turning points of history show such a combination of calculating statesmanship and luck. William was a stranger to England. He knew that no English statesman understood as he did the grand strategy on the Continent, in which, however, England would have to be made to play its part if it were to be saved. He knew that the temporary combination of Whigs and Tories could not be expected to last forever, that there would be uneasiness and plots for the return of James.

There was no one whom he could fully trust. He had no love for England and the English never loved him, but he knew the desires of England as its native Stuarts had not, and that if he were to carry England with him in his great adventure he would have to align himself with the wishes of the people. In nothing did he show himself abler than in understanding the prejudices and politics of the foreign country which fate had brought him to rule.

The Revolution Settlement, characteristically, did not involve the drawing up of any new constitution but consisted merely of a number of separate acts to meet grievances or dangers evident from the past. Among them was a Bill of Rights declaring, among other things, that it should be illegal for the Crown to suspend laws, maintain a standing army without Parliamentary consent, interfere with free elections or with freedom of speech in Parliament. A new Triennial Act declared that no Parliament should continue more than three years without a fresh election, while the Mutiny Act, which had to be renewed each year, for the army, and the provision that the Crown should have no permanent revenue except for normal civil purposes, insured that Parliament would have to meet annually. A Toleration Act which gave freedom of worship legally to all except Unitarians and Catholics, satisfied the mass of the nation and settled the religious question.

The transition from the attempted tyranny of James to the constitutional government of William was thus made easily and smoothly in England. This was equally true of all the colonies but there was an important difference. There was no attempt made to interfere with their local liberties, although the fact that Massachusetts was at the moment without a charter enabled one step to be made toward uniformity. The new charter of 1691 provided for a royal governor, and a popularly elected lower House as in

331

other colonies, but in other respects marked a distinct advance in democracy and religious toleration.

With the exception of Rhode Island and Connecticut, which elected their own governors, all the American and West Indian colonies now had the same form of government, consisting of a royal governor, an upper House not usually elected by the people, and a lower one always so chosen. The governments might thus be considered as little replicas of the English King, Lords and Commons, with local rights and united with each other and England only through the Crown, although in general the home government was acknowledged to have the right to regulate trade.

The Revolution, however, had subtly readjusted the relations of the different parts of government in England. Henceforth the Crown was fundamentally to be subject to Parliament, which soon came to mean the Commons. Thus it came about that although the colonies, as the Dominions are today, were theoretically united through and subject only to the Crown, yet as the Crown had become subject to Parliament, the colonies were to find themselves in practice falling more and more under the control of the same power which controlled the Crown.

With the possible exception of the trade regulations as embodied in the Navigation Acts, it had been tacitly assumed that the local colonial legislatures in each colony were as free to legislate as Parliament was in England, which was very different from being subject to another legislature three thousand miles away and in which they were not directly represented. The significance of this result of the Revolution of 1688 was not at the time realized either at home or in the colonies, but the unnoticed change was pregnant with dire results for the future.

The only immediate difficulties, however, which faced William after England had peacefully accepted him and Mary as sovereigns were in Scotland and Ireland. In neither did he display the statesmanship which he did elsewhere, but as his whole life had been centered upon the problems of the Continent his knowledge of both the past and present of each of these countries was probably not as good as that which he possessed concerning England,

and in each case there were unfortunate precedents and prejudices. Moreover the dangers were immediate and pressing. On the Continent events were moving rapidly. In April, 1689, Louis declared war on Spain and the next month the Treaty of Grand Alliance against him was entered into by the Emperor in Germany and by Holland. William was anxious to have England join at once, as she did later, and move against Louis, but could not leave a Jacobite and rebellious Scotland and Ireland in his rear.

In Scotland, Graham of Claverhouse and the Duke of Gordon rose in favor of James, defeating the troops sent by William in the battle of Killiecrankie, although the Scottish Parliament had declared for the new monarchs. It had dictated its own terms, and the interminable religious question had reached a settlement, as it had in England, though much yet remained to be adjusted. Presbyterianism had been restored, but toleration provided, and the Church, no longer politically dominant, was removed as an interference with the natural development of a Parliament.

Scotland, however, was as yet almost two countries, made up of the Lowlands and the Highlands. The former were far from what they are today, with their rich farms and flourishing cities. All Scotland was poor, and largely owing to the English Acts of Trade, there was almost no commerce. The Highlands were much behind even the Lowlands and were wild indeed, still controlled by the clans and the clan spirit. It had been the Highlanders who had defeated William's troops, but after the victory they had retreated to the glens with their booty, and a wise use of money gradually brought one chief after another over to William's cause.

Practically all had agreed to submit except one MacIan Glencoe who, although he intended to do so, had not on the final day allotted. The King's chief minister in Scotland, the Master of Stair, asked permission, which unhappily William gave, to extirpate the entire clan, which he not only did but did after abominable treachery in the famous "Massacre of Glencoe" in a wild and somber glen. Even the Lowland Scotch had always treated the Highlanders as savages for whom no mercy could be expected, but the cry of horror which went up indicated the beginning of a more humane and civilized attitude. Although feeling was embittered, Scotland was now safe for the time.

The story of William in Ireland is even blacker. The native Irish were Jacobites and Catholic, and when James landed there in March, 1689, in an effort to regain his throne, they rallied round him. Many of the English and Scots settlers took refuge in the towns of Londonderry and Inniskillen, and the former had to stand a long siege from the forces of James. For fifteen weeks, faced by stark famine, living on dogs and rats, and even by chewing leather, the besieged held out until an English fleet brought them food and raised the siege. James was also defeated near Inniskillen but was still able to hold his own against the English forces in the field.

So long as this danger lasted, William's hands were tied for any operations against Louis on the Continent. Ireland must be conquered at any cost of delay, and William decided to head an army against it in person. Fortunately Louis, who did not realize as William did the importance of the Irish crisis, again blundered. Owing to a severe defeat of British and Dutch fleets off Beachy Head, the French for the time controlled the Channel, but Louis failed to prevent the transporting of William with his army and supplies across the Irish Sea. On July 1, 1690, William won a great but not decisive victory over the Irish in the battle of the Boyne, and James again lost the chance to hold his throne by scuttling off to France from Ireland as he had from England. Louis had now awaked to the importance of the operations, and sent troops to reinforce the Irish, but step by step William completed the conquest.

Meanwhile, the Irish Parliament, made up almost wholly of Catholics, had passed laws restoring the lands confiscated in 1641, making the Roman Catholic Church supreme, and Ireland practically independent of England. By this time a considerable part of the population of Ireland was English and Scotch. It has been estimated that not less than 50,000 settlers had gone from England in Cromwell's time alone. Like the Highlanders in Scotland, the native Irish were still regarded as wild, and the country as open to colonization as America. But unlike America, it lay at England's back door, a few hours away. England could not afford that it should be independent when independence meant a hostile Catholic state ruled by the exiled dynasty in alliance with the power which was threatening the life of England and all Europe. But that does not excuse what was now to come which forms perhaps the most infamous page in England's history and one of the blackest in that of Ireland.

Not only did the English Parliament exclude all Catholics from the Parliament of Ireland but subordinated all its acts to the English legislature. In the next few years the treaty of Limerick, which had closed the rebellion, was discarded. The Penal Laws provided that no Irish children could be educated by Catholic teachers in schools or private houses or sent abroad for the purpose, without their parents forfeiting all lands and goods; that Catholics could not own firearms, or a horse worth more than £5; that all Catholic bishops and priests should be banished from the island; that no Catholic could marry a Protestant, and if such a marriage occurred with a Protestant woman all her property was immediately to pass to her Protestant relations; and that practically all the lands in possession of "rebels" were to be confiscated unless they passed to a Protestant heir.

These infamous laws were followed by others in 1699 that ruined Ireland's growing trade and manufactures. No wonder that an eminent English historian calls this story "the darkest blot in the whole history of the British Commonwealth."

Scotland was soon to become joined, as we shall see, in a full and happy union with England but no such fate was ever to be in store for Ireland, for though union did come there could be no lasting and happy one for a race peculiarly tenacious of national memories and with such centuries of cruel memories to recall. In every other quarter of the globe where the English have ruled, it is almost impossible to point to one where, in spite of blunders or of selfishness, she has not left some legacy at least of good. Ireland, at her very door, is the one terrible exception.

Meanwhile, William had returned to London on his way to

335

lead the army on the Continent, for England had joined in the war on France. Mistrustful, as we have seen, of many of the English statesmen, he had caused both confusion and jealousy by advancing many of the Dutch who had come over with him at the time of his accession. Most of the English leaders were, it is true, still in touch with James at his Court of St. Germain, and it was as difficult to know whom to trust as it was for the leaders to know whether William or James would win in the end. Most of us in these days who have property to handle for ourselves or others are apt to consider that the times are of almost unprecedented uncertainty and anxiety, but it is well to recall that in almost every generation in earlier periods men have had to pick their way between courses which might, in a wrong choice, lose them not only their property but possibly their heads.

That the leaders were in touch with both camps did not mean that they were disloyal, and if both Marlborough and Admiral Russell wrote to James, they were nevertheless to prove the salvation of William and of England, although in 1691 William had stripped Marlborough of all his offices. The next year Russell had under his command the combined Dutch and English fleets. James had planned an invasion of England with French aid, had issued a manifesto, and had gone to the harbor of La Hogue where the powerful French fleet was in waiting. Russell had been offended by William and was in correspondence with James. What would he do?

The destiny of England hung on the answer. When the French fleet came out he shattered it and burned twelve of the best ships under the eyes of James in the harbor where he had been waiting to embark. Henceforth during the wars which were to end the chances of the exiled Stuarts and the ambitions of Louis and France, the seas were open to the Allies without hindrance, and English troops and supplies could be transported to the Continent with impunity. On land, however, Louis still dominated. He captured the great border fortress of Namur and defeated William at Steinkirk and Landen.

But in this duel to the death material wealth was to count

heavily, and it is reported Louis had said that it would be the last piece of gold that would carry the day. The French economic condition was steadily growing worse. The days of the great Colbert were over, and in spite of his wise measures French trade was decreasing whereas that of England, as we saw in the previous chapter, was advancing rapidly. The steady stream of precious metals pouring into Spain was doing her no good because she had developed no internal industrial or commercial life, and the gold and silver she imported passed on to other nations to purchase needed goods.

England, with no mines, was growing rapidly richer by means of business, and this new wealth, unlike the old landed property, was liquid. The war in the years to come was eventually to be won partly because of the statesmanlike foundations laid by William, partly because of the military genius of Marlborough together with Prince Eugene and partly because England became "the paymaster of Europe" and held the Alliance together with subsidies. The financiers and the innumerable merchants and business men were as important as the troops in the field.

1692 is memorable for the beginning of the National Debt. Kings and governments had borrowed before but only for short periods with the understanding that incoming taxes would pay off the loans incurred. Rich as England was becoming, taxes alone could not support the great burdens which she was to have to carry for herself and her Allies. Her credit, with a free government based on consent, was good, and the device was hit upon of borrowing for a long or indeterminate period. We are so unhappily used to long-term government debts today all over the world, that it is hard to realize the difference that the new method made in placing vast sums at the disposal of Parliament, an advantage not shared by the enemy.

Another great step forward was the formation of the Bank of England in 1694. The goldsmiths, followed by private bankers, had taken money on deposit and loaned it out, but their resources were limited and they had to keep them very liquid. The new bank, however, when formed at the suggestion of the Scotchman,

William Paterson, met with such instant success that the great volume of its deposits enabled it to carry on business on a much larger scale and in a more modern way. It had the prestige and credit of the government behind it, as well as the deposits of government funds, and attracted deposits from numberless individuals who had hitherto preferred to hoard their money. The resources thus placed at the disposal of the government formed another factor for final success.

Another minor cause was the reform of the currency in 1696 under advice of Sir Isaac Newton. The practice of "clipping" coins had been common and difficult to detect so long as they had smooth edges. This was obviated by the very simple device of having a milled edge which would immediately show if the coin had been cut. In a business community confidence in the currency is a point of prime importance.

The government also had to be reorganized. When William returned to London after his defeat at Landen in 1693, he found Parliament in confusion. He had come to the throne with the help of both parties, and had naturally chosen his ministers from each. Deciding that this had been a mistake, he discharged all the Tories and installed Whigs, but he found that in order to carry on the war efficiently it was necessary to have ministers from among the majority in Parliament, and as parties changed he had to change his ministers. England had groped another step forward toward government by a Cabinet responsible to Parliament.

Another advance, taken apparently somewhat casually, was the refusal of Parliament to renew the Licensing Act, thus doing away with the necessity of getting a license from the government for the publication of any book or newspaper, and suddenly conferring complete freedom on the press. Nothing could show better than the ease with which this transition was made the distance which toleration of ideas had gone during the previous twenty years.

The death of Queen Mary was a personal blow for William who had cared for or trusted few persons, and also led to new dangers. In 1695 he had given the French the greatest check they had received in fifty-two years by recapturing the fortress of Namur, but in England the corruption of many of the ministers, William's rewarding of his Dutch friends, and other causes had created much discontent among both the people and those of high rank who felt that they had not been rewarded as they had hoped.

The Jacobite plotting continued, and William now alone on the throne occupied a more vulnerable position than when the daughter of James had shared it with him. The former King now suddenly moved to Calais, there was stirring in all Jacobite circles, and a very serious plot was uncovered to murder William as he should return to Kensington Palace from hunting. The abortive attempt to kill him did much to restore his popularity, and in the treaty with France at the Peace of Ryswick, ending the war, Louis acknowledged him as King of England. Various factors again combined, however, to make him once more unpopular, and to William himself the remaining few years must have seemed to indicate failure to achieve his one great object, the downfall of France.

He well knew that the Peace of Ryswick could be only a truce, but, as usual at the end of a Continental war, England wished to forget it and to return to normal life. The problem of the division of the Spanish Empire still overshadowed all else, and Louis as well as William recognized the dangers in the situation. In 1698 the two Kings signed a Partition Treaty according to which the larger part of the empire was to devolve on the Electoral Prince of Bavaria, but the death of that young man the next year upset the plans. Meanwhile, Parliament had been at work reducing the English army to 7000 men, thus weakening at the same time William's strength in negotiating with Louis. Surrounded as he was with possible traitors, Parliament forced him to dismiss his Dutch guard, and the harassed King even considered abdicating and returning to Holland.

There was also trouble in Scotland, where a company had been formed to send out a colony to the Isthmus of Panama, or Darien as it was then called. It was an extremely foolish undertaking,

339

because both of the climate and the fact that the territory was part
of the Spanish Empire, but Scotland had taken a national interest
in it hoping that it would help to establish its commercial life.
When most of the colonists had been killed by disease and the
rest by the Spaniards, William, unjustly, had to bear the full
brunt of Scotch resentment and disappointment because he refused to go to war with Spain to save the colony.

Under these difficult conditions he negotiated and signed a new
Partition Treaty with Louis in 1700, but in a few months the
long-dreaded event of the death of the King of Spain occurred,
and Louis, finding that the King had bequeathed the entire empire to Louis's grandson Philip, accepted the inheritance and tore
up the treaty with William.

War would now sooner or later be inevitable again but there
were other difficulties. A few weeks before the death of the
Spanish King, the young Duke of Gloucester had also died in
England. These deaths, including that of the young Elector of
Bavaria, were to have profound effects upon the history of England and of the world. Gloucester was the last surviving child of
Anne, who was next in succession to her sister Mary and to William on the throne of England. Mary was dead, and Anne was
now childless, so the problem of the possible successor again became acute, and was the first to occupy the attention of the Tory
ministry which William had appointed.

The Act of Settlement of 1701 was another proof that divine
right had passed as a tenable doctrine and that the nation firmly
believed that Parliament had the right of designating the monarch and the line of succession. Nevertheless, if the country was
determined that there should be no Catholic on the throne, the
idea of hereditary right was still strong, as it is today, and the
succession was settled on Sophia, Electress of Hanover, and her
descendants being Protestants. She was a granddaughter of James
I, and the nearest Stuart heir, not a Catholic, other than William
and Anne. There were many other stipulations made in the Act,
chiefly designed with reference to possible dangers incurred by
having as sovereign one who also held a Continental throne and

possessions. Much is made of the fact that the British Constitution is unwritten, but the Act of Settlement is only one of many written documents which form parts of it, and very important parts.

William had been blamed by the Tories for having made the Partition Treaties with Louis, and a number of the Whig members of his former Cabinet, as it now at last began to be called, were impeached. Louis, however, played into the hands of the King and those in favor of renewing war, by seizing with Spanish help all the border fortresses along the line of the Spanish Netherlands. The Netherlands in the hands of Spain had ceased to be dangerous to England, but to have them in the possession of France was a direct threat to her across the narrow sea.

The war feeling rose, Parliament voted troops and money, and William made the fortunate decision to put Marlborough at the head of his forces. Louis was dreaming again of controlling Europe, with his grandson in possession of all the Spanish Empire, including its possessions in Italy and the Netherlands. The Franco-Spanish combination now threatened universal domination, and in 1701 William signed the Grand Alliance which bound England, Austria and the Dutch Republic to fight together against the common danger.

The day before, the exiled King, James, had died in France, and Louis at once roused all England to fury by acknowledging James's son James as King of England. William dissolved Parliament, the Tories were defeated in the ensuing election, and a Parliament with a small Whig majority came in, which at once raised the army to 40,000, and took steps to increase the navy. The final crisis with France and the inevitable war for which William had been preparing so long had at last come. He was planning to cross the Channel to command in person when in riding at Hampton Park his horse stumbled in a mole-hill and threw him. It was the last time that death, which had so often intervened in his affairs at critical moments, was to do so, for in a few days it claimed him for its own. All his plans had come to fruition and he himself had never before been so popular, but it may have been well for England that his career ended at this precise point. Great statesman as he was, he was far from possessing the military genius of Marlborough, who also rose to unexpected heights of statesmanship, and whom William had named his successor in command.

Marlborough was undoubtedly one of the greatest of Englishmen but opinions as to his personal character vary widely, from the vicious attacks of Macaulay to the vigorous defense and even adulation of Winston Churchill in the *Life* of his great kinsman, yet unfinished though six volumes have been published. Opinions as to leading men often differ, but the controversy over Marlborough was rendered more bitter than usual by party bias and the conditions of the time which required that the leaders keep in touch with both the Courts of St. James's and of St. Germain at the same time, leaving them open to the vilest suspicions however unfounded.

In any case when placed in command and put to the test Marlborough, like Russell, bent his whole magnificent energies and abilities to serving the cause of England and its chosen dynasty. Although constantly hampered by having to conciliate his touchy German allies and the cautious Dutch, as well as frequently by the political situation at home, few men have wielded greater power. During the period of discredit with William, he and his wife had won the unbounded confidence of the Princess Anne, who had now become Queen, and for many years the almost complete ascendency of the Duchess over her royal friend was of inestimable value in gaining her support for Marlborough's daring and far-reaching plans.

He was as great an organizer as he was warrior and statesman, and his constant care for every detail regarding the welfare of his men won him the devoted loyalty and confidence of all the troops who fought under him. He was also the first and perhaps the greatest of military commanders to understand the grand strategy of a world war and of how to co-ordinate land and naval operations. Moreover, his success was to a large extent due to his changing warfare from the static condition of slow sieges of fortresses into one of quick mobility in the field, and if he suffered much from certain hampering qualities in his allies he had a devoted and brilliant aid in Prince Eugene.

There was little decisive about the first two years of the struggle. On land all the cards seemed to be in the hands of Louis though he was helpless on the sea. In Italy, Eugene had had to retreat, and in Austria, Bavaria as an ally of France was threatening Vienna, with the Hungarians in revolt. The war thus far had been of the old slow type, though Marlborough had secured the lower Rhine as far as Bonn. Attacks against Spain by an Anglo-Dutch naval expedition had brought no results except the capture of the treasure fleet, and the entrance of Portugal into the war on the side of England.

But the genius of Marlborough was to be made manifest. He planned to save the Emperor in Austria by so daring a march across Germany to the Danube that he felt constrained to hide the plan from both the Dutch and the statesmen in England who would not have allowed him to take the risk. There was also to be an attack on France from the Mediterranean and on Spain through Portugal, thus striking at the enemy from three sides at once, a piece of grand strategy which was rendered possible only by his own ability and the fact of English sea power. He carried out his own part with brilliant success, deceiving the French first by a feint, and then marching across Bavaria, and in August, 1704, winning the magnificent victory of Blenheim, completely shattering the combined French and Bavarian forces, who lost 14,000 men and 11,000 more as prisoners, including among the latter the French commander, Marshal Tallard. Austria was saved, the French had to retreat westward across the Rhine, and Bavaria had ceased to be a factor to be reckoned with.

In the Mediterranean the French fleet was defeated in the battle of Malaga, not again venturing to sea, and the capture of the Rock of Gibraltar in the same month as Blenheim gave England control of the gateway to the great inland sea. In the following two years the Spanish campaigns, under the brilliant but irresponsible Earl of Peterborough, resulted in the over-running of several provinces and for a time even Madrid itself was occupied.

In the same period, Marlborough, in the Netherlands, broke through the line of French fortresses, and in the battle of Ramillies (1706) won an even more brilliant victory than Blenheim, the French army suffering losses five times as great as those of the Allies. As a result, practically all the fortified towns of the Netherlands fell into Allied hands. In Italy, Eugene had also had a series of successes and was driving the French out of the peninsula.

In the field, everything had not only gone in favor of the Allies, but few countries have had to take such a drubbing as France did. The pride of Louis was at last broken. He asked for peace, and even offered to surrender Spain, but unfortunately in war there are always two fronts to consider, the military and the political. Great war after great war has shown that politicians can and frequently do spoil the fruits of victory. In England, when Anne came to the throne she had preferred the Tories to the Whigs and made a Tory Cabinet, even Marlborough having rather unwillingly to declare himself a member of that party. Political necessity, however, forced her first to make a combined Tory and Whig Ministry and then gradually after the Whig victory at the polls in 1706 to choose a completely Whig group of advisers. Marlborough and Godolphin, who at the Treasury had been of great help in carrying on the war, went over to the Whigs, but that party, which had flourished on war and was the inveterate enemy of Louis, refused the opportune moment to make peace. They would have none of it.

Anne disliked the Whigs and had accepted them only because the Constitution was now shaping itself in such a way that she had to accept them to carry on government. Marlborough, by turning Whig, had weakened himself with her. In addition she had tired of her dear friend the Duchess and her domination and had given her affection and confidence to a much inferior person, a Mrs. Masham, an indigent cousin of the Duchess, who had secured for her a minor post at Court. The Whigs, moreover, partly because of their foolish attempt to impeach a clergyman, and partly because of their opposition to the making of peace, which was much desired by the nation, lost their popularity, and the Tories came back with the election of 1710. A completely Tory Ministry was now formed, including Harley and the brilliant Henry St. John, the latter to become better known as Lord Bolingbroke.

Meanwhile, the disasters of the French continued. They lost the desperate battle of Malplaquet, and the Allied forces had penetrated far into French territory. The Tories were willing to treat for peace with the humbled Louis who was begging for it, but in the Parliament of 1711 the Whigs had very nearly a majority again, and threatened control by a political deal with the Tory Lord Nottingham, agreeing to vote for the Occasional Conformity Bill if he would vote to continue the war. The Lords disagreed, and the two Houses thus found themselves in opposition. On the advice of Harley, Anne deprived Marlborough of all his offices and created twelve new Tory peers, a precedent of great significance, being another indication of the predominant power of the Commons in any deadlock with the Upper House.

The Tories could now carry out their policy of peace, which they desired to do without consulting the Dutch and by leaving them in the lurch. The Duke of Ormond, the peace envoy, however, disclosed his instructions and on his own responsibility saved the Ministry from that unnecessary ignominy. Finally on March 31, 1713, the peace treaty of Utrecht was made between the French and the Allies.

By its terms the British were to retain the Rock of Gibraltar, which has never since changed hands; Nova Scotia and a complete title to Newfoundland; and received from Spain the enormously valuable sole right, known as the *Asiento*, to import and sell Negro slaves in Spanish America. Certain changes among the Continental powers were also of indirect benefit to England, such as the substituting of the distant and landlocked Austria for Spain or France in part of the Netherlands.

The treaty was indeed an important landmark in the long rise of England to world power. France had become an exhausted land of misery, and although remaining a great nation would not again threaten the control of Europe for nearly a century to come. Spain had ceased forever to be a great power. The Dutch had spent much of their strength and wealth, and would no longer be formidable rivals. Not only because of her acquisitions, but also from her increase in wealth, modernization of business method, immensely increased prestige, and above all her undisputed control of the seas, England was now far in the lead in the race for the trade and empire of the world. When William had landed at Torbay to "take England on his way to France," the power of the great Louis had seemed impregnable. Now it lay shattered in the dust, and as a result of the far-seeing vision of the Dutch King, England had become the leading power on the globe.

Although the Whigs should have been willing to make peace several years earlier, and the Tories deserve the credit for its final accomplishment, the policies of the latter were in general to prove disastrous to them. From 1710 on both Oxford and Bolingbroke were bent on making their party all powerful and destroying the Whigs. An Act was passed that no one who did not hold land to the value of £200 a year income could sit in the House of Commons, and the Occasional Conformity Act also excluded a large number of Dissenters. Because the Whig interest was mainly trading and Dissenting, another blow was struck, this time at the Bank of England. In order to diminish the power and prestige of that institution, a new company, the South Sea, was formed to take over about £10,000,000 of the national debt with a monopoly of South American trade as a Tory make-weight to the Whig Bank.

In 1714 the worst attack was made on the Dissenters, which recalls the Penal Code of Ireland. The children of Dissenters had already been excluded from all public schools and the universities, but the Dissenters had founded schools of their own. The new Act now prohibited any one from teaching who was not licensed by a bishop of the Church of England, and this Act, which prevented any child of a Dissenter receiving any public education except that of the Church, was passed by the Tory Commons by a vote of two to one though by only a small majority in the Lords. Whig leaders were also infamously attacked. Marlborough, who with William had wrought the miracle of the overthrow of France and laid the foundation for the world power of England, was unjustly accused of misusing funds and was forced to exile himself to the Continent. Another Whig leader, Sir Robert Walpole, was similarly accused and, although the case broke down, was imprisoned in the Tower.

There was worse, however, in store, and England on the threshold of a new and glorious career was in truth in grave danger. The physical condition of the childless Queen made it appear that her death might not be long delayed, and the Tory leaders were conspiring to overturn the Act of Settlement and bring back the Stuart Pretender, the so-called James III, to the throne if he would renounce Catholicism. Marlborough's place at the head of the military forces was given to the Duke of Ormond, who was a Jacobite, and he was also made Lord Warden of the Cinque Ports which would enable him to betray the south coast harbors. Oxford and Bolingbroke, who did not take religion seriously, were amazed to find that the Stuart Prince did, and that he refused flatly to change his creed for a crown.

Even so, Bolingbroke, although not Oxford, was willing to proceed with the plot, of which Queen Anne was ignorant. Unlike the great Elizabeth she did not possess an able mind, but like her she had much objected to any talk of who was to succeed her.

The Electress Sophia had died, and her son, George, the Elector of Hanover, was the heir. The Whigs, who had of late years been excluded and persecuted, realized that their only hope lay in him, and he in turn realized that his main strength would lie in them. The Tories who had controlled Anne realized that their power would crumble on her death unless James instead of George could be brought to the throne. The desperate Bolingbroke was willing to take the chance even if James would not change his religion, and he secured the dismissal of the more honest or vacillating Oxford from the service of the weak and now mortally ill Queen. For a moment he seemed all powerful for evil, for the Whigs had been preparing for eventualities, and if he had brought James across the Channel, England, with the world at her feet, would have had to sacrifice everything to another civil war.

Fortunately death, so active in this chapter, again threw the deciding card on the table. Within four days after Bolingbroke's triumph over Oxford and before he had had time to make his arrangements, the simple-minded "good Queen Anne" died in Kensington Palace. Her death had been assured for the previous forty-eight hours, and there had been a meeting of the Privy Council in an adjacent room. Council and Cabinet were not yet wholly disassociated, and, even in the Cabinet, ministers were frightened and undecided. The Whig Dukes of Argyle and Somerset, who were Councillors but not members of the Cabinet, together with other Whigs, turned the scale and took control in the meeting of the Council.

Lack of time, and the resolute action of the Whig leaders, defeated Bolingbroke's plot. Military measures were immediately taken. George was summoned with all speed to come to London, and was peacefully proclaimed King. The benefits of the "glorious Revolution" and of the successful war were thus saved. Although Bolingbroke, able, brilliant, dissolute and daring as he was, has yet his defenders because of certain general ideas as to government, it would appear impossible to defend his conduct in connection with his plot to overturn the will of Parliament as expressed in the Act of Settlement and to reintroduce the exiled Stuarts.

Whatever the merit of certain theoretical ideas as to who should govern and how, who could predict what ideas might emerge from the hell-broth cauldron of certain civil war? It was personal ambition that persuaded him to try to overthrow the will of the nation as expressed in Parliament and to cast away the gains of ten years of bloody and costly warfare. The quiet acquiescence of the whole people in accepting the House of Hanover was the best proof of what the nation desired. Although

Bolingbroke went to France to serve the Pretender he became disgusted with that service but was never again to hold office in England.

He had also ruined the Tories and for nearly a half century the Whigs were to maintain almost undisputed control over government, although often a minority party. That very fact kept them moderate and they were not to use their power in such high-handed fashion as had the Tories in their brief reign. What Bolingbroke had achieved was that for nearly two generations the new House of Hanover was to put its whole trust in the Whig party and deeply to distrust every Tory, for that name had become too nearly synonymous with Jacobite.

That George was acknowledged King as quietly in Scotland as in England, in spite of some later Jacobite risings, was due to the most important event in Anglo-Scottish relations. About the beginning of Anne's reign negotiations had been started looking toward the actual union of the two Kingdoms, so often approached in the past but never achieved. The English were at first unwilling to grant the equality of trade laws and privileges which the Scotch naturally demanded. In 1703, the Scots Parliament passed the Act of Security which declared that the successor to Anne in Scotland should not be the same person who would be the sovereign in England. Anne as Queen of Scotland had to sign the Act and there followed a war of threats between the two nations.

Fortunately good sense finally triumphed on both sides of the border, and Scotland having secured what it had demanded for its trade and, on the other hand, having consented to the English Act of Settlement regulating the succession to the two thrones, the Act of Union was formally signed by both nations in 1707. Scotland retained her own independent Church and her laws, but there was henceforth to be but one Parliament, that at Westminster, for the government of the two nations, now at last merged in one. The Scottish peers were to elect sixteen of their body to sit in the House of Lords and the people were also to be represented by forty-five members in the Commons.

The political advantage to England was great. Engaged at the time in the death struggle with France and distracted by Jacobite plots, she could ill afford to renew the age-old danger of a hostile Scotland on the north bound to France and the Stuart cause. On the other hand, though the pride of many of the Scots was touched, the gain to Scotland was even greater in the long run than to England. From the back-water of her national but restricted life she swung at once into the broad sea of imperial and commercial opportunity on which England was embarking. The character and ability of her citizens were at last to have opportunity consonant with their quality open before them, and not only did they benefit by it but so did the intellectual, public and business life of England and the entire Empire.

It is hard to overestimate the contribution which Scotland has made to the common life since the happy day for all when she consented to abandon her isolation. The people of Great Britain have been made up, as we have seen in different periods of our story, of many strains, and among the most important of the qualities which they have contributed to the common life and character must be reckoned those which have come with the Scotch. In the American colonies the Scotch-Irish, as the Scots who had lived in Ireland for some generations and then passed to America were called, are recognized as having been the finest frontiersmen the New World has known, and the same qualities contributed by the race north of the Tweed have helped to build up the Empire in every quarter. In addition, their deep religious spirit, their stern self-discipline, their love of learning for its own sake, and their keen mentality, as well as their history, literature, and wealth of legend and romance, have all made an inestimable addition to the general stock of the united British race.

The exigencies and events of the great European war had, for the time being, a less fortunate effect on the American colonies. Across the Atlantic French and British fleets fought each other, with crews almost decimated by tropical sicknesses, for the capture of one or another of the West India islands of both nations. Increasing piracy and buccaneering, in addition to the ravages of legitimate warfare, temporarily ruined the prosperity of all the islands. Conditions in the English navy seemed to be at their worst on the American station, and it was largely owing to its inefficiency that the genuine efforts made by the continental colonies of Massachusetts and New Hampshire to support the mother country resulted rather in ill feeling and contempt than in a better spirit of imperial co-operation. It was due to the British that two colonial companies sent to their aid in Jamaica were uselessly sacrificed. Moreover, the colonists, who had for several years been making notable efforts to attack Canada, while the Indian allies of the French were ravaging their borders, were finally disgusted with the complete fiasco of the naval expedition under command of Sir Hovenden Walker and the incapable General Hill, the brother of the Queen's favorite, Mrs. Masham.

Massachusetts, the most independent in feeling of all the colonies, the sore spot of empire, had burdened herself with debt and made genuine and repeated efforts at last to assume a loyal and responsible place in the imperial structure only to be shown the seamiest side of English administration and inefficiency. Marlborough might win brilliant victories, the navy in the Mediterranean might rake in Minorca and the Rock of Gibraltar as spoils of war, but the direct contact of the men of New England with the armed forces of Britain bred only contempt and dislike, which was not to be without far-reaching effect in the future.

On the other hand, the final result of the war, because it so greatly strengthened the position of England, strengthened also that of the rest of the Empire, and it was a matter of no slight importance to the entire world that in the race for mastery in far and foreign lands it was the British and not the Dutch or Spanish or French who were to win. None of the other contestants had ever been willing to concede the self-government and local freedom to its colonists that were almost unconsciously accorded by the English, and, as we shall see, if a large part of the first overseas Empire was at last to break away into complete independence, it was quite as much due to the freedom which had been granted to its citizens as a natural result of the British system as it was of attempted tyranny which would not have been considered so in the colonies of any of England's rivals, who from the very start had never tasted the sweets of local liberty.

Anne's short reign of scarcely a dozen years has left a perhaps over-rated effect on popular conception of the arts, in such terms as Queen Anne furniture, architecture and other matters. It was in fact too short a period to consider as of separate importance and was rather one of brief transition, yet it had its character. It is true that many notable buildings were being erected, such as the great palace of Blenheim for Marlborough, designed by Sir John Vanbrugh, and it was in Anne's reign that Sir Christopher Wren completed the present St. Paul's Cathedral in London with, if not the finest, certainly one of the finest four, domes in the world. Wren, however, who had found his great opportunity in rebuilding London after the Great Fire of 1666, had been at work a long time, and the Wren churches which are scattered over the city and considered his characteristic work are of a quite different type from his more ambitious undertakings in London, Oxford and elsewhere. When, in domestic architecture, we think of Queen Anne or the Georgian into which it was now to merge, we think not of such great piles as Blenheim or Castle Howard as of the essentially homelike, simple and almost dull exteriors of the internally extremely comfortable houses which still line so many streets and squares.

Indeed, the reign of domesticity, of "reason" and of "common sense" was coming in. The eighteenth century was, on the whole, to be a period of absorption in politics and commercial expansion. The coming age of Samuel Johnson in literature, for example, was not, like the Elizabethan or even the Victorian, to be compact of fire and imagination. The tone was already being set under Anne, and charming as are the writings of Addison and Steele or at times as vitriolic as can be those of Swift, they deal largely with daily matters of fact in a manner carefully avoiding high emotion.

In that day, when Parliamentary debates were not yet reported, but when the minds of men were largely concentrated on politics, the weekly issues of *The Spectator* or other writings of the day were eagerly scanned for news, and the services of the authors were in demand by political leaders. Addison, like most of them, was a Whig although the Tories secured Swift. Another writer who, though his most continuously popular book has been *Robinson Crusoe,* was also largely used for his political pamphlets and other work, was Daniel Defoe. One of the great influences which these and other men exerted, aside from that on public opinion as to affairs, was greatly to increase the numbers of the reading public. It has been estimated that before them there had been not much more than about five thousand people in England who read what might appear in print, but the enormous popularity of the issues of *The Spectator,* containing the famous "Sir Roger de Coverley" papers, *The Tatler,* and other well-liked sheets, as well as the mass of pamphlets on political topics constantly appearing from the press, won so many readers as to make a permanent change in both English political and intellectual life.

It was essentially an age of prose, and carefully measured prose at that. For a century or so "enthusiasm" was to be bad form, in social life, religion and art. It may be suggested that it was, possibly, the ostracism of high imagination that was later to lose the American colonies to the Empire, but if the vaunted "common sense" of the period was not always to prove so very sensible in truth, it gave the nation a breathing spell and rest between two great periods of profound disturbance.

CHAPTER XVI

THE EARLY GEORGES

AFTER THE TREATY OF UTRECHT, one of the French diplomats who had taken part in the negotiations tried to end the ceaseless wars which had so long devastated Europe by the formation of what we would today call a League of Nations. But it was impossible then, as it has proved in our own day, and in part for the same reason.

It meant the establishment of the territorial *status quo,* which was humanly impracticable partly because Europe was a maze of small states under some four hundred separate rulers, and in part because leading nations were rapidly growing in energy and ambition and wished to extend their power in various parts of the world in which their interests conflicted. In spite of the fact that the period of this chapter, approximately that from 1714 to 1760, was comparatively peaceful up to 1739 and filled with wars thereafter in Europe, America and India, the whole of the half century was really one long continuation of the duel between England and France.

It attains an additional unity in England because of the long continued dominance of the Whig oligarchy, and the steady development of constitutional and particularly Cabinet government under the earlier Georges, the first of whom did not even speak the English language, and perforce had to leave matters largely in the hands of his ministers. Before making a rapid survey of the events of the era we may take a glance at the life and character of the English of the day which will help us to understand

354

both the successes and failures of these important decades leading up to the end of the first British Empire.

Winston Churchill in his book on Marlborough remarks that "to understand history the reader must always remember how small is the proportion of what is recorded to what actually took place," and he might have added, how little even of what is recorded can be set down in a condensed narrative. The period of the early Georges is full of contradictions, and although it invites definite labels it does not answer to them. It has been called lethargic, dull, heavy and unimaginative, and in many ways it was, yet we have to find place for the lives and achievements of such men as Chatham, Clive, Warren Hastings, Wolfe, Oglethorpe, Fox, Garrick, Gibbon, Pope, Goldsmith, Johnson, Reynolds, Gainsborough, the two Wesleys, Priestley, Hunter, Newcomen, and many others who were enlarging the Empire, advancing science and the arts, or beginning the modern humanitarian movement, and who indicate a national life anything but lethargic and dull.

There is, however, some truth in all the adjectives used to describe the era. There were many kinds of Englishmen with very diverse interests, and it is easy to distort the picture of England as a whole by selection and emphasis. Perhaps we can give the best idea of the variety of the nation by the method of contrast.

There was, more marked than ever before, the contrast between town and country. London had for long been growing, as we have noted from time to time, into the great metropolis of the kingdom, but with the Georgian period we have the modern conception of "town," that full, varied life of all classes which so fascinated Samuel Johnson and in another century was to fascinate Lamb, as it has done countless others. The city itself was fast taking on some of its modern aspects. Great landlords were developing on long leases the sections around the squares which usually bear the family names, Cavendish, Hanover, Grosvenor, Berkeley, and are still among the well-known squares of today that were then beginning to be new residential districts.

355

Kensington Gardens were developed and the Round Pond made, beloved of children ever since. Bookshops, coffee houses and taverns, such as the "Mitre," frequented by Johnson and his circle, were becoming numerous, and were centers for social, literary and political gossip, although the more modern club was also coming into fashion, a number being scattered along Piccadilly and Pall Mall.

The town, forming a contrast with the country, was itself full of contrasts. There was high society, with often affected manners, its costly mode of living, its wigs and exaggerated costumes, and its excessive gambling. There was the middle class of many grades, often strict and Dissenting, and the crowds of poor who lived in squalid quarters and provided so many of the subjects for Hogarth's pictures.

Not only in the busy streets, in which traffic was a serious difficulty, but in the more exclusive parks, such as St. James's, all classes could be found, jostling one another, but the London "mob" was on the whole good-natured, and though it might hoot after persons, especially foreigners, who were extravagantly dressed, there was evident that ability of all classes somehow to get on with one another which is still characteristically English in its special quality. Class distinctions were sharply drawn, but because of their complete acceptance in many points, there was more ease of relationship in many ways between high and low than in the next century after the French Revolution, when the class warfare on the Continent tended to undermine to some extent the former completely accepted class differences in England.

Besides London, which was always *the* "town," there were growing up many small but fashionable watering places and spas such as Bath, where Beau Brummell ruled society and did much to improve its tone, Harrogate, Cheltenham, Tunbridge Wells, Brighton, Scarborough and others. Both fashion and travel over improved roads, many of them toll turnpikes, were spreading over the island. It is of the life in all these which we are apt to think as typically eighteenth-century, but, in contrast, that century saw the best of the old village life, and was largely dominated by the country, with its squires, its Justices of the Peace, its county families and magnates.

Agricultural, village and small-town life had advanced considerably in prosperity and comfort without as yet having suffered from the industrialism to come, and country communities were still remarkably self-contained. Arthur Young and others were making their agricultural investigations and improvements, as were Robert Bakewell in improving the breed of cattle, and others in different directions. We spoke earlier of the smallness of cattle in the preceding century, but this one was to see the breeding of the famous "Durham Ox," weighing 3800 pounds or about 1200 more than the average butcher's ox of today.

Better roads, the rise of town life and other causes conspired to make farming—and almost every one in the country farmed, including the squires, the parson, and the great landlords—change from farming for subsistence merely to farming for markets. Improvements in method might therefore mean large increase in money income, and the effect on rural districts was notable. It may also be noted that fox hunting, which has loomed so large in English life, was coming in, though grouse shooting was still confined to the Scots.

Social gradations of rank were delicately distinguished from top to bottom and every one "knew his place," but here, again, counting on that basic assumption, there was a much closer intermingling of different grades than in the next century. A parson could dine with his tailor, and a local magnate, known as the "King of Ashbourne," counted among his friends who visited at his mansion two retired innkeepers, two tanners and a gentleman farmer.

On the other hand, a well-to-do farmer making an income of £800 a year, in spite of having a large house with drawing room and other apartments for state occasions, might dine and spend the evening with his wife in the great kitchen, the servants dining at another table, and busy at their tasks later. Throughout the century, seats in Parliament, as well as commissions in army and navy, and the plums of government positions were practically all reserved for the upper class, largely for the great families, of whom there were perhaps seventy, and their many relations and connections. Nevertheless, owing to the odd English texture of classes, which has astonished all Europeans, there was surprisingly little class animosity on the part of the excluded, and an extremely strong national feeling on the part of all.

For example, conditions in the rank and file of army and navy were execrable. In the latter, food and treatment were so bad that it was difficult to get men willing to enter the service, and, especially when a war might call for multiplying their number fivefold, the press gang, which was nothing less than kidnapping, was resorted to. Crews were often largely made up of poor material, such as the scum of London and other ports picked up on the streets by force, yet when a ship with such a crew swung into action the men would fight for England with dauntless courage, energy and patriotism.

The enormous gulf which separated the privileged classes from the lower can be illustrated glaringly by this branch of the military service, in the matter of division of prize money when an enemy vessel was captured. For example, when in 1762 the *Hermione* was taken, the total sum available for division was about £520,000, of which the Flag officer (who had not been present) and the Captain each got about £65,000; the Lieutenant £13,000; the Warrant officer well over £4000, whereas the entire crew received only £480 to divide among them all.

Conditions among the very poor were also bad and inhumane. The system of Poor Relief included the "farming out" of paupers to those who took care of them at so much a head or other similar methods which naturally resulted in cruel treatment and lack of food for those unfortunates who were thus turned over to a low class who took up such work. Conditions among the debtors imprisoned, often for small sums and who could be incarcerated for life until the debt was paid, were almost equally bad. There was naturally much crime, but the criminal law, with its unequal punishments and its long delays, has been called by

358

an authority "a mere sanguinary chaos." In dipping down into these levels of life we are getting as far away from the Georgian drawing room where bewigged young beaux in satin and silk talked and flirted with the ladies of fashion as we are when we have to find place for Clive in India or Wolfe in Canada, but it is all part of the eighteenth century.

As we have noted before, no period conforms to a single rigid pattern throughout, any more than does a "Frenchman," an "Englishman" or an "American." Nevertheless, there are certain recognizable traits which, taken as a whole, do set each off from the other. In the early Georgian period, if we have to find place for Fielding's *Tom Jones* or Sterne's *Tristram Shandy*, we feel instinctively that the writer who represented the period more characteristically than any other was Alexander Pope. A poet made rather than born, and the greatest master in English of the heroic couplet, we find in his *Essay on Criticism, The Rape of the Lock,* his *Essay on Man* and other works, both the presence and lack of qualities which are characteristically Georgian. Without passion, spontaneity, high imagination, philosophical insight, or sympathy, he had wit, lucidity, grace, a calm wholly unperturbed by "enthusiasm," though a biting irony, and had made himself master of an unsurpassed technique in his own field. Largely because of that last fact and of the ease with which his flowing couplets catch the attention and remain in the mind, few poets other than Shakespeare are so often quoted. We are tempted to say, if we momentarily ignore quite other qualities of the period, that he is the eighteenth century incarnate.

In spite of the delicate drawing rooms, it was a period of heavy, even gross, eating and drinking. Many of the faces which look down on us from the portraits of the day recall the "John Bull" of later personification. Among the upper classes gout and port went hand in hand, while among the lower the enormous increase in the use of gin was responsible for untold misery. Not only the masses, in their more sodden way, but the upper classes had also largely deteriorated. This may well have been due to the fact that leadership had to a great extent been assumed by a selfish

359

class which had legislated and held office for the sake of its own interests and property. In fact, this age of prose may also be called the age of property. As we study the lives of all too many in all classes, we seem to hear, as Tennyson's "Northern Farmer" heard in the hoof beats of his cantering horse,

"Proputty, proputty, proputty—that's what I 'ears 'em say." As a reviewer in *The London Times,* speaking of this period, pointed out some years ago "it is hardly too much to say that everything had become private property—the Parliamentary seat, the municipal chain, the miter, the parson's cure, the officer's shoulder knot, the College Fellowship, and the Professorial Chair." With all this absorption in getting money and all sorts of life jobs which brought in money and which the holder could, in many cases, buy and sell, there went a coarsening of the moral fiber and the personal morals of the nation.

The remarkable rise in population, which was to be a feature of the next century, had already begun, as had also, in a small way, the industrial revolution, and the amount of machinery used was attracting attention by 1757. In another few generations the face of England was to be changed, for better or worse, but in this period the country still rested firmly on agriculture with liquid wealth increasing mainly from trade, commerce and banking. For the first time, English life with all its variety of character can be studied in the new form of the novel taking shape under the hands of Fielding, Smollett and Sterne, while Boswell's *Johnson* is almost an encyclopedia of the mind of the unbending Tory as weighty and solid as the Durham Ox himself, who rather than change one iota of opinion preferred later to lose the American colonies.

The new King, George I, who was proclaimed peacefully in August, 1714, was to influence English Constitutional development more by what he lacked than by the qualities he possessed. Sensual, heartless and avaricious, without counterbalancing abilities, he was accustomed to playing the martinet in his small German possession. He had little understanding of the nation and the government he had been called upon to head solely because the choice of him alone could satisfy the English desire to settle the succession by Parliamentary choice of a Protestant monarch with as little disturbance to hereditary right as the case allowed. As his wife, on account of a suspected amour, was, by his orders, spending her life in prison, he brought no Queen with him, the lack being ill made up for by two unprepossessing German mistresses, one lean and the other very fat, dubbed by London wits the "Maypole" and the "Elephant."

One of the most important facts about the new King was that he did not speak the English language. Hitherto the monarch had always sat in the Council, but after trying for a while to continue the practice and to talk with such ministers as could understand his bad Latin, George gave it up, with the consequence that the power and prestige of the Prime Minister were much enhanced and the royal power was in important respects transferred to the Cabinet, which was in turn controlled by the Commons. The modern form of Cabinet government is now seen to be fast emerging, although after his accession in 1760 George III was to try to get back some of the prerogatives lost by his predecessors.

It was the Whigs who had brought in the House of Hanover, whereas leading Tories had played with Jacobitism and treason. It was therefore natural that the new King should form his Council of Whigs, turning out all Tories, and thus the long period of Whig ascendancy began. The great Whig families, however, were not in general as popular in the country as the Tory, and, especially in view of the fact that the King himself proved unpopular and unable to win the affection or respect of his subjects, the Whigs should have been careful in the moves they made with regard to their opponents. The first they made, the impeachment of the Tory Lords Oxford, Bolingbroke and Ormond was an unfortunate one. The latter two statesmen fled to France and were attainted of treason while Oxford got off with two years in the Tower. But this unnecessarily high-handed use by the Whigs of their new power led to an increase of Jacobite sentiment which might have had serious results.

The other move was far wiser. As we have pointed out in several earlier sections, there had been a long movement of decentralization of power from London to the country by means of the local but important functions of the Justices of the Peace, unpaid country gentlemen who formed a body utterly different from a bureaucracy paid and controlled from the center of government. For the most part these squires had been Tory, and the Whigs did not dare to arouse the resentment of their innumerable localities by replacing them with men of their own party. Thus although the "Whig Oligarchy" might rule the nation in many respects, the countryside remained largely under the control of the Tories, limiting to a considerable extent any attempt to tyrannize by the Oligarchy.

In 1715 and 1716 many of the Tories in England, combining with the Jacobites in Scotland, planned a rising, and in January of the latter year the Stuart Pretender landed on the Scottish coast. Both he and his leaders, however, were incompetent, and the unenterprising Prince, who had made a bad impression even on the loyal Scots, returned to France. The Whigs, nevertheless, did not dare to face the electorate in the election due in 1718, and to secure themselves in office passed the Septennial Act which provided for four additional years of life for the Parliament then sitting and thus secured a respite, although badly straining the Constitution. The King, however, refused to exercise his prerogative of veto, and signed the bill, the royal veto power then passing forever from the British form of government.

Partly owing to personal jealousies and ambitions, and partly to disagreement over Continental diplomacy as well as domestic policies, the Whig leaders split for a while, and Walpole, who was soon to enter upon a long reign of power, had to accept a lower office than he had enjoyed. The period of peace, following the great wars, had, as usual, inaugurated a great speculation. Stock companies were formed for almost every conceivable object, their shares rising rapidly in the market.

It was much like America in 1929. In particular the stock of the South Sea Company, already mentioned, rose from 100 to

1000, and when the crash came thousands of all classes were ruined. There was intense wrath against the Cabinet, one member of which was sent to the Tower, another committed suicide, and two others died suddenly. The crisis was grave, and Walpole was called to rescue both government and nation, for he was one of the few who had given warning of the impending crash. The result was to be twenty-one years of continuous office.

The new Minister was entirely cynical but he realized the profound need for making a healing peace both at home and abroad. The object was essential for the recovery and strengthening of the United Kingdom, with uncertainties threatening from the Continent and an increasingly unpopular foreign dynasty on the throne at home. If Walpole did not hesitate to maintain the position of government by a system of heavy corruption, that was at least better than the use of military force, and he did succeed for two decades. When George I died in 1727 and his son came to the throne as George II, Walpole found a staunch supporter in the Queen, Caroline, on whom her husband greatly depended.

In spite of personal quarrels between ministers, Walpole's unfortunate effort to enact a hated excise tax, and opposition by Bolingbroke, who had been allowed to return to England, Walpole maintained his position, and wisely kept England out of the Continental brawls, conserving her wealth and man power for greater struggles which he saw ahead in the farther future. His position, however, was much weakened in 1737 when Queen Caroline died and the intense dislike between the King and his son, the Prince of Wales, broke into open quarrel, the Prince organizing a Court party against his father. Even the Queen had said of her son that he "is the greatest ass and the greatest liar and the greatest *canaille* and the greatest beast in the whole world, and I heartily wish he were out of it." Unfortunately he was not, and the opposition he formed undermined Walpole to a considerable extent.

Moreover, in another two years, 1739, the English had a fit of war mania against Spain, and insisted upon entering upon the war known as that of "Jenkins' ear" because a seaman of the

name claimed to have had his ear torn off by Spanish customs officers, though the war was really based on trade causes and national hatred. Walpole was opposed to the whole adventure and
being still for peace might have done well to resign and leave the
odium of the brief and rather inglorious struggle to some one
else. However, he remained until beaten by a vote of one in an
election petition, when he gave up office at the beginning of 1742,
and retired to the House of Lords as Earl of Orford. In tiding
Britain over its dangerous period of transition, he had rendered
great service but in the struggle for empire looming ahead, he
would have been unfitted by both age and nature. Nevertheless,
the fact that Britain could play its great and successful part in
that when it came was due in large measure to his policy of peace
and conservation.

Like many another statesman Walpole was fitted for one phase
of national and political life and not for another. During the
quiet years during which he headed the government, England
had had the chance to adapt itself to changed conditions, and the
far from popular Hanoverian House had become firmly established on the throne, as it might not have done under the leadership of a more brilliant and uneasy spirit than Walpole's.

The Minister, like many others of the upper class of the period, expressed intense distaste for "enthusiasm." Nevertheless,
under the fashionable calm there was a powerful ferment at work,
both intellectual and emotional. The age of Voltaire in France
and of Berkeley, Butler and Hume in England was a highly
sceptical one in religion. The warmth of Christianity was tending
to be replaced by the intellectualism of Deism, and Presbyterians
were passing rapidly over to Unitarianism. This, however, is but
part of the picture. The religious revival, which we may date
from about 1735, had its deep effect not only in Wales, where re-
awakened religious fervor marked the real renaissance of Welsh
national thought, life and spirit, but also elsewhere.

In England we have to note the rise of the immensely important Methodist movement, as led by John and Charles Wesley,
which stirred in particular the sluggish religious emotions of the

working and poor classes, largely neglected by the Church. Tireless in their journeyings, and preaching to huge throngs in the open air, the influence of these two brothers was incalculably great on the life of England. Lay preachers were sent in every direction; schools, missions and charitable works were inaugurated, and the masses were given a glimpse of that vision without which a people perishes. Quite as much as William Pitt they may be considered as the founders of a new England.

As a result of the spirit developing it is noteworthy that it was in this period, usually considered as particularly venal and material, that the last of the original thirteen colonies was founded on the mainland of America, and that unlike any other it was founded neither for commercial nor sectarian reasons but from motives of pure philanthropy. General James Oglethorpe had become deeply interested in the evil conditions of the prison life of the day, particularly with respect to debtors, and it was especially in order to give to such unfortunates an opportunity for a new start in life that he obtained a charter and founded the colony of Georgia in 1733. Although his efforts to restrict the use of spirits and to prohibit that of slaves were unavailing, and two decades later his colony was taken over by the Crown, the noble venture was a monument to one aspect of the earlier eighteenth century which is too much neglected.

On the fall of Walpole no one minister was powerful enough to replace him and in the new Ministry Lord Carteret and the Duke of Newcastle, neither of them an able statesman, were too jealous of each other for either to be really Prime Minister. Meanwhile the War of the Austrian Succession had broken out on the Continent, and although at first King George was involved as Elector of Hanover and not as King of England, France declared war against England in 1744, and sent the Young Pretender to invade that country. Partly owing to a storm, such as has so often helped to protect the English coasts, the expedition was a complete failure, but the next year the young Prince, Charles Edward, landed in the West Highlands of Scotland, and the episode known as "the Forty-Five" had begun.

Raising a small force, he advanced to Edinburgh, where he was welcomed, and on September 21 defeated the English at Preston Pans. With 6000 men, the Pretender then crossed the border hoping that England would rise in his favor. However, it failed to do so and was entirely apathetic in the Stuart cause, though there was a financial panic in London. Charles had to retreat again to Scotland followed by the Duke of Cumberland with a much superior force, and in April, 1746, Cumberland beat the insurgents at Culloden Moor, inflicting such needless and bloody revenge as to give him the name of "the Butcher."

Charles, his cause now ruined beyond retrieve, wandered many months in the Highlands, a hunted fugitive. Eventually he escaped to France, living until 1788, and his brother, Henry, who had become a Cardinal, until 1807, but never again did the Stuarts make any effort to regain the English throne, and with the death of Henry the male line of the House was ended. It may be noted, however, that there are still living descendants of Charles I through his daughter, of whom the present King of Italy is one.

For the English, the military operations of the War of the Austrian Succession were neither brilliant nor important. The new Ministry, with the Pelhams in control, displayed no ability although before the end of the war they forced the King to accept young Pitt as a member of the Cabinet, against bitter royal opposition. Although England controlled the ocean highways, almost no use was made of the navy while money was lavished on the indecisive war on the Continent. Nevertheless, it was across the seas that the most interesting events were taking place.

In America, the New Englanders, particularly those of Massachusetts under the vigorous lead of Governor Shirley, raised about 4000 troops, and with no help from England except a few ships from the West India squadron to control the line of communication, besieged and at last captured the supposedly impregnable French fortress of Louisbourg, a brilliant colonial contribution to imperial defense and war that should have spelled a lesson for the British government.

We must now turn to the other side of the world, where events of stupendous importance for the future were taking place. Along the coast of India there were the trading stations of the British and French, and even yet of the Dutch and Portuguese, of which those of the two former were much the more important. The British were concentrated at Bombay, Madras and Calcutta, while the French had only two posts, Pondicherry not far from Madras, and Chandernagore not far from Calcutta. The French, however, although less strong in India had the advantage of a naval station in the island of Mauritius, and in the third and fourth decades of the century had been assuming a more aggressive attitude toward Indian trade and affairs under Labourdonnais, a naval officer, and Dupleix, Governor of Pondicherry.

Up to about this time there had been no question of Indian empire for either power but merely of trade rivalry, in which, however, the favor of native rulers could be made useful, nor had the East India Companies of both nations allowed the wars in Europe to extend to their Indian settlements. India herself was now undergoing profound changes which were to have effects equally profound on Britain, and to understand the future relations between their two peoples we must study for a few moments a civilization as different from that of Georgian England as it is possible to conceive.

It is somewhat misleading to speak of the two peoples, because for almost untold centuries India has held in its vast embrace a welter of many different races, varying greatly in their languages, their mentality, character and stages of civilization. Races, tribes and languages may almost be numbered by the hundreds. Although there is a considerable infusion of Aryan blood among the peoples of the North, those of the South appear to have had none whatever and to have originally belonged to a wholly non-Aryan stock. This is speaking generally, for in the past few centuries there has been much admixture, though the amount varies greatly from section to section. There are also a number of religions, though what largely holds India together, other than power superimposed from above, is Hinduism.

367

On the other hand, this has also emphasized differences between individual Indians to an extent that no other race or group of races has known, by the remarkable system of caste. It is impossible here to describe at length this peculiar but all-important institution, which certainly has lasted for over 2000 years and appears part of the order of nature to a Hindu. In general we may say that a caste is a group set apart from others by its rules and usages, involving many factors, though not always the same, such as race, trade or occupation.

The number of castes has been variously estimated at from two to four thousand, and the whole system is extremely complex. Every Hindu is born into one of these castes, and must forever remain in it. Any member who breaks the rules of his caste becomes an "out-cast," cut off from all relationship with those of his own or any other caste. Not only is intermarriage between members of different castes forbidden but in many cases other forms of social intercourse. On the one hand, the system has given such a rigidity to Indian life that in spite of wars and changes in rulers the deeps of that life go on as unruffled as the deeps of the sea by the storms on its surface. On the other hand, it has also made it difficult for Indians to act together to overthrow conquerors, and has added another disunity to those of race, language and character.

For some seven centuries before Europeans first appeared to trade, the larger part of India had been subject to the military rule of conquering races, that of the great Mogul Empire, the last of a long series, being in power when our story opened. As these last conquerors were Mohammedans, another element of disunity was present in that the great Hindu population was governed by those of an alien race and religion among whom the caste system did not exist. None of the successive conquering and ruling powers had ever attempted to unify the people or to build a firm government dependent on factors other than the power of the ruler of the day. The Mogul Empire has been, perhaps, the best, but even under it, while a certain degree of peace had been maintained, there had been no impartial justice for the individual subject, and taxes consumed about one-third of the revenue of the people, who were at the mercy of the great officers who were locally in authority in various parts of the unstable empire.

In the first half of the eighteenth century, the Mogul Empire collapsed, and coincident with the wars in Europe and America, India became a seething chaos. While some of the viceroys of provinces, such as the Nawabs of Oudh and Bengal and the Subadar of the Deccan, continued to pay nominal allegiance to the Mogul at Delhi, they had in fact become independent. Moreover, the warlike tribe of the Mahrattas began to overrun the peninsula, levying heavy tribute on penalty of destructive plunder. One-quarter of the entire revenue of the Deccan alone had to be paid to them. The remnants of the Mogul power were no match for them, and they might have built an empire on the ruin of the former had they shown any capacity for rule. They did not, however, and merely plundered in every direction on a colossal scale.

The Afghans also poured in through the undefended passes of the northwest frontier, and when Nadir Shah, who had already made himself master of Persia and Afghanistan, sacked Delhi, he gave the death-blow to the Mogul Empire, although he withdrew through the passes again, claiming lordship only of the vast Punjab, where his power was threatened by the Sikhs. Nadir Shah's own empire broke up across the mountains, and by 1760 the Mahrattas had made themselves masters throughout almost all India, though seeking only to plunder and not to govern. India, with its possible 200,000,000 of population, was in terrified anarchy.

This situation naturally reacted on the little trading posts of both French and English which became increasingly insecure and liable to attack from avaricious princes. Meanwhile, war had been declared between their two countries in 1744. The British used their superior naval strength to sweep French commerce off the seas. Labourdonnais and Dupleix retaliated, and in 1746, in a joint expedition captured the English Madras. Dupleix had promised the ruler of the Carnatic that if captured the place

369

would be turned over to him but broke his word, and when the Nawab sent an army of 10,000 against him he defeated the mob with only 500 trained troops.

A land and sea attack by the British against Pondicherry was a failure, and in the eyes of the natives all prestige had been transferred to the French. Then came peace in Europe, and in the Treaty of Aix-la-Chapelle, 1748, the French agreed to return Madras to the English in exchange for Louisbourg in Canada. The curtain, however, had been drawn up and the stage was set for the great Indian drama of the next generation.

Had the British Government made proper use of its navy, both Madras and Louisbourg might have been retained, and the return of the latter to France was a sore disappointment to New England. The latter in especial, though it was true of all the colonies, was beginning to feel that its interests were being subordinated to those of England, to an unwarranted extent. In 1733 its trade had been threatened with extinction by the passage of the Molasses Act with its prohibitory duties on the import of molasses from other than the British West Indies, though the British islands could not supply the New England merchants with enough to turn into rum for the triangular trade with the West Indies and Africa. It was on this trade that they depended to secure exchange with which, in the absence of staple exports of their own, to buy the English manufactured goods they were forced to purchase by the prohibition of domestic manufacturing.

It is true that the law simply could not be enforced but its passage had indicated that New England's interests were to be sacrificed to those of the island planters, and now again, by the exchange of Louisbourg for Madras it appeared that they were again to be sacrificed to those of the East India Company. Throughout the intervening period, there had been growing evidence that the home government was drawing tighter the commercial and other legislation which was tending to drive the American continental colonies into determined opposition. Moreover, there was now pouring into the Middle Colonies in particular a stream of immigration of Germans and Scotch-Irish and others who had either no knowledge of the mother country or an intense hatred of her for the wrongs they had suffered.

The peace of 1748 had been only a truce. In fact, it was not even that, for there was much unofficial fighting before the formal declaration of war again between Great Britain and France in 1756. In India, Dupleix was taking advantage of the anarchic conditions to back such native aspirants to thrones as would support the claims of the French if aided—and controlled—by small forces of trained French troops. It was a new policy and had been so far successful by 1751 as to appear to threaten the complete destruction of English interests in India.

In that year, the new English governor, Saunders, placed a young clerk in the company's service, Robert Clive, only twenty-six years old, in charge of an expedition to attack Arcot, the capital of the Carnatic. With only eight officers, of whom six, like Clive himself, had never seen service, and with but 500 troops of whom 300 were Indians, Clive captured Arcot, and then stood a siege of nearly two months against the overwhelming force of 10,000 troops of Chanda Sahib, the ruler, who had been forced by the danger to his capital to withdraw these from the siege of the British in Trichinopoly. The next year that place was relieved by a force under Major Lawrence and Clive, and a French force defeated. Nevertheless, the French appeared still to be stronger than the English and to be the coming power in India. The British were not yet making proper use of their naval strength, and the future looked dark for the East India Company and British trade when the two European nations finally declared war. This was followed by repeated defeats of the French and the ultimate recall and ruin of the great French Governor Dupleix and the end of his dream of a French empire in India.

In America affairs were also going badly. During the early years of settlement, the British had fortunately been confined to the rather narrow strip between the ocean and the Appalachian Mountain ranges. Thus settlement had been concentrated, and the settlers had devoted themselves mainly to agriculture and trade. On the other hand, the French claimed all the vast regions drained by the St. Lawrence and Mississippi Rivers, an imperial domain too vast to be settled, and had dissipated their energies in exploration and the fur trade. By the mid-eighteenth century, however, the well-settled colonies along the central Atlantic seaboard, particularly Virginia, were beginning to look across the mountains to the rich lands of the Ohio Valley, and a clash between the French who claimed that country and the English frontiersmen and land companies who insisted on crossing over into the territory was bound to come sooner or later.

The Duke of Newcastle, who had succeeded his abler brother, Henry Pelham, as Prime Minister on the latter's death, had neither the ability nor energy to carry on an extensive war such as was now developing in various parts of the world, but did send out an expedition under the brave but stubborn Braddock to cooperate with the colonials in opposing the French on the Ohio. The story of Braddock's defeat is one of the commonplaces of school history, and was almost contemporaneous with the loss of the island of Minorca to the French in the Mediterranean. The failure of Admiral Byng, who was not the traitor he was assumed to be, but who had not struck a blow against the French fleet in defense of Britain's important naval base, aroused intense indignation. The panic into which Newcastle had been thrown by his own incompetence was indicated by his suggestion that the King call over troops from Hanover to protect England from invasion!

Newcastle resigned and the Duke of Devonshire formed a new Cabinet in which Pitt was practically Prime Minister, although soon forced out temporarily by the hostility of the King. There was a fresh energy in public affairs and war was declared with France, which country had fortunately also embarked on a war for the breaking up of Prussia under Frederick the Great, so that her strength was divided. Nevertheless, Britain seemed unable to make headway, and a new Ministry was again formed with Newcastle as head, who if he could not manage a war was a master in handling of patronage and the House of Commons. Owing to overwhelming popular demand, Pitt was also recalled to office. It was his task to manage the war, and he threw himself into it with an energy and capacity that no other statesman of the time could have displayed.

Granted his egoism, his dictatorial ways, his love of the theatrical and all his other foibles and defects, the elder Pitt was undoubtedly one of the great Englishmen of history. He understood both Europe and the Empire as no other statesman of his day. The grandson of Thomas Pitt, who had played his part in Indian development, he also seemed instinctively to understand the character of the American colonials. Closely allied with the trading classes, and known as "the Great Commoner," he inspired the mass of Englishmen who had accepted the bribery and corruption of political management as a necessary evil which could be tolerated in good times (much as Americans used to tolerate municipal corruption in their politics) with a new ideal of patriotism and public service.

Spurning the customary spoils of office, Pitt became the idol of ordinary people, as also a dangerous portent to those who did not share his views as to public office being a public trust. Moreover, he had a marvellous gift for choosing men to serve under him, and not only did he choose them according to their ability and regardless of their rank or influence, but he also rewarded them according to the same standard. The result was an intense loyalty to him, especially on the part of his younger officers in the services and other subordinates. Finally, he himself was an indefatigable worker and an administrator of the first rank. In four dazzling years, after place-hunting statesmen had been bungling and fumbling the British nation into disaster, Pitt raised it to perhaps the highest and most dominant position it has ever occupied in the eyes of the world.

During those years, success followed success until the English themselves were amazed. Before 1760 Canada had been conquered in America, Louisbourg was retaken, and in the famous attack against Quebec Montcalm was forced to surrender to Wolfe on the Plains of Abraham. The brilliancy and daring of the performance, the importance of the result, considering the numbers involved, and the tragic death of the youthful English commander in the moment of victory, have surrounded the fall of the French citadel with a halo of glory and romance. Fort Niagara, Ticonderoga, Crown Point were also captured, and in the Ohio Valley, Fort Duquesne, now Pittsburgh, had fallen to the English, and the French power in America was prostrate.

Although the thirteen colonies had not been entirely inactive in their own defense they contributed little as compared with previous and much less important crises, and for the most part the Assemblies showed a huckstering and provincial spirit that had much to do with the problem of imperial defense which was to loom so large a few years later and to be one of the leading causes of the Revolution. In part, the difficulty came from the jealousies and ill-feeling existing between the several colonies and sections.

They had, in fact, little sympathy with, or knowledge of, each other, and except for a common language and the tie to Britain they represented almost as different civilizations and outlooks as may be found among the nations of Continental Europe. There were barriers of all sorts, religious, cultural and economic. Puritan New England, for example, a land of traders and small farmers, had little in common with Quaker Pennsylvania, Catholic Maryland, or Anglican Virginia, or with the sort of culture which had developed on the large slave-operated plantations of the South.

In 1753, with the possible coming struggle in view, the British government had asked the colonies to hold a joint meeting of the Governors of Virginia, Pennsylvania, Maryland, New York, New Jersey and New Hampshire with the Indians in the effort to evolve some common Indian policy and to make a joint treaty, a plan which was soon made to include some form of general political union among all the colonies. But nothing came of this suggestion.

The colonists themselves attempted at Albany in 1754 to form some such union, but jealousy and provincialism again proved insurmountable obstacles, and it was evident that if war with the French and Indians should come on a large scale nothing more could be expected, if even that, than that each colony would make some effort to protect the citizens and settlements within its own boundaries. Any general campaign would have to be conducted by the British government. The situation was rendered even worse by the often conflicting policies pursued by the several colonies toward the Indian tribes on their borders or with whom they traded.

Picking up again the thread of the main story of the war we may note that Pitt, in addition to his brilliant campaigning on land, was also at last using the British navy, and let loose against the French its forces under Rodney and Hawke, the latter winning the notable victory of Quiberon Bay. The French, who had threatened to invade England, were now powerless at sea, and in the West Indies the islands of Guadeloupe and Marie Galante fell to the British, as had the French trading posts on the African coast. On the Continent, the battle of Minden was a crushing blow to the French in their war against Prussia.

In India, the stage of action was the great province of Bengal. The old ruler died in 1756, and his grandson, a degenerate nineteen years old, who succeeded him, and who wished to drive all Europeans out of India, marched against Calcutta with an army of 30,000 men. Capturing the small garrison there, he placed an uncertain number of his English prisoners, said to be about 150, in a small dungeon for the night without air or water. The horrors of the sufferers in the heat of an Indian June can never be told, and it is estimated that about 125 died before morning in what has ever since been known as "the Black Hole of Calcutta."

Meanwhile, Clive, who had been in England, had returned with a small fleet under Admiral Watson, and on the second day of 1757 recaptured Calcutta, making a treaty with the young ruler, Siraj-uddaula, which the Indian had no intention of carrying out. He had, however, by his greed and cruelty alienated the chief men of the province, who conspired to place an old friend of his father on the throne, Mir Jafar, and Clive entered into the conspiracy. In the anarchic conditions then prevailing in India and with the French using the native rulers, the English had to do likewise or turn India over to the French. It was probably fortunate for India that the English were to win at the game the

French had started, for whatever their qualities, the latter race has shown no such ability in governing subject peoples as has the British.

Unfortunately, the transaction was marred by Clive's drawing up two treaties, a true and false one, the latter to be shown to a Hindu, Omichand, who had learned of the conspiracy and had threatened to divulge it to Siraj-uddaula unless bought off with a huge sum. It may be questioned, however, whether a blackmailer can complain of the methods used against him. However, it was agreed that Mir Jafar should be placed on the throne, pay the British about £3,000,000, and transfer a large district around Calcutta to the East India Company to be governed by it. Whether Mir Jafar could be depended on was a question, but Clive took the risk, and at the battle of Plassey, completely defeated Siraj-uddaula, whose Bengali troops simply fled, the young ruler being later killed by the son of Mir Jafar. That ruler was now under control of the Company, as was the entire province of Bengal which he nominally ruled.

A French fleet, sent out in 1756, arrived in April, 1758, and undertook to besiege Madras, but was forced to withdraw by the arrival of a British squadron, and the naval victories in Europe had decided that control of the sea was henceforth to lie with the English. There was some further fighting, but one by one the French posts fell, and when the most important of all, Pondicherry, was captured in 1761, the possibility of French control in India had passed forever, and that of the British Empire had begun.

It had come accidentally, due to the necessity of dealing with the unscrupulous and wholly untrustworthy rulers of the various provinces who had succeeded to the power of the Mogul Emperors. The situation was an extraordinary one. Neither the British people nor the government, nor, indeed, the East India Company had desired conquest. As yet there was no conquest in fact, but by control of the rulers of Bengal and a large part of Madras, the Company had become responsible for government and policy without itself being the direct governing agency. From one point of view, there was power without responsibility, and from another, responsibility without power.

Yet here was an empire at the feet of a trading company which was itself a corporate creature of the British government. It was far less clear to the men of the time than it is to us that vast problems were bound to be raised for solution. Meanwhile, the Company was by no means altogether pleased with the prospect opening before it, for the cost of the forces, which would be necessary to garrison and hold the empire so unexpectedly acquired by it, threatened to consume all the trading profits, to say nothing of the diversion of the energies of its employees from business to politics. But there was no alternative except to abandon the lucrative trade entirely.

In any case, France beaten to her knees in Europe had lost both her American and Indian Empires to the English, and although a peace treaty was not to be negotiated for nearly three years, the fighting was over and the treaty would be dictated by the victors. Suddenly, on October 25, 1760, the King died, though for so little had his influence counted that his death had only a negative effect. That effect was that the throne was now inherited by his grandson, an obstinate young man of twenty-two, George III, who would insist on playing quite a different role in the State from that of the first two sovereigns of his dynasty.

CHAPTER XVII

THE END OF THE FIRST EMPIRE

GEORGE III, though almost wholly German in blood, was the most English thus far of the Hanoverian House on the throne of England. He had been born and brought up in England, and in many respects had the qualities, good and bad, of the ordinary Englishman. He was honest, according to his own view, a hard worker, opinionated and obstinate, but, again according to his own view, a patriotic upholder of the British Constitution as he understood it, and sober judgment after this long lapse of time cannot endorse the contemporary belief of many that he was a conscious tyrant.

He was profoundly influenced by two ideas. One was to reinstate the Crown in the position which had been accorded to it in the Revolution Settlement of 1689, and the other was the conception of "the Patriot King" which had been promulgated by the brilliant Bolingbroke who in one way and another had always exerted a baneful influence on British history.

There is no doubt that in the 1689 Settlement it had been intended that the king should be at the head of the executive department of government. A constitution, however, is not static but a constantly changing organism to fit the needs of a people, and in the seventy years intervening, greatly helped by the peculiar circumstances of the first two Georges, the Cabinet had developed into the real executive head, the ministers being responsible to the majority in the Commons. Cabinet government is probably the supreme contribution of England to the practical science of politics. It enables the nation, and far more important, the Empire, to retain all the obvious advantages of the Crown as the symbol of national history, aspiration and unity, while at the same time placing it above the strife of party feeling and providing an executive—the Cabinet—which is controlled by majority rule.

Although the Cabinet had developed as an invaluable part of the mechanism of government, it could not as yet be said to be responsive to the will of the nation, in spite of the fact that it was to the majority in the House of Commons. Until the Reform Bill of 1832, still long in the future when George III ascended the throne, that majority was made up chiefly of members elected from "pocket boroughs" under the control of leading families, and by bribery and corruption. Indeed, it may be said that although the Cabinet had to have a majority in the Commons, the King could still choose his own Ministers, and those Ministers could create a majority. Parties in the modern sense had not yet evolved, and in their place were the "factions" of which George Washington was later to warn the citizens of his own newly born nation. In England these factions took the form of family groups, with a sprinkling of independents, and were known as the Bedford Whigs, Pelhamites, Rockinghamites, Shelbournites, and so on. So great was the desire for places, honors and pensions, that Ministers had little difficulty in making a majority in the Commons once they were in the Cabinet and in a position to hand out the coveted prizes. Had the Cabinet reached the stage of development when it really represented the will of the nation instead of merely that of such a majority of Parliament, George would not have been able to arrest the course of constitutional history for nearly twenty years. Like many Englishmen and most of the statesmen of his day, George, honest according to the accepted rules of the game as then played, was wholly lacking in constructive imagination. He worked on the immediate situation as he saw it, and believing, truly, that the power of the Crown had been limited to a degree far beyond that contemplated in the Revolution Settlement, he determined to regain the lost position which to him meant not tyranny but restoring the Constitution, and in fact he kept carefully within it.

Bolingbroke in his theory of a "Patriot King" had promulgated the belief that the monarch should be free of party and gather around him as he chose the ablest men of any party to serve as his Ministers, rising above party and freeing himself from the exorbitant claims of the office of Prime Minister as that office had developed. There was, indeed, something to be said for the idea, and Pitt as well as other leaders who objected to the long ascendancy of the Whig Oligarchy agreed with it. The Whigs had rendered great services to the nation and done much to bring forward the modern constitutional arrangement between King and Cabinet, but, maintaining their control of the Commons by virtue of patronage and corruption, the Whigs, as many felt, by their control of *both* Crown and Parliament threatened the liberty of the nation.

Britain under the new King had many problems to face which had been created by the events of the previous decades, and among these the domestic constitutional problem loomed large. In spite of the breaking up of the Whigs into groups, they all had in common the wish to maintain the hold they had fastened upon the country. In the absence of an opposition party the only alternatives were for the King to try to follow the course laid down by Bolingbroke or for Parliament to reform the franchise so that the Commons would really become representative of the people at large. As that appeared to be out of the question at this stage, the King took it upon himself to break the Whig control. It may be noted, however, that he did not attempt to break down the Cabinet system in two important particulars. He did not sit in Cabinet meetings himself, and he accepted the fact that on the whole his chosen Ministers must be responsible to the majority in the Commons. In the absence of electoral reform, the nation could not create the majority. It had to be created by the Whig Oligarchy, which had ceased to have the confidence of the nation, or by the King himself, using the same means of "management" as the Whigs had, that is, bribery and corruption.

The granting of honors and offices theoretically belonged to the Crown, and it required no stretch of the Constitution for the King to take their bestowal into his own hands. The confused and sordid political alignments and realignments of the next twenty years must be considered not so much as the efforts of a King seeking to impose his tyrannical will on the nation as of the nation itself groping after some means of continuing the development of an executive which should be based on neither the unfettered will of the sovereign nor the selfish desire of a faction which had fastened itself on the people to hold on to its places and incomes.

The struggle, which is too intricate to go into in all its details of two decades, was to end in the eighteenth century in the reorganization of a strong Tory opposition party, and in the nineteenth in the reformation of Parliament. The contest proved, however, that there could be no such thing as Bolingbroke's Patriot King, and that a monarch who would try to rise above party in his choice of Ministers and yet to control Parliament by manipulation could only himself become the leader of a party or faction, and lose both for himself and the nation the advantages of constitutional monarchy. That was the lesson of the earlier part of the long reign of the unhappy and unpopular King, who in the beginning at least seemed forced to make his unsuccessful effort.

Meanwhile, the Seven Years' War continued. Pitt, who had wished to declare war with Spain in 1761, had resigned when the proposition was defeated, although Spain herself declared war the following year. In the general election, the King had declined to allow Newcastle to use the royal patronage and money to build up a Whig majority and had used them himself, with the result that about a quarter of the new Commons looked to the King and not to the Whig leader for their orders. On Newcastle's resignation, the King named the unpopular Scottish peer, Lord Bute, in his place, and during his brief administration peace was at last made, February 10, 1763, at Paris.

By the terms of the treaty, Great Britain retained Canada, Nova Scotia and Cape Breton in America, and received from

France a clear title to all the western lands to the Mississippi (except New Orleans), together with Senegal and several small West Indian islands. From Spain she received another American colony, Florida, and also the return of Minorca. The decision to retain Canada and the West instead of the rich sugar islands of Guadeloupe and Martinique marked a departure from former colonial ideas and was the subject of a bitter pamphlet warfare. Although many selfish interests were involved, the decision was in the main a victory for those who were henceforth to regard colonies as a market for British manufactures rather than as sources of raw materials. It was, however, to have unexpected results.

The balance, already badly upset between the British sugar islands and the needs of the New England traders, was now to be hopelessly lost, and the prohibitive Molasses Act of 1733 became more impossible of enforcement than ever. Moreover, the removal of the French danger to the north and west of the American continental colonies was considered by many to portend an increasing restiveness and independent spirit on their part. In my opinion this was to prove of less importance than the unanticipated problems raised by the vast new possessions which no one expected, and the failure to solve which was to have such fatal ending.

The problems, some arising from the new territorial acquisitions, and some wholly disconnected with the war, which faced the King and the British Government in the period of this chapter, were indeed of a variety and importance, as well as novelty, which would have severely taxed the ability and imagination of the best British statesmen of any period. For the most part those in power during their attempted solution were not great men, and in recalling the failure to arrange some settlement with the "thirteen colonies" in America it is only fair to say that the handling of the other problems reflected a considerable degree of credit on the successive administrations.

The domestic problem of responsible or Cabinet government we have already mentioned. In the absence of a well understood and developed two-party system, that had to be worked out slowly and clumsily by the method of trial and error. The other problems had to do with Ireland, India, Canada and the older American colonies, and we shall take them in order so as to provide a better background of understanding for the one great failure. To a considerable extent, events in each part of the globe were influenced by those occurring elsewhere, particularly by the revolution in America, but for the sake of clarity we shall have to treat them independently.

In Ireland we may dismiss the agrarian risings which began in a serious form in 1761 and which were to be repeated at intervals until well into the nineteenth century. These were not political in nature, but there were to be great constitutional changes during the period of the controversy with America. When George came to the throne, Ireland already had a Parliament of her own, but almost wholly subject to that of England and to the Privy Council. There was no limit to the length of time the Irish Parliament might sit, except that of the life of the King, but at the request of the Irish it was limited, in 1768, to eight years.

By 1776 there had been growing discontent, partly due to the example of the American colonies, and when in that year a new Parliament was elected those who desired substantial changes in the relations with England found a leader in the extremely able Henry Grattan, a Protestant, though he was to advocate strongly the relief of the Catholics from their disabilities. In 1778 the administration of Lord North, which has so much in America to its discredit, not only relieved the Irish Catholics from many of the worst conditions which had weighed so heavily on them, but also proposed extraordinarily liberal trade measures for the island, though the latter were not carried out owing to the intense opposition of both English and Scottish business houses.

The Irish situation was becoming dangerous, however, owing to the fact that England had had to withdraw most of her troops for the war, and, with both France and Spain as enemies, there was danger of invasion by either or both of them.

Ireland, for her own defense, raised over 40,000 volunteers, the number rising to over 80,000 by 1781, mostly Protestants.

Economic and political demands followed the formation of these important bodies of citizens, and the influence of the struggle going on in America can be traced in the "non-importation agreements" entered into, and even in a "Declaration of Independence" introduced by Grattan in the Irish Parliament, 1780, although the North government had meanwhile passed legislation which gave Ireland complete equality with England and Scotland for trade both within and without the Empire.

Contrasted with all the previous periods in which we have touched upon the Irish question, there was now growing up a distinct Irish *national* sentiment, in spite of continued Catholic disabilities. Grattan and the other Irish patriots, although demanding complete independence within the Empire, had not suggested withdrawal, and recognized the link of the Crown. In 1782 the Whig Ministry following the resignation of North granted all that was asked, giving up as Grattan said "*in toto* every claim to authority over Ireland," although they expected to make a treaty (which was never made) establishing some sort of working arrangement between the two kingdoms.

In view of the long and embittered history of Anglo-Irish relations, and of the attitude of George III's government toward the American colonies, one has almost to rub one's eyes when reading of this Irish settlement of 1782. With trade equality, which Scotland had obtained only at the cost of Union and giving up her local Parliament, and with complete independence except the acknowledgment of George as King of Ireland, that country seemed at last to have attained all the advantages with none of the disadvantages of Empire membership. If it seemed too good to be true, it was at least unfortunately too good to last.

Aside from other points, the fact that Ireland was now free to adopt policies diametrically opposed to the interests of the greater United Kingdom which she faced across a few miles of narrow sea might prove a disastrous anomaly. Nevertheless, if, as ever, her geographical position and other factors were to prove her misfortune, it is interesting to note that the most complete freedom which she ever enjoyed under British rule until the present day, was granted to her ungrudgingly by the government of George III.

The Irish problem, if never solved, had been familiar to English governments for centuries. We must now turn to another facing the government which was not only new but which has never been presented to any other imperial power on any scale so comparable as to make the problem similar—that of India, although in this period that problem was still in its early stages.

From 1760, when Clive left for England until his return to India in 1765, conditions in that country were disgracefully bad. As we have seen, the Nawab of Bengal had the nominal responsibility for government without power, whereas the East India Company had the power but without responsibility. As might have been expected, government by the Nawab broke down, and the employees of the Company scrambled only to make their fortunes as rapidly as might be, and the opportunities for plunder of one sort or another staggered imagination. Mir Jafar proved a bad ruler even under the conditions which made native rule almost impossible, and when the local representatives of the Company deposed him in favor of his son-in-law, Mir Kasim, they not only demanded enormous sums in cash but secured the administration of the richest three Bengal provinces. In these, for the first time, the English (but, it must be noted, not the English government) united responsibility to power with the result that administration greatly improved.

Mir Kasim also made an effort to better the administration in his remaining provinces, but in spite of the sympathetic aid given to him by the Governor, Vansittart, and Warren Hastings, the remainder of the Company's leading representatives insisted on demands that threw the Nawab into revolt, and the Company replaced him with Mir Jafar again. The confusion in Bengal led the Nawab of the great state of Oudh, together with the nominal Mogul Emperor, to fish in the troubled waters, but they were defeated by a small force of Company troops at Buxar in 1764, the Company thus extending its control over Oudh as well as Bengal, and even over the Emperor himself.

385

The situation, however, was intolerable, and in 1765 Clive, now a peer, was sent out to develop a better system. The new one put in force, honest in its conception, did not work in practice. The native rulers were to be responsible for the maintenance of order and for military affairs, while the Company was to have charge of the collection of taxes, a dual form of control which had been customary in India, with the exception that the Company now substituted itself for the former native collector of revenue, although it farmed out the collections. This function was expected to produce such a large revenue that for the first time the government in England took a hand in the affairs of the Company.

Under Charles Townshend, Chancellor of the Exchequer in 1767, who was just then, as we shall see later, having his troubles with America, Parliament demanded that £400,000 a year of the loot should be paid to the British Government. Little could be done under either Clive, even with his immense prestige, or his less able successor Verelst, against the evils which had developed locally, and in 1770 there came the worst famine ever known in this land of famines. It has been estimated that one-third of the population died, and the stories which reached England, true or not, that Englishmen were making heavy profits from the hideous calamity aroused intense resentment.

Moreover, the Mahrattas were again on the move and dangerously menacing the Company's interests. In the South, a Mohammedan adventurer, Hyder Ali, had acquired power, was threatening Madras, and had brought on wars among the several potentates of that section. The sea of Indian life, like an ocean, was being churned into tempestuous waves by the storms passing over its vast surface. The Company, both from these causes and from internal mismanagement and graft, was facing bankruptcy by 1772 instead of the enormous prosperity which had been anticipated. The one outstanding figure, for honesty and ability, of the sorry years that had passed, was Warren Hastings, who was now sent out to retrieve the situation and to reorganize the relations of the Company to the local rulers and governments.

In a little over two years Hastings succeeded in giving Bengal the best government any Indian province had ever had. He arranged for honest collection of taxes on a fair basis; established courts of law; made Bengal safe from the Mahrattas; and firmly attached to the British the great state of Oudh. Although he could not correct all abuses he did marvellous work not only in rehabilitating the Company, but in introducing decent government for the benefit of the Indians themselves. The beginning had been made of the modern services based upon a sense of responsibility toward the native peoples.

In England also a new spirit was stirring, although the India Act of 1773, which marked the first effort of control of the Company and its possessions by Parliament, was to have disastrous results though well-intentioned. While it left the Company in political control it provided for a certain amount of supervision of its political activities by the home government. It also foolishly introduced English law through a Supreme Court in India to which any one could have recourse against employees of the Company; and set up a Council of five members, including the Governor-General, who were to have equal votes in the management of affairs.

Unfortunately the new members of the Council, who arrived in Calcutta in 1774, included Philip Francis, the reputed author of the *Letters of Junius,* who was consumed with personal ambition and a jealousy, amounting to a disease, of Hastings. Nothing could convince this young man, who like two other of the new Councillors had never had any experience or knowledge of India, that Hastings was not a complete rascal and tyrant. As the other two almost invariably sided with Francis, Hastings found his hands so tied that he was unable to continue his reforms, although the meddling trio could not undo all that had been accomplished thus far.

However, they invited any one to make charges against the Governor, even accepting an infamous forgery by a worthless native, Nuncomar, who claimed that Hastings had taken enormous bribes. When after trial before the Supreme Court Nuncomar was hanged, the enemies of Hastings, with no shadow of evidence, even accused him of having procured Nuncomar's death. Such were the conditions under which the Governor had to do his work, though the situation was much improved by the death of one of the hostile Councillors in 1776, and the return to England of Francis in 1780 to carry on there his campaign of slander and lies.

It was fortunate that the position of Hastings had been strengthened, for in the five years between 1779 and 1784 he, and he alone, preserved against seemingly hopeless odds the empire of India for Britain. There was a terrific struggle against both the Mahrattas and Hyder Ali, and after the declaration of war by France in 1778 it was known that a French fleet was on its way to India to back the native powers in their struggle against the Company, whose treasury was almost empty, although Hastings was still expected to remit handsome dividends to England. The Rajah of Benares, who was dependent on the Company for his throne, had to pay about £500,000 for protection, but even so Hastings had to carry on war with no help from England, now fully occupied with the world war into which the American rebellion had drifted.

By seizing the French posts he deprived the French fleet of a base and rendered it impotent. By fighting and diplomacy he also managed not only to maintain the British power but greatly to increase British prestige. In the course of the struggle occurred the incident which, with the protection money or fine levied on the Rajah of Benares, was to form the chief basis of the later impeachment of Hastings.

The province of Oudh owed the Company a large sum of money which the Nawab was unable to pay because his mother and grandmother, known as the Begums, had unlawfully retained the vast treasure of the Nawab's late father, with the permission of Francis and the other members of the Council hostile to Hastings. There was no doubt of the Nawab's rightful claim to his inheritance, and after Hastings had lent him troops to collect the treasure unjustly retained by the ladies of the family, the Nawab paid the debt he owed the Company, a payment sorely needed in the crisis.

Hastings, single-handed, had not only saved India without the slightest territorial or other loss, but during his years as Governor had laid the foundations for a better political order. Almost alone among the Company's servants he understood the Indian problem and had a genuine sympathy with the native Indian population. He was forced to do much he otherwise would not have done by the rancorous folly of the Council and the stupidity of the governors of Madras and Bombay, who involved the Company in dangerous situations from which Hastings had to extricate it. Statesmen in England, however, notably Burke and Fox, were beginning to feel that the problem of India was too vast and offered too many temptations for the government to remain in the hands of a commercial company. Other Governors, more avaricious or less clean-handed than Hastings, should not be trusted to use Company troops to collect such vast sums as he had from the Rajah of Benares or the Begums, and the Coalition Ministry of 1783 introduced a bill to deprive the Company entirely of the government of India and to vest it in a Board of seven Commissioners appointed in the bill at first and later to be appointees of the Crown.

Although owing to the venal political question of patronage the bill failed to pass, the dozen or more years during which Britain had been mishandling the American problem had seen a notable advance in both administration and public opinion with reference to better government in India and the rights of the native population and rulers.

Without the slightest intention of engaging in more than profitable trading, like scores of other companies formed about the time of the founding of the East India Company, that Company had been led by a long series of circumstances, none of which could have been foreseen, into the position of being practical sovereign over rich and populous states with an old though thoroughly decadent civilization. It was an anomalous position which could not be permanent, but the problem had no precedents for guidance, and in feeling their way toward a solution neither the Company nor the government had done badly under Hastings.

Pitt succeeded in having passed in 1784 a far better India Bill

389

than the earlier abortive Coalition one. According to its terms the Company kept all patronage, except the appointments of the Governor-General and one or two other high officials, in its own hands, but although the government of India was nominally left also to the Company it was really controlled by the King's Ministers. This dual form of control was to last until 1858.

There was yet another problem which the British Government had to face, this time as a direct result of the Peace of Paris in 1763. That was the problem of Canada and the vast American western hinterland. The latter, except for a few military posts here and there, was practically uninhabited by white men, but the population of Canada was about 60,000, of whom all but a couple of hundred or so were French Catholics. The attitude of the British Government toward them, even before the treaty of peace, was and continued to be, exemplary. The instructions to the military Governor recited that "these newly-acquired subjects, when they have taken the oath, are as much His Majesty's subjects as any of us, and are, so long as they remain deserving of it, entitled to the same protection." This pledge was fully redeemed by all later legislation in spite of the small Protestant population, chiefly from New England, who made preposterous demands that they alone should rule the new province.

The British Government, by the Proclamation of 1763, established four new distinct governments in the New World, those of Grenada (West Indies), East and West Floridas, which were unimportant historically, and that of Quebec. The Proclamation was intended to be only a stop-gap until further legislation could be prepared, but in fact this was not accomplished for another eleven years, due largely to the usual procrastination of the eighteenth century. Viewed in the large as a temporary measure, and in great part even as a permanent one, the Proclamation was a statesmanlike document.

Not only was the religion of the conquered respected to the full, but also the entire system of French law under which they had been accustomed to live, it being wisely decided that to force English law upon them would work great and unnecessary hardship. How far in advance of the general ideas as to colonial administration of the times such legislation was may be judged by what would have happened to an equally large body of alien Protestants had their colony fallen into the hands of either France or Spain.

The one point which may be justly criticized, especially in view of the unexpectedly long time that the legislation remained in force, was the inclusion of the entire West and Mississippi Valley in the government of "Quebec." From the beginning of American settlement, the Indian question had been ever present, and the colonies had never been able to agree upon any joint policy, as had been demonstrated over and over. That question was now of far greater importance and complexity than ever, due to the enormous additional territory, with its native inhabitants who had been under French rule or in French alliance, and the British Government intended to undertake its solution.

Until a policy could be worked out, it was decided, and embodied in the Proclamation, that there should be no settlement in the new lands "westward of the sources of the rivers which fall into the sea from the West or North-West." In other words, the inhabitants of the original thirteen colonies were prohibited from crossing the Appalachian range to take up lands, the effect of which prohibition on American sentiment we shall note later. Nor was any individual to be allowed to purchase any Indian lands in future, such purchases being permitted only by officers of the Crown at a public meeting of the Indians involved according to Indian law. This just system, which has ever since been maintained in Canada, coupled with the closing of the western lands, was undoubtedly highly beneficial to the newly acquired regions, however much, with the toleration of Catholicism, it may have been offensive to the inhabitants of the older colonies.

Various difficulties developed, however, and in 1774 the Quebec Act was passed which by apparently permanently extending the province to include all the "West" of the American colonies and confirming the Catholics throughout the vast domain in their rights and privileges was to cause more trouble among the older settlements although satisfactory to the overwhelming majority of Canadians.

The Governors appointed, in especial Carleton, had been men of probity and ability, and unusually wise administrators. Unfortunately judgeships and other minor offices had become subject to that besetting sin of the century, political jobbery, but on the whole, the handling of the problem of how to administer an enormous new territory with large populations of alien civilized people and of savages had been accomplished with skill and honesty, although without sufficient consideration perhaps of the reaction on the inhabitants of the other colonies. This brings us to the final problem of the period, and to its great failure.

After the Peace of 1763 the most immediately pressing question was that of imperial defense. The British territory on the American mainland alone now extended from the Gulf of Mexico to Hudson's Bay, and from the Atlantic to the Mississippi. There was a line of frontier forts stretching for between 2000 and 3000 miles, and a force of 10,000 men was deemed the least possible to protect this enormous extent of new lands with its recently conquered alien population and the savages who had to accept a new supremacy. It was obvious that the troops would have to be regulars supplied by Great Britain. The long history of intercolonial jealousy and refusal to cooperate or to maintain standing forces would have been sufficient proof of that had not new evidence been at once forthcoming in the very year of peace.

In the Northwest the formidable native uprising known as Pontiac's rebellion began and lasted for over a year. There were again the old troubles. Pennsylvania refused to supply any troops. New York, New Jersey, Massachusetts and Connecticut insisted that two-thirds of any they supplied should be kept within their own borders and the brunt of the work fell on the British.

But there were other dangers besides those arising from the Indians. France and Spain had been beaten and despoiled but might attempt to regain their lost possessions. France had invaluable naval bases in the West Indies, and Spain, at New Orleans, held the mouth of the Mississippi. In the Seven Years'

War the colonies had helped to protect their own territories, but the rest of the continent, now British, had been won not by them but by the British army and navy operating in many parts of the world. The question was, who would pay for the maintenance of the necessary garrisons?

The problem at first aroused little interest in England. Bute had resigned after peace had been made, and Pitt, still in dudgeon, having declined to accept office, the King appointed the Great Commoner's brother-in-law, George Grenville, a plodding, honest, unimaginative, industrious man of the business type who thought in figures rather than in terms of human nature. For a while public interest was centered on the case of John Wilkes, a clever, scurrilous adventurer of no morals, who had been elected to Parliament and whose writings and sayings had brought down the wrath of the King and his Ministers. Although expelled from Parliament and condemned by the courts, he fled to France, and attained a considerable degree of popularity largely because of the unpopularity of the King who had attacked him. The British public was paying much more attention to the rascally Wilkes and his doings than it was to the taxation of the American colonies.

The case of Wilkes is, however, of deep interest for the light which it sheds on the struggle for liberty which was, in fact, absorbing the attention of many in England as well as in America. Parliament, unrepresentative of the people in any real sense, and controlled by the King and Ministers, was lapsing into tyranny over Englishmen at home and not merely overseas. The majority in the Commons, created and maintained by the means we have noted earlier, refused to accept the fact of the people's sovereignty.

In 1768 Wilkes, who had returned from France, was elected to represent Middlesex, but in February of next year was expelled by the Commons. Twice again he was elected and twice the Commons refused to allow him to take his seat. Here was a distinct constitutional crisis. If Parliament could overrule the choice of the people in electing their representatives, then there was no longer such a thing as popular government, and the King and his coterie could control the Commons. The bad character of Wilkes was forgotten in the struggle by the people who rallied under the cry of "Wilkes and Liberty." Both the caustic pen of Junius and the violence of the London mob were enlisted on his side. Placed in prison, he was elected Alderman, and finally the freedom of Parliamentary election was vindicated.

The Americans were as deeply moved by these events as the people at home, and Wilkes was, for a while, the most popular man in the colonies. Had he been of better character, and had the liberty parties in England and America not been geographically divided by the ocean, there might well have been a new civil war in England itself instead of a conflict between the two branches of the race. But Wilkes was no Pym or Hampden, and although Parliament at last had to give way to the demands of the constituents at home, the subjects over the ocean were left to continue the fight alone, so that the contest instead of resulting in a constitutional victory for the Empire against Parliament brought about the unhappy cleavage between those who had won in one section and those in another who were still refused the freedom which they demanded. The forces on the side of liberty had been divided. The threat to freedom of the subject by Parliament was the culmination of the steady growth in the power of that body from the days of the struggle with Charles I, and the result of the control of that body by King and Ministers instead of by the people.

The approaching civil war may thus be traced in its fundamental causes in part back to the civil war of the seventeenth century. There were, however, other factors, one of which was the somewhat contemptuous regard which many of the English at home have always felt for the Englishman as a colonial. Although some, after the victory of "Wilkes and Liberty" in England, still understood and sympathized with the American demands, most were inclined to disallow the justice of them, and the struggle became, in a few years, not a national movement but, like the Civil War in America itself in the next century, sectional strife.

Grenville, in his plodding way, undertook to tackle the American problem. He had opposed Pitt's conduct of the war because of the enormous expense involved and was now deeply worried by the amount of the national debt, which had risen to about £130,000,000, a huge sum for those days. The tax on land in England was up to 20 per cent, and the cost of the military and civil administration in America had jumped from £70,000 to £350,000. It seemed only common sense to him, and to most Englishmen, who indeed did not think much about the matter at all, that the Americans should pay some of this increased cost, as the British had driven the French from their borders and planned to defend them against the Indians.

In spite of the establishment of a Court of Admiralty in America and a stricter enforcement of the trade laws, the added revenue from duties would raise only about one-seventh of the amount required. The American colonists would raise neither troops nor taxes, so Grenville proposed to lay a tax on them by Act of Parliament, the famous Stamp Tax. The tax, which called for small payments on certain legal documents, cards, dice, newspapers, liquor licenses, and other things, was estimated to yield about £100,000 a year, of which part would fall on the island colonies. There was no opposition in England by Pitt, the Whigs or others, and even the colonial agents made none, such men as Benjamin Franklin and other American patriotic leaders seeing little or no objection. Even so, Grenville waited a year for the colonists to propose some other plan, should they prefer one, but none was offered.

In 1765 the law was passed with practically no voice raised against it, and every one was wholly unprepared for the storm which almost at once swept over the colonies. The opposition aroused was intense and was probably the greater on account of the revision and attempted enforcement of the trade laws, although Grenville's effort in that direction can scarcely be criticized. If there were to be control of trade at all, the revision was a fair one, especially in the replacement of the old prohibitive duty on molasses by a new moderate duty which could be paid without damage to the New England trade. One difficulty in practice was that the old duties had never been paid whereas the new ones would have to be.

Trade regulations had always been accepted, so when the cry went up "no taxation without representation," a distinction had to be drawn between such taxes as those called for by the Stamp Act and those regulating trade, or between, as it came to be phrased, "internal" and "external" taxation. During the next decade, as the unhappy dispute dragged out its course, the distinction was to prove untenable, and wider and wider ground had to be occupied for the rationalizing of the colonial position. For the moment, the Americans won, and the Non-importation agreements entered into in the colonies so injured English trade that the Whig Ministry which succeeded that of Grenville repealed the Stamp Tax the next year, 1766, though adding a declaratory clause asserting the unqualified right of the British Parliament to tax the colonies.

In the joy over repeal, however, little attention was paid to that, and at this critical moment it was not yet too late to reconsider the whole question of imperial relations. Unfortunately, the declaratory clause could be seized upon by radical agitators in America for use later, and in England much ill-feeling had been aroused among the landed interest smarting under their 20 per cent taxes. The background for the continuing dispute was to become about as bad as possible on both sides of the water. Like the constitutional struggle under the early Stuarts it was to be made impossible of friendly settlement by treating it in the narrowest spirit of legalism. The England of James and Charles had been outgrowing the doctrine of divine right, and the American colonies were outgrowing the doctrine of plantations controlled and operated always primarily for the benefit of the mother country. They had reached the stage at which, in sentiment at least, they were ripe for, and would have been content with, what we now call "Dominion Status."

It is customary to say that such a conception was at that time beyond the range of British statesmanship, yet the American colonies would have been amply satisfied with the position accorded to Ireland and which we have already described. A century and a half later Lord Cromer was to write that "the principle that lies at the root of all sound administration . . . is that administration and commercial exploitation should not be entrusted to the same hands." Yet that is precisely what Britain insisted upon in the case of America although she had given her old foe, Ireland, the status of a modern Dominion.

It was natural probably that political thinking in America should be more advanced than in England, and if England could not conceive of Dominion Status America could, and ten years before the Irish settlement of 1782 writers in New England newspapers were suggesting the lines, not only of the temporary Irish settlement, but of the whole future of the Empire. One in *The New Hampshire Gazette,* for example—and there were others—suggested that all local legislatures should be independent of each other but that the King should be the head of all. "The Government thus united," he wrote, "in one Sovereign, though divided into distant Parliaments, will be actuated by one Soul. . . . If the supreme Legislature is considered as only in the Majesty of the King as the common Head of all his Parliaments, and exercising his authority with their consent, while none of them encroaches upon the rights of the rest, harmony will reign through the whole Empire; every part will enjoy freedom and happiness; it may be extended farther and farther to the utmost ends of the earth and yet continue firmly compacted until all the kingdoms of the World shall be dissolved."

The first vision of the future Empire was vouchsafed in America, but British statesmen were not reading the New Hampshire, Massachusetts and other *Gazettes,* and if they had been, the ideas set forth would hold little appeal to the English country gentlemen who were to be of more and more influence in the struggle. In America there was a very small minority, mostly built up by Samuel Adams in Massachusetts, Patrick Henry in Virginia, and other radical leaders, who increasingly aimed at complete independence, but even after a dozen years of agitation, according to John Adams, only one-third of the colonists were in favor of separation from the mother country, one-third remained Loyalists, and one-third were indifferent.

Judging by the number who usually prefer a quiet life and their own personal concerns to taking active sides in political movements, the indifferent one-third may be largely increased at the cost of diminishing each of the other thirds. In other words, the British government had over a decade in which to deal with a very small minority of discontented "die-hards," but by playing into their hands and by increasing their numbers by blunder after blunder it brought on the final catastrophe.

It is of no use to accuse the Americans of being unreasonable. They did, indeed, receive naval and other military protection from their connection with the Empire, but on the other hand they knew that their trade, which on the whole they had allowed England to regulate, was a large source of wealth to that country. Moreover, although the logical distinction between internal and external taxation might break down, two and a half millions of men who inherited the English traditions could not allow themselves to be taxed directly by a Parliament three thousand miles away, only partly representative of the seven millions or so at home, and in which those in America themselves had not, and by the nature of the case could not have, representation of their own interests.

The problem of proportional contribution by taxation to imperial defense has never been settled, except by default, and it must moreover be recalled that at this time Britain was asking to tax the colonies in part for the defense of the huge new territory she had acquired but in which by prohibiting settlement and land purchase and in giving privileges to the Catholics, she was running counter to two of the strongest feelings in practically all of America—the desire for expansion and the maintenance of Protestantism, even where it was not narrow Puritanism.

The Stamp Act had been repealed by the short-lived Ministry under Rockingham, which in this particular action received the support of Pitt and a new member of Parliament, Edmund Burke, who made his maiden speech on the American question. Pitt agreed with those Americans who had taken the position that Parliament had the right to regulate trade but not to tax the colonies "internally," but Burke, who was to prove one of the ablest members of the Commons and one of the greatest political thinkers of his day, took the far broader ground that taxation in such a case was not a legal quibble but a question of expediency, and that the lasting good-will of America and the harmonious development of the Empire were worth far more than any small taxes to be collected by force or at the cost of deep and lasting resentment.

The King, still experimenting with his theory of government, accepted the resignation of the Rockingham Ministry soon after the repeal of the Stamp Act, and at last Pitt, now made Earl of Chatham, formed a new combination with the irresponsible Charles Townshend as Chancellor of the Exchequer. Chatham, after his brilliant career and the great services he had rendered to the nation, was now entering upon that unhappy decade or so before his final passing. Incapacitated much of the time by the gout, and mentally no longer his old self, he became impossible as leader or colleague. His cabinet was a heterogeneous collection of individuals rather than the executive of a party, and although in his own absence, his colleagues for the most part disagreed with Townshend, the idea of Cabinet solidarity and joint responsibility had not yet developed far enough to cause them or Townshend to resign, and the Chancellor had his way.

That way savored of a cheap cleverness. As the Americans had objected to "internal" taxation, Townshend said he would impose only "external," and so secured the passage of Acts levying a new series of duties on lead, painters' colors, paper, tea and other articles. So sure was he of no trouble that he reduced the English land tax by one-quarter and so had to find the loss of about £400,000 elsewhere. The country gentlemen who had been relieved of the burden could be counted upon not to assume it again without much bad feeling. Townshend had got himself into a position where he would have to offend either the English country party or the Americans. Even today the stay-at-home Englishman is apt to consider himself as superior to the colonial, and the country gentlemen of 1767 had votes in Parliamentary elections and Parliament whereas the Americans had none, a point for obvious consideration. It was evident that the attempt to tax the colonies would continue.

Delicate as the question had become, another blunder was now made. The American taxes were stated to be not even for the maintenance of the army but to pay the salaries of governors and judges, which meant that all local political control would pass from the colonial Assemblies to Parliament. The spirit of Hampden who had fought the imposition of the ship-money tax, though it was only twenty shillings for him, was again evident in America. So violent was the reaction that the following year, 1768, it was felt necessary to place two regiments of British soldiers in Boston, and when in 1770 a collision occurred between them and some of the citizens, resulting in the loss of three lives, the government retreated and repealed all the Townshend taxes except that on tea.

It was unstatesmanlike to acknowledge that the Americans were strong enough to cause repeal and yet to continue to assert the principle to which they objected. For the next three years, however, in spite of the fact that the colonists refused to a large extent to use the tea with its threepence duty, there was no open resistance, though feeling became increasingly bad in both countries. In 1773, as we have seen, the East India Company was in serious straits, and Lord North, who had succeeded Townshend on the death of the latter, conceived what he thought the clever plan of widening the market for India tea, and so helping the Company, by not charging the shilling duty in England on tea to be re-exported to America, retaining only the colonial threepence duty of 1767, so that Americans would actually pay nine pence less per pound, less freight, than consumers in England.

The Americans, however, regarded the plan as a ruse to make them buy freely and thus tacitly acknowledge the right of Parliamentary taxation. In addition, a point often overlooked by

English historians, it was provided that the tea was to be sold by certain merchants only, named by the British Government, which merchants, particularly in Boston, were disliked Tories who had taken the British side in the controversies. Thus the measure raised afresh not only the question of taxation but the new ones of monopoly and coercion.

The first ships bringing consignments of the tea under the new Act met with varying receptions in the different colonies. Only in Massachusetts was violence used, and there, after a controversy with the Governor, a band of citizens, rather carelessly disguised as Indians, boarded the ship at night and dumped about £10,000 worth of tea into the harbor of Boston. It was a lawless action, which even in America was condemned by many who had been opposed to the course of British policy, and in England the anger of people and Parliament reached a high pitch, although Burke again pleaded for conciliation and a broad view of Empire relations.

"I am not here going into a distinction of rights," he said, "nor attempting to mark their boundaries. I do not enter into these metaphysical distinctions. I hate the very sound of them. Leave the Americans as they anciently stood. Be content to bind America by the laws of trade; you have always done it. Let this be your reason for binding her trade. Do not burden them with taxes; you were not used to do so from the beginning. Let this be your reason for not taxing. These are the arguments of states and kingdoms. Leave the rest to the schools, for there only they may be discussed with safety."

However, few could take such views, and even some of the best friends of the colonies now deserted them. A series of punitive measures were introduced and passed in Parliament without difficulty, though against considerable minorities. One closed the port of Boston to all commerce until the "Tea Party" had been paid for by the colony; another provided that local authorities must make provision for the quartering of British troops wherever they might be posted; others that if the British Government considered that an accused person might not receive a fair trial in an American colony he could be transported for trial across the ocean to England; another that jurors should in future be appointed by sheriffs instead of elected as formerly; another that the Massachusetts charter be modified so that members of the upper House of the Legislature should be appointed by the Crown instead of elected by the Assembly; and that no town meetings, except one annually for the election of officers, should be held without permission of the Governor. It was about this same time that the Quebec Act was passed, although it had no connection with the American crisis. General Gage, in command of the troops in Boston, was made Governor of the colony and began to erect fortifications.

There had been many minor causes of fear and growing dislike of England, such as dread of the establishment of Bishops and the Anglican Church; the continued hemming in of the colonists by the Proclamation Line of 1763, which seemed to be made permanent by the Quebec Act, which prevented the expansion westward of an increasingly rich, energetic and populated seaboard; and other factors. Some of these varied in the different colonies, and even in the seaboard and frontier sections of the same colony. One of the mistakes made by the Governors in reporting conditions to the home government was in underestimating the combined strength of all these causes of dissatisfaction, and also the belief that on account of their differences the several colonies could not be induced to act together but that at least each group, if not every colony, would negotiate independently for selfish interests.

The fact proved, however, that the utterly unwise and unnecessarily ruthless revenge taken on the entire colony of Massachusetts for what was, after all, an act of violence on the part of only a handful of its citizens, made all the colonies, from New Hampshire to Georgia, feel that their own liberties were in danger from British policy. As Burke had pointed out, that policy was new, and it appeared evident that if Parliament was to have unlimited powers of taxation; if it could transport Americans to England to be tried before hostile judges and juries; if it could not merely regulate trade but seal up flourishing ports; if it could override charters and alter the forms of government; then there was to be no more liberty for Englishmen in America who were already more than a third as numerous as Englishmen in England.

Within a few weeks after these disastrous Acts had been passed, a Congress made up of representatives from every colony, except distant Georgia, met at Philadelphia to consider the situation. Meanwhile cargoes of food and other supplies poured into Massachusetts from other colonies, and it was evident that if British policy had accomplished nothing else it had performed the miracle of uniting the jealous commonwealths in one cause—that of self-protection and hostility to the mother country. In the past, owing in very large degree to the charters granted them by the British Government, to the distance from England, to the levelling democratic conditions of the frontier, Americans had been the freest people in the world and the most accustomed, even with their limited franchise, to taking active part in their own self-government.

They were not a people suddenly to accept subjection to a distant Parliament in which they were not represented. In America, the Congress drew up an emphatically worded Declaration of Rights, and in England Chatham and Burke pleaded for conciliation, Burke especially in speeches of the most moving eloquence. But it was all of no avail. Suggestions of proceeding forward to Dominion status were as little heeded as were Burke's suggestions of retracing steps to leave the colonies in the relationship which had formerly held them so long in peace.

On April 19, 1775, a small expedition sent from Boston by Gage to secure some ammunition stored at Concord came into touch with the colonials, and was driven back into the city with heavy losses. The "shot heard round the world" had been fired, and blood had at last been shed, not as before in mere brawls but, at Lexington and Concord, between British troops on a war errand and Britain's American citizens in arms.

The Civil War between the two great sections of the race had opened. Throughout the struggle there were to be distinguished

English leaders who were to plead the American cause. There were also many who recognized that, as George's effort to play the part of a "Patriot King" degenerated more and more (not simply from his own character but largely by force of circumstances and the fundamental impossibility of Bolingbroke's conception) into personal rule through second-rate Ministers and by corruption of Parliament, the cause of liberty in America was closely linked to that in Britain.

On the whole, however, Britain was more united than the colonies, and it would be a mistake to believe that any considerable or important section of the British people were on the American side. On the other hand, to a great extent, the British, including not only the rank and file but not a few high military officers, showed that they had little zest for the work of warring against their fellow subjects for the purpose of depriving them of liberty, which in part accounted for the fact that the King had to hire German mercenaries for the distasteful job, a fact not yet forgiven in many an American village where "Hessian" is still the vilest name one small boy can think of to call another.

In the colonies there was a much wider division, and we have already mentioned the proportions of those who were for and against the war, especially when it came down to one for complete independence. It has been estimated that about 100,000 Tories in all emigrated from America, of whom perhaps about 60,000 became later the Empire Loyalists who did so much toward making Canada England's premier Dominion. For the most part, the Tories belonged to the conservative, upper economic and social classes, though they were to be found in all, and the loss to the colonies caused by their emigration can be compared only to that suffered by France in the flight of the Huguenots.

The well-known story of the military operations of the war may be briefly told. It falls at once into two phases, the first during which Britain was engaged in suppressing a colonial rebellion, and, the second, in which, owing to the entry of certain European nations into the struggle, she was fighting for her life in many quarters of the world against a host of enemies.

Until this second phase practically assured the success of the American cause, it depended almost wholly upon the courageous and steadfast character of one man—George Washington, one of the greatest the English race has produced. There have been far abler statesmen, and as a general he cannot compare with, for example, Marlborough, but it was one of the fortunate moments in history when the Continental Congress chose him as Commander-in-Chief of the American forces. A rich Virginia planter, with limited experience of public or military life, he was to demonstrate, in many a seemingly hopeless situation during the eight years of war ahead, how sound judgment, tenacity of will, and a strength of character visible to all men, may control destiny more effectually than technical training or brilliancy of mind.

In 1775, after taking charge of the rather motley local levies which were besieging Gage in Boston, he forced the evacuation of all British forces from that town after the battle of Bunker Hill, and though an attack on Canada under a subordinate failed, the fact that American troops had fought at Quebec and Montreal had a certain effect on American morale, as did also the failure of a British attack on Charleston, South Carolina.

The main interest of 1776 is political and not military, for in July of that year the Congress adopted the Declaration of Independence, which asserted to all the world that the imperial connection between Great Britain and her thirteen colonies had ceased. Canada and the West Indies had remained loyal, and the limits of the Civil War were thus definitely fixed. Part of the misunderstanding between the two sides had come about from the fact that the Americans, living under conditions completely different from those in England, had slowly but imperceptibly been becoming a different race with different outlook and characteristics, a process which has continued to the present day, an extremely important point which is even yet all too often overlooked, resulting in unexpected misunderstandings.

That the process had already gone far by 1776 is evidenced by the Declaration, which, in its sweeping generalities, is utterly unlike any statement drawn up in the history of England itself. As

405

we have so often stated, the English face each situation as a practical problem of the moment, to be settled as an incident and not as a theorem, and with words, if they have to be used, limited strictly to the occasion in hand. The introduction to the Declaration, with its "We hold these truths to be self-evident—that all men are created equal; that they are endowed by their Creator with certain inalienable rights; that among these are life, liberty and the pursuit of happiness," etc., was as un-English a document as it is possible to conceive, yet it was drawn up by Englishmen practically every one of whom had, a few months before, been a loyal subject of King George III.

It was saturated through and through with the ideas, and even with the phrases, of Locke and other English philosophers, but it was nevertheless un-English as a state document in a national crisis. It was, however, to have an emotional effect on the minds, the imaginations and aspirations of men in many lands which no English document from Magna Carta onward ever had. At any rate, the Americans had now crossed their Rubicon, and the war was no longer one over trade regulations or theories of taxation but for breaking or saving the Empire.

The campaigns of 1776 and 1777 went badly for the Americans. Washington, who had withdrawn to New York after driving the British out of Boston, was defeated by General Howe in the battle of Long Island (August, 1776), and had to fall back into New Jersey, though a victory in a surprise attack on the Hessians at Trenton at Christmas gave the troops cheer. The next year the British developed an ambitious but fatal plan which in its final consequence was to result in the independence of America. Howe was in possession of New York and the mouth of the Hudson, and it was planned that he should advance up the valley of that river to meet Burgoyne and some 8000 troops coming down from Canada by way of Lakes Champlain and George, thus cutting the New England section off from the rest of the colonies. Howe figured, however, that he would first have time to strike a blow at Washington who had moved farther south. Having transported his troops by sea to Philadelphia Howe did defeat the Americans at the battle of the Brandywine and forced Washington into quarters at Valley Forge, where the Americans suffered intensely during the winter of 1777–78 while Howe and the British passed a gay social season in Philadelphia, then the most delightful city in America.

Clinton had been left with some forces in New York but not sufficient for him to secure control of the Hudson Valley, and when, after a most difficult march through the wilderness, Burgoyne reached Saratoga, neither the troops expected from the West under St. Leger nor those from New York were on hand to afford him any aid. Howe himself, and the sorely needed troops, remained inactive in Philadelphia for seven months. The result of the complete breakdown of the plan, which had been much too complicated, aside from Howe's inexplicable conduct, to be carried out with precision under American conditions, was that Burgoyne had to surrender with his entire army.

This disaster was to end the first phase of the war. France had already been giving assistance to the American cause but had declined doing so openly or making any formal alliance. Burgoyne's surrender, however, in October, 1777, finally decided her, and in February she allied herself to the revolting colonies. Lord North was now willing to yield all but independence and begged to be relieved of office. The King, however, was insistent, and even Chatham, although willing to concede all else, could not bring himself to agree to the breakup of the Empire. In his last speech in Parliament he pleaded against a motion for withdrawing troops from America, and in the course of it fell unconscious in a fit of apoplexy, dying a month later.

The war now changed in character, and in 1778 there was no decisive fighting in America, the scene shifting to the sea. The British navy had been neglected, and the French were superior on the water, but little was accomplished. The British lost Dominica and Grenada in the West Indies but captured St. Lucia; and a small force from New York, whither Howe had retreated after his disastrous winter in Philadelphia, captured Savannah.

The following year a new enemy complicated matters for the

British when Spain joined the war against her, and began the famous siege of Gibraltar, which was to last three years, although the Rock was to be saved in the end by the heroic gallantry of its commander, Eliot. The troubles in India, which we have already noted, were now at their worst, and there was also fighting along the African coast, where French captured English posts and vice versa.

In 1780 Russia, Denmark, Sweden, Prussia and the Emperor all arrayed themselves against England in the League of Armed Neutrality, and Holland declared war, though the others did not go to that length. Nevertheless, their insistence on their rights as neutrals, which they claimed had been infringed by Great Britain, hampered the operations of that power as previously carried on. The British campaign in America directed northward from the Southern states appeared, however, to be promising, and at sea Rodney had managed to relieve Gibraltar, defeat a Spanish fleet, and drive a combined French and Spanish one back to Europe from the West Indies.

The year 1781 opened well for the British both on sea and land, as well as in India, but was to prove the fatal year of the contest. The British troops operating from the South had met with considerable success and devastated much of the countryside but the American General Greene had reversed the tide, and the British General Cornwallis was finally obliged to take up a defensive position on the Virginia seacoast on the peninsula of Yorktown.

In spite of Rodney's fine work, the navy had not been well handled by the Government, and now a series of mistakes, including one by Rodney himself, lost control of the sea to France. Cornwallis, who had hoped for the appearance of an English fleet to give him succor, instead was attacked by the American and French land forces and a French fleet under de Grasse. On October 19, 1781, he surrendered all his forces. Although almost two years were yet to pass before Britain made peace with her foes, Lord North was right in exclaiming, when the news from Yorktown reached him: "O God, it is all over."

The independence of the United States was assured and there was no further fighting on the American mainland. At sea, however, the French captured St. Kitts and Nevis, and the Spaniards took the Bahamas, Jamaica being saved in a desperate naval battle won by Rodney. Gibraltar was saved but Minorca fell to the French and Spanish after a siege of six months by their combined forces.

Although the British had put up a magnificent fight against half the world, there had been growing dissatisfaction in England with the conduct of affairs and especially the mounting cost. The obstinacy of the King, however, in insisting upon the prolongation of the war during the year after Yorktown met with no response from the people, who were weary of the struggle, and saw ahead only continued expense and no gains to be made. Negotiations for peace were begun in 1782, and under the short Ministry of Shelburne took the form of definitive treaties with all Britain's enemies in the latter part of 1783.

In general, but with some exceptions, the whole situation returned to what it had been before the war. France retained her conquests of St. Lucia in the West Indies and Senegal in Africa, while Spain kept the important Mediterranean island of Minorca and reacquired Florida. Most important of all, the independence of the thirteen American colonies was acknowledged, and the United States of America was accepted as a new member of the family of nations, her territory extending from Canada to Florida and from the Atlantic to the Mississippi, the entire interior of British America, except Canada, thus passing to the successful rebels.

It is futile to consider in history what might have happened had events taken a different course from what they actually did. Independence and the freedom to organize their own economic life as they chose and to exploit the continent, probably made for a much more rapid increase of wealth and population in the United States than would have been the case if they had remained colonies, a fact that was by no means to prove an entirely unmixed blessing to the new nation. On the other hand, had the problem of imperial administration been handled more wisely, the separation might have been long delayed though probably inevitable in the long run. Under such conditions it might have come about peacefully in the different atmosphere of the nineteenth century, but it also might have been brought about only by a more terrible war. The "ifs" of history can be but fireside musings.

At this tragic crisis in the history of the Empire we may pause to take a rapid survey of the ground we have thus far covered in our story. It has been a long road we have travelled over rapidly since in the mists of prehistory we dimly discerned a peninsula jutting to the northward from the European continent into the stormy seas, later by geologic changes to be cut off from the mainland and to become an island, thus creating one of the fundamental factors which have influenced and determined all the later story we have had to tell. We have also had to note other nonhuman factors, such as the climate, which have helped to mold the British character and ways of life. Even the wild winds and storms have played their parts at critical moments, such as when the Armada threatened invasion or William was carried past his landing place and the Revolution with all it meant to England and the world was saved by a sudden shift in the gale.

We have also seen how many strains have gone into the making of what we now call the British race. We found that we yet know too little of the very earliest inhabitants to trace much to them, or even to the mixed elements of population which came in with the Romans, but in later periods we have been able to discover more distinctly the origins of some of the traits mentioned in the Introduction as we have noted those contributed successively by the Celts, the Saxons, the Danes, the Normans and others who came to plunder or to settle the rich lands of the British Isles. We have seen also how all these contributed to form the English speech and the infinite variety of British literature in language, thought and spirit. These peoples, living together in war and peace, gradually fusing, likewise helped to develop one of the notable traits of the British, their tolerance of one another and of differing local laws and customs, as was exemplified, for example, early in the story, in the Danelaw and almost at the end in the treatment of conquered French Canada.

Another thread running through our tale has been the increasing devotion to personal liberty, in which Britain led the rest of Europe, so that not only did the British in their own island become the freest and least regulated people in the world but also as they won in the race for empire and scattered their governments over the world, personal freedom and local liberty became the British gift to a large part of it. We have seen in addition the Constitution develop slowly down the ages, mostly from the peaceful settlement of one problem after another, and how the instinct for self-government also grew from the practice of talking things over and compromising on immediate disputes rather than fighting and generalizing. Though impasses did occur, no other constitution has so long a record so little stained with violence or blood.

Another aspect of the story has been the marvellous growth and expansion of the nation from the days when complete darkness fell on the record as the Roman Empire shrank and the last recalled legions left an abandoned and decayed land to descend into barbarism once again and undefended from a succession of plundering hordes who had never known the order and civilization of the Roman world. We have watched them come and burn, sack and murder, slowly themselves developing a new civilization after centuries of turmoil and growing pains. Then came the Norman Conquest to weld the people together under the iron hand of William, and to bring them again into touch with the more advanced and organized culture of the Continent. We have also noted the beginning of Christianity, and seen how both Church and State became centralized and powerful. The feudal system did its appointed task, declined, and gave place to the freer organization of the modern period.

We have had to follow the struggles and ambitions of English rulers and the English people to build up imperial possessions on the European Continent until the nation finally woke from that dream, to break loose from the desire to rule any land across the

Channel and equally to resent any attempt by any power, temporal or spiritual, to control it from thence. Under Henry VIII we heard the bonds break which had bound the English Church to the Papacy, and also, through the story, we have traced the slow growth of tolerance of religious belief, and the difficult disentangling of religion from politics.

After the turning of their ambitions from the Continent, and their refusal to be in any way controlled by it, we found the English suddenly launching out upon the seas under Elizabeth, and subsequently building up an empire in many parts of the world —in distant India, the West Indies and the American mainland. Moreover, their trade was seeking outlets in every corner where a profit was to be made, and with the wealth, power and national spirit which had been growing, we have also watched how England became the arbiter of Europe, and finally destroyed the seemingly invincible power of the great French monarchy under Louis. While Holland declined, France fell, and the great Spanish Empire decayed to a third-rate power, little England had steadily been rising.

We cannot recite again all that we have tried to recount in our brief survey of some eighteen hundred years of recorded history, with its successes and failures, among the latter notably Ireland and the handling of the American problem, but we may recall for a moment some of the great days. There were Crecy, Poitiers, Agincourt, the defeat of the Invincible Armada, Grenville's last fight of the *Revenge*, and many another military exploit, such as Blenheim and Ramillies, which did so much to build up the British feeling of invincibility. Of another sort, there was the day when the boy King, Richard, talked to Wat Tyler at the head of his threatening mob, saved the Kingdom, and exemplified in dramatic fashion the English way of talking things over. Other days, of yet another sort, were those when the barons faced King John at Runnymede, when Hampden refused to pay his ship-money tax, or when the Commons defied Charles I, and the Speaker was held in his chair while resolutions were passed in defiance of the royal order to adjourn.

412

In our backward glance we have been able to touch upon only a few points, and the story has now brought us to the place where much of what had been accomplished in building up an empire at least seemed lost. Although there is no use denying the great gash which had been made in the Empire by the breaking away of the American continent south of Canada, yet it was to prove, in truth, to be far from ruined. In the next volume we shall have to trace the growth of a still greater Empire, developed largely in the intellectual climate of a new age. Nor had any of the other and more spiritual gains of the long centuries we have surveyed been lost. That fact is to be evidenced by the culmination of the new Empire in that Commonwealth of free nations and of vast possessions which is the Empire of today, glimpses of which had been vouchsafed during the angry and hopeless discussions which led to the disruption of the first one, and the schism between the two great branches of the English-speaking race.

INDEX

INDEX

416

INDEX

Bombay, India, 315, 389; acquisition of, 308; English post, 367
Boniface VIII, and Edward I, 88
Bonner, Bishop, placed in Tower, 184
Book of Martyrs by Foxe, 236
book shops, 356
books, brought with the new church, 30
Boroughbridge, battle of, Lancaster defeated at, 92
Boston, General Gage in, 405
Boston "Tea Party," 401
Boswell's *Johnson*, 360
Bosworth Field, Richard III killed at, 131
Bothwell, Earl of, Mary Queen of Scots carried away by, 202
Boulogne, given to the English, 185; given up, 186
bourgeoisie, 83
Bouvines, battle of, 63
bowmen, of William's army, 45
Boyle, founder of Royal Society, 324
Boyne, battle of the, victory of William over the Irish, 334
Braddock, defeat of, 372
Bradshaw, digging up of body, 314
Brandywine, battle of, 407
Bretigny, Treaty of, 99
Brighton, as a resort, 356
Bristol, trading center, 147, 275; merchants of, 138, 225; building in, 141
Britain, Roman invasions of, 5 f.; subjugation of, 7 f.; rising under Boadicea, 8; nature of Roman civilization in, 9 f.; visited by Emperor Hadrian in 119, 9; status of peasant in, 11; government of, 14; Roman Empire fades out of, 14; Celtic strain in, 20
Britons, characteristics of, 6, 12, 21 f.; not wholly destroyed, 21
Bronze Age, in England, 4
Browne, Robert, leader of the Brownists, 211
Browne, Sir Thomas, writings of, 298
Brownists, beliefs of, 211, 256
Bruce, Robert, Scotch leader, 79, 81; Stirling captured by, 92; and Mortimer, 94; death of, 95
Bruges, wool exported to, 96; effect of English wool on, 135
Bryce, James, quoted, 94
Buckingham, Duke of, 258, 260, 261, 317; rebellion led by, 131; favorite of James I, 248; Charles I and, 250; assassinated, 262
building, Roman love of, 12
buildings, wooden instead of stone, 24; Saxon, compared with Roman, 25
bull fighting, 140
Bunker Hill, battle of, 405
Bunyan, *Pilgrim's Progress* by, 235, 322 f.
burgesses, 81, 83, 97
Burghley, Lord (*see* Cecil)
Burgoyne, General, in America, 406, 407

Burgundians, migration to England, 10
Burgundy, Duke of, 124, 125; the new, 125, 126, 127, 128
burh, a, 25
Burke, Edmund, on the problem of India, 389; American colonies and, 398, 401, 402, 403
burial customs, 18
Bury St. Edmunds, monastery at, 40, 63
business men, English, 135 f.
Bute, Lord, 381, 393
Buxar, Nawab of Oudh, defeated at, 385
Butler, age of, 364
Byng, Admiral, failure of, 372
Byrd, William, composer, 233

"Cabal," the, 317
Cabinet, the, 314, 341; emergence of, 313; formed, 339
Cabinet government, 354, 378 f., 380; emerging, 361
Cabot, John, 147
Cade, Jack, rebellion of, 128 f.
Cadiz, attempt to capture, 259
Caernarvon Castle, 77
Cæsar, and the Belgæ, 4 f.; first expedition to Britain, 5 f.; next expedition to Britain, 6 f.
Calais, 99, 124, 128, 163, 339; siege of, 98; lost to the English, 192
Caledonians, could not be beaten by the Romans, 9
Calcutta, 387; English post, 367; march against, 375
Calvin, John, 198
Calvinism, 182, 198 f., 268; agreed to by Mary, 202; William of Orange's religion, 327
Cambridge, 142, 167; University at, 73
Campion, Thomas, Jesuits headed by, 206; executed, 207; songs of, 237
Canada, 351, 381, 382, 383, 390, 391, 392, 404, 405, 406; conquered by British, 373
Candish, Thomas, or Cavendish, 220
Canon Law, the, 57
Canterbury, British defeated by Cæsar near, 6; Roman town, 12; headquarters of the Church at, 30; pilgrimage to, 59; captured, 111
Canterbury Tales, by Geoffrey Chaucer, 118
Canute, ruler of England, 40; rule of, 41
Canynges, leading merchant of Bristol, 138, 141, 144, 146
Cape Breton, 381
Cape of Good Hope, 218, 220
Caractacus, brave opposition to the Roman advance by, 7
Carew, Thomas, lyrics of, 298
Carey, Sir Robert, posting to Scotland, 227
Carisbrooke Castle, Isle of Wight, Charles I imprisoned in, 279

417

INDEX

dress, 298; Anglo-Saxon, 24; Elizabethan, 228; in eighteenth century, 356

drinking, heavy, 25, 140

drinking horns, 25

Drogheda, stormed by Cromwell, 285

Druid priests, massacring of, 8

"drum and trumpet" school of historians, 101

drunkenness, fines for, 298

Dryden, John, poet, 322

Dublin, English settlement around, 78

Dublin, 273; Cromwell at, 284

Duchess of Portsmouth, mistress of Charles II, 318

Dudley, Henry VII's agent, 146; imprisoned, 160

Dudley, Lord Guilford (see Warwick, Earl of)

Dudley, Lord Robert (see Leicester, Earl of)

duke, the Norman, 39

Duke of Medina Sidonia, commander of the Armada, 209

Dumnorix, escape of, with cavalry, 6

Dunbar, battle of, 80; victory at, 286

Dunkirk, harbor of, Armada takes refuge in, 210; surrender of, 295; Charles II sells to France, 314 f.

Dunstable, John, musical composition of, 144

Dunstan, Archbishop of Canterbury, 37 f.; influence of, 38

Dupleix, Governor of Pondicherry, 367, 369, 371

Durham, "harrying of the north," 47, 267

"Durham Ox," the famous, 357, 360

Dutch, the, 316, 317, 318; aided by Elizabeth, 208; in the Far East, 251; the Amboyna Massacre, 252; in the New World, 254; possession ceded to the English, 307; London blockaded by, 317; William advances the, 336

Dutch East India Company, 251

Dutch guard, dismissed, 339

Dutch Republic, 287, 341, 346; rise of, 205; Parma conquers much of, 207

Dutch States General, 314

Dutch trade, 289

Dyer, "My mind to me a kingdom is," 237

Eadgyth (Matilda or Maud), 53

earl, rule of borough by an, 36

earldoms, Saxon, created, 37; destroyed, 48

East Anglia, kingdom of, 22

East India Company, 222, 225, 251 f., 315, 367, 370, 376 f., 385, 386, 387, 388, 389, 390, 400; rise of, 321

East Indies, 218

Easter, date celebrated, 28

Eastern Association, formed, 275

Eastland Company, the, 225

eating and drinking, 359

Ecclesiastical Commission Court, 325

ecclesiastical courts, lay courts separated from, 49; Henry II and the, 58

Ecclesiastical Polity, by Thomas Hooker, 236

Edgar, son of Alfred, death of, 39

Edgar, grandson of Edmund Ironside, 45

Edgehill, battle of, in Charles I's favor, 275

Edict of Nantes, 325

Edinburgh, 269, 273; Edwin's Burgh, 27; burned, 113; Mary returns to, 200 f.; rioting in, 268; capture of, 286; advance of Young Pretender, 366

Edmund, Earl of Lancaster, 85

Edward, son of Edgar, assassinated, 39

Edward, son of Ethelred, chosen king, 41; death of, 42

Edward, son of Edmund Ironside, 42

Edward I, reign of, 71 f.

Edward II, born in Caernarvon Castle, 77; reign of, 90 f.; Ordinances accepted by, 92; murdered at Berkeley Castle, 93

Edward II, by Marlowe, 238

Edward III, 84; reign of, 94 f.; Hundred Years' War begun in reign of, 95

Edward, son of York, crowned King Edward IV, 129; entertained by **Canynges**, 141

Edward V, murdered in the Tower with his brother, 130

Edward VI, 152, 155; birth of, 176; reign of, 180 f.; becomes ardent Protestant, 185

Edwin, King, converted by Paulinus, 28, 43

Edwin, Northern earl, vengeance on, 47

Edwin's Burgh (Edinburgh), built by King Edwin, 27

Effingham, a Catholic, 211

Egbert, King of Wessex, over-lord of England, 31

Egypt, trade with England, 3

Eikon Basilike, describing sufferings of Charles I, 297

Eleanor of Provence, Henry III married to, 67

election, of a king, 61, 75

Electress Sophia, death of, 347

"Elephant," the, German mistress, 361

Eliot, John, leader in commons, 259, 261; Petition of Right by, 262 f.; imprisoned in Tower, 264

Eliot, commander at the siege of Gibraltar, 408

Elizabeth, 152, 190 f.; declared illegitimate, 176; excluded from the succession, 187; character of, 193 f.; Philip of Spain and, 199 f.; Scotland and, 200; Mary, Queen of Scots, compared with, 201; rebellions and plots under, 203; excommunication of, 204; plot against

INDEX

INDEX

Kent, Belgic tribes of, 7; landings in, 19; Ethelbert of, 22; and kinship, 24; Augustine in, 28; converted to Christianity, 28; harried by William of Normandy, 45

Kentish jewelry, 24 f.

Ket, Norwich captured by, 185

Khiva, Jenkinson's exploration, 219

Kildare, the Anglo-Norman Earl of, the King's deputy, 156; imprisoned in the Tower, 157

Killiecrankie, battle of, 333

Kimbolton, impeached, 274

king, in the feudal system, 37; rules locally, 48; election of a, 61

"King of Ashbourne," the, 357

King of Ireland, title bestowed, 158

King Henry V, by Shakespeare, 101

King James' Version of the Bible, 235

King John, by Shakespeare, 239

King of Mercia, 23

King's Bench, 88

King's Chapel, Cambridge, 142

King's Council, the, 146

"King's Courts," 55 f.

"King's Peace," not yet in existence, 37

King's prerogative, 265

kingship, mystical quality of, 29

kinship, in Anglo-Saxon society, 23 f.

knight, the, 81, 83, 84

Knights of King Arthur, 19

Knights Templars, 91

Knole House, 231, 232, 233

Knox, John, angered by Mary, 202

Kyd, Thomas, dramatist, 238

labor, 103, 105, 224; dislocated, 181; slaves for, 308

laboring class, 104

Labourdonnais, naval officer, 367, 369

Lady Jane Grey, 186 f.; character of, 187; proclaimed queen, 187; executed, 190

La Hogue, James II at, 336

Lake Champlain, 406

Lake George, 406

Lamb, Charles, 355

Lambert Palace, pillaged, 111

Lament of Deor, The, quoted, 38

Lancaster, Duke of, power of, 100; the Savoy of the, 111; Spanish throne claimed by, 113; property confiscated, 115

Lancaster, Earl of, 91 f.

Lancaster, House of, 85, 115, 116, 126, 129, 130, 131, 152, 153

Lancaster, Sir James, expedition of, 222

land, and the rich middle class, 224; confiscation of, 47; "common," 55; Church, 86, 174; renting of, 103

land tax, reduced, 399

Landen, William defeated by Louis at, 336

landlord system, in Ireland, 285

landscape, change in English, 44

Langland, *Vision of Piers Plowman*, by, 106

Langton, Stephen, Archbishop of Canterbury, 62 f.

language, becomes Teutonic, 21; court, Saxon and Danish, 41; French, preferred by Edward, 41; English, used by lower class, 51; French, used by upper class, 51; English, alteration in, 86 f.; English, used by Parliament and the law courts, 101 f.; English, growth of, 117

Latimer, Cambridge student, 167; Bishop, burned at the stake, 191

Latin, language of the Church, 51; spoken, 12

Laud, Archbishop, 272, 273; relied on by Charles I, 265; imprisoned in the Tower, 271

Lauderdale, member of the "Cabal," 317

law, Danish, contribution of, 35; Henry's reform of the, 56 f.; "common," of England, development of, 57; of Canute, old, 84; basis of, changed, 87 f.; profession of, secularized, 88; two systems of, 260; in India, 387; French, allowed in the French colonies, 390

law courts, French language used in, 51

Lawrence, Major, command of, 371

lawyers, new class of, 91

League of Armed Neutrality, 408

League of Nations, 354

learning, love of, brought with the new church, 30; furthered, 35

Leeward Islands, 303

legal cases of Scotland, 79

Legatine Court, opened in London, 169

Legatine powers, 171

legends, Arthurian, the, 20; *Mabinogion*, 20

legionnaires, in England, 9

Leicester, Earl of, Elizabeth and, 201; aid to Dutch under, 208

Leicester Abbey, Wolsey's death at, 170

Leith, captured by Elizabeth, 200

Lennox, Duke of, Regent in Scotland, 207

Leofric, of Mercia, power of, 42

leprosy, disease of Bruce, 95

Leslie, Alexander, leader of Scottish force, 276

Letters of Junius, Philip Francis, reputed author of, 387

Levant, fine English cloths sold in the, 135

Levant Company, the, 225, 226

Levellers, extreme democrats called, 283, 284

Leviathan, by Hobbes, 297

Lewes, battle fought at, 69

Lexington and Concord, battle of, 403

liberty, battle of, 64 f.; struggle for, 393; cause of, 404

Licensing Act, not renewed, 338

Limoges, town of, attack on, 99

427

INDEX

Philip II of France, 60, 62

Philip IV of France, 79

Philip VI of France, alliance with young Bruce, 95

Philip II of Spain, 207; husband of Mary, 189, 190; and Elizabeth, 199 f.; ready to invade England, 209

Philip III, of Spain, 212

Philip IV, of Spain, death of (1665), 316

Philippines, death of Magellan in the, 218

Piccadilly in London, 356

Picts, in England, 19; become aggressive, 14; ravages of the, 17; in Scotland, 27

Pilgrimage of Grace, 173

Pilgrim's Progress, by Bunyan, 235, 322 f.

Pilgrims, the, 256

Pinkie Cleugh, battle of, 182

piracy, 138, 219, 350; in Elizabethan days, 209; sack of Panama by Sir Henry Morgan (1671), 307

Pitt, William, Earl of Chatham, 355, 365, 366, 375, 380, 381, 393, 395, 398, 399, 403, 407; one of the great Englishmen of history, 373; Prime Minister in new Cabinet, 372; India Bill passed, due to, 389 f.

place names, 18, 21, 25

Plains of Abraham, Wolfe at, 373

Plassey, battle of, 376

Plymouth, English fleet collected at, 210; settling of, in 1620, 255; landing at, 256

Plymouth Company, the, 254

"pocket boroughs," 379

poetry, 298; Saxon, 25 f., 38; Elizabethan, 237

Poitiers, victory of, 98 f.; battle of, effect of, 131

Poitou, lost to England, 62

Poland, under a dictator, 324

Pole, Cardinal, the Papal Legate, 190

political ideas, of the Saxons, 23 f.

"political instinct," English, 257

political theory, English have not cared for, 23

Pollard, A. F., *Evolution of Parliament*, by, 83, 176; quoted, 151

Pompeii, room decorations in houses, 10

Pondicherry, French post at, 367; British attack against, 370

Pontefract, castle of, 116

Ponthieu, retained by English, 99

Pontiac's rebllion, 392

"Poor Priests," the, 107

Poor Relief, system of, 358

Pope, the, a "foreigner" to the English, 173

Pope, the, Henry VIII breaks with, 149, 166 f.

Pope Clement VII, 167 f.

Pope Gregory XIII, favors Elizabeth's assassination, 204

Pope Pius V, excommunication of Elizabeth by, 204

Pope, Alexander, 355; *Essay on Criticism*, *The Rape of the Lock, Essay on Man*, 359

"Popish plot," the, 311

population, 222; under Roman rule, 9; of Silchester, 12; in London, in the Antonine age, 12; in Verulanium, 12; of England, 46; rise in, 360

Portsmouth, Buckingham assassinated at, 262

Portugal, at war with France, 315; Philip annexes, 206

Portuguese, beaten by the East India Company, 252

posting system, established (1572), 227

poverty, increase in, 224

Prayer Book, the, 274, 292; first used, 184; revised version of, 185; Edward's Second to be used, 197; restoration of, 309, 310

prehistoric days, in England, 1; in Ireland, Scotland, Wales, 2

prerogative, use of a, strong feeling against, 310

Prerogative Courts, 260; abolished, 312

Presbyterian system, 198, 276; established, 268

Presbyterianism, 273, 274, 276, 277, 278, 309, 310, 333, 364; plot to abduct Charles I, 279

press gang, the, 358

prices, rise of, 181

"Pride's Purge," 280, 283

Priestley, achievements of, 355

Prime Minister, 313, 380; prestige of, 361

primogeniture, rule of, 52, 83

Prince of Wales, quarrel with George II, 363

principle of consent, in British history, 23

printing, invention of the, Continent, 143

prison life, ideas of reform, 365

private enterprise, 139; in India, 253

privateers, 219

"Privilege," 274

Privy Council, 269, 291, 348

prize money, division of, 358

Proclamation of 1763, 390

Proclamation Line of 1763, 402

procurators, Roman, in Britain, 8

property, Crown, 49; English, 65; transferred to the Church, 30

prose, English, 105, 353; Elizabethan, 236; political tracts, 297

Protestantism, 144, 173, 182, 398; beginning of, 165; return of English, 198; struggle between Catholicism and, 199 f.; persecution in Netherlands by Spain, 204; James I and, 245; persecution, 325; in Ireland, 383

Provisions of Oxford, the, 69

Prussia, against England, 408

public baths, 12

Punch, "the British character" in, 24

puppet shows, 228

Purchas, collections of voyages by, 236

432

INDEX